THE CITY OF ADELAIDE,

with the Acre Allotments numbered.

Surveyed by

Col. Light.

Scale of 8 Chains or 1 Mile

1 Mile

ADELAIDE 1836-1976

ADELAIDE 1836-1976
A History of Difference

Derek Whitelock

 University of Queensland Press

© University of Queensland Press
St. Lucia, Queensland, 1977

Typeset, printed and bound by Academy Press Pty. Ltd.

Distributed in the United Kingdom, Europe, the Middle East, Africa, and
the Caribbean by Prentice-Hall International, International Book
Distributors Ltd., 66 Wood Lane End, Hemel Hempstead, Herts., England

National Library of Australia
Cataloguing-in-Publication data

Whitelock, Derek.
    Adelaide 1836–1976.

    Index.
    Bibliography.
    ISBN 0 7022 1401 9.

    1. Adelaide—History—1836–1976. I. Title.

994.231

Contents

Illustrations

Preface

"Kind of Different", the state publicity department says, breezily, of Adelaide and South Australia. Since we have had the luck to live in or near Adelaide since 1968, first in an embowered Unley Park villa, then amid the lovely green undulations of the Adelaide Hills, I have come to realize that Adelaide *is* different. Pleasantly, distinctively different from the rest of Australia: the fact is admitted, generally with affection, all round.

I was curious to know why this is so. It cannot just be geography, topography and climate, although these certainly help. As an historian, I assumed that the reasons for this Adelaide distinctiveness must lie entwined in the city's historical origins. So I began to delve and read and interview and wander about the city. An invitation from the Adelaide City Council to write a book on the history of Adelaide gave the project the necessary force and cohesion.

The idea was to produce a study which would differ from the customary local government-backed history, which can tend to overemphasize the activities of mayors, councillors and politicians, and civic deliberations. These have their honoured place, of course, and so they do in this book. But I was, above all, concerned to write a broad history of a community with attention to all the elements I could encompass. Thus I have written in detail on such matters, often neglected in civic histories, as popular amusements, sports, the environment, newspapers, and community attitudes, prejudices, and strengths. Such aspects of a city's history seem to me of equal importance to its politics and commerce.

There is an overriding factor in this study. Clearly, a *total* history of Adelaide or anywhere else can never be written to everyone's satisfaction. The writer would soon be overwhelmed by details and conflicting views and bemused by the complexity of it all. So I chose a theme, the aspect which had intrigued me from the beginning, and called it Adelaide's sense of difference. While trying to provide a reasonably detailed and wide-ranging study of Adelaide's historical growth from foundation to the 1970s, I have throughout, where appropriate, looked for and stressed matters and events which seemed peculiarly Adelaidean. And I have tried to explain how this distinctiveness came to be.

The plan determined for the book was a deployment of facts and interpretations which might be a useful compromise between the old chronological method of writing civic histories and a more discursive and selective approach. As is shown by the table of contents, the first part is largely chronological, advancing on a broad front from about 1836 to the late 1850s. Under the heading "Foundation", this section covers the comparatively self-contained formative years of Adelaide. The second part, "Adelaide 1859–1970: a Brief Chronicle", is a summary of major events and experiences in the city from the achievement of self-government up to quite recent times. "Mosaic of a Community", the third part, is a collection of studies of various aspects of Adelaide life and interest from the beginning to modern times. The fourth and final part examines Adelaide in the 1970s and draws some conclusions on the whole study.

Incidentally, throughout this book, by "Adelaide" I have usually meant the whole metropolitan area, not just the few square kilometres within the Parklands which is the actual city of Adelaide and the nucleus of the whole. Further, I have sometimes stretched the term to include the state of South Australia, or at least its settled parts, for this, even more than the other Australian states, is very much a city state, with the capital heavily dominant over the country.

Finally let me say that I am well aware that I have had to omit or inadequately treat many, many things about Adelaide which are very important to some people. My excuses are space and time, and a feeling that Adelaide, like beauty, may lie in the eye of the beholder.

This book gave much pleasure in the writing. My hope is that it will give at least some pleasure in the reading.

Acknowledgments

During the three years or so in which this book was prepared, I incurred many debts of gratitude to people who most courteously helped me. While the opinions advanced in this study, and the conclusions reached, are my own, I was often enlightened and guided by others far too numerous to list. I should like to thank them warmly now collectively and in particular, for research assistance and counsel, the following: The Lord Mayor and Corporation of the City of Adelaide which originally invited me to write this book and which, through a special committee (the Lord Mayor, Mr. John J. Roche, the Town Clerk, Mr. Russell Arland, and Aldermen J.V.S. Bowen and G. Joseph), gave me indispensable practical and financial help and encouragement and, through its research and clerical staff, facilitated the production of the manuscript and the illustrations in innumerable ways; Alderman W.L. Bridgland; Mrs. Helen Mullins, Ms. Cherry Watkins, Mr. Adrian Graves, and Mr. Len Mathews of the Town Hall staff who were especially helpful in collecting and preparing illustrations from the rich Town Hall Archives; Mr. J. Suckling; Mr. and Mrs. R.M. Gibbs, who gave invaluable advice and research assistance; the Premier the Hon. Don Dunstan and Sir Arthur Rymill, for particularly enlightening interviews; Mrs. Sadie Pritchard and Miss Elaine Potts for help with illustrations; Mr. Ashley Cooper; the late Mr. Ian Mudie; and Mr. Hugh Stretton of the University of Adelaide. And I should like to thank my wife, Alison, who helped and encouraged me all the way.

1

FOUNDATION

Proclamation

Colonization is an imperative duty on Great Britain. God seems
to hold out His fingers to us over the sea. But it must be a
colonization of hope; not, as has happened, of despair.

Samuel Taylor Coleridge, 1834

If I can get pious people sent out to that land, the ground will be
blessed for their sake.

George Fife Angas, 1836

Adelaide—and South Australia—began with the highest hopes. "The object", Edward
Gibbon Wakefield had written, "is not to place a scattered and half-barbarous
colony on the coast of New Holland, but to establish ... a wealthy, civilized society." The
reality, on that hot summer's afternoon of 28 December 1836 when the Province of
South Australia was proclaimed, was rather less grand. But it had a kind of homespun
nobility.

The scene was a huge gum tree on a grassy plain studded with peppermint gums
and melaleucas, near the sand dunes of Holdfast Bay. There, by the mouth of the
Patawalonga Creek, the little storeship *Buffalo*, South Australia's *Mayflower*, swung at
anchor, the ensign listless in the hot antipodean air. In the background marched the
600 metre high Mount Lofty Ranges, named by Lieutenant Matthew Flinders as he industriously charted his way up and down St. Vincent Gulf in the *Investigator* in 1802.

The wooded crest and tawny spurs of the ranges, the huge powder blue dome of
the sky, the yellow kangaroo grass of the plain, humming and clicking with insects, the
queer trees and odd birds, the startling clarity of the South Australian light, in which
unaccustomed English eyes still blinked, the black natives peering from the scrub, the
heat and the space and the strangeness—all this seemed a far cry from the
philosophical and commercial debates over tea or sherry in stuffy London rooms which
had led to Proclamation Day.

Yet after rhetoric, some idealism, some hard bargaining, much muddle, and many
lost tempers, the founding fathers' enterprise to establish a model colony in the Great
South Land had got this far. The South Australia Act of 1834 had approved the foundation of a rather special colony. A governor, Captain John Hindmarsh, had been appointed by the Colonial Office, with the agreement of a specially appointed board of
commissioners, whose resident commissioner, James Hurtle Fisher, sailed with Hindmarsh on the *Buffalo*. The South Australian Company, formed in 1836, had strong influence over economic matters in the new colony while the Colonial Office had vague
administrative suzerainty, had funds of 320,000 pounds, and had already sold large
slabs of the Adelaide Plains, site unseen, on the strength of Captain Charles Sturt's
enthusiastic report of his explorations in 1829.

By Proclamation Day nine colonizing ships, including the *Buffalo*, had disembarked tired and bemused settlers and officials by the scrub of Kangaroo Island, where the South Australian Company had set up a whaling station, or on the dunes of Holdfast Bay. Unsteady after over twenty weeks' pitching over the oceans in foetid little ships, they waded through the waves in their stovepipe hats and crinolines, pitched their canvas tents amid the clutter of disembarkation and had their first confrontations with Australian heat and insect life. Cultural shocks must have been severe. John Morphett, soon to achieve success as a businessman and land agent, had arrived earlier with the surveyors on the *Africaine* and recalled later: "I can recollect perfectly well the disconcerted and dismal look with which most of the first party regarded, from the deck of the ship, the dried and scorched appearance of the plains, which, to their English ideas, betokened little short of barrenness".[1]

Still, most of the first settlers seemed to have been in high spirits, and all must have been relieved to be safe on dry land, however alien, after such a voyage. Unlike the unhappy outcasts who first settled New South Wales and Van Diemen's Land, or the ignominious speculators by the Swan River, these followers of Angas, Torrens, and Wakefield had an uplifting cause. From the outset, South Australia was to be a pure moral contrast to the rum and convictism of the eastern Australian colonies and the fecklessness of the surviving Swan River settlers. It was to be, as Anthony Trollope observed when he visited Adelaide in the 1870s, a "happy Utopia",[2] of free religious conscience, progress, and profit. There were to be no convicts and almost no alcohol. Land was to be paid for, at Wakefield's "sufficient price", by respectable gentry who would employ industrious labourers. Immigrants would be screened for sobriety, savings, and morals.

Morphett typified the high hopes when he wrote to the commissioners on 25 November 1836. He was impressed with everything he saw, including the trees of the coastal plains near Rapid Bay. "These are principally blue-gum, which is a most elegant tree of great magnitude, growing only in rich land ... we measured one of these lords of the Australian forest, and found it to be twenty-one feet in girth. Fourteen and fifteen feet is a very common size, with a straight trunk in many instances sixty feet high."[3] On settlement, Morphett was lyrical: "I do most confidently believe that the shores of South Australia will furnish, not only a happy and prosperous home for thousands of England's sons, and of 'the finest peasantry in the world' ... but that the colonization of South Australia will furnish to civilization another resting-place, whence she may spread her magic influence over a large and hitherto untrodden portion of the globe."[4]

Some, at least, of the settlers were inflated with such sentiments, as they left their tents and trudged, perspiring in their best clothes, through the kangaroo grass for the proclamation. The governor, in the blue and gold and epaulettes of a naval captain, appeared in such state as the *Buffalo* and the tent and shanty town could provide. Four-square John Hindmarsh, a veteran of the Napoleonic Wars (he had even lost an eye, like his hero Nelson, at the Battle of the Nile) was, in the words of Lord Auckland, "zealous, good-tempered, anxious to do right, brave and well used to hardship—perhaps not remarkably clever, but altogether not unsuited to the conduct of a new colony".[5] Auckland was right enough about Hindmarsh's character, but shatteringly wrong about his suitability to be South Australia's first governor. Prickly and impetuous, Hindmarsh was a man of action, used to the quarterdeck autocracy and instant lower deck obedience of Nelson's navy. He had served ten of his golden years at sea fighting the French. He had been promoted by Nelson himself on the *Victory*, and had been in the thick of powder and shot at many a stirring sea battle, from Cadiz to Trafalgar to Mauritius. He had been instrumental in the capture or destruction of more than forty enemy ships of the line and much merchant shipping.

Later, in 1834, Hindmarsh had enjoyed more muted glory in the Egyptian navy, where he had become well acquainted with Adelaide's favourite son, Colonel William Light. This Hamlet of South Australian history had been the nominee for governor of their mutual patron, Colonel Sir Charles James Napier, after Napier had withdrawn his own acceptance of the governorship when the Colonial Office refused his demand for more troops to guard the colony. Napier recommended Light for the position. He had served with Light during the Peninsular War and considered that he would "give an eclat to the appointment which might be useful to the colony".[6] However, Napier had earlier mentioned the vacancy to Hindmarsh when they met in Portsmouth. The unemployed Hindmarsh had with him, ironically, a letter of introduction from the luckless Light. And Hindmarsh had shown all his old naval talent for quick and decisive attack by posting up to London, gaining influential support, and securing the job in three days before Napier's preference was known. Much was made of his bravery on the old *Bellerophon* at the Battle of the Nile. This was natural enough. Hindmarsh was a man after the Admiralty's heart, and in those days both the Admiralty and the War Office looked to the governorships sprouting all over the expanding British Empire as honourable berths for the superabundant veterans of the Napoleonic Wars. Subduing savages, safeguarding settlers, and carrying out government orders, with attendant pomp and circumstance, was much preferred to frustrated retirement on half pay in the shires. This tradition of making distinguished military men imperial governors was to prevail in South Australia and elsewhere right up to the 1970s.

In the 1830s there was no real alternative. Veterans as diverse as Sir Ralph Darling in New South Wales, Sir George Arthur in Van Diemen's Land, and Sir James Stirling in Western Australia had all won their spurs against Napoleon and gained their reward in Australian government houses. Moreover, South Australia was a huge unknown quantity to the London authorities. Most of them regarded New Holland as a bore or an expensive nuisance anyway. ("Pray where is South Australia?" a prince of the blood asked during the debate on the South Australian Bill. "Somewhere near Botany Bay", surmised the lord chancellor.) Lord Glenelg, the colonial secretary, probably felt the infant colony might need a military hero to defend it. So the eager Hindmarsh got the job and the sensitive Light was too late. The captain showed his appreciation by naming the settlement at Holdfast Bay, Glenelg, which has the distinction of being spelled the same both ways. It was said of Glenelg that "he reduced the art of doing nothing to a system, and when he abandoned that attitude what he usually did was wrong". With hindsight we can say that he was wrong about Hindmarsh. Either Napier or Light *must* have been better (although, then, who would have planned Adelaide?). Adelaide in its foundation years was to sour many tempers and that of Hindmarsh was the first.

It seems not to have occurred to Glenelg and his advisers that a strong-minded seadog, used to speaking his mind in a gale, was hardly the ideal mentor for a crowd of theoretical colonists. Hindmarsh was not the man for philosophical debate on land settlement and immigration. He had little sympathy with the crypto-republican theorists, and the fatal division of authority between Government House and the resident commissioner was to rend his administration. "I rather fear", said John Brown, the emigration agent, after meeting Hindmarsh, "we shall have a little quarterdeck government, but this must be provided for."[7]

Hindmarsh did his best. He bustled about London, met and, surprisingly, liked Wakefield and pronounced that he supported his system, although he clearly did not understand it. Perhaps with a sore conscience, he recommended his rival Light for a position in the colony. Torrens offered him the surveyor-generalship of South Australia at the miserly salary (the commissioners were consistently mean on pay) of 400 pounds a year. Light, like Hindmarsh had been, was out of work and accepted the post in February 1836.

Life had been exciting and exacting if not rewarding to William Light.[8] He was the illegitimate son of an illegitimate son. His mother, Martinha Rozells was spoken of as a princess of Kedah but was almost certainly a Portuguese Eurasian. It is interesting to reflect that the half-caste Light might not have been allowed to settle in Adelaide during the days of the White Australia policy. His father Francis, an adventurer in the Raffles mould, had founded the East India Company settlement of Georgetown on the island of Penang, which now has sister city status with Adelaide. Planning was in the brief Light dynasty's blood. Like so many Napoleonic War veterans of his type, the colonel was a man for all seasons. One of his friends remarked that he was "a man of extraordinary accomplishments, soldier, seaman, musician, artist, and good in all". Before his quickly dimming twilight in South Australia, Light had served in India, Spain, Portugal, and Egypt, and had travelled widely. His ability and charm had made him popular with military men from Wellington downwards. Although circumstances prevented him from fighting at Waterloo (and perhaps saved him for Adelaide), Light had fought in forty engagements in the Peninsular War without a scratch. One of his exploits in this bloody war is so full of dash and daring, and so well described, by Sir William Napier in his *History of the War in the Peninsula*, that it deserves quoting yet again here. On 19 March 1814, the advancing British cavalry were held up by a line of French skirmishers at Vic Bigorre near Tarbes. Napier wrote:

> Lord Wellington was desirous to know whether a small or a large force thus barred his way, but all who endeavoured to ascertain the fact were stopped by the fire of the enemy. At last Captain William Light, distinguished by the variety of his attainments, an artist, musician, mechanist, seaman and soldier, made the trial. He rode forward as if he would force his way through the French skirmishers, but when in the wood dropped his reins and leaned back as if badly wounded; his horse appeared to canter wildly along the front of the enemy's light troops, and they thinking him mortally hurt ceased their fire and took no further notice. He thus passed unobserved through the wood to the other side of the hill, where there were no skirmishers, and ascending to the open summit above put spurs to his horse and galloped along the French main line, counting their regiments as he passed. His sudden appearance, his blue undress, his daring confidence and speed, made the French doubt if he was an enemy, and a few shots only were discharged, while he, dashing down the opposite declivity, broke from the rear through the very skirmishers whose fire he had first essayed in front. Reaching the spot where Lord Wellington stood, he told him there were but five battalions on the hill.[9]

Yet in most other matters Light was less than lucky. He was swindled out of his Penang inheritance. He had married, in 1824, a rich beauty, Mary Bennett, an illegitimate daughter of the Duke of Richmond, whose main distinction was that he was descended, illegitimately yet again, from Charles II. But Mary had left him taking her money with her. He had been severely wounded at Corunna when fighting for the Spanish revolutionaries. He was suffering from tuberculosis before his appointment as surveyor-general. He had been unlucky over that, too, for he might have been governor. And he was doubly unfortunate in the wretched rate of pay offered by the commissioners.

Light was to die, penniless and dejected, in his "city in the desert" within three years of Proclamation Day. He was to be involved in harassing controversies, and was pestered into resignation. His morals, for he lived with a mistress called Maria Gandy, were deplored by the godly founding fathers. Yet, as he expected he might, Light has probably received more honour by later South Australians than any of the other progenitors. There is a special place in the sedate Adelaide heart for this doomed,

Byronic colonel with a whiff of the Indies and the theodolite through which he looked with such imagination.

Meanwhile, luck continued bad for Light after his appointment. The commissioners, none of whom had been within 26,000 kilometres of the vast wilderness they had acquired by act of parliament, were explicit about the capital city Light was to plan. They described it to him in his letter of instruction. The site should have:

1st.   A commodious harbour, safe and accessible at all seasons of the year.
2nd.   A considerable tract of fertile land immediately adjoining.
3rd.   An abundant supply of fresh water.
4th.   Facilities for internal communication.
5th.   Facilities for communication with other ports.
6th.   Distance from the limits of the colony.
7th.   The neighbourhood of extensive sheepwalks.
The above of primary importance, the following of secondary value.
8th.   A supply of building materials, as timber, stone, or brick, earth and lime.
9th.   Facilities for drainage.
10th.   Coal.

The commissioners further instructed Light: "You will make the streets of ample width, and arrange them with reference to the convenience of the inhabitants and the beauty and salubrity of the town; and you will make the necessary reserves for squares, public walks and quays." This last was fair enough: it was a great deal better than the deafening silence from London as to how Sydney or Hobart should be laid out. It was a sensibly vague outline. Perhaps the commissioners realized that their new surveyor-general, who won golden opinions from men like Napier, had the vision and ability to do the rest.

However, since most of their money had come from purchasers of colonial land, the commissioners were detailed about country surveys. Such sections were to be of " ... 134 acres each, of a form convenient for occupation and fencing, with a reserved road adjoining each section; and you will provide in the best manner you can for the after division into 80 acre sections of such of these lands as may not be selected by the holders of the first 437 land orders."

Moreover, as if all this were not enough, Light was expected to have a close look at Kangaroo Island, and then to examine carefully the central areas of the South Australian coast charted by Flinders and other explorers. He was especially recommended to study the potential of Port Lincoln, with its deepwater harbour, as well as the eastern coast of Gulf St. Vincent about which Sturt had reported enthusiastically. As well, of course, Light was to survey the Murray mouth and Encounter Bay area.

To do all this, the commissioners allowed this fifty-year-old cavalryman a miniscule surveying party, with George Kingston—completely incompetent, by most accounts—as his deputy, and two small ships, the *Cygnet* (239 tons) and the *Rapid* (162 tons). In case they had any spare time, the surveyors were also urged by the commissioners to report in detail on the soil, climate, vegetation, wildlife, and the natives, who were to be "lifted up from degradation" by the colonists who would follow Light.

In our own times, when it takes an army of bureaucrats several months to decide upon the site and name of the proposed new city of Monarto, let alone plan it, we can only boggle at the difficulties Light faced. Geoffrey Dutton writes: "In that two months Light was expected to have examined all the good harbours on 1500 miles of coast, founded the first town and as many secondary ones as he had leisure for, surveyed the town acres and to have completed a complicated survey of about 100,000 acres of country sections!"[10] And this in virtually unexplored country, in the middle of a hot summer, and among natives already alienated by the riff raff whaling and sealing gangs who lived like down-and-out pirates on Kangaroo Island. Light wrote later amid the bitterness of resignation to Wakefield on 16 May 1838: "There never was so large a colony entrusted to the judgment of one man to *found*."

But Light's cup of tribulations was still not full. The commissioners, who vividly proved the adage that a camel is a horse drawn by a committee, were to pursue him with much armchair advice. Before leaving England, Light was obliged to confer with Hindmarsh on the site for the first town. Worse, Light was "to pay due regard to his opinions and suggestions, without, however, yielding to any influence which could have the effect of divesting you in any way of the whole responsibility of the decision". Such a fence-straddling proviso would have been dangerous enough with any colleague. With Hindmarsh, it was disastrous. Light dutifully consulted the governor who, liking blue water near him, plumped for Port Lincoln as the spot for the capital. He had been smouldering about this for some time. On 10 March 1836, Brown noted in his diary: "It appears that the Governor is dreadfully annoyed at the Commissioners leaving the selection of the Town to Col. Light and the Surveyors".

Thus, with trouble brewing behind him, Light set sail in the *Rapid* on 1 May 1836. After a pleasant passage during which he gained the esteem and loyalty of his staff, he arrived off Kangaroo Island on 17 August. Thence he sailed to Encounter Bay, later to be advocated as the site for the capital by Hindmarsh and his party. Light rightly pronounced it unsuitable. The Murray mouth was, and has remained, useless as a harbour because of its exposed position and the formidable rollers that surge into it from the south. Light sailed the *Rapid* north to Rapid Bay, which he named after his handy little ship, then further north up the gulf searching for the chimerical "Jones' Harbour" which had been mentioned by Collet Barker. By the time he had found the Port Adelaide River, the small but adequate harbour upstream, and the attractive Adelaide Plains, the first settlers were already arriving and expectantly pitching their tents. Before choosing his site, Light still had to hurry over to Port Lincoln, where he soon concluded that the shoals by the harbour mouth and the arid hinterland ruled it out. But Light already had more than an inkling as to where his new city should be. He was later to call the plains round the Torrens River a "little paradise", and he wrote in his diary: "My hopes were now raised to a pitch I cannot describe." Then back to Holdfast Bay (Light had named it), where the *Africaine* had disembarked officials like Robert Gouger the colonial secretary, John Brown, and some seventy-four colonists.

The *Africaine*, one of the first of the South Australian immigrant ships, was fairly typical of them: Gouger and Mary Thomas, wife of the government printer, kept detailed diaries of the voyage and the modern reader can re-live their odysseys through their pages.[11] The *Africaine* was a mere thirty-eight metres long, and her decks were only three and a half metres above the waves. The forty steerage passengers existed together in a gloomy area next to the hold, equipped with bunks and a long table. The upper decks were packed with farmyard animals, including seventy sheep. The food—apart from the occasional flying fish—was mainly salt meat and weevily biscuit. The water casks soon became foul. When one keg was opened the escaping gas was lit by a sailor's lamp and exploded "with a tremendous flash and report". The shortage of water meant that for the five months of the passage most of the voyagers went unwashed. The *Africaine* butted and wallowed her way over the Atlantic, round the Cape of Good Hope, and through the Roaring Forties of the Southern Ocean, tossing her landlubber settlers, sheep, and chickens from side to side, on into the vast unknown.

The weather was stormy and hot, the passage had been a gruelling one, and the landfall at Kangaroo Island had not been happy. Two young settlers had perished of thirst in the scrub. They were sick of salt pork, many of them had incipient scurvy, and they were probably frightened by the vast, un-English land and sea-scapes all round. By the time Light had returned from Port Lincoln, tired and ill, the settlers and officials were raising a chorus of complaints about their canvas tents and reed huts. Plagued by "oppressive" heat—on one day the temperature exceeded 105 degrees Fahrenheit—and the "cruel perseverance" of the flies, Gouger pitched his tent near the surveyors. He wrote: "Troops of mosquitoes entertained us with their music and we, in return, entertained them with a full repast, and in the morning we were well-nigh in a fever from their visitation". Five inch long centipedes perturbed the colonial secretary and "enormous ants and very small frogs abound also in our tent ... and the changes from heat to cold have been somewhat extraordinary; in one instance, within twelve hours the thermometer ranged between 105 degrees and 50 degrees, both in the shade". Mrs. Gouger was six months pregnant.

"Wild dogs", Mrs. Thomas recalled, "were numerous at Glenelg, and often prowled about our tents at night howling most hideously." Many of the first settlers were to stay encamped by Holdfast Bay for a year during the wrangles and delays over the site and survey of Adelaide. William Jacob, one of Light's surveyors, described the "Piggish life" they led in the tents. Meanwhile, there were compensations. For all the privations, which were much less severe than those on shipboard, the original settlement had its idyllic aspects. George Stevenson, the first editor of the *South Australian Gazette and Colonial Register*, noted in the diary he kept with his wife:

> We were all delighted with the aspect of the country and the rich soil of the Holdfast Plains. Mount Lofty and the hills before us are wooded to the very summits, 1,500 feet at least above the level of the sea. On the plain, there are numerous splendid trees of the eucalyptus species. The *Banksia rosa marinafolia* was in great beauty—we found the pea, buttercup, the camomile daisy and geranium, the flax plant, the Kangaroo grass in great abundance. The parrots and parroquets were very numerous. In a short walk we startled several coveys of quail ... nothing in fact can be richer than the soil. I have seen the Pickaway plains of Ohio and traversed the Prairie of Illinois and Indiana, but the best of them are not to be compared with the richness of the Holdfast Plains. Fifty bushels of Indian corn or wheat could be grown at the first turnover. The water is in plenty, and four or five feet of digging is required to obtain an abundant supply ...

Recalling Proclamation Day, the *Register* of 3 June 1837 showed how the new arrivals rejoiced at anything reminiscent of England: "The lupin, buttercup and several of the wild flowers of our own country, were met with and hailed with delight."

The idyll was not to last long. There had been trouble on the *Buffalo*. Hindmarsh had hoped for a more dignified conveyance than this 589 ton sixth-rate storeship. From the start he had a poor opinion of the colonists. At best, the journey would have been long and uncomfortable, but its rigours were worsened by Hindmarsh's dithering over the route and the fact that he showed more concern for the comfort of his large family (three daughters, a wife, and a son), his dogs, and his variegated livestock than for his passengers. Stevenson, always waspish, spoke for them all in his diary:

> They have no place where they can walk or breathe unpolluted air. The bulwarks of the *Buffalo* are six feet high. On both sides of the main deck are rows of filthy hogs kept in pens, generally in a horrid state of dirt and uncleanliness. The emigrants can only walk alongside of these animals and inhale the stench from them. They are forbidden either side of the quarterdeck, although the officers and passengers have the poop, or what remains of it unoccupied by hay-trusses and hen coops, to themselves. These things make a deep and ineffaceable impression on the individuals most directly affected by their operation, and will tell eventually. A voyage like this calls for the exercise of more philosophy than falls to the common lot. Zeno was never at sea in an emigrant ship.[12]

And even Zeno may have forgotten his stoicism when bitten by one of Hindmarsh's pack of dogs which roamed the *Buffalo* nipping everyone except the Hindmarshes. The Governor often cut the water ration, although the emigrants noted that the livestock had plenty to drink. He shouted and bullied. He plunged into what was to be a virulent series of quarrels with Fisher. He upset the Methodists by putting the ship about with much flapping of sail, in the middle of their on-deck prayer meetings. For a month the mainsail was kept reefed, lengthening the voyage, so that, Stevenson complained, Hindmarsh's "cow and mules in the longboat may not suffer by the draught of wind ... Of what importance is making sail to their health and safety!"

Hindmarsh began to bicker with Fisher about the site of the capital. When Stevenson observed that the commissioners' instructions to Light had been quite clear, "The polite and dignified remark in answer was he 'did not care a —— for any order of the Commissioners, and he would fix the seat of Government where he pleased.'" None of this was promising for colonial tranquillity as the *Buffalo* discharged the emigrants, the governor, the governor's family, and the governor's unpopular livestock at Holdfast Bay. Mrs. Hindmarsh's piano fell into the sea. Hindmarsh had weathered many storms during his career, but none more tempestuous than the one which his own tetchiness and circumstances were about to provoke in South Australia.

But on Proclamation Day itself, at least, all seemed sweetness and light—although Light himself was not present at the ceremony. Hindmarsh had sent Kingston to summon the surveyor-general to the proclamation that afternoon. Light demurred. "I heard of the Governor's arrival, but having much to do, had not time to go to Holdfast Bay.[13] Perhaps Light was annoyed by the peremptory summons: more likely, he realized that Hindmarsh would soon begin quibbling about the city site. Light stayed with his theodolite while the governor enjoyed his drums and trumpets. It was a bad augury.

Down at the bay, the settlers temporarily forgot the mosquitoes and the sore eyes in the euphoria of foundation. There was solemnity and a sense of high endeavour. John Stephens wrote in his *The Land of Promise* (1837): "The renunciation of his native land, and the adoption of another country is the most important step that a man can take, and one, moreover, which can seldom be retraced, and never without much inconvenience and loss." Probably such thoughts were uppermost in many of the settlers' 'minds. They must have known, most of them, of the failures at Swan River and of the violence and hardship of the eastern colonies. They were determined that this province would be different—a model for rational colonization and a New Jerusalem for Nonconformists. Even so, it must have been reassuring to see "buttercups" peeping at them from the kangaroo grass and the sight of Hindmarsh in his finery and the marines reminded them of English law and order on this margin of wilderness.

Mrs. Thomas wrote an admirable description of Proclamation Day:

> December 28, 1836. This was a proud and, I hope, will be a happy day for South Australia. Early in the morning it was announced that the *Buffalo* had arrived from Port Lincoln, accompanied by the *Cygnet*, which had gone thither to escort the Governor, Captain Hindmarsh, to Holdfast Bay. This made us all alive, and soon after Mr. Thomas received notice to attend at the tent of Mr. Gouger, the Colonial Secretary, where His Excellency the Governor was expected to be at three o'clock to read his Commission and proclaim the colony.
>
> It was requested that we would prepare ourselves to meet the procession, as all who could were expected to attend. We went accordingly, and found assembled the largest company we had yet seen in the colony, probably two hundred persons.
>
> The Governor's Private Secretary read the Proclamation under a huge gumtree, a flag

was hoisted, a party of marines from the *Buffalo* fired a *feu-de-joie*, and loud hurrahs succeeded. A cold collation, of which we partook, followed in the open air.

The Governor was very affable, shaking hands with the colonists and congratulating them on having such a fine country. After the repast, he mounted on a chair and gave the first toast, "The King", which was received with three times three, and followed by the National Anthem, led by Mr. Gilles ... The health of His Excellency was then proposed and drunk with loud and universal cheering, followed by "Rule Britannia". Then "Mrs. Hindmarsh and the Ladies" was proposed by Mr. Gilbert, and also received great applause, as did several other toasts.

The Governor then gave the following:—"May the present unanimity continue as long as South Australia exists", which made the plain ring with acclamations. At about 5 o'clock His Excellency and lady departed to the ship, and some officers and others followed in another boat. They all seemed highly delighted with our village as I may now call it, consisting of about forty tents and huts, though scattered about without any regularity. Everyone fixed his present abode wherever he wished, knowing it would not be of long duration.

The *South Australian Record* commented with more bombast:

The landing of the little band in their new country recalls the awful emigration of Noah, and the promise that painted his horizon, and that of Moses. It reminds us of the Tyrians at Carthage, of Aeneas and the dominion of the west which, tradition tells us, was founded by him: of the stout-hearted Britons who built up the great, though still young, nations of America; and, nearer to the present scene, the colonies of Australia, whose errors of constitution have served as an impressive lesson, while their unexampled prosperity points to the commercial fortune of the new settlement ... To those who, from a distance, contemplate the placing of a people where late there was a blank on the great map of the world, and who have the glorious expectation of seeing, within the short space of a man's life, in one and the same spot, a desert, a settlement, and a busy city, every act ... is full of meaning, intrinsic or extrinsic. It forms the bright strong line between desolate barbarism and busy civilization. It is the first act in realising the dream of the philanthropist, the emigrant, and the ambitious commercialist, who, like Alexander ... find the civilized world too small for their activity and their desires.

Stevenson, who had endured the *Buffalo* and her captain, contrasts with the rodomontade of the *Record*:

A dozen or so of drunken marines from H.M.S. *Buffalo* discharged several muskets in honour of the occasion; a table manufactured impromptu out of boards supported on barrels, salt beef, salt pork and an indifferent ham, a few bottles of porter and ale, and about the same quantity of port and sherry from the crypts of the *Buffalo*, completed the official banquet which graced the advent of British rule to the shores of South Australia.

His wife observed that during the ceremony "not a *Buffalo* face, at all events, was to be seen unwrinkled by a frown, or not distorted by a sneer. Sad, sad, this!"

If a little makeshift, this was at least more impressive than the foundation days in the other Australian colonies. There were no leg-irons here, or speculators itching to grab land for nothing or next to nothing. The Aborigines had been coolly elbowed out of their lands by Whitehall ukaze, but at least the proclamation, thanks to Glenelg's influence, contained high-sounding sentiments about how they should have "equal rights and an equal claim with the white man upon the protection of the Government".

The junketing was now over. The explorations and theorizings which had made the settlement possible, and which we shall examine in detail, were giving way to the explicit facts and work of settling emigrants. Whither should the people of the shanty town at Glenelg move? Where was the capital to be?

By Proclamation Day, Light had made up his mind. The trouble was that Captain Hindmarsh, who bore down on him on the afternoon of the next day, had made up his mind, too. But before looking at this clash between artist and man o'war, we must consider more closely the human and physical background to this nervous cluster of Britons raising their flag in the antipodes.

The Physical Setting

By raising the Union Jack and having its proclamation read, Hindmarsh now ruled for Britain an enormous land mass. The governor and his three hundred or so colonists had but vague ideas about their new acquisition. They knew South Australia was big. They knew that there were hundreds of kilometres of coastline both east and west of Holdfast Bay thanks to the navigations of Flinders and others. They knew that the River Murray emptied into the sea by the dunes where Barker had perished eighty kilometres to the south, and that this river rose thousands of kilometres away in the interior. They knew that the plains below the hills were good settlers' country, and that there was timber and potential sheep runs in the hills themselves. They knew, from recent experience, that the South Australian summer is hot. They had already seen and wondered at strange plants, trees, animals, and birds. They had seen the Aborigines who, in possum skins and wallaby cloaks, gazed at these sweltering newcomers in their frock coats and stifling dresses across an abyss of evolution.

Such was the sum total of the settlers' knowledge of their new home. As to what lay beyond the ranges, they could only speculate on unimaginable vastness. Moreover, they were for years to be more concerned with building their new capital and importing the paraphernalia of British civilization as speedily as possible.

The state of South Australia now comprises almost a million square kilometres.[1] England, with its 130,000 square kilometres would fit into it comfortably six times over. Its western border with the even bigger state of Western Australia lies along the 129th meridian of east longitude, spanning the Nullabor Plains and the immensity of the Great Victoria Desert. Its northern boundary, equally straight as a ruled line across the map, lies south of the 26th parallel of south latitude and stretches 1,200 kilometres from the Tomkinson and Musgrave Ranges to the salt flats of the Lake Eyre Basin. The eastern boundary extends along the 141st meridian for 1,325 kilometres. South Australia's southern boundary is natural—roughly 3,500 kilometres of rugged coastline fretted by the Southern or Indian Ocean, sprinkled with islands like Kangaroo Island, Australia's third largest, and including the long dunes of the Younghusband Peninsula, the northward probing identations of St. Vincent Gulf and Spencer Gulf and the high cliffs that rim the Bight.

South Australia's relief is rarely as dramatic as that of the eastern states, there being few areas over 600 metres high. Cross-patterned warping and faulting, elevation and submergence in the Pleistocene period created the most striking features of the state, including the Flinders and the Mount Lofty Ranges.

Climatically, South Australia can be roughly divided into two areas. The northern region, which is warm and dry, has high summer temperatures and an erratic rainfall of less than 250 millimetres a year. The smaller, southern region, which includes the Adelaide area, has a climate that is often described as Mediterranean, but is in fact subtropical with moist, cool winters and hot, dry summers. Very few areas in this region receive more than 890 millimetres of rain a year. Adelaide receives about 530 millimetres and most of the settled areas from between 380 and 640 millimetres a year. South Australia is generally warm and sunny, and although some of its southern areas, including Adelaide, sometimes endure cold and wet winter weather, it merits its reputation as the driest state in a dry continent. Thirty-nine per cent of Australia as a whole has less than 250 millimetres of rain a year, but over 82 per cent of Southern Australia is thus deprived. On average, Adelaide has 13 days a year when the temperature exceeds 38 degrees Celsius (100 degrees Fahrenheit).

When the first colonists came, the vegetation could be divided roughly into five types according to areas. In the northeast and northwest, the very dry areas, spinifex grass is the chief plant, and there are huge stretches of sandy ridges and gibber (stony) plains devoid of any vegetation at all. Mulga scrub, a type of acacia, prevails over much of the north, succeeded further south by thickets of mallee, a kind of dwarf eucalypt, she oak, and tea tree. Saltbush is the dominant plant on the Nullabor. The comparatively well-watered region where the settlers first landed, the wetter parts of the Flinders and Mount Lofty Ranges, and the south east portion of the colony were a colonists' paradise of eucalypt forest and open, grassy plains studded with tall trees. Originally the Adelaide Plains were covered with open, savannah type woodland, and the forest was continuous on the highlands of the ranges. Much of the soil was excellent in the Adelaide Plains as many settlers remarked. The explorer Barker had commented on the "rich, fat, chocolate-coloured earth". In the first settlers' letters there were many delighted comparisons between the Adelaide landscape and a nobleman's park at home, a popular simile. That observant Quaker traveller, James Backhouse, went for a walk in the Glen Osmond foothills in 1838 and wrote: "Some of the kangaroo grass was up to our elbows and resembled two years' seed meadows in England, in thickness; in many places, three tons of hay, per acre, might be mown off it."[2]

There was plenty of fresh water for the settlers. It could usually be found merely by digging a well, or by going to one of the many creeks, like the Sturt, Torrens, Para, and Onkaparinga that flowed down from the hills. As settlement spread, the Murray and the artesian resources of the north were used.

Dr. R. Schomburgk wrote of the mallee later:

> The monstrous and dismal look of an extensive scrub is depressing, especially when viewed from an eminence. The equal height of the vegetation, the dull glaucous colour of the foliage, look in the distance like a rolling sea reaching the horizon—at least the first sight of the Murray scrub, extending hundreds of miles, produced this impression on my mind. Everyone avoids the scrub as much as possible—many have lost their way there and perished for want of water.[3]

As for wildlife, settlers like the Stevensons and Morphett looked with pleasure and interest upon the eucalypts, banksia, wildfowl, and flowers of the plains. There were numerous kangaroos, wallabies, wombats, and other marsupials. Cormorants nested in colonies in the mangroves and pelicans and herons flapped majestically over the reedbeds. Wild duck, emus, quail and shrikes—soon to be dubbed magpies by the homesick settlers—were plentiful, as were a bewildering and beautiful variety of parrots. Less agreeable were the equally numerous snakes and centipedes, of which the settlers soon developed a healthy dread.

The hills and plains were a world removed from the pinched streets and overcrowded shires they had left behind, and over all was the beaming sun and clear air, which had a most un-English effect upon their surroundings. As the artist George French Angas (son of the founding George Fife Angas) wrote of the sunset at Rapid Bay in his *South Australia Illustrated* (1846): "The rich violet of the hills at evening—the intensely deep blue and purple of the distant landscape after sunset—and the pink eastern sky, through which the full moon rises like a silver shield on a bed of roses, are effects of an atmosphere peculiarly Australian."

THE ABORIGINES

> So many miseries have been sustained by those unoffending creatures in different parts of the continent that I felt particularly anxious that the annals of our province should be unstained by native blood.
>
> *Robert Gouger, 1837*

The first white settlers were relieved to find that the local tribe, the Kaurna, was friendly. One of the Kaurna, Panartatja, was taken out to a ship, and, in classic Bennelong fashion, made much of and dressed in European clothes. He later learned English and called himself Jimmy Rodney. One of his sons, Philip, died in the Adelaide Hospital in 1897, and appears to have been the last authentic male survivor of the Adelaide Kaurna tribe. In other words, a mere sixty-one years of European urban settlement was quite sufficient to eliminate, almost without trace or cultural memory, an indigenous community.

The native population of South Australia before 1836 has been variously estimated to have ranged between 10,000 and 14,000. Kangaroo Island had no Aboriginal occupants, beyond the Tasmanian Aboriginal women slaves brought there by the sealers, although relics of earlier native occupation have been found. There were only a few hundred Kaurna, and about five hundred Aborigines on Yorke Peninsula. Understandably, Aboriginal settlement was densest where the food supply was most reliable—along Encounter Bay and the Coorong, and along the banks of the Murray, where Sturt noted many, sometimes warlike, tribes, some of them numbering two or three hundred. The nomadic tribes of the interior were to remain undisturbed until dust rose about the hooves of the advancing sheep flocks, or explorers struggled over the forbidding deserts.

It was the more sophisticated Kaurna and Narrinyeri peoples of the habitable coastal regions who first felt "the fatal impact" of the Adelaide pioneers. And it is largely to the occasional descriptive writings of the first settlers that we have to look to get even a garbled idea of what the first South Australians were like. From these it appears that the Kaurna and similar peoples were a peaceable, friendly, robust group, living at ease with their environment and totally devoid of Western interest in progress and possessions. The women were usually treated in a way that would appal modern liberationists—they looked after the children, dug for roots, grubs and berries, made camp, carried the few movable goods and were often savagely beaten about the head. The Aborigines believed in an animistic spirit world and expressed their feelings, sense of worship, and legends through singing and dancing and through complicated rites.

They painted themselves, usually with white or red ochre, and rubbed their skins with shark and fish oil. They adorned themselves with feathers, branches, and down. In hot weather they were often naked, at other times they wore garments made from reeds and animal skins. They slept behind a semicircle of branches in fine weather, and during the winter they made more permanent homes in caves, under trees or in wurleys of boughs. They were usually on the move, and usually found ample food by hunting for fish, shellfish, marsupials, birds, fruits, and insects. They often fired the scrub on the ranges to flush game from cover.

One thing is certain—that despite the good intentions of the officials like Gouger, quoted at the beginning of this section, most of the pioneers regarded the Aborigines as shiftless, benighted heathen. The settlers thought their customs at best picturesque, at worst obscene or barbaric. When it was found that the Aborigines would not work as servants in a way satisfactory to Englishmen, then they became a problem. They should be herded on to reserves, dressed in old clothes, and converted to passive Christianity. Or they should be got rid of, like pests.

Wakefield's theories and Sturt's discoveries were sad events for the Kaurna and their like. The meeting with the whites, once the novelty had worn off, became a confrontation between totally different worlds. The weaker went to the wall and for the Kaurna there remained only an increasingly debased twilight existence on the fringe of the fine new city dedicated to progress and profit. While the banks were built, they lingered for a time on the parklands and the beaches, then they faded away. Few of the newcomers had the perception of men like Sturt or Edward John Eyre, or even Governor Hindmarsh, who wrote to Angas on 15 February 1837 of the Aborigines:

> Many natives have visited us, bringing with them their women and children, and altogether exhibiting confidence that is quite pleasing. Instead of being the ugly, stupid race the New Hollanders are generally supposed to be, these are intelligent, handsome and active people, being far better looking than the majority of Africans. The women exhibit a considerable degree of modesty. A party of about twenty, who came down a few weeks ago, and who brought the first women and children I had seen, were placed under the shade of a tree in little family groups. When I first came up to them, I soon became acquainted with their names, which were musical and pretty such as Alata, Ateon, Atare and Melanie.[4]

In our times, the tribes which produced Hindmarsh's "intelligent, handsome and active people" are long gone. During the intervening period there was cultural attrition, disintegration, rape, and murder. Gouger's hopes that the annals of the model colony would be "unstained by native blood" were never realized.

Even as late as 1936, the Aborigines were still regarded with patronizing indulgence, as anthropological curios, as this concluding sentence of the chapter on Aborigines in the *Centenary History of South Australia* shows: "Taking them altogether, they are a loveable race, good humoured and kind, but they are incapable of mixing successfully with the European population, and so require guidance and care, like grown-up children."

Discovery

In 1627 a Dutch East Indiaman, the *Gulden Zeepaard*, Francois Thyssen commanding, nosed its way from Cape Leeuwin along the cliffbound western coast of South Australia as far as the islands of St. Francis and St. Peter. These mariners named the dun coloured expanse "A Landt Van P. Nuyts" in honour of the "Councillor Extraordinary of India" on board, Pieter Nuyts. But they obviously did not think much of the unprofitable deserts they had found. They were interested in rich Oriental civilizations, ripe for mercantile plucking, such as they found in the Indies. The French admiral, D'Entrecasteaux was the next unimpressed inspector of the cliffs of Pieter Nuyts Land, observing in 1792: "It is not surprising that Nuyts has given no details of this barren coast; its aspect is so uniform that the most fruitful imagination could find nothing to say of it." At least one fruitful imagination had, however, made use of this Here Be Dragons part of the unknown world: Jonathan Swift in his *Gulliver's Travels* located Brobdingnag, the land of the giants, in southern Australia.

The first British explorer, Lieutenant James Grant, sighted the extreme east coast of present day South Australia in 1801, and named Cape Northumberland, Mount Schank, Mount Gambier, and Cape Banks. The following year, the "Great Denominator" of Australian exploration, Matthew Flinders, made his famous voyage along the "Unknown Coast" in the *Investigator* between Nuyts Archipelago and Encounter Bay. There he met the French explorer Nicolas Baudin who had charted the coast from Western Port to the bay. Flinders, who popularized the term Australia incidentally, and who is warmly remembered in South Australia, sprinkled the map with homely East Anglian names like Port Lincoln and Sleaford. He reported that the coastal plains round the gulfs seemed good colonizing prospects. He sighted and named Mount Lofty, later to be the watchtower of Adelaide. On 22 February, Flinders landed at Nepean Bay on a large island at the mouth of St. Vincent's Gulf, both, like Yorke's Peninsula and Spencer's Gulf, named after Admiralty notables. The hungry sailors were delighted to see mobs of kangaroos watching them innocently from the scrub. Flinders wrote in his journal:

> It would be difficult to guess how many kangaroos were seen, but I killed ten; the rest of the party made up the number to thirty-one taken on board in the course of the day, the least of them weighing 69 and the largest 125 pounds ... The whole ship's company was employed this afternoon on skinning and cleaning the kangaroos, and a delightful regale they afforded after four months privation from almost any fresh provisions. Half a hundredweight of heads, forequarters, and tails were stewed down into soup for dinner on this and succeeding days ... In gratitude for so seasonable a supply I named the southern land Kangaroo Island.[1]

Nepean Bay, Kangaroo Island, was to be the site for the first British settlement in South Australia.

There were no important explorations of the area between the departure of

Baudin and Flinders and Captain Sturt's dramatic descent of the Murray in 1830. Vaga-
bond sealers and escaped convicts found a haven on Kangaroo Island and began the
demoralization of the mainland Aborigines. A Captain Jones apparently discovered the
Port Adelaide River but was imprecise about its whereabouts.

Captain Charles Sturt, another Peninsular veteran, was despatched on 10
November 1829 by the government of New South Wales to solve the "problem of the
rivers" in the interior. Sturt's vessel was a whaleboat; his companions seven soldiers
and convicts. Yet he managed to traverse a huge blank on the map by means of the
Murrumbidgee, Darling, and Murray rivers. This last "broad and noble river" as he
called it, Sturt named after Sir George Murray, colonial secretary.

Sturt and his party survived many hazards to reach Lake Alexandrina (the future
Queen Victoria's first name), whence they walked over the sandhills to Encounter Bay
on 9 February 1830. The shallow and treacherous Murray mouth, guarded by a great
semicircle of rollers sweeping in from the Southern Ocean, disappointed Sturt. It would
disappoint many later men who hoped for a large port on the Murray estuary. The
party was too exhausted and short of supplies to brave the rollers and attempt to sail
back to Sydney by sea. Nor had Governor Darling's promised support ship arrived. The
alternative they chose, and it must have seemed a grim one as they slumped on the
sand, was to row the entire 1,500 kilometres back upstream to their depot on the Murrumbidgee. On 12 February, they began to row back against the current. They survived
many hardships to reach Sydney six months later.

Sturt wrote of this and earlier explorations in his *Two Expeditions into the Interior of
Southern Australia*, published in 1833. In this he regretted the need for haste in returning,
which prevented him from examining the western shores of Lake Alexandrina.

> We were borne over its ruffled and agitated surface with such rapidity that I had scarcely
> time to view it as we passed, but, cursory as my glance was, I could not but think that I
> was leaving behind me the fullest reward of our toil in a country that would ultimately
> render our discoveries valuable, and benefit the colony for whose interests we were
> engaged. Hurried, I would repeat, as my view of it was, my eye never fell on a country of a
> more promising aspect or of more favourable position than that which occupies the space
> between the lake and the ranges of St. Vincent's Gulf, and continuing northerly from
> Mount Barker stretches away without any visible boundary.[2]

The Mount Barker Sturt mentions was named after Captain Collet Barker who was
sent by Governor Darling to explore the coasts of St. Vincent's Gulf as Sturt had recommended. Barker arrived at Cape Jervis with a small party on 13 April 1831. They
walked observantly over lightly timbered meadows, climbed through ravines to the
summit of Mount Lofty, named the Sturt River, where they caught fish, and examined
the inlet of what was to be called the Port Adelaide River. Inevitably, Lake Alexandrina
and the Murray mouth attracted them, and there the expedition ended in tragedy. As
Hodder describes it:

> Captain Barker judged the breadth of the channel to be a quarter of a mile, and being anx-
> ious to take bearings and to ascertain the nature of the strand beyond the eastward, he
> determined, notwithstanding the remonstrances of his people, to swim across. Unfor-
> tunately, he was the only one of the party who could swim well enough for the purpose.
> He stripped and swam across with his compass fastened on his head, with difficulty gain-
> ing the opposite side, and then he was seen to ascend the hillock and take several bearings.
> He then descended on the further side—and was never seen again. For a long time his
> comrades waited in anxious suspense; then some of them heard, or thought they heard, a
> sharp sudden cry. Evening advanced without any sign of Captain Barker's return, but
> when night set in the terrible explanation came. Upon the sandhill the doomed man had

ascended, the natives had lighted a chain of small fires, around which their women were chanting a melancholy dirge. It struck upon the ears of the listeners with an ominous thrill, and assured them of the irreparable loss they had sustained.[3]

It was later stated that natives had speared the unfortunate captain and thrown his body into the sea. Sturt surmised in his book that "the cruelties exercised by the sealers towards the blacks along the south coast may have instigated the latter to take vengeance upon the innocent as well as the guilty".

The sandhill by the Murray mouth was named Barker's Knoll. Flinders's observations, Sturt's brief sightings, some explorations by a Captain Hart and the more thorough survey by Barker all pointed to the conclusion that the eastern coastlands and ranges of St. Vincent's Gulf were good for settlement. Sturt summarized the situation in his book:

> It would appear that a spot has at length been found upon the south coast of New Holland to which the colonist might venture with every prospect of success, and in whose valleys the exile might hope to build for himself and for his family a peaceful and prosperous home. All who have ever landed upon the eastern shore of St. Vincent's Gulf agree as to the richness of its soil and the abundance of its pastures. Indeed, if we cast our eyes upon the chart and examine the natural features of the country behind Cape Jervis, we shall no longer wonder at its differing in soil and fertility from the low and sandy tracts that generally prevail along the shores of Australia.[4]

This report was fuel to the fire of colonizing fervour in England.

The Background to Settlement

There will never be a single convict sent thither ... See what sort of a society we are likely to have ... Emigration will be disarmed of nearly all its terrors.

Advertisement of the South Australian Company, 1835

The novelty of the scheme of colonization propounded, the untried character of the principles upon which it was proposed to establish the colony, the limited nature of the territory to be occupied, combined to give the Parliament and the public an idea that the well-meaning projectors were visionaries and enthusiasts seeking to establish a Utopian settlement.

Edwin Hodder, The History of South Australia (1893)

England under the Regency and the reigns of George IV and William IV was entering upon one of the more expansive and creative phases of her history. Rivulets were beginning to run which would become broad and fast-flowing rivers in the Victorian period.

A depression followed the exertions and expense of the Napoleonic Wars. The Industrial Revolution, productive alike of unprecedented wealth for the industrialists and unprecedented poverty and insecurity for the rapidly growing proletariat, was in full spate. The population was increasing fast. Ill-considered changes in the Elizabethan Poor Law, which meant supplementing the wages of poor families from the rates, had helped this growth. Unemployment, overcrowding, and simmering discontent, which sometimes exploded in violence, were chronic features of society. Religious dissenters were tired of being discriminated against. A parliament composed mainly of squires made bread dear by taxing imported corn.

There were to be slow, typically British, ameliorations and compromises, such as the Reform Bill of 1832 and the erosion of the Corn Laws, but in 1829, when proposals were first made for colonizing South Australia, England was still for many people an excellent place to emigrate from.

Despite—or perhaps because of—the defensive conservatism of an establishment much shaken by the runaway libertarianism of the French Revolution, there was also in England a strong liberal and philanthropic ferment. This resulted for example in the anti-slavery movement and legislation to improve some of the worst excesses of the factories and gaols. The Utilitarians, followers of Jeremy Bentham, had considerable influence. There was a powerful evangelical groundswell of opinion led by dominant figures like William Wilberforce for this, for all its hypocrisies, was an intensely religious age.

It was natural, then, that colonization should attract its advocates. To the conservatives, and they usually prevailed at the Colonial Office, the thirty British colonies seemed costly irritations, more than likely to separate from the mother country in time just as the United States had done. The old mercantilist theory which had justified the first British Empire had been discredited by the American example and by the publication of Adam Smith's influential *Wealth of Nations* in 1776. The British have usually been reluctant imperialists, pushed into foreign occupations by the exigencies of war or opportunism on the spot by men like Raffles and, in Penang, Francis Light. The Australian colonies, for example, had been set up, and then only half-heartedly, because they were useful receptacles for criminals. Or because, if Britain did not raise the flag over the eucalypts then the old enemy, France, would. Vision, popularity, and sentiment about Empire would have to await the un-English enthusiasm of Disraeli and the high noon of Victorian pomp.

Still, colonization in the 1830s had its appeal to conservatives because it promised to remove surplus population (a dread to thinking Englishmen since the publication of Thomas Malthus's *An Essay on the Principle of Population* in 1798), especially the paupers who strained the rates. Moreover, it promised to dish the French who, as Flinders had found, were taking a competitive interest in Australia. In 1817 and 1819 Poor Law committees agreed that paupers should be exported at public expense and some were, to Canada, from 1823 onwards.

The theorists who were to set up South Australia as the first model of a new look colony shared the conservatives' concern about excess population and French rivalry but had a much more idealistic view on the challenges of colonization. They visualized colonies as profitable but also philanthropic enterprises which would offer scope to overcrowded Englishmen, extend British influence and civilization, and eventually strengthen rather than weaken the homeland. The more utopian among them dreamed that well-planned colonies would recreate new Britains without the blemishes of the old, like Wentworth's vision of a "new Britannia in another world". And it was Edward Gibbon Wakefield,[1] perhaps the most imaginative thinker in the history of British colonization, who provided the framework to their dreams. Wakefield, born in London in 1796, was well qualified by breeding to give voice to the humanitarian intellectualism of his time. His father, a Quaker, was a close friend of Bentham and of Francis Place, the radical. His grandmother, Priscilla Wakefield, was one of the founders of the Savings Bank in England. Edward Gibbon, the monumental historian, was a relative, and Elizabeth Fry, the prison reformer, a cousin. A brilliant, erratic youth, Wakefield managed to abduct and marry one underage heiress, but came to grief when she died and he hurried to Gretna Green with a rich schoolgirl named Ellen Turner. Wakefield had abducted her under false pretences, the Turner family had him arraigned for illegal abduction, and Wakefield was consigned to the notorious Newgate Gaol for three years. The young man was discredited and his career in the public service blighted. He narrowly escaped transportation.

Most men would have wilted under such ignominy but the reverse brought out Wakefield's Quaker industry. His surroundings and enforced leisure gave him the chance to marshal his thoughts and a life's cause. Cousin Elizabeth visited him and helped turn his thoughts towards penal reform and the sufferings of his wretched companions. He developed a vivid style of writing and wrote influential essays on the futility of capital punishment and the need for reformation rather than punishment. These prompted *The Spectator* to observe:

The imprisonment of Mr. Edward Gibbon Wakefield in Newgate will probably prove a source of the most essential benefit to the country. If ever a man redeemed the wrong he had done society, by conferring upon it a vast benefit, it is Mr. Wakefield. We would call upon all generous minds to forget that this ingenious and enlightened enquirer had ever been detained within the walls of a prison except for the purpose of a philosophical investigation.

Ironically, Adelaide and South Australia as we know them would not exist were it not for Newgate Gaol and Wakefield's penchant for adolescent heiresses.

Wakefield in his cell read all he could find on Australia with such effect that he published a "Sketch of a Proposal for Colonizing Australia" followed in the autumn of 1829 with eleven famous letters in *The Morning Chronicle*. These were republished anonymously next year under the editorship of Robert Gouger as *A Letter From Sydney*. Gouger became Wakefield's strong right arm in the campaign for systematic colonization. He too had been imprisoned for debt in the King's Bench prison. There he had met a Captain Dixon, who excited him with his tales of voyaging round Kangaroo Island. Thus two at least of Adelaide's most respected founding fathers were ex-convicts. Wakefield had been no nearer Botany Bay than its posting house, Newgate, but he wrote as a colonist who had travelled widely there and had taken up 20,000 acres (8,100 hectares). This verisimilitude together with his pungent style made the book a political and literary sensation. The general opinion of the Australian press was that its author was "a penny-a-liner from Grub Street" who had written it "within sound of Bow Bells". One editor, however, thought that on colonial life it "contained more real and more accurate information than any other which has yet been given to the public".

Wakefield's ideas on "systematic colonization" as he called it were not completely new. Experiments with land and emigration had often been suggested for colonies. But the power, clarity, and comprehensiveness of his theories enhanced by cogent prose appealed to Englishmen ashamed of the mess they had so far made of New Holland settlement. Squatting and land grabbing, "shovelling out paupers", and dumping convicts offered a seedy contrast to Wakefield's philanthropic and scientific vision of a society of well-regulated gentry and free and honest yeomen.

Wakefield's plans had three main principles: the sale of land; the use of the resultant income for sponsoring immigrants; and the granting of some measure of self-government. The first two at least had direct application in South Australia. Supplementary principles were that land should be sold at a fixed minimum price, or above; that settlement should expand in contiguous blocks (the "concentration" principle); that the volume and pace of immigration should be related to the available land; and that the settler should have a say in such matters as the appointment of officials and land sales. Altogether he offered a seductive package attractive to a wide range of English urges.

Firstly, necessity. None could deny that England was becoming overpopulated, not only with paupers but also by "respectable" people denied outlets for their talents. Wakefield wrote in his essay "On the State and Prospects of the Country" in the *Quarterly Review*: "All trades, pursuits and professions are becoming more and more overstocked; and multitudes of persons, of all degrees and ages, are moving about, without employment, useless to themselves, and a burden to the public."

Secondly, philanthrophy. Hitherto, Wakefield argued, while the British population had been rising by "3 and 400,000 annually", only about "7 or 8,000 at utmost" people a year had been "removed to our colonies". Moreover, while "No pains should be spared to teach the labouring classes to regard the colonies as the land of promise", the authorities should stop considering them as depositories for "desperate or needy men". They could have balanced populations. He added: "THE GREEK COLONIES CONTAINED A MIXTURE OF ALL CLASSES OF SOCIETY." As it was, Australian society had acquired "the sentiments and manners of jailers and turnkeys". With systematic colonization, the colonies would become "extensions of older societies". Prosperously balanced and content with their measure of self-government, such colonies would not wish to rend themselves away from Britain as the United States had done. They would support her in her advancing years. "Britain would become the centre of the most extensive, the most civilized, and, above all, the happiest empire in the world." All this was very agreeable to philanthropists.

Thirdly, science. In the 1830s science, or natural philosophy as it was usually called, was even more fashionable than it is today. Wakefield's implicit claim that his theories were scientific, based upon pure reason, helped to ensure a sympathetic response. With precision and accuracy, this alleged New South Wales land holder argued that the colony's economy was unsound because of the scarcity of labour, especially skilled labour. No one would work as a farm labourer when he could get a free land grant easily. Convict labour was neither plentiful nor satisfactory. Convictism demoralized the infant society. Autocratic temporary officials had little sympathy with or understanding of colonial life.

Wakefield argued that the answer to all these problems lay in proper planning, particularly with regard to the disposal of land. Instead of allowing land to be seized by the first ruthless fortune hunters, as in New South Wales, or to be sold too cheaply, as in the Swan River settlement, the authorities should insist upon a "sufficient price". Wakefield suggested two pounds an acre. A suitably high price would restrict abortive land distribution and attract capitalists with funds and experience. Wakefield had many practical and persuasive proposals on how the money from the sale of colonial lands could be used to bring over skilled labourers and trades people as immigrants. All this seemed impeccably scientific.

Fourthly, profitability. Wakefield was man of the world enough to know that vision and philanthropy needed to be laced with opportunities for capitalist enterprise for his scheme to succeed. His theory was practicable enough to indicate to pious business men like Angas that excellent returns upon investment might be had in an orderly, well-planned Wakefield colony. It was better than the reality, say, of Van Diemen's Land where, as Augustus Prinsep had written: "If the history of every house were made public, you would shudder; even in our small menage, our cook has committed murder; our butler, burglary; and our housemaid, bigamy."[2] Businessmen could support "scientific colonization" with the gratifying sensation that they were adding both to progress and their own prosperity.

It is not necessary here to narrate in detail the various attempts to launch Wakefield-style settlement in South Australia. All have been well described elsewhere. It is sufficient to note that Wakefield's writings, his own great propagandist ability, and the support of friends like Gouger soon created a ferment of interest. From 1829 until his death in 1862 Wakefield was to devote his life to his crusade as master builder of the new British Empire. Because of his Newgate record he had to work, as he put it, "like a mole, in out-of-sight obscurity", but he was brilliantly effective for all that. The two colonies of South Australia and New Zealand, where he died, again in "out-of-sight obscurity", were his brain children, and his was the moving spirit of the famous Durham Report which made possible the growth of the British Commonwealth of Nations.

In reality the plans of South Australia were not all pure Wakefield. But they were sufficiently his inspiration to make us regret that his memory receives far from sufficient honour in Adelaide and South Australia. His influence prevailed strongly enough to give Adelaide its sense of difference.

Meanwhile, with Wakefield fresh out of Newgate, the questions were where and how to build his new utopia? With Gouger active on his behalf, Wakefield soon rallied progressive thinkers to his cause, a mixture of Utilitarians, businessmen, members of parliament, and general enthusiasts, some of whom had been at Trinity College, Cambridge, together. The influential William Hutt, the merchant Jacob Montefiore, a connection of the Rothschilds, and Colonel Robert Torrens, M.P. and ex-marine, were prominent here. All have given place names to Adelaide.

Torrens wrote later that "the colony of South Australia, devised by Mr. Wakefield, was planted by me". A tireless publicist and organizer, anxious to export surplus population, especially from his native Ireland, Torrens worked for a "self-supporting system" of colonization. On 15 February 1837, a little over a year after proclamation, Torrens voiced one of the main ideals of the systematic colonizers during a Commons debate on emigration: "In giving effect to extensive and improved plans of colonization, we are multiplying the British nation; we are rocking the cradles of giant empires; we are co-operating in the schemes of Providence; and are its favoured instruments in causing Christian civilization to cover the earth as the waters cover the sea."[3]

Another favoured instrument ardent to help Providence and rock imperial cradles was George Fife Angas,[4] a pious Northumbrian merchant banker with a lifelong passion for forming societies and pushing philanthropic causes. His was to be a major influence upon Adelaide and South Australia. It was largely due to Angas's business acumen that the colony attracted capital, and it was his strong dissenting principles that ensured the moral tone of the province and the separation of church from state. God and Mammon were perfectly reconcilable in Angas's philosophy. He wrote in a circular of 1835 about the South Australian project: "The world has to be Christianized, and the machinery employed in the present day ... is far from adequate to the attainment of that end ... Emigration is according to the manifest design of Providence. ... That I am sincere in my convictions above stated I can give no stronger proof than the fact that I am a large land holder of land in the colony; as an investment it is better than any I can obtain in England."

Wakefield and his supporters made a number of attempts to interest the government before they achieved success with the South Australian Colonization Act of 15 August 1834. There was Gouger's National Colonization Society, founded in 1830, then the South Australian Land Company, headed by Torrens, formed in 1831 when Sturt's gratifying reports on South Australia reached England. The company beat its head for three years against the conservatism of the Colonial Office. The powerful under secretary, James Stephen, thought their plan for self-government "republican", an ominous word in Whitehall at that time. He also suspected it would become a financial burden. The Duke of Wellington believed that Britain already had enough colonies, although he later changed his mind when Wakefield adroitly suggested that the capital of the new colony should be called Wellington. (In the event, King William preferred to name it after his queen, Adelaide. The duke had to wait until Wellington was named after him in the second Wakefieldian colony of New Zealand.) Bentham approved of the Wakefieldian proposals. *He* suggested that the new colony be called Felicitania, a good indication of the founders' hopes.

Further good reports on South Australia from the explorers and the passing of the Reform Bill of 1832 improved the prospects for the systematic colonizers, who attracted more Whig and liberal support. They discussed their plans at the Adelphi in London. In 1834 the South Australian Association was formed and the sedulous efforts of Gouger, Torrens, and others, with Wakefield pulling most of the strings, at last brought about the South Australian Colonization Act. Colonial Office caution ensured unhappy compromise between the misgivings of a government which had burned its fingers at Swan River and the aspirations of the Wakefieldians. To Wakefield's disgust, South Australia was not to be a virtually independent chartered colony. Authority was to be divided. The Colonial Office was to appoint a governor who was to be responsible for affairs of state other than land sales and immigration. These were to be under the control of a specially appointed board of commissioners, set up in 1835 with Torrens as chairman and Rowland Hill, of later penny post fame, as secretary. The board was to preside over the sale of all land alienated from the crown at a price of not less than twelve shillings an acre, much less than Wakefield's ideal "sufficient price". The income from the sale was to go into a fund for "conducting the emigration of poor persons from Great Britain and Ireland".

The territory allotted under the act comprised 802,511 square kilometres. The western boundary was the 132nd meridian of east longtitude and other boundaries were much the same as they are today. All this huge area was designated as "waste land", the implication being that the resident Aborigines had no sovereign rights to it. The new colony, or province, as it was first called, was to be open to settlement by British subjects. No convicts were to be sent there, which meant that garrison troops were unnecessary. Some local participation in government would be allowed when the population reached 50,000.

The government protected itself further against untried principles going wrong by denying finance; the colony had to be self-supporting. The commissioners were authorized to raise 200,000 pounds against future general revenue to finance the first settlement and the foundation of government, and 50,000 pounds against the sale of land to begin the emigration programme. There were two conditional clauses which were to bedevil the whole enterprise and delay settlement by at least a year. Before the board could exercise its powers, government securities to the value of 20,000 pounds had to be lodged as a guarantee of the venture. And land to the value of 35,000 pounds was to be sold prior to settlement.

The commissioners proved to be energetic publicists. During 1835 they offered land in the new colony at 2 pounds an acre including rights to an acre in the new city for every 80 acres of country land. Investors could buy a city acre plus an 80 acre country block for 81 pounds in a bargain package. When only half the necessary land was sold (land at that time was selling at 5 shillings an acre in New South Wales), they dropped the price to the permitted minimum of 12 shillings an acre. Finally, Angas, a member of the board, saved it from early collapse by forming the South Australian Company as a philanthropic but also hard-headed business venture. The company bought up the balance of the land and in December 1835 sufficient land had been sold and the 20,000 pounds guarantee was lodged with the Treasury. The South Australian Company was not officially connected with either the government or the commissioners, but its intervention had made the project financially viable. Its vigorous land, banking, mercantile, and whaling activities were to have an important influence upon the colony.

Thus by the end of 1835, "systematic colonization" was at last possible. Hindmarsh became governor, Light surveyor-general, and Kingston his deputy. J.H. Fisher (later Sir James and first mayor of Adelaide), a lawyer who had helped to sell land, was appointed resident commissioner. Gouger became colonial secretary. Osmond Gilles, a shrewd and wealthy financier who was prepared to charter ships, became colonial treasurer.

There were further harrowing delays while the Colonial Office, for example, had last minute worries about the treatment of Aborigines, but in early 1836 the pioneer ships set sail. First to go were the South Australia Company's four ships to set up a whaling depot at Nepean Bay, Kangaroo Island. They were followed in May 1836 by Light with the *Cygnet* and the *Rapid*. In June away sailed the peppery Hindmarsh, the eye of a growing cyclone of controversies, in the *Buffalo*, with the immigrants.

The situation bristled with difficulties. Most importantly, the South Australia Act had been a compromise between the Wakefieldians and the government, satisfactory to neither. The division of power between Hindmarsh and the commissioners was almost to pull the young colony in two. There had been haste and last minute expediency. Money had been borrowed at a high rate of interest to fulfil the government's conditions so the enterprise was saddled with debt from the outset. There was incompetence and frayed tempers as amateurs, some talented, some not, some interested only in making money, others full of ideals, administered a novelty. Fisher and Hindmarsh squabbled on the *Buffalo*. A disputatious board struggled to administer an unworkable act of parliament. Light was to be driven to distraction and illness. The company's whaling settlement on Kangaroo Island, managed by the reckless Samuel Stephens, was fated to be unprofitable. A bad situation was made worse by the board's policy of allowing its underpaid officers to take part in commercial ventures.

The province's parvenu leaders were, too, a queer assortment if one cracks away the varnish of later respectability. Hindmarsh, for instance, bullish, confused, and on the make; Gilles, rich, bibulous, radical ("We'll have no kings here!" he once exlaimed), and on the make; Fisher, fussy, snobbish, and on the make; Brown, an extremist with a fiery mastery of polemics; above all that acidulous Scot with a shady background, whom Light called "the Paragon of Blackguards", Stevenson.[5]

Then there were the settlers themselves, uprooted, demoralized by the voyage, worried if they had done the right thing, concerned about what their unseen land would be like—when it was surveyed.

A peck of troubles was descending on the quiet plains of St. Vincent's Gulf. Still, the gloom, rancour, and frustration had always been shot through with rays of hope and promise. There was a power and a faith in the founding fathers that would help them surmount all their obstacles. Above all, a magnificent country awaited them. Once arrived, much of the worry would dissolve in the excitement and work of pioneering.

Settling In, 1836-40

The reasons that led me to fix Adelaide where it is I do not expect to be generally understood or calmly judged of at present ...
I leave it to posterity ... to decide whether I am entitled to praise or blame.
Colonel Light, 1839

South Australians began at the wrong end—they commenced by building a town before there was any country population or country produce to support it.
J.F. Bennett, 1843

... it must be admitted that for some years the outlook for the Province was a very black one.
William Harcus, 1876

The first few years of Adelaide's history were traumatic. There were bitter dissensions and many blunders. There was a hectic land boom which, when it burst, ruined many speculators. The division of authority between an incompetent governor on the spot and an incompetent board of commissioners 26,000 kilometres and six months by ship away in London caused discord and delay. Hindmarsh, Fisher, and Light were only three of the founding fathers whose reputations, or at least peace of mind, suffered in the turmoil.

THE SITE OF ADELAIDE

Fortunately, during the weeks after Proclamation Day, the ailing surveyor-general still had the drive and resolution to make bold, decisive strokes. While the colonists were still recovering from the libations at Gouger's tent, Light was at work laying out the site of Adelaide.

Light and his team had already decided on the best location before the *Buffalo* arrived. While Hindmarsh was enjoying his Proclamation Day, Light was encamped by the Torrens and was busy, as he recorded in his journal "examining the plains and looking out for the best situation for the capital". Earlier, on 21 November, he had explored the southern reach of the Port Adelaide River, concluding that this was "one of the finest little harbours" he had seen. The channel held three or four fathoms of water and could be deepened by mud barge. There were creeks and inlets among the mangroves which could be used for ship-building and other harbour activities. Light wrote to the commissioners: "Although my duty obliges me to look at other places first before I fix on the capital, yet I feel assured, as I did from the first, that I shall only be losing time. The eastern coast of Gulf St. Vincent is the most eligible, if a harbour could be found—

that harbour is now found, more extensive, safe and beautiful, than we could ever have hoped for."[1]

About twelve kilometres inland from the Port Adelaide River Light and his party had found a pleasant expanse of slightly elevated, lightly timbered and fertile land traversed by the River Torrens and a number of other creeks. There was ample land for city growth. There were timber and limestone for building, clay for bricks, and ample supplies of fresh water. If not actually by a harbour, the site was not far from both Port Adelaide and Holdfast Bay. The soil was rich and deep. Light's artistic eye could not have missed the fact that the Mount Lofty Ranges, "the enchanted hills" as he called them, provided a superb backdrop. There were fine potential sheepwalks and farmland all round and communications could be established with any future settlements by the Murray. Thus almost all the exacting conditions laid down by commissioners for the capital were fulfilled.

The most obvious disadvantage of the site was the distance from the Port Adelaide River. Founding fathers had a natural preference for harbourside settlements and the squabble over this was to be Light's bane. However, the plain between the site and the harbour was firm and level and as Light's assistant B.T. Finniss wrote in 1837: "as wealth and population increased Adelaide would soon approach nearer the harbour than six miles. Those miles would then become a vast suburb studded with shops and warehouses." He was prophetic.

The surveying party had really decided on 18 December that the plains beyond Holdfast Bay would be the best location for the capital. Kingston was to claim that it was he who had pointed out to the colonel the exact location. We can dismiss this as rodomontade. Finniss, who could see through him, wrote to Montefiore in August 1838: "I should not be surprised to hear that Mr. Kingston contrived to persuade the Commissioners that he surveyed all the town himself, and even pointed out the eligibility of the site to the surveyor-general."

Adelaide—that is, the physical city, the streets, the squares, the location—is William Light's creation. There was no doubt about this either in his own mind, or among the detractors who were soon to criticize him for his choice of site. He was to suffer blame for this during the three years of life left to him: posthumously, he deserves most of the credit.

On 30 December, Hindmarsh, Fisher, and Light inspected the site. At first, the governor approved. He wrote to Glenelg on the 6 January 1837 that the location was of "great beauty and promise", surrounded by "beautiful park-like scenery and rich, fertile ground, fitted for all agricultural purposes". Even the harbour was "very secure once in", "upwards of seven miles" and "capable of carrying many ships". Moreover, from the harbour there was "easy communication over a perfect flat" to the city. Before he left the surveyors, however, the governor began to meddle. He thought that the site should be removed two miles nearer to the harbour. Light, too reasonable by half, agreed. He and Kingston however, decided that night that the new position would be unsuitable because of flooding. Light reverted to his original choice and began his city survey the next day, 31 December 1836.

They were only a small party. It is easy to visualize them: small, overdressed European figures against a huge antipodean background. They would have been knee deep in kangaroo grass as they pushed their wheelbarrows and hefted their theodolytes among the big trees. The sun beat down, flies buzzed round their sweating heads, insects hummed in the grass, and curious parrots screeched from the eucalypts as they worked. They were short of men, good food, equipment, and, above all, of time. They had no horses. They worked under immense pressure, for they knew that the first immigrants were already demanding to take up their selections and that hundreds more were arriving soon. They were upset even while doing the city survey by organized opposition to the site. The wonder is that Light was able to complete the survey at all under such circumstances: the marvel was that he did it so well. Despite illness, and the disruptive meddling of Hindmarsh and others Light completed his survey of the town and its 422 hectares by 11 March 1837.

Light laid out Adelaide on the gridiron pattern that was to become popular in many Australian towns,[2] a pattern with its faults but one at least no more troublesome than any alternative. He planned fifty-one streets with a minimum width of 20 metres, many of them up to 30 metres wide. As for his noble boundary terraces, these were from 40–50 metres wide. His city was in two main sections north and south of the Torrens. North Adelaide from north to south extends for more than a kilometre, and from east to west about 800 metres. It consists of 138 hectares. The larger South Adelaide, which Light correctly visualized would develop as the commercial centre, covers 283 hectares and measures from north to south about one and a half kilometres and nearly two and a half from east to west. He allotted 190 hectares for government land and 227 hectares for streets, footpaths, and the squares.

In addition he set aside swathes of virgin plain for his famous parklands, dividing the two Adelaides with a belt of greenery along the Torrens and girdling the entire city. Naturally, he but vaguely adumbrated the outer edges of the parklands. In time they comprised no less than 688 hectares, making a total area now administered by the Adelaide City Council of 1,528 hectares or more than 15 square kilometres.

Light endured wounding criticism at the time both for the location and the plan of Adelaide. Hindmarsh was obsessive that the choice of site should have been his as governor and that it should be by a harbour. The situation at the Glenelg shanty town where impatient immigrants sweltered and swatted mosquitoes while waiting for their selections was ideal for controversy.

The officials of the South Australian Company, led by Stephens, complained that their property was spoiling at Holdfast Bay and the port and demanded a city location handy both to a harbour and fresh water. Certain landed proprietors were unhappy about the inland site and angry at the delays. Stevenson, the governor's general factotum, soon revealed a genius for sowing discord. He and Strangways, Hindmarsh's private secretary, left Finniss and other surveyors stranded on Kangaroo Island by their improper removal of the *Cygnet*, thus further delaying the work. Some settlers grumbled that the surveyors were idle, although anyone who had gone to the Torrens would have seen them, in Woodforde's words, "working like slaves".

On 19 January, Light was obliged to interrupt his survey to be questioned at a council meeting at Holdfast Bay for neglecting his duty. Hindmarsh ordered him to abandon his city work to survey the harbour. Light refused. By now, he must have realized that this settlement of philosophical business men in the bush was going to cause him more trouble than any of his chequered experiences in the war or in Egypt. In his *Brief Journal*, for instance, he recorded:

> ... I was incessantly treated with some hints at my want of ability in the performance of my duty. One gentleman (I am told) said that he considered himself a ruined man through Colonel Torrens and myself, but principally through me! and that he would publish my proceedings in all the newspapers in England! ... I had also the satisfaction of hearing, that the Governor had found great fault with it [i.e. the site of Adelaide], and that I had not paid sufficient attention to my survey.

Gouger wrote to Light from the Bay:

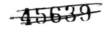

> You may tell Hindmarsh if you wish it, Light, that … he frequently told me "he would be d——d if the capital should be here." Some days afterwards he qualified this by adding "unless a sufficient number of acres are also surveyed at the Harbour"; and once when his ire was greatly kindled he said that "rather than have the capital at the place you fixed upon, he would order all the Government officers on board the *Buffalo* and sail away with them to Port Lincoln".[3]

Stevenson walked out to inspect the Adelaide site (and got lost walking back to the bay) and recorded in his journal:

> The position is very good for a farm, but for a commercial city seven miles from a harbour—that will never do. There is, besides, nothing but the eucalyptus, or bluegum, altogether worthless for any purpose of building or enclosure. The trees are very few and mostly damaged by fire. The choice of the capital, therefore, has been made in a spot where there is no fuel, seven miles distant from a harbour where there is no fresh water. Oh, had we but a Yankee surveyor to help us, all would be well.

Stevenson, abetted by his wife, was becoming the storm centre of this dismal controversy. An able and plausible man, he had Hindmarsh under his thumb. In the confusion of the Holdfast Bay settlement, he took his chance to seize considerable behind-the-scenes power. He controlled the press, and he more or less controlled the governor. Thus he was able, in Dutton's words, "to realise the dream of many a journalist, not only to comment but to contrive". Stevenson could write with readable ferocity, and Colonel Light together with all members of the anti-Hindmarsh party were to reel before the thunderbolts launched against them through the *Register*.

Stevenson vented his indignation against the surveyors in his journal: "Some order must be taken with these pig-headed gentry." He fomented discontent among some of the section owners. His argument now was that the South Australian coast should be thoroughly surveyed before a decision was made on the capital site—an impossible condition. Edward Stephens of the South Australian Company supported him, as did the governor who began to insist on a survey of the port. On 4 February he wrote to Light: "I … think it's very likely you may be correct in your estimate of the mangrove swamp: yet as mercantile people think *proximity to a port* the one great thing needful, why not indulge them by surveying 500 acres wherever you may find the best landing place on the Harbour?"[4] He went on to suggest that these 500 acres (202 hectares) could be one half of the thousand Light had been authorized to survey at the capital or additional to them. He urged that they be divided between Adelaide and Port Adelaide "with this inestimable advantage that it would settle at once every discontented feeling on the subject". Light had his crosses to bear; and Governor Hindmarsh, twiddling his thumbs on the *Buffalo* off Glenelg, sending him chops from his "last sheep" one minute and undermining him the next, was the heaviest.

More rancour and backbiting followed until finally the "discontented feeling" came to a head in a public meeting of the preliminary purchasers. A letter had been circulated, signed by Edward Stephens and others but written by Stevenson, calling for a postponement of the capital's foundation until the coast had been thoroughly surveyed. Hindmarsh agreed to the meeting, although he knew full well that he had no authority over the choice of site. He displayed his meddlesome ambiguity further by urging the colonists not to retard the survey, yet also urged that land should be surveyed at Port Adelaide.

The meeting was held on 10 February. Stevenson was in the chair. His supporter, Strangways, moved: "That it is the opinion of this meeting that the site at present selected for the chief town of the colony, being at considerable distance from navigable waters, is not such as they were led to expect would be chosen." But a long report from Light on the advantages of Adelaide and Port Adelaide backed by letters from Captain Duff of the *Africaine* and Captain Fleming of the *William Hutt*, both praising the port as a good harbour to which fresh water could easily be conveyed across flat, clear land from the city, finally swayed the meeting back to sanity. There was vehement discussion. Finally an amendment to Strangways's resolution was put:

> That this meeting considers that in the site selected by the Surveyor General for the first town, he has secured, in a most satisfactory manner, those advantages which the Commissioners·and the first purchasers in England contemplated as essential—a central point in the province, in the neighbourhood of a safe and improvable harbour, abundance of fresh water on the spot, and of good land and pasturage in its vicinity, with a probable easy communication with the Murray, Lake Alexandrina, and the most fertile part of New South Wales, without fear of any injury to the principles of the colony, from too near an approach to the confines of the convict settlement.[5]

This amendment was carried by 218 votes to 127. The votes represented the holders of land orders. Thus Stephens, for the South Australian Company, cast 110 votes for the minority, and Morphett's block represented 115 votes of the majority. Hindmarsh, egregiously, had voted through Stevenson against the amendment. Light later commented in his *Brief Journal*: "where the Governor begs of the gentlemen not to retard the survey, his name appears by proxy in the minority for that very purpose."[6]

The meeting had been useful. It had cleared the air. Stevenson and his schemes were scotched for the moment. Light and Fisher had agreed to survey some acres at the port, and twenty-nine were surveyed, so some salve was applied to the governor's wounds. It is pleasant to think that the majority of the landowners had the vision to realize that Light was right. Certainly they must have been appalled at the prospect of further delay and dissension. The long-suffering colonel was enabled to complete his Adelaide survey.

But this was by no means the end of the controversy. When the commissioners heard, months later, of the meeting they rejected what Torrens called "the pernicious cabal which was raised against the site of the town". They also wisely rejected any proposal to locate the capital in the western part of the province, such as at Port Lincoln. They still hankered after the Murray mouth. This is not surprising. The Murray looked impressive on the map, which was the nearest most of them ever came to their distant possession. They dreamed of a city port, a New Orleans of Australia, exploiting the resources of the enormous area drained by the Murray system. If Adelaide were the nearest possible site then they would support it, but for a time they seem to have hoped that a more convenient site might be found. They did not know that the Murray is almost unique among the world's great rivers for the difficulties and disappointments of its estuary. Light knew of them, but his opponents had to find out the hard way.

That troublesome trinity, Stevenson, Strangways, and Hindmarsh were soon at the head of a movement to abandon Adelaide as the capital and locate one on some mythical harbour by the Murray mouth. Stevenson used the *Register*. During November 1837, for instance, a sealer named Walker claimed that he had found a good harbour south of the Murray mouth. The man must have been either drunk or a rogue, for the dangerous and unbroken sands of the Younghusband Peninsula stretched for 145 kilometres south of the outlet. However, his tale was just the sort that the anti-Light party wanted to hear. Stevenson blazoned Walker's story over the *Register* and Hindmarsh pestered the surveyor-general for details. In the end, Light repeated his sound arguments against the Murray mouth region.

Hindmarsh persisted, sending agents to explore the area who reported favourably on Victor Harbour. Strangways, for instance, thought Victor Harbour could be the first town and entrepôt for the Murray. However, the drowning of the province's first chief justice, Sir John Jeffcott while trying to pass through the Murray mouth in a small overloaded boat, dampened colonial enthusiasm. So did the sinking of a number of vessels at Victor Harbour in rough weather.

Then the Goolwa channel was discovered, which gave rise to the idea of a canal communication with Encounter Bay. To cut a long and petulant story short, Hindmarsh eventually went to the extraordinary length of suggesting to the Colonial Office the removal of the capital to Encounter Bay. He had a notion that the shallow and unsafe Coorong would serve as a channel. The fury of the land owners, whom he had not consulted, when this proposal was made public shredded the last rags of the governor's prestige, but by then he was being recalled himself. The site of Adelaide was not changed, but the governor was.

"I was never sanguine on any point but one", wrote the weary Light in October 1838, "and that was the eligibility of the site of Adelaide." Light lived long enough to see his stand vindicated. For example, Finniss wrote to Montefiore in August 1838: "If Colonel Light had not stood firm when an attempt was made to change the site of the town, the colony would have been a failure, the first colonists would have been ruined, the capital of the Company would have perished, and public feeling would have ruined the Commissioners."[7]

On this, the Rev. John Blacket in his *History of South Australia: A Romantic and Successful Experiment in Colonization* (1911) quotes the reminiscences of William Jacob, whom he calls "a sturdy old pioneer". Jacob had come out with Light as assistant-surveyor in the *Rapid*, helped lay out Adelaide, and eventually resigned and went into private practice with the colonel. Jacob recalled:

> When Colonel Light showed us the site he had selected for the capital he was confident that it was the best possible one. He said to me: "I never expect the present generation to approve of it; but posterity will do me justice." And I may add here that after sixty-five years' experience I am not aware of a single instance in which Colonel Light's judgement is at fault. The survey of the city was commenced at the corner of North Terrace and West Terrace by Light, and I was employed at the eastern end ... Some of the settlers at Van Diemen's Land who had come to inspect it told Light that grain would never grow on it. His reply was, "We will not only grow grain, but all the products of Spain and Portugal."[8]

After Light's resignation, the faithful Jacob helped him in 1839 to lay out the site of Gawler. In his plan for what was to be, after Adelaide and Port Adelaide, South Australia's third town, Light showed again his acumen and originality. Parklands along the North and South Para river banks enclosed Gawler, and it retains to this day a distinctive and gracious atmosphere. Jacob recalled how the colonel, near death, remarked: "Jacob, if you live an ordinary life you will see these plains enclosed." Light's vision stretched at least a generation beyond that of his contemporaries.

Finniss and Jacob were, of course, friends and supporters of Light. The second governor, Gawler, was not so well disposed. He was to appoint Sturt surveyor-general rather than reinstate the colonel. Therefore his tribute after Light's death is the more telling. Gawler wrote to the commissioners in October 1839:

> There is one circumstance in Colonel Light's official conduct in this colony which is becoming more and more apparent to his honour—this is the wisdom of his personal choice with regard to the site of the early Capital. For the influence which that choice has had towards the rapid progress of the prosperity of the province his memory claims the warmest gratitude from every lover of South Australia.[9]

At last, the infant Adelaide was secure in her cradle by the Torrens. The plots to transport her bodily to a new nursery at the tip of Eyre Peninsula, or Encounter Bay, or by the marshes of the Murray mouth, were frustrated. Adelaide could now grow. Slowly, for many decades, but surely, buildings would flesh out that big 400 hectare survey skeleton. Adelaide had had a stormy birth, but her future was safe. At the Port Phillip settlement further east, it had taken a much larger and better paid and equipped surveying staff five months to lay out the 240 acre (97 hectare) site of Melbourne. It was eight months before land sales could be held. In contrast, Light and his little band, despite all their harassments and difficulties, had completed their task in two months.

One more word from that elegant *Brief Journal*:

> It was generally supposed that planning and measuring out a thousand acres for a capital was so easy a job that it would be completed in a few days—and the disgrace heaped upon me again became warm. I leave this matter to be judged of by experienced surveyors in England, remarking at the same time that they must bear in mind that we were in a country perfectly in a state of nature, and the obstructions for this work were greater on this particular spot than on any other part of the plain. It may be asked then, "Why choose it?" I answer, "Because it was on a beautiful and gently rising ground, and formed altogether a better connection with the river than any other place."[10]

Sir Archibald Grenfell Price's praise of Light in his *Foundation and Settlement of South Australia, 1829–1845* (1924) deserves quoting here. He points out that Light's surveying party had been allowed only "a hopelessly short time". They landed only twelve weeks before the *Africaine* and eighteen before the *Buffalo*. Light had wanted at least six months for preliminary work, and two years to complete the whole task. A disaster had been averted because of his "sound geographical knowledge, innate topographical instinct, courage, and patience." Sir Archibald concludes on the capital city site controversy:

> The later history of the state makes it difficult to discover any other locality in which colonization had a similar chance of success. The shipping disasters of Encounter Bay, the desperate struggles and slow progress of the settlements at Port Lincoln, and Kangaroo Island, the deserted roadsteads, rugged country, and sparse population of the Cape Jervis Peninsula are an eloquent testimony to the geographical genius of the first Surveyor-General. Light has for long received his due as the founder of Adelaide, but on the greater list of the founders of South Australia his is no mean place.[11]

POLITICAL AFFAIRS

> The good folks in power in the *free* republic of South Australia
> appear to be a most unruly, quarrelsome sort of gentry.
> The Perth Gazette, *24 April 1838*

Before examining the social history of Adelaide in its earliest years, we will follow the chequered careers of some of the dominant founding fathers to their close. While the immigrants were trundling their wheelbarrows up the dusty track from Holdfast Bay to pitch their tents and build their mud-walled, reed-thatched huts on the city acres, controversies still raged among their leaders. As Blacket observed: "To the young colony the dark figure of dissension came." Dissension had already got off to a rousingly good start on the voyage out and amidst the wrangles over the site of Adelaide. It would continue to thrive over the chronic vexations of divided authority, for as long as Hindmarsh was governor and the commissioners muddled and incompetent.

On 21 April 1837 the governor set up house in Adelaide itself and began to cause trouble from the centre of things. A three-room, mud-walled hut had been built for him as vice regal residence by sailors from the *Buffalo*. It was not an auspicious start. Fisher, who was by now bitterly anti-Hindmarsh, accused the governor of "trespass and depredation" when these mariners gathered reeds and cut down some pines on public land so that they could build this shack. Moreover, either their drunkenness or lack of skill made them build it without a chimney. One had to be added from the outside later. Hindmarsh was further embarrassed when it was pointed out that some of the window panes in his hut bore the initials of Morphett, from whom they had been stolen.

The first great obsession of the colonists and their leaders had been the town survey and the controversy over the site of Adelaide. The second obsession was over the country surveys, and this was to drag on over many weary months. All the problems and mistakes resultant from the haste and confusion of the commissioners' first phase of planning were to be accentuated here. The settlers—and more were coming all the time—had had to wait long enough for their town sections. They had to wait much longer for their rural land. The country surveys proceeded so slowly that it was not until May 1838 that the first ballot for country sections was held. In the meantime, the colonists had to fume and fret in and around Adelaide, while their resources dwindled.

THE END OF LIGHT

The central figure in the country survey controversy was once again the unfortunate William Light, with a dissenting chorus made up of Hindmarsh, Stevenson, Kingston, and the distant muddled twittering from the Board of Commissioners in London. The story has been well told, notably by A.G. Price, Geoffrey Dutton, and R.M. Gibbs. However, the salient points need to be mentioned here for the delays over the surveys had serious consequences for Adelaide. The whole future of the colony depended upon primary production. This depended upon land settlement—and there could be no settlement until the land had been properly surveyed.

Light had been able to survey Adelaide on foot. He could not hope to survey the vastness beyond the city limits until he had proper transport. Eventually, a few bullocks were imported from Van Diemen's Land and Light, his health worse then ever, his staff dispirited and underpaid, began another Herculean labour for the board. The commissioners expected him to survey thoroughly at least 40,500 hectares. They had promised the preliminary purchasers the choicest areas, and they had given promises about pasturage which involved surveying hundreds of additional square miles.

Light and Fisher soon agreed that the work would take years, that more staff and equipment were needed, and that the meddling Hindmarsh should be recalled. They sent Kingston back to London on the *Rapid* to see the commissioners and ask for these things. Meanwhile, Light pushed on with the survey and had 24,300 hectares completed by December 1837, when Hindmarsh was still badgering Glenelg for permission to move the settlement. When Kingston returned in June 1838, 60,750 hectares had been surveyed, an extraordinary achievement.

But Kingston—"a vulgar overbearing upstart" in Light's opinion and incompetent, at least, by most accounts—had played him false. Instead of support and sympathy from the commissioners, he brought back reprimands for Light, a rejection of his requests, and an impossible demand. Either he should abandon his trigonometrical survey for an allegedly quicker "running survey" or he should hand over control of the surveys to Kingston and confine himself to coastal examination. Light resigned at once. He was sick, harrassed, and had had all he could take from the commissioners and especially their secretary Rowland Hill. He was misunderstood and insulted both in London and in Adelaide. Jacob recalled how Light received the commissioners' instructions. "He was given a week in which to consider the matter. His reply was, 'I don't want five minutes to consider it; I won't do it'."[12] Almost all the surveying staff resigned with him and Kingston blundered on. In time he was forced to revert to the trigonometrical survey. In time, too, the country surveys took as long to complete and cost as much as Light had said they would. In the meantime, the board bitterly and publicly blamed Light for the delays.

The last months of Light's life were miserable. Although his health was worse than ever, he formed with Finniss the surveying firm of Light, Finniss and Co. He surveyed Glenelg, the Port Adelaide harbour, and Gawler. He took part in exploring expeditions into the hills, once penetrating as far as the Lyndoch valley in an attempt to find a passage to the Murray, but his strength was failing. There were a number of attempts to reinstate him, in Adelaide, where there was a large public meeting in his favour, and in London, but all failed. The new governor, Lieutenant-Colonel George Gawler, had the chance to make Light surveyor-general once more when he arrived in Adelaide in October 1838, but he preferred to appoint Captain Sturt.

Light's life was petering out in illness and bitterness. He still retained many good friends, such as Morphett and Jacob, and Maria Gandy nursed him devotedly. A terrible blow was the destruction by fire of his reed hut in January 1839. The flames devoured nearly all his lifelong collection of papers, journals, and sketches. (However, a number of his early notebooks and journals, which give some insight into his extraordinary character, were found recently in the Town Hall archives.) He built himself a cottage at the misspelled Thebarton, named after Theberton in Suffolk where his family had lived. There he found some solace in demonstrating that excellent vegetables could be grown on Adelaide soil if it were mixed with river mud. Even here, he was pestered by roaming stock, and by Aborigines, who once paraded round his hut with his precious potatoes on the end of their spears.

He was desperately poor, having spent much of his own money in his survey work, with no hope of redress. He was obliged to sell sketches to make ends meet. His depression was worsened by the continuing innuendoes of enemies like Stevenson and a rankling feeling of being unjustly used. In his last letters, he railed against "the sages of Adelaide" who had worried him so. One he wrote to George Palmer in February 1839 is typical:

> My health is so very bad that I am not in a state to be of service to anyone. I am so ill that I feel I shall never recover, and I only pray that the Almighty may spare my life long enough to vindicate my honour against all the aspersions that have been thrown against me ... No one could have worked more zealously and conscientiously than I did, and Mr. Hill actually accused me of wilful neglect of duty ... So much noise was made against me for not finishing all the surveys in time to please a lot of idiots. Governor Gawler came and knocked off the preliminary surveys almost entirely, began other plans which I shall expose when I get home, and not a word was said, a proof that the attacks on me were personal, originating from Hindmarsh and his Private Secretary, Mr. George Stevenson, editor of the *Gazette*.

He would never see "home" again, of course, but his honour was vindicated by the publication of his *Brief Journal* and tardy general recognition of his achievements.

Gawler called on him—"He received me with the greatest good feeling"—as did staunch friends like Dr. Woodforde and the members of the original surveying party.

But the colonial chaplain found it inconvenient to visit a man who lived openly with a mistress. Finniss wrote:

> My wife and I called frequently to see him and she read prayers to him, which he listened to with reverent attention. He said to me that he had been suffering much pain with his cough ... I called on the Rev. C.B. Howard, our Chaplain of Trinity Church, and suggested to him that, as the Colonel was evidently dying, he might call on him and offer a prayer at his bedside. Mr. Howard replied: "It is not the practice of our Church to attend to the sick and the dying unless they express penitence and desire the services of the Church."[13]

Thus sanctimonious small-mindedness pursued Light to the end. His thoughts must often have been bitter as he lay in his sweltering hut thousands of miles from "home". He had lost his inheritance, his wife lived with another man, he had been driven from office, most of his writings and sketches had been burned. True, he had founded his city in the wilderness and some people honoured his choice. But in 1839 Adelaide was still a seedy collection of shacks, tents, and stores, its streets muddy scratches through the grass, its squares a tangle of gum trees and wombat holes. It gave little intimation of the beautiful city it was to become. And even then there were influential critics like Stevenson who still questioned his surveyor's skills. Little wonder that Light liked to recall the freer, more expansive days of derring do in the Peninsular Wars and dreamy wanderings round the Mediterranean. He loved to talk about famous friends and acquaintances of his military past, such as Wellington and Napier, probably contrasting them with his petty bourgeois colonial persecutors. Light died of tuberculosis on 6 October 1839, aged fifty-four.

With the colonel dead—and leaving debts of 620 pounds—South Australians at last united to honour him. Gawler allocated 100 pounds towards the cost of a memorial and closed all government offices on 10 October, the day of the funeral. "The largest body of colonists ever congregated in this Province", as the black-bordered *Register* put it, "joined the funeral procession that wound from Thebarton Cottage to Trinity Church. Minute guns were fired, all business ceased and the flag at Government House flew at half mast." Light was buried, as he had asked, in Light Square, in a leaden coffin containing a copper breastplate carrying the inscription "Founder of Adelaide". Four hundred and fifty gentlemen mourned at his graveside.

Kingston designed a curious Gothic memorial to his old master. Not surprisingly, it crumbled away and was replaced by the present rather dreary monument surmounted by a theodolite which covers his grave in Light Square, in a down-at-heel area of the city. The dashing bronze statue designed by Burnies Rhind in 1906 recalls the colonel, or at least his more confident military image, better. Originally raised in Victoria Square, the statue now crowns Montefiore Hill. There Light points compellingly at his vision: although one wonders what his spirit thinks of the hill quarries, insurance skyscrapers, and suburban sprawl also encompassed in the famous view. The authorities wisely chose as his epitaph on the statue base the last paragraph of Light's preface to his *Brief Journal*, quoted at the beginning of this chapter, in which he asks posterity, not his contemporaries, to judge his work.

The colonel's name is officially commemorated by Light Square, the muddy little Light River, and Colonel Light Gardens, an interesting piece of surburban town planning. His fine self-portrait is in the National Gallery, Adelaide and an elegant room in the Town Hall is the Colonel Light Room. In 1858, his friend George Palmer gave a silver bowl to the mayor and corporation as a gift from himself, Jacob Montefiore, Raikes Currie, and Alexander Elder with the inscription: "Presented to the Mayor and Corporation of Adelaide that they may thereout drink in Australian Wine to the memory of Lieut. Col. Light, the first Surveyor General of South Australia, by some of the original members of the Colony." Council authorized a sum "not exceeding 10 pounds to be expended in Colonial wine and biscuit that the citizens may drink to the memory of Colonel Light". Dutton writes: "once a year this is still carried out, a pleasant tradition, especially in a country that had so few."[14]

Other founding fathers are vaguely respected, if they are remembered at all. Light, for his vision, and his misfortunes, is the one who is genuinely loved in memory.

THE DEPARTURE OF HINDMARSH

If Light's last years were unhappy, so too was the South Australian career of his old foe, Hindmarsh. From January 1837, straight after the proclamation, up to his recall in June of the following year, the governor locked horns with James Fisher, representative of the commissioners and the second source of power in the province. The division of authority and the haste and inadequacy of the first surveys were bad enough. The position worsened as settlers poured into South Australia with their land orders, only to find that they had to live like gypsies in the Adelaide immigrants' camp until the surveys were completed. By May 1837, sixteen vessels from England had landed upwards of a thousand immigrants, and five vessels from Sydney and Van Diemen's Land had bought further settlers. In November of the same year the population had risen to about 2,500. In 1837 there were only about one and a half hectares under crop.

The spark to the whole explosive mixture was struck by the enmity between Hindmarsh and Fisher. Hindmarsh was in David McLaren's opinion "a reputable character with a considerable degree of natural shrewdness" but "accustomed to command, jealous of his prerogative and ill advised". Sir John Jeffcott thought Fisher "a wily attorney, the worst class of person that could have been selected for his office" who "by the splitting of hairs on every insignificant point wished to place the Governor in a false position".[15] The two were poles apart, and what Jeffcott called the "dreadful dissensions" between them almost completed the ruin of the young province.

To Hindmarsh, Fisher was a scheming civilian, full of Wakefieldian principles and totally lacking in respect for the king's officer and vice gerent. To Fisher, Hindmarsh was a booby who hindered progress. He especially resented Hindmarsh's meddling with the city location and the country surveys. And like many of the colonists, he distrusted and feared the governor's private secretary, Stevenson. This forceful Scot, perhaps the most intellectual of the founding fathers, had also received from Hindmarsh the important positions of clerk of the court, justice of the peace, protector of aborigines, registrar of shipping, agent for Lloyds, customs officer, and postmaster. As well, of course, he edited the *Register*. Small wonder that Stevenson was seen by many colonists as the pluralist Richelieu to Hindmarsh's ineffectual Louis XIII. It must be added, however, that he was more competent in all these positions than most of his immediate successors.

Hindmarsh seemed fatally incapable of commanding respect. McLaren wrote to Angas in September 1837 that "owing to doubt as to Hindmarsh's powers in the colony, it is likely to be a scene of confusion and turmoil, and the laughing-stock of neighbours for some time to come". Leaders of the governor's party were Jeffcott, Gilles the treasurer, Strangways, and Stevenson. Supporters of Fisher included most of the colonial officials such as Brown, Light, and Mann, the advocate-general. The partisans clashed over all kinds of issues, trivial or great. One battleground was the Adelaide street naming committee which met in May 1837. Hindmarsh and Fisher each thought that it was his prerogative to decide on the names. Brown wrote:

> The Governor brought a pocketful of naval heroes, but, afraid of proposing them himself, got Sir John Jeffcott to try. King William Street and Victoria Square were assented to by all, but when we got to "Duncan" and "Howe" as the proposed names for the next streets, we divided, and "Grote" and "Wakefield" reigned in their stead. I am rather ashamed of myself for having any hand in the business, but votes were wanted, or it would have been a journal of our Governor's life and adventures. As to this business, however, he cannot keep quiet.[16]

Names for the squares appear to have been chosen finally as accolades for persons connected with the foundation of the province, or whose names would add international lustre. Hindmarsh, James Hurtle Fisher (Hurtle Square), Light, Wellington, and Woolryche Whitmore, a commissioner, each got a square. The same principle seems to have applied to many of the street names. Officials, theorists, and commissioners were commemorated in streets like Wakefield, Brown, Jeffcott, Currie, Gouger, Hutt, Hindley, McLaren, Flinders, Sturt, and Rundle. Some few were named with a more poetic fancy, such as Byron Place and Coromandel Place, named after the *Coromandel*, which arrived in January 1837 and from which sailors deserted, to be captured in the valley later known as Coromandel Valley. Blenheim Street was named after the victory over the French.

If the rival parties could quarrel over street names and the purloined window panes in the governor's shack, then on more serious matters, such as the surveys, they were almost at daggers drawn. Gouger actually came to blows with Gilles in Franklin Street. Hindmarsh peremptorily suspended Gouger from his legislative council and replaced him with a supporter, Strangways. Even the neutral McLaren was driven to protest that the new colonial secretary was "utterly incompetent" and had made seven mistakes in one document, including the misspelling of his own name.

Another unseemly row, this time between Brown and the governor, revealed again the divisive effects of divided authority. An immigrant had died in Emigration Square, as a section of the parklands where new arrivals camped was called. The weather was hot, and Hindmarsh ordered Brown to see to the burial. Brown refused, arguing that as emigration agent responsible to the board he was concerned with live settlers, not dead ones. Fisher supported him. Hindmarsh then suspended Brown. Fisher attacked the government with a public handbill. Hindmarsh denounced Fisher as seditious through a proclamation. The colonial storekeeper finally saw to the interment.

Hindmarsh next turned his broadside on another Fisher follower, Mann, who resigned from the council. Hindmarsh installed George Stephens in his place, a man who knew nothing about law but who, like the other two replacements, had the excellent qualification of being a suitor of one of the Hindmarsh girls.

Official Adelaide was in a continual uproar with these dissensions, with Stevenson blasting the Fisherites in many issues of the *Register*. This passage from the *Register* of 23 March 1837 is typical: "We are quite sure", he asserted, "that we consult the feelings of every respectable individual in the province leaving the foul abuse of the Governor which Mr. Mann has vomited forth ... to the contempt such impotent calumny deserves ... " Of course, Stevenson went on at length to notice it and reply with equally foul abuse. All these wrangles were bad for Adelaide, South Australia, and the bewildered settlers who wanted to get on with making their fortunes, as promised, if only the authorities would let them.

Hindmarsh's tempestuous course was soon run. The slighted Gouger and Kingston, representing Fisher and the enraged surveyors, were only two of Hindmarsh's many critics who, by September 1837, were petitioning the commissioners in London for his recall. The board was receiving reports of Hindmarsh's incompetence and high handedness from every quarter. There was even a public meeting in London of the South Australian Society which called for his replacement with a governor more susceptible to Wakefield's principles. Glenelg bowed to the pressure and Hindmarsh left South Australia for ever on 14 July 1838.

One can almost feel sorry for Hindmarsh. He was in an extremely difficult position and he was opposed by men who, if not "the contemptible bad set" he called them, were often fractious and self-seeking. He had had an honourable career before 1836, and after his misfortunes in Adelaide he was to soothe his pride with a knighthood and the governorship of Heligoland—although he did little notable beyond writing a report on its bird life. In private life he could be amiable. Mrs. Thomas recalls in her diary a "ridiculous circumstance" involving the Hindmarshes during a church service. "His Excellency, Mrs. Hindmarsh, and the whole of their family were listening to a sermon from Mr. Howard, when the supports of the bench suddenly gave way, and the occupants were all laid on their backs, to the evident amusement of many of the congregation. Some laughed outright, as did the Governor himself, and even Mr. Howard could not suppress a smile at seeing the vice-regal family in such an undignified position." Hindmarsh seemed to attract such misadventures. The Hindmarsh who pottered among his olives and orange trees in his garden, who wrote kindly and perceptive letters about the Aborigines, and who sent chops to Light seems a likeable old seadog. We can sympathize with him in his ludicrous mud-walled government house where centipedes fell from the ceiling and guests, who did not realize that he was in debt to Angas, complained about the stinginess of his hospitality.

But so far as Adelaide, South Australia, and most of the men who had to work with him were concerned, Hindmarsh was a menace. His efforts to remove the capital to Port Lincoln, Port Adelaide, or Encounter Bay were all wrong-headed. He helped drive Light, the most outstanding man among them, into resignation. For all his administrative incompetence, he was adept at feathering his family's nest. He married his daughters off strategically and his land buys in Adelaide netted the handsome sum of 12,000 pounds after his recall.

Hindmarsh arrived in Adelaide on the *Buffalo*, and left on the *Alligator*. The names of his transports evoke appropriate images of cantankerous and dangerous stubbornness.

Pending the arrival of Gawler, the new governor, George Stephens, Hindmarsh's future son-in-law and advocate general, administered affairs.

In his first address to the Legislative Council, Stephens described a gloomy situation. He feared that officials would migrate to other colonies because "there are no funds in the treasury". The marines who had provided something of a "Pirates of Penzance" atmosphere in Adelaide, had left with Hindmarsh on the *Alligator*. Therefore, "this province, with a population exceeding four thousand persons, is abandoned to the protection of eighteen policemen ... while there are now twenty-one prisoners confined in the weather-boarded building used as a gaol, and perhaps twice that number of desperate runaway convicts in the neighbourhood of the town."

However, by being diplomatic and lending 200 pounds of his own money, Stephens managed to hold things together until Gawler and his wife and five children arrived in the *Pestonjee Bomanjee* on 2 October 1838 and were conducted by enthusiastic settlers to the government hut.

GAWLER

George Gawler (1795–1869) resembled Hindmarsh in that he was a war hero—he had served with distinction in the Peninsular War and led a charge at Waterloo—but there the resemblance ended. He was a pious, restrained, thoughtful man, who in 1820 married Maria Cox, "a lady as religious as himself". While stationed in New Brunswick, Canada, the Gawlers had set up a Sunday school and religious classes. He had written respected articles and pamphlets on military matters. Unemployed and a lieutenant-colonel in 1838, Gawler seemed just the godly sort of intellectual that Angas and other commissioners needed to restore order and progress to their chaotic colony. One other advantage Gawler had over Hindmarsh. He was to combine the duties of governor and resident commissioner in his own person. Torrens had successfully asked Glenelg that the "evils of undefined and divided authority" should be done away with.

Fisher was superseded as resident commissioner on Gawler's arrival in Adelaide. Unlike his old antagonist, Hindmarsh, Fisher was to remain in South Australia and prosper there as a successful lawyer, the first mayor of Adelaide and member, speaker, and president of the Legislative Council.

Thus Adelaide was no longer to be the sparring ground for two rival rulers although Gawler was still responsible to two masters, the Colonial Office and the Board of Commissioners, with unhappy results.

Brisk, confident, and high-principled, the new governor set about his task with energy. As usual, the distant commissioners had tied his hands. He was limited to an ordinary expenditure of 8,000 pounds a year, with the right to call on the commissioners for an extra 2,000 pounds, later raised to 4,000 pounds, to avoid destitution. He could also draw on credit of up to 5,000 pounds if confronted by "fire, pestilence, attacks from pirates, incursions of convicts from other colonies, or seditious risings". On his appointment, Gawler had had an interview with James Stephen of the Colonial Office who advised him that the Wakefield self-supporting system was a failure and that he should rely upon government assistance. Gawler imagined, with results fatal for his career, that this meant he had a blank cheque for necessary expenditure.

When he arrived, the province was on the point of collapse. There was no public money. Officials were unpaid. Adelaide was a disgruntled shanty town of 4,000 immigrants living in makeshift accommodation and hundreds more arriving each year. As for the controversial surveys, 8,500 hectares of the preliminary purchases had still to be surveyed in areas reserved south and east of the capital. The authorized expenditure for 1838 had already gone—12,000 pounds in the first six months. A weaker man might have got back on to the *Pestonjee Bomanjee* and sailed rapidly back to England.

But Gawler rushed into this graveyard of reputations, assumed responsibility for everything, spent money in a way that would appal the commissioners when the bills arrived, and produced results. He perceived at once that the major problem in the colony was the delay over rural settlement and primary production. He persuaded Sturt to come from New South Wales to work as surveyor-general, and in the meantime he took over the surveys himself. He appointed more, and better, colonial officials and raised their salaries. He set up a police force. He took a vigorous part in exploration. By 1841 the mapping of 18,000 square kilometres had been completed and more than 200,000 hectares divided into sections at a cost of 65,000 pounds or more above his total authorized expenditure for the period.

To raise the gubernatorial prestige in Adelaide, Gawler had Hindmarsh's wretched mud hut demolished and built a more imposing twelve-roomed government house, the eastern end of the present building. The governor tried to economize by omitting screens and verandahs, but it still cost 10,000 pounds and some Adelaide people grumbled. Mrs. Gawler thought it "a pretty looking, comfortable house ... not at all suited for a Governor's House".

To give the insecure colonial administration what he called "a permanent outfit", the governor also built a gaol, police barracks, and hospital, a customs house and wharf at Port Adelaide, as well as houses for public officials and missionaries, outstations for police and surveyors. He used the plentiful immigrant labour for these public works, for clearing fallen timber from the city and parklands, and for building roads to the port and through the Mount Lofty Ranges.

Throughout his thirty-one months of office, Gawler was preoccupied with the problems of the immigrants. By the time he was recalled, on 15 May 1841, South Australia's population had grown from about 4,000 to 15,000 people. Many of these had been sent out by the board with free passages financed by the Land Fund—during 1839 alone 4,600 had come out this way—and it was Gawler's duty as resident commissioner to settle these newcomers in and try to turn them into productive members of the community. He had to transport them from the port to the city, feed and clothe them, care for the sick, and employ them at reduced rates if the labour market could not absorb them. Eventually he was forced to limit government assistance to rations for a week and free housing for a month. In August 1839 he advised the commissioners that the expenses of the Emigration Department were out of control.

The unhealthy land boom which had obsessed Adelaide citizens for many months eased after 1839. Cash and credit were scarce, explorations seemed to indicate that good land was limited, and British speculators were becoming interested in New Zealand. However, Gawler's many problems were compounded in 1840 by crop failures in the other Australian colonies on which the province still mainly relied for food. The cost of living rose rapidly. Gawler's reaction was to increase government expenditure to stave off collapse. The result was bankruptcy and a radical constitutional overhaul of Wakefield's wayward province.

In January 1840 the ineffectual board of voluntary commissioners had been replaced by three salaried commissioners, with little good effect. As Gawler's bills came home to London to roost, the commissioners were disturbed to see that he had spent in all over 200,000 pounds. At the same time, the Land Fund was exhausted and the whole enterprise was in debt. South Australia was thrown on the mercy of the Colonial Office, where officials like James Stephen had always been skeptical of the self-supporting principle. Parliament appointed a select committee to inquire into the province's affairs and eventually recommended a loan of 155,000 pounds which was later converted into a free gift. Meanwhile a head had to roll, and there was general agreement it should be Gawler's. Torrens, forced to resign from the board, wrote: "The high minded soldier who led the storming party as Baddajos ... has been dismissed from his government for having exceeded his instructions. The Commissioners who disobeyed the Act of Parliament have been retained in office ... Colonel Gawler has no friend at court. He has no political connection, no family ties with members of a Whig Cabinet."[17]

Like Light and to a certain extent Hindmarsh and Fisher before him, the hapless Gawler was made the scapegoat. During his administration, South Australia's major problem, the lack of a productive rural population, had been eased. Over 5,000 settlers were now farming. Almost 6,500 hectares had been enclosed and 2,700 hectares were under crop. These made possible the magnificent harvest of 1841 which helped put Adelaide back on an even keel, but for which Gawler's successor, Captain George Grey, unfairly got the credit. Gawler's vigorous activism at all levels had restored public confidence in Adelaide, where he was well liked. He had seen, quite rightly, that only vigorous action and heavy expenditures could save a settlement demoralized by bad planning, bad luck, survey delays, and violent dissensions among the leaders. Unlike Hindmarsh, he had ruffled few feathers. No colonist had worked harder than he.

Mrs. Gawler, hearing rumours that her husband was to be replaced by Grey—"a mere boy ... a captain, too, of only two years' standing"—wrote bitterly to Admiral Hawker on 30 March 1841. She said that "Numbers affirm that they will quit the Colony if the present Governor goes" and went on:

> The Commissioners know but little of the step they are about to take ... in the removal of my husband from this Colony, for never was a man, nor will be one, who gives his whole mind to the welfare of the Province as he does ... Since our arrival here he has not realised one penny; on the contrary, his sacrifice has been very great, for it is impossible to live on the Commissioners' pitiful allowance of 1,000 pounds per annum. I should like any one of them to try it even now when provisions are lower.

Mrs. Gawler described the progress of the province:

> We are now using flour grown in the Colony and of a very superior quality. Agriculture is progressing rapidly and families are fast going out of the towns to live on their sections and fencing is carried on now to a great extent, between this and Glenelg the land is nearly all fenced in, and when we arrived it was a barren plain—and the same occurs in every direction for about seven miles out of Adelaide ... two most valuable lead and silver mines have been discovered and likely to bring great wealth into the Colony. Then we have beautiful slating for roofs, stone and bricks for building, in short the progress of a Colony only four years old is beyond all human expectation.

Then, the bitterness welling up again, Mrs. Gawler exclaimed: "Oh, 'tis an ungrateful world we live in!"

GOVERNOR GREY

All Gawler's achievements, sacrifices, and piety availed him little in London where heavy bills and reports of extravagance united the commissioners in the urge to salvage their own reputations at the expense of the man on the spot. And just as Kingston had undermined Light before the commissioners and got his job, so did Grey, an able, hard, and ambitious young man, serve his own ends by destroying Gawler. Captain Grey (1812–1898) had stayed with Gawler in Adelaide for three weeks in 1840 after some adventurous and futile explorations in Western Australia. The hospitable Gawler had taken pride in showing the young man his public works and in talking of his problems and plans. His kindness was abused. Back in London and looking to further his career, Grey heard of the commission of inquiry and sent a memorandum on how he would restore South Australia to prosperity and work in full harmony with the Colonial Office. *He* would not cause any extravagance.

It was pleasant for the authorities to hear from an alleged expert on Australia that the blame was Gawler's. A myth was created that the governor had been disobedient and spendthrift. Certainly, in retrospect, Gawler might appear naive, autocratic, and occasionally careless, but it is hard to see how anyone could have done much better in this difficult situation. Nonetheless, Gawler was curtly dismissed and Grey was appointed governor: the dismissal and the supplanter arrived together in Adelaide on 15 May 1841. Grey read his commission from Government House steps, and the Gawlers were herded into the guest room once occupied by their usurper. It must have been a black and bitter day for the colonel.

Light had his city to immortalize him, and some late recognition. Fisher and Kingston stayed on to prosper and achieve civic eminence and knighthoods. Even the disastrous Hindmarsh got Heligoland and a knighthood. Poor Gawler received none of these good things. He returned under a cloud and remained under it until his death in 1869. He was denied further public employment. After four years of eccentric semi-independence, South Australia had become an ordinary colony controlled by the Colonial Office which had paid off the commissioners' bad debts. The commissioners had been abolished. Grey could rule like the governors in other colonies.

Gawler was the convenient scapegoat for everything—for the theorists' mistakes, the board's incompetence, and the Colonial Office's indifference. He found some consolation in religious and charitable works but never got the government's endorsement of his claim that, thanks to his efforts, South Australia was "the only cheap and brilliantly successful colony in modern history".

Life in Early Adelaide, 1837-41

Read all you can about South Australia and believe one quarter of the same.

Immigrant's letter home, 1839

S o far the emphasis has been on the stresses, successes and failures of the notables among the founding fathers, the theorists, legislators, administrators, officials and the like. What about the raw material of the Wakefield experiment, the cannon fodder of colonization—the men women and children who had chosen to make Adelaide their home? What were their experiences in this raw provincial capital during the period from Proclamation Day to the establishment of local government?

Adelaide abounds in early records. This was no convict camp, like the first Sydney and Hobart, or service centre for squatters, like the infant Melbourne. Adelaide's origins were doctrinaire and highly moral. Some early visitors took pleasure in contrasting prudent Adelaide with the rakehelly cities of the east. T. Horton James, for instance, in his *Six Months in South Australia* (1838): "There are no huge barracks in Adelaide full of wicked and condemned men—no female factories, or penitentiaries— no enormous gaols and permanent gibbets in the public streets—there are no poorhouses often calling for enlargement—nor lunatic asylums with their drear and solitary cells, offering their living sepulchres to the sad victims of vice and rum."[1]

ATTRACTIONS OF THE MODEL PROVINCE

Many of the nineteenth century English not only considered themselves moral but loved to moralize. The example of this young city with a queen's name establishing itself amid a welter of good intentions in a continent notorious for convictism and land grabbing was too good to miss. Moreover, the South Australian Company, the Colonization Commissioners, general investors, and even, at times, the Colonial Office, were eager to attract immigrants from Britain and to preach about the success of systematic colonization. Finally, the immigrants themselves were anxious to convince themselves that they had been right to take the fateful step of emigration and suffer the hardships of the voyage south. And they belonged to an articulate generation with the happy knack, since largely lost, of describing their experiences in direct and agreeable prose. So a great deal of ink was spilt on early Adelaide, numerous journals, reminiscences, newspaper articles, and books were written about the model province, and many of these have been rescued from near oblivion in facsimile form by the State Library of South Australia.

The feel of early Adelaide comes over strongly from these writings. Why did the immigrants come to South Australia? Most motivations were probably a compound of despair or dissatisfaction with prospects at home, a desire for greater religious or political freedom, an urge to forget past mistakes and begin anew in a freer environment, a desire to get rich quickly—all, perhaps, with a dash of adventure. There was something atavistic in all this. England had become a nation as a result of emigration: the movement of Anglo-Saxon tribes across the North Sea seeking pastures new in the land of the Britons. The United States was the result of British emigration to a new frontier.

Emigration to North America from the British Isles increased greatly during the early nineteenth century. To emigrate to Australia, so far distant and with its convict connotations, called for more than usual firmness of mind, or desperation, on the part of the emigrant. Dutton writes:

> The men who explore new countries are usually shrewd enough to come home again. Those who settle in them are usually on their beam ends, whether financially, politically, or psychologically. Those who are doing well at home stay there. Thus the settlers of the new country have two lives: the one at home which was unexciting if not unsuccessful; the one abroad which may casually call forth genius, or at least unused reserves of bravery, endurance and ingenuity.[2]

Certainly, the colonization of South Australia made opportunities for riches, land ownership, knighthoods and even local immortality for men who, had they stayed at home behind their English ploughs or desks, might have remained in the vast anonymity of history. Moreover, South Australia must have seemed outstandingly attractive for an Australian colony, at least to the type of immigrant the founding fathers wished to attract.

Against the unsavoury confusion of the other Australian colonies, it seemed a high principled and businesslike venture. The South Australian Act guaranteed that no convicts would be allowed in, so the settlers would be spared what William Smillie called in his *Great South Land* (1838) "the fearful demoralization prevalent in the convict colonies". The founders also promised religious freedom and an early achievement of political responsibilities. Godly settlers were specifically preferred. George Fife Angas proclaimed: "If I can get pious people sent out to that land the ground will be blessed for their sake."

That great London centre for Nonconformist activists, Exeter Hall, where meetings to publicize South Australia were held, was the spiritual home of the Adelaide founding fathers. Morphett wrote to the commissioners in 1837: "This is the country for a small capitalist, with sober and industrious habits. His family, which in England is often times an encumbrance, will be a fortune here; and he will attain a rank in society, which in England is rarely attainable."[3] In his *Savage Life and Scenes in Australia and New Zealand* (1847), George French Angas, the artistic son of the founding father, struck similar chords:

> In Adelaide, all the comforts and luxuries of life may be obtained; and an individual who is pining in the cold-catching and uncertain climate of Great Britain—struggling to keep up the necessary appearances of fashionable life, and to be a "somebody", upon a very limited income—may by changing his abode to the genial climate of South Australia, live like a little prince and become a "somebody", with the same amount of income upon which he could barely exist in England.[4]

Horton James thought the province had "a soil and climate resembling Castile", and was favourably impressed with the health and cheerfulness of Adelaide's "labouring classes". As for the women, "they compare very favourably with the rubbish of Sydney;

and a person coming from the eastern colonies could not fail to be struck by the superior ruddiness, simplicity and purity of the South Australian damsels." Smillie quoted a settler's comments on the "first-rate soil, black as ink, and fit to plough up without any preparation".

Stephens in *The Land of Promise* deplored what he called "the rude system of solitary emigration" to America and quoted *Tait's Edinburgh Magazine*: "South Australia is, at present, in the ascendant to what is to us a most interesting class of emigrants— respectable labourers and artisans, and intelligent and educated small capitalists, aspiring to improve their conditions, or to keep their places in society, after the struggle has become hopeless in the Old World." Stephens also quoted "an Irish writer" who rhapsodized that "in South Australia at least the climate of Paradise appears to have survived the Fall". Like all the other commentators, Stephens assured his readers that Adelaide was poles apart, morally, from a Sydney seething with "the most demoralised men on the face of the earth". He believed: "The state of morality in a country is tolerably well indicated by the consumption of ardent spirits. In Great Britain it amounts to one gallon and a fraction to each individual; in New South Wales, to the enormous quantity of seven gallons."

Even the angler would rejoice in Adelaide. According to Stephens there were "plentiful and delicious" fish in the Torrens, and as for sea fishing! "It is not an uncommon occurrence to take three or four hundred weight in one cast." This is a fisherman's story, but catches were good in those long gone unpolluted waters round Adelaide. The *Register* reported on 2 November 1839: "About a fortnight ago the fishermen at Glenelg had the good fortune to enclose and draw to land a draught of fine fish of the kind dignified here by the name of *salmon*." There were over 6,000 salmon caught and the fishermen got 40 pounds for them.

The *Register* was always anxious to extol Adelaide's merits and attract immigrants, for it was distributed in England by the commissioners. In the 12 August 1837 issue, for example, Stevenson wrote at length for the benefit of "Intending Migrants". He lyrically described the climate, soil, and morality of the province, then thundered:

> We want no idlers here—no drunkards. But steady, sober men, who are not ashamed to live "by the sweat of their brow", will be welcomed, and cannot fail to make themselves independent in a few years.

Stevenson wrote further:

> The hills are covered with a species of wood, called in New South Wales *stringy bark*, of as much use and as easy to work as American pine. It splits freely, is fit for all "country purposes", and fences made of it beat the Yankee ones "all to nothing". There are hundreds of thousands of acres of this timber, plenty of it within seven or eight miles of the town, and if we had 20,000 immigrants a year for the next century, there would be enough for them all.

He was on firmer ground when he wrote on farming prospects near Adelaide:

> Very little difficulty is found in clearing the land, as there is scarcely any scrub or brushwood. Four bullocks possess strength enough to turn up any part of the soil I have seen.

Stevenson, an excellent gardener himself, went on to claim that maize would flourish on the plains and that potatoes, peas, beans, cabbages, and turnips "are thriving delightfully". Hindmarsh's oranges, figs, and olives had wintered well and "the vine is sure to flourish".

Our oxen and horses, hard worked and hard ridden, as they necessarily are, grow fatter every day; and the sheep we have imported from Launceston, whose bones, when they were landed, seemed only to be held in place by the skin, have never required more than a few weeks to get into excellent condition. I have seen mutton exhibited at the butchers, which would not have disgraced Leadenhall Market.

Stevenson thought pigs and poultry flourished "better than I ever saw them in the richest districts of Yorkshire or Westphalia. They require very little feeding."

Dingoes had been a nuisance on the plains but: "There is scarcely now one to be seen or heard; and in a year ot two it is likely that we shall get rid of the animal altogether. The kangaroo is in great abundance, and can be purchased at from 9d to 1s a pound ... The black swan, wild duck are in great variety; quail, plover, cockatoos and parrots abound. The harbour and gulf swarm with fish." Mrs. Stevenson wrote in her diary that when they first camped on their one and a half hectare town section, between the present Melbourne and Finniss Streets, a pack of dingoes attacked the food in their camp fire frying pan. Stevenson fired his blunderbuss to disperse them. One of the jobs for the unemployed in the early days was dingo hunting. The wild dogs were even hunted for a time on horseback as surrogate foxes before the survivors retreated into the ample wilderness, leaving the plains to the pigs, sheep, and cattle. The kangaroos, too, soon had to vacate these grassy levels as settlement intensified. As they were edible and the first citizens were short of meat, they usually went the hard way. Smillie recalled:

> While I was exploring, I killed my first kangaroo, it was a monstrous "old man" as they are called here; the white lurcher fixed him, but the kangaroo took him in his forepaws and dashed him to the ground as if he had been a puppy; luckily my mastiff was in time to have a spring at him, the kangaroo was not able to throw him about quite so easy, but actually held him at arm's length until I came up. I put my shoulder under his tail, and with a great effort capsized him, and cut his hamstrings. Before I succeeded in this he gave the white dog a kick that sent him up in the air three or four feet. When the kangaroo came down, the dogs fastened on his throat and soon made an end of him. The old man weighed more than a hundredweight and a half—when fighting he stood as tall as I.[5]

Most of the letter, journal, and book writers enthused about the Adelaide climate. Smillie quoted Kingston as saying: "Though the heat is at present intense, it has no injurious or debilitating effects upon our constitution. I am generally occupied from 6 a.m. to 3 p.m. without cessation and ... have not had a minute's illness since we landed."

"The climate surpasses France", maintained Morphett. "There are no creatures to fear." Horton James displayed a talent for tourist literature. He proclaimed: "I have sometimes in the mornings of April and May, whilst inhaling the pure and balmy air of Mount Lofty, felt a positive pleasure in mere animal existence, in the act of breathing." However, James deplored the summer dust which "reduced to an almost impalpable powder ... penetrates every article of clothing, from its extreme fineness". Smillie went so far as to suggest that the province would appeal to sick or bored people, or to those on the verge of retirement. "For such persons a new scene is opened up. They need no longer pine under a quiet monotony at home, in Devonshire or on the Continent; but may repair to a region where they can engage in an agreeable activity, and can enjoy a climate obviously fitted by nature to foster and cheer declining life."

Beguiled by literature like this, the settlers came in thousands across the heaving seas in their little ships. They came for adventure, or to live "like little princes", or to escape insoluble problems or "a quiet monotony" at home, or to transform their large families from "an encumbrance" into "a fortune", or to become "a somebody", or to get away from the poor house, or to swell the ranks of Nonconformity abroad. Whatever their motives, they came to Light's skeleton of a city sketched on the levels below Mount Lofty, to make or break themselves on colonization.

The emigrant ships deposited them at Glenelg or Port Adelaide. At Holdfast Bay, the dunes were empty. The town of Glenelg was not established until 1839, when wealthy citizens like Morphett began building villas there. In the interval, it was almost deserted, its only permanent building a grog shanty called the Reed Hut. A poor introduction, this, to Angas's pious province, especially as the thirsty new settlers were overcharged for drinks. J.B. Neales was dismayed by the Reed Hut when he ordered refreshments for himself and the two sailors who helped him with the baggage. "The charge was a staggerer, gin and water 4d, porter for the two men 5/6."

From Glenelg a track made by the wheels of bullock drays snaked over the grass-lands to Adelaide and the settlers followed it. Transport was often difficult to find. When the self-reliant Pastor Finlayson arrived at Glenelg on the *John Renwick* in 1837, he placed his possessions in a watercask and rolled it to the site of the future suburb of Hindmarsh.

The settlers often arrived in a grievous condition. On 27 November 1838, Sarah Brunskill wrote from an emigrant ship to her parents in Ely about the tragedies of the passage: "Eight children have died since we left London ... and had it not been for the leeches I should have gone also ... The warm weather here brings out swarms of small flies, cockroaches and bugs ... There is another child dead today, making in all 17, and I believe all could have been saved with care and proper medical attention." Mrs. Brunskill had lost two of her own children. She added: "The ship is like a little town, so much scandal and ill-nature and prying into each other's affairs, you would hardly believe. We have found the preserved meat the last eleven weeks so bad we cannot eat it ... "

South Australia sometimes had a grim aspect at the first sight. Pastor Finlayson, as he watched from the deck of the *John Renwick*, was glad, "as a Scotsman", to see that the province had hills, even though they seemed "parched and white". He wrote in his journal:

> We were truly glad to get to the termination of our voyage, but after dark a grand and (to us) mysterious fire began to kindle on the hills ... It spread with amazing rapidity from one hill to another until the whole range before us seemed one mass of flame. We looked at each other, and the knowing ones shook their heads and declared that it was a signal for the native clans to gather for the purpose of destroying the white intruders ... It was, in-deed, a grand and fearful sight, and many sat on deck all night long expecting to see bands of naked savages coming down on us. The new settlers soon learned that at the end of the summer the poor natives were in the habit of firing the grass that they might secure rep-tiles and animals for food. The incident above recorded, however, filled many with a lasting dread of aboriginals, and for the first few months the whole settlement of Adelaide kept watch and ward against a "black attack", which never came. The fear of an assault was not an unreasonable one, as the new arrivals did not know what enemies dwelt beyond the hills, but the natives soon lost whatever warlike spirit they may at first have possessed, and cringed and whined in an unmanly fashion.[6]

A Mrs. Mahoney, daughter of Ross Reid who settled at Gawler, years later wrote of their voyage to Adelaide in 1839. Her father paid 20 pounds passage for each of his servants, 80 pounds for himself and 70 pounds for his wife and 40 pounds for the children.

> Wine was included, champagne being given every Sunday. The milk not being assured, we bought a cow ... We also brought four pigs, fowls, and a supply of American flour in casks,

casks of pork, oatmeal, firkins of butter ... We dropped anchor on 15th January, 1839, in Holdfast Bay. Being summer, the hills had a dried-up appearance which, with the wretched foreground of sandhills, made the country look very barren, but when we landed and crossed the sandhills it looked very different. The splendid gumtrees were still growing in all directions but much the finest were in and about Adelaide. My father and Mr. Murray landed and walked up to Adelaide, seven miles. The former returned the next day saying he had succeeded in renting a three-roomed wooden house, and had bought the only conveyance then for hire; it was a sort of inside Irish car; also he hired a cart for the luggage. So we packed up, got into the boats and when as near as they could get to land the sailors jumped out and carried us the remainder of the distance. I walked with the two elder boys. I can now see the pretty pair of bronze shoes I had on ... quite worn out, and my feet sore by the time we walked the seven miles.

PORT MISERY

Holdfast Bay, which had no wharf until 1839, was a bad enough landfall. The immigrants were often soaked upon landing, or had the mortification of seeing their packing cases floating in the waves. Port Misery, the aptly named disembarkation point in the Port River, was even worse. The immigrants contemplated eerie tangles of mangroves, a black and viscous creek, banks and shoals of mud. The mosquitoes were so fierce that Alexander Tolmer recalled in his *Reminiscences* that, for once, his wife begged him to light his pipe. The Tolmers arrived on the barque *Brankanmore* in 1840. Their luggage was "thrown promiscuously on to the muddy beach" by cheery sailors who carried the ladies and children ashore from the boats. The men were usually obliged to wade through the mud. British to the last, they carried parasols to protect themselves from the sun. It took the immigrants two hours in a bullock dray to reach Adelaide— and "under a broiling sun". J.W. Bull having been carried ashore "pick-a-back" had to walk to the city in tight wellington boots.[8]

The journey in from the port to the city usually seems to have been pleasant and several early arrivals, doubtless relieved to have got there at all, wrote of their pleasure at seeing the clumps of tall eucalypts, the line of trees by the meandering Torrens, and the universally admired rampart of the ranges. Stephens, for example, wrote of the "belt of magnificent gumtrees" growing by the river and "the white flowers of the marsh mallow" by its banks. The site of South Adelaide was a well-wooded "slight eminence" sixty feet above sealevel.

When the inquisitive Horton James first came to the city site, he saw few "substantial buildings". One, owned by the South Australian Company, was built "on an enormous scale". Other brick buildings were owned by "the enterprising Mr. Gilles", Mr. Hack, and Mr. Thomas and there were "a couple of new taverns".

Most of the pioneers lived as best they might on their scrub-covered city sections or by the bosky banks of the Torrens. Gouger, after his travails in a tent by the Glenelg dunes, was lucky: he had a portable hut opposite the site of Trinity Church. Hindmarsh had his barn-like, thatched government hut with the chimney tacked on.

Finniss, Light's survey assistant and good friend, pitched a tent by the Torrens after pushing his possessions up from the bay in a wheelbarrow. He paid a boy ten shillings to trundle his wife to Adelaide in a "wicker boat placed on wheels". He later claimed that he had built the first wooden hut in Adelaide, as well as the first wooden house, brought out in sections on the *Tam o'Shanter*. Still innovative, he added to this the first Adelaide brick building—a kitchen and oven, on which Mrs. Finniss cooked "excellent white stews" made from parrots.

Hailes wrote of Adelaide in 1839 in his *Reminiscences*:

> At that time it resembled an extensive gypsy encampment. Not the semblance of a street existed on the land, although all the main streets had been duly laid out on the plan. It was in fact an extensive woodland, with here a solitary tent and there a cluster of erratic habitations. There were canvas tents, calico tents, tarpaulin tents, wurleys made of branches, log huts, packing case villas and a few veritable wooden huts ...

Wallabies, until they were shot for the pot, hopped over the sites of Hindley and Rundle Streets. Some of the most "erratic habitations" were thrown up by the latest arrivals at Emigration Square. When the rain swept in from the Gulf, families would huddle together under umbrellas, sails, thatches of reeds, anything that would protect them. Writing of the "semi savage state of life" of the first Adelaide citizens, Stephens observed: "The appearance of the dwellings of the first settlers was very singular, both the walls and roofs of some were composed of mud and grass, others of rushes or brushwood, and the walls of others again were formed of a mixture of limestone, marl and red earth."[9] John Ottaway recalled early memories in the *Register* in 1908:

> We had ... to rough it; but we were none the worse for that. It made us self reliant, and little boys had to be miniature men. I distinctly remember our first home—a miserable shanty indeed; no fireplace and a mud floor. Our cooking was done in the open until my father took the liberty of cutting an opening in the wooden wall and building an outside chimney and fireplace of turf. On top of the chimney a sort of funnel of bark was erected to create a better draught and so we were able to indulge in the luxury of a warm fire. Our roof was none of the best, but mother was equal to the occasion, when the leaky places admitted the rain, by placing tin plates and dishes in position on the bed to catch the rain. We got our drinking water from the Torrens, three-quarters of a mile distant.[10]

Immigrants tended to pitch their tents together according to the ship they came in; thus there was a "Buffalo Row" and a "Coromandel Row". Bull noticed several heaps of empty liquor bottles between the tents and observed that the settlers wanted to relax a little before the serious business of colonization—like a young donkey frisking about, as he put it, before being trained for work.

The government depot at Emigration Square, presided over by John Brown, was a primitive reception centre for labourers and their families whose passages had been paid from the Land Fund. Mr. Gawler used to distribute improving tracts among the weatherboard shacks. Blacket records the impressions of one discontented immigrant:

> How very inferior to what was promised at Home are the comforts and attentions bestowed upon the newly-landed immigrant. Brought from the discomforts of shipboard, he is lodged in a square of not exceeding 10 feet, exposed to wind, heat, cold, in all their dangerous changes. And often into the same small square are crammed two families, destroying morality and causing misery and death. It is necessary that the authorities should go around that Augean stable, Emigration Square, and regulate the occupancies.[11]

Emigration Square, originally called Forbes' Square, stood on the west parklands near the site of the present observatory. "This is a historic spot", declared Blacket, "that must not be lost sight of." It has been.

FIRST CONTACT WITH ABORIGINES

Naturally, there were many references to the Aborigines in the early letters and journals. The local Kaurna tribe seems to have been friendly and no doubt got a lot of amusement from watching the formidably overdressed British as they made their first efforts to build wurleys or catch kangaroos. In 1836 Finniss at Rapid Bay watched with admiration while "Jim", his Aboriginal friend, cut toeholes up the trunks of towering gum trees so that he could poke the possums from their holes. The natives watched for sharks from the cliffs while the surveying party swam in the sea and helped Mrs. Finniss nurse her baby daughter, born in December 1836. Finniss emulated the Aboriginal cooking methods, singeing the fur off possums and other game in the flames of a wood fire, then covering it with hot ashes to bake.

Colonel Light got on well with the Rapid Bay tribe, but disliked the Kaurna, who cut down and burned his trees at Thebarton. He wrote to Palmer: "I never saw less interesting people. They are exceedingly cruel to their women, and they are certainly the dirtiest people I ever beheld."[12]

Blacket, who must have spent many hours with his notebook among reminiscing pioneers, records the first impressions of the Aborigines from one "lady pioneer" at Glenelg:

> The natives eat rats, snakes, or anything they can find. They will come and shake hands, very friendly. They ask for biscuit and say "good night", which they know to be a sort of salutation so say it any time ... They are very superstitious and very idle, lying under a tree all day; but in the evening they have a dance or merry-making they call a "corroboree."

Another lady recalled:

> When we landed a few friendly natives appeared. Unattractive they certainly were, bedaubed with red and white paint and dirty matted hair. Nor did they exhale the odours of Araby.[13]

It is a pity that no one seems to have recorded the natives' views on these patronizing newcomers, sweating in their swathes of serge and calico, as they blandly divided the Kaurna land among themselves. Compensation, if it was thought of at all, was a few biscuits and maybe a little illicit rum and some half-hearted efforts later to set up an Aboriginal reserve on land that the settlers did not want, yet.

A "GYPSY ENCAMPMENT"

Many of the settlers were homesick. One expressed his wistfulness in verse:

> Thou art very fair, my adopted land,
> With thy dome of cloudless blue;
> And I have found on thy distant strand
> Hearts that are warm and true;
> But I love thee not with the feelings deep
> That I love the Isle where my fathers sleep.
>
> Thy birds, it is true, are of splendid wing
> With tints that are gorgeously bright,
> But to most is denied the tuneful string
> Which falls on the ear with delight
> 'Neath the shady oaks that wave in the west
> In the far off land—the Isle I love best.[14]

And, of course, many of the immigrants complained bitterly. One wrote:

> I have not been able to get a job, nor any hope of any. I am reduced to a great distress, provisions being enormously high—bread, 3s a loaf; potatoes, 3s 6d a gallon; beef and mut-

ton, 1s a pound; butter, 3s 6d a pound; cheese, 2s per pound; porter, 1s 6d a quart. I have
conversed with several who came out on the first ship, and they assure me that everything
they have attempted has turned out a failure. How can anything grow in dust and sand
and eternal drought? There is not a river in the colony. Rents are twelve times as high as
in England. A hovel in which you would not put a good horse, 1 pound a week. Still, many
persons say that they are doing well; but there is no bottom in the whole affair, and it is a
cruel deception practised on the people in England. A cabin passenger of mine shot himself
three weeks after arrival.[15]

Blacket quotes complaining letters from Adelaide published in the London *Times* in
1840. Their writers complained about everything: flies, heat, mosquitoes, inflation,
loneliness, high mortality at Emigration Square, and so on. One said: "I suppose you
are getting very favourable reports from some of the old inhabitants, who wish to invite their friends to come to this fairy isle, where in summer time you can scarcely get a
drink of good water, with a burning sun all day long, the north wind as hot as fire,
blowing the sands in clouds enough to stifle you and to burn the eyes out of your
head."[16] The editor of the *Times* himself was moved to say of such complaints: "It shows
the wretched condition of those unhappy creatures to whom the land of promise has
been so niggardly in its performance."

Elizabeth Davison, who arrived on Christmas Day 1839 after "a long tedious
journey of twenty-two weeks", wrote in her diary:

We went to board at Mrs. Bathgate's, the best house in Adelaide. We were much disappointed in Adelaide, and the country round it appears to be nothing but a sandhill. The
weather was so hot it was almost unsupportable and not a blade of grass or anything green
except the gum trees, to be seen. Provisions of every kind very dear and house rents enormous. We paid Mrs. Bathgate 9 pounds a week for our board till we could get into a four
roomed box that we had taken for 100 pounds per annum.[17]

Horton James made fun of Adelaide's plan:

The Town of Adelaide, as depicted on the maps, is a very *beau ideal* of all possible cities—
there is an elegance and a vastness of design about it, that makes one almost blush for the
comparative insignificance of London and Stamboul, of Paris and Canton; but on going to
the spot, like so many other works of art and imagination, it resembles the picture very
slightly—it is altogether on too large a scale; and of all the follies committed by the inexperience of the surveyor-general, who is, nevertheless, in every other respect, a most
gentlemanlike, entertaining and intelligent person, next to its inland situation, this
monstrous extent of Adelaide will turn out to be the most fruitful of complaints. You may
lean against any tree in the city and exclaim:
"This shadowy desert, unfrequented woods
I better brook than flourishing peopled towns."

James exercised his wit further by telling how he wandered through the forest in
search of Victoria Square. He came upon a fowler shooting parrots in a gum tree who
told him that the scrub all round represented the central square of the city. James concluded by declaring: "there is not the remotest chance that this most unnatural abortion can ever come to any good."

It is easy for us, with hindsight, to dismiss James's criticisms as short sighted and
impertinent. Light asked posterity to judge him, not his contemporaries. But there must
have been many who agreed with James while Adelaide was in its struggling, shanty
town phase. The contrast between plan and reality was harsh.

The "gypsy encampment" or "hutting" phase lasted about eight months, roughly
coeval with the period of Hindmarsh's governorship. At the time experiences were
often unpleasant enough but the old pioneers who reminisced to Blacket had warm

memories of the tents and wurleys. Blacket wrote:

> Everything was new. There was no snobbery. The settlers led a free, unconventional sort of life. Servants were difficult to get. Those who came out soon got married. Ladies had to do what is termed menial work. A pork barrel, end up, or a packing case served as a table. Tin pannikins were used for tea. Ship's biscuit and salt pork was the staple food. Sometimes there was a welcome variety in the form of wallaby or native birds. Even baked snakes or lizards were indulged in. Of vegetables and fruits there were few. Some of the immigrants pickled the leaves of the mesembryanthemum, or "pig's-face" ... The settlers had their social gatherings in tents and in huts.[18]

It is touching to think that a city which was to become associated with almost excessive propriety began in this raffish jamboree among the bushes, when even the most respectable founding father was prepared to eat baked snake when hunger pinched. Among its summer dust and winter mud, earliest Adelaide was almost a commune.

However, the richer and more enterprising settlers soon began to distinguish themselves. On 27 July 1837 the *Register* praised the home-building progress of the shrewd Osmond Gilles: "There is a cottage at the south eastern part of the town, planted and fenced round with a substantial English iron fence. The garden is laid out in front, and the roof is adorned with a cupola, surmounted with a weathervane; the door, too, is graced with a handsome knocker—the *tout ensemble*, in short, would not disgrace the neighbourhood of Richmond." How Treasurer Gilles, doing extraordinarily well from his trade and land deals, must have gloried in that weathervane, that handsome knocker, that snug little cottage while his friends still perched on their upended packing cases in leaking tents!

EXPANSION

Governor Gawler's vigorous expansion policies and the heavy influx of immigrants wrought a quick change. In December 1837 Adelaide consisted of about 300 houses and huts. These had doubled by the end of the next year. The first official census in late 1840 gave the total metropolitan population as 8,489—1,932 of whom lived in the municipal villages and 66 on private sections within the municipality. The rest lived in the city—5,297 in South Adelaide, 629 in North Adelaide, and 631 on the parklands.

Stephens noted that East Terrace, with its fine view of the hills, "appears to be the favourite spot for villa residences". He quoted a contented settler:

> My temporary house is putting up on acre 257, with Mount Lofty in front of us ... a lower range of beautiful hills a littler nearer, and, between this and the town, a beautiful valley studded with trees and covered with the richest herbage. The town slopes, in natural terraces, downward to the valley and I have nothing between me and the view. It is more like the richer and more verdant of the views in Cumberland, than anything else I know.

Gawler spent heavily to erect solid and durable buildings, both to give the province a respectable base and to absorb some of the unemployed immigrant labour. Before his recall, he had given Adelaide several good public buildings, including the central portion of the present Government House, a "plain but handsome" treasury building, and Adelaide Gaol, as well as a vastly improved road system. He also established municipal government, the first of its kind in Australia.

Under the Hindmarsh regime Adelaide was far from self-supporting. Provisions and livestock had to be imported from Cape Colony in South Africa or the eastern colonies at heavy cost. Finniss was obliged to pay 90 pounds for a horse from Van Diemen's Land. The delays over the country surveys had forced most of the settlers to stay in Adelaide living on their savings. Some of them even had to auction off their agricultural implements and dairy equipment.

Here again, Gawler's vigour rescued the province. The acceleration of the country surveys and the laying down of roads to outposts like Encounter Bay allowed the settlers to fan out into the country, till the soil, and depasture their stock. On 3 April 1838 Joseph Hawdon and his party were welcomed to Adelaide. They had overlanded 325 bullocks, heifers, cows, and horses sixteen hundred kilometres from New South Wales from a station on the Hume, across the Goulburn and Murrumbidgee rivers, and down the Murray. The journey had taken ten weeks and opened up a valuable line of supply from the east. Henceforth pastoral progress was rapid. The numbers of sheep rose from 38,000 in 1838 to 200,160 in 1840; of cattle from 2,500 to 15,100; and of horses from 480 to more than 1,000. *The South Australian Almanac* of 1840 shows that there were substantial flocks and herds in rural areas as scattered as Mount Barker, Willunga, Para, and Port Lincoln.

The colonists soon realized the province's potential for Mediterranean fruits. Stevenson wrote in the 1840 *Almanac* that South Australia was becoming "the peculiar country of the orange, the pomegranate, fig, olive, vine, and every species of grain most prized as animal or human food". He prophesied that the grape, thanks to the climate and topography of the Adelaide region, "will ... become one of the staples of South Australia".

THE GERMANS

German settlers, first variant among the almost wholly British immigrants to South Australia, were prominent among the pioneering endeavours in farming and market gardening. While the British up to 1840 tended to cling to Adelaide, these dour Lutheran refugees from religious persecution in northern Germany moved out into the countryside. Angas, always sympathetic to nonconformity, always eager to direct moral colonists to South Australia, sent out the first batch of German settlers in 1838 in the ship *Prince George* under the leadership of Pastor Augustus Kavel. They settled on some of Angas's land by the Torrens, naming their village Klemzig after their Prussian home. Many hundreds followed, and distinct German townships sprang up, as at Hahndorf, Lobethal, and throughout the Barossa Valley. The *Register* of 8 June 1839 spoke approvingly of the "patient and enduring habits" of the Lutherans, noted that they were being employed in large numbers by graziers round Mount Barker, and concluded: "striking is the effect of these Teutonic accents arising amid our solitary places".

Within a few years, the German communities were well entrenched, not always with the approval of British observers. George French Angas wrote of them in 1846 in his *South Australia Illustrated*:

> Though frugal and industrious to an extraordinary degree, they are a slow, plodding class, with many conventional prejudices, and frequently exhibit considerable selfishness and ingratitude. Their houses and cultivation are in the style of their own country, and living as they do entirely to themselves, amalgamation with the English portion of the settlers is of rare occurrence. Poultry, butter, vegetables and fruit, are frequently brought into Adelaide for sale by the women, whose picturesque style of dress, and simplicity of manners, obtain for these peasants a considerable share of custom.[19]

Clannish they were, and odd and uncouth they might have appeared to xenophobic Britons, yet the arrival of these Germans was timely for South Australia. The province was battling to survive. The Lutherans had the tenacity to turn parts of the daunting wilderness into productive fields and, later, vineyards. Moreover, they knew that behind them in Silesia and Prussia was religious harassment, fines, even imprisonment. Unlike many of the British, the Germans did not pine for home as they built their slab huts in the hills.

THE TIERSMEN

If Adelaide was dubious about the Germans at first, it was dismayed by the incursion of settlers from the eastern colonies. Wanderers from New South Wales followed the routes of the overlanders into the godly province and lurked in the hills or Tiers, and became known as Tiersmen. Several "Vandemonians" worked for the South Australian Company at its Encounter Bay whaling station. The *Register* of 8 June 1839 deplored the "profligacy and intemperate habits" of the Tiersmen which made them "unfit to be received into any establishment". The point was, of course, that most of these easterners were escaped convicts or ticket-of-leave men, many of them Catholic Irishmen with the reverse of that patriotic ardour for things English which animated Adelaide. The *Register* often warned its readers of these papist wolves of the hills, poised to pounce on the Methodists of the plains.

Adelaide was zealous to preserve its no convict image and probably over reacted against the Tiersmen. This was natural enough in a lonely province with no troops and only a vestigial police force. No doubt the Tiersmen did push up the crime rate. Tolmer in his self-congratulatory *Reminiscences* observed that "The state of crime in the colony when I joined the police was appalling".[20] The Tiersmen were committing "black-faced" (masked) robbery, stealing cattle and driving them to their camps in the Black Forest between Adelaide and Glenelg, or up into the gorges of the Tiers. Tolmer tells us how he rode boldly into the ranges to bring many an escaped convict to justice, and then was responsible for security at the subsequent public hangings. One bushranger, a man called Hughes, offended everyone by smoking his pipe on the scaffold and ignoring the homilies of the clergymen. When the trapdoor opened, he still refused to do the decent thing and stood with his feet on either side of the gap. Then, Tolmer writes, "the Rev. Howard went forward and kicked his foot off".

Adelaide's first public execution took place on 2 May 1838. The victim, Michael Magee, was an escaped convict from New South Wales who had shot at a sherriff, J. Smart. Magee was hanged on a tall gum tree on the parklands before the Colonial Store, avidly watched by an enormous crowd. Hangings were as great a crowd puller as football matches today. The Magee execution was horribly bungled by a masked and apparently misshapen hangman. Horton James described it, and mordantly noted that the crowd was "half of them women".

THE *MARIA* MASSACRE

Apart from wild Tiersmen, Adelaide was also agitated by newspaper reports of Aborigines spearing shepherds up the river or on the pastoral runs near Port Lincoln. The most notorious incident here was the massacre of the crew and the passengers of the wrecked brig *Maria* on the Younghusband Peninsula in July 1840. Five men and seven children were murdered on the dunes, allegedly by members of the Milmenrura or Big Murray tribe. Gawler sent out the police commissioner, Major O'Halloran, Tolmer, and a party of police to administer summary justice. The mangled bodies were found and buried and over the graves O'Halloran had a gallows of she oaks constructed. Two uncomprehending Aborigines were given a drum head trial before their fellows and the nooses were slipped over their necks.

"Black men!" the major told the Aborigines. "This is the white man's punishment for murder ... They must hang until they fall to pieces."[21]

One wonders what the natives thought of this civilized ritual as the corpses swung in the winds of the lonely Coorong. The *Maria* affair probably did untold harm to race relations in South Australia, especially after its sensational misinterpretation by Simpson Newland in his popular novel *Paving the Way* (1893).

This execution without trial was to cause a controversy in the pages of the *Register* and among Evangelicals in England, and to tarnish Gawler's reputation further. He was actually charged with murder and had to be pardoned by the queen. The commissioners had been eager to claim that: "The colonisation of South Australia by industrious and virtuous settlers, so far from being an invasion of the rights of the Aborigines, is a necessary preliminary to the displacement of the lawless squatters, the abandoned sailors, the runaway convicts ... that now infest the region." Perhaps, like Captain Barker, the unfortunates from the *Maria*, had suffered for unrecorded outrages against the natives by white intruders.

One prominent settler at least could wander among the natives of the Lake Alexandrina region after the *Maria* massacre without feelings of revenge. This was Johann Menge, the extraordinary Lutheran sage, geologist, and hermit who preferred the wilderness to Adelaide. He wrote as a "Friend to the Aborigines" to the *Register* of 26 September 1840 of an encounter with natives near the Murray Mouth. "I smiled at them, I shook their hands; I put a little biscuit into their mouths—sat down at their fires—gave them gum ... This so did away with any feeling of ill-will that when I bid them good-bye, they repeated it, 'good-bye', as long as they thought I could hear it, with joyful shouts."

THE ABORIGINES

But people like Menge were exceptional indeed. Most of the colonists no doubt were well disposed enough towards the Aborigines—providing they gave up their culture and nomadic ways and became respectable Methodists, of the second grade and deferential. The founding fathers made comparatively strenuous efforts to treat the natives better than had their counterparts in the other Australian colonies. The office of protector of Aborigines was set up, occupied by men like the explorer Edward John Eyre who had some limited success with his charges at Moorunde station on the Murray. However the policy was, and remained so for many years, strongly paternal. The assumption was that the Aborigines should adapt themselves to British ways. To most modern readers, the nineteenth century colonial writings on Aborigines, even the most well meaning, reek of condescension and dogmatism. George French Angas in his *South Australia Illustrated* was typical of benevolent observers when he wrote:

> In South Australia the native inhabitants have been far better treated than in any of the other Australian Colonies; a wise and humane legislation on their behalf under Governor Grey, has tended to promote their welfare, and the peace of the Colonists, and a friendly feeling is thus established between the degraded denizen of the soil, and the intelligent and

christianised European; whilst the schools established for the native children of both sexes, are developing a new era and the dawn of civilisation, amongst these benighted and sunken creatures.[22]

Much of this was humbug. There was little real "friendly feeling" between the "intelligent christianised European" and "these sunken creatures" in Adelaide or anywhere else in Australia. The Aboriginal schools Angas refers to never amounted to anything much, largely because those pupils who did not return to their old tribal ways were not accepted as equals by the settlers. Racial prejudice was strong from the beginning, accentuated here by the defenceless nature of the Aborigines. Had they been warlike, like the Maoris or the Zulus, the Aborigines would have achieved more respect and better conditions. As it was, demoralized by the cultural confrontation, decimated by imported diseases like small pox, syphilis, and measles, they went to the wall.

Angas added: "Independently of their want of cleanliness, there is a perceptible odour about these people which is offensive and is frequently rendered more intolerable by the shark and whale oil with which they anoint their bodies." It probably never crossed his mind to wonder if there was anything offensive to the Aborigines about the tobacco smoking, spirit drinking, violent, polluting newcomer.

Mrs. Conigrave recalled of the Aborigines on Hindmarsh Island in the 1850s: "The blacks at that time greatly feared the white man's gun." She also recorded what was probably a fairly typical white attitude to the natives: "A Lady settler once said in my hearing: 'Give them a tail and you have a monkey complete'".

Bull tells how early in 1837 the only two horses in the province (one of which was owned by John Morphett) had disappeared and that a search party was organized, led by C.W. Stuart, the stock overseer, and Allen who was later to supervise the first botanic gardens in Adelaide. Near the mouth of the Onkaparinga they came upon a group of natives, whose leader they jovially named Tam o'Shanter. Bull writes:

> For some time Mr. Allen addressed the black leader, repeating that they had landed to introduce Mr. Wakefield's principles of colonization, and that they begged to apologise for this intrusion on their country etc. etc. Tam o'Shanter, not understanding Mr. Allen's polite speech, got impatient and stepped up to Mr. Stuart, and first took from his head his cabbage tree hat and touched up his hair, and then opened his waistcoat and shirt front to examine his skin; then lifted up one of his feet like a vet., examined his boot. The others also had to submit to a similar examination—at which Mr. Allen expressed great anger, saying he had never been treated in such a manner before.[23]

One can perhaps sympathize with Mr. Allen's indignation at being inspected like one of his botanical specimens, and also with Tam o'Shanter at being lectured to on Wakefield's principles, which were difficult enough for the English to understand. But this incident makes a refreshing change from superior Europeans studying the Aborigines like peep show curiosities. The truth probably was that each side seemed absurd to the other.

(Incidentally, earlier on this expedition the white men had thrown away on to the beaches some empty bottles which Bull saw as "the first tokens of civilization in that part of the country.")[24]

The anonymous author of *South Australia in 1842*, who had spent four years in the province, was informative on the local Aborigines—"stout, good-looking, and well made, with the exception of their legs, which are slender"—and was at pains to show that the founding fathers had "humane designs" for them, in contrast to the eastern colonists. He wrote:

> The number of the natives ... is very few. In an area of 2,800 square miles, including

Adelaide, there are only 650—280 males, 182 females and 188 children. This is attributed to perpetual quarrels among them—to polygamy, infanticide and other causes; indeed the number is on the decrease.

He did not go into the "other causes" of the decline, but clearly these were the debilitating effect of white settlement. He continued:

Various measures have been adopted for their improvement. A location for them, in the immediate neighbourhood of Adelaide, was formed in 1837; yet, although they are supplied with food, not more than 160 or so, can be induced to live there, and the particular individuals are frequently changing. They have been assisted in erecting six cottages; and in January, 1842, they had a plot of ground of three acres, cultivated by themselves, in which potatoes, carrots, maize and melons were then growing. On 23rd December, 1839, a school for the native children was opened. In June 1841, the average attendance was 19; the progress made, was such as to show that there is no deficiency in mental capacity. The girls have received instruction in sewing from a number of ladies, chiefly connected with the Wesleyan Methodist congregation ... The adults are still more inattentive to religious instruction than the children, and can scarcely be induced to attend the Lord's-day. A few have been employed during the whaling season, at Encounter Bay, in pulling the whale boats, but no dependence can be placed on them.

He noted that when the first settlers arrived, the Aborigines wandered about in a state of "perfect nudity". One can imagine the effect this had on the pious pioneers: but the missionaries, mainly Evangelical Lutherans from Dresden at first, and the ladies of the Wesleyan Methodist society soon had them covered with cast off trousers and dresses.

The authors of this and other propagandizing pamphlets probably wrote to please English readers anxious to "improve" the Aborigines.

The gradual disappearance of the Aborigines was a fact of colonial life noted by most nineteenth century observers. Sometimes they noted it with regret, sometimes, as in the case of Anthony Trollope, as a phenomenon as natural as the ebb and flow of the tide. Trollope, the warm-hearted novelist, concluded in his *Australia and New Zealand*:

It is their fate to be abolished, and they are already vanishing. Nothing short of abstaining from encroaching upon their lands—abstaining, that is, from taking possession of Australia, could be of any service to them ... Of the Australian black man we may certainly say that he has to go. That he should perish without unnecessary suffering should be the aim of all concerned in the matter.[25]

Bull, who knew the South Australian situation pretty well, was a little more shamefaced about this virtual genocide, but consoled himself by seeing Aboriginal extinction as God's design. He wrote:

The question of the displacement of the aboriginal race has always been attended with great difficulties, but is one of those necessary processes in the course of Providence to bring about the improvement of the human race and the promised latter days. From my own experience with our natives, low as they have sunk, I am convinced that, with ample means granted, and time, much good may be worked on them; but at the same time the introduction of civilised habits seems to be fatal to their continued existence, independently of the vices and disease we have brought among them, to our disgrace, which have hastened their destruction.[26]

"He has to go." One of "those necessary processes in the course of Providence". Round Adelaide, as in all settled parts of Australia, the Aborigines decayed and dwindled down to the modern era of subsidized existence on reserves and mission stations. The last of the Kaurnas died in 1897. Meanwhile, during Adelaide's first few years the

Aboriginal tribal system quickly broke up. Bull deplored Hindmarsh's regulation forbidding the employment of Aborigines, and the "scanty means" available to the protectors of Aborigines. He claimed that the establishment of schools for Aboriginal children (they were in the parklands and at Walkerville) in the city was a mistake, for the adults camped there too "and thus the worst vices of the town were only too readily acquired and adopted by them".

The citizens grumbled about Aboriginal activities on the parklands. In the *Register* of 19 August 1840, for instance, "A townsman" protested about "a whole body of natives hewing and cutting away at the fine trees opposite Government House". The editor agreed with him, deploring the "wholesale destruction" of trees by Aborigines with "absolute impunity". He also bemoaned the "nuisance of their beastly corroborees" and wished they would take their "discordant orgies" out into the bush.

Bull concluded by regretting that more intelligent measures had not been taken. "We had been received as friends, and now where are the original lords of the soil, and what are the state of the few who remain in any of our settled districts?"[27]

EXPLORATIONS

There was much news of other kinds apart from what early writers called "difficulties with the Aborigines". The wilderness round Adelaide gradually lost its mystery as the settlers pushed outwards. In July 1837 Bingham Hutchinson, after two attempts, climbed to the summit of Mount Lofty. This required, as the *Register* of 8 July 1837 reported, "considerable exertion and perseverance, as well as a night's rest among the hills". Hutchinson's account went on:

> Our progress was slow, and attended with great difficulty, from the luxuriance of the plants and underwood by the side of the brook, being in many places over our heads, and the lower parts interlaced with creeping plants ... We discovered a great many new and beautiful plants; grass trees abounded ... We discovered several mushrooms, two of which I ate, to satisfy myself of their wholesomeness, and we also saw today the first snail.

The explorers saw plenty of evidence of native burning off of the scrub, but saw no Aborigines. They observed six dingoes.

Later that year, Robert Cock led a party which explored the lovely country between Adelaide and Lake Alexandrina. They discovered and named the Angas River. Often they stopped to gaze, as Cock wrote in his journal, "with wonder and delight on the richness of the country". Next year, he explored parts of Yorke's Peninsula. In November 1838 Strangways took a party to discover the source of the Torrens and the Gawler River, and in 1839 C.C. Dutton penetrated to Coffin Bay. Governor Gawler himself was a keen explorer, and nearly perished during an expedition to the north when Mount Bryan was named after one of his party who disappeared without trace. By 1840 there was a thin skein of settlement over the province along the coastline and inland for a hundred kilometres from Adelaide. Eyre began his bleak wanderings in the north.

The author of *South Australia in 1842* estimated that there were about 500 "farm steadings" in the province and 400 sheep stations. He described a thriving new farm, established by John Barton Hack at Echunga Springs near Mount Barker. "Mr. Hack has enclosed four paddocks, containing 620 acres—has an extensive farming and dairy establishment, twelve acres of garden and orchard, with plantations containing upwards of 1,000 vines and fruit trees". He quoted a letter from "a highly respectable

Scotch gentleman", Alexander Lorimer on the secrets of success in pioneering round Adelaide:

> The particular class of persons to whom I would, with all confidence, recommend South Australia, as a proper field, is good practical Scotch farmers who possess a sufficient capital. Such farmers, with families able to assist them, are, above all others, the best qualified individuals for this colony. Those who feel themselves really comfortable, in every respect, at home, I recommend to stay where they are; and South Australia is certainly no place for dissipated young gentlemen, with little capital and less judgement.

And indeed, "good practical Scotch" like the Elders and the Barr Smiths were to do extraordinarily well for themselves in South Australia, whereas "dissipated young gentlemen" completed their ruin in the rugged bush or amid the inflation and uncertainty of early Adelaide.

ACHIEVEMENTS

By 1840, Adelaide was sliding into the economic crisis which brought about Gawler's recall and his replacement by Governor Grey and a policy of ruthless retrenchment. For many months to come, the city was to be racked by crises in business confidence, fluctuating prices, and uncertainties about the future. The Wakefield system was to be abandoned and some of the old distinctive official attitudes which made the province so interesting to progressive thinkers and philosophical visitors were to be discontinued. Such periods of exhaustion and confusion soon after the first settlement were a fairly common feature of colonization in Australia and New Zealand.

However, good luck, geographical circumstances, the continuing momentum of some of the original ideas on what South Australia should be like, and the determination of many like-minded pioneers were to preserve in large measure Adelaide's sense of difference.

Gawler had driven himself and his staff to exhaustion and had spent 200,000 pounds to give the province a reasonably secure anchorage from which it would weather the economic storms to come. The protracted problem of the surveys was solved. The province had good communications, and had started on the road which would bring it to agricultural and pastoral prosperity. There was a new wharf at Port Adelaide and a road connecting it to the city. The record land boom had eased and most of the flood of immigrants had been transformed into productive settlers. The rancour of political argument had abated, although it was to revive in lively if a little more muted form during the administrations of Grey and Robe. Some of the newly tilled land was bearing twenty to thirty bushels of wheat to the acre.

Kingston's map of Adelaide in 1841–42 shows that the city had made progress during the few years since its troubled beginning. Settlement had concentrated near the water supply of the Torrens—in the northern end of South Adelaide, especially along Rundle and Hindley streets, and in the southern end of North Adelaide. The city had Gawler's fine new public buildings, distilleries, and flour mills, the buildings put up by the South Australian Company such as the Bank of South Australia, and several shops and offices. In the month of May 1841, there were 1,960 houses, shops, stores, and other buildings in Adelaide according to a return of the town surveyor, "capable"—in the words of the *South Australia in 1842* pamphlet—"of affording comfortable accommodation to a population of 9,000 souls, and of yielding a sufficient sum for the purposes of municipal government at a moderate rate".

Besides, Adelaide had churches, schools, a mechanics' institute, a theatre, societies such as a natural history society and an agricultural society, a chamber of commerce—even a botanic garden. Hitherto South Australia had been governed by a necessarily autocratic governor and his staff and nominated council. The founding fathers had, for their times, strong democratic beliefs. From the beginning they had planned that Adelaide should have a form of local government as soon as circumstances warranted this. Despite the setbacks they had endured and the economic problems which were soon to worsen, there was still a strong momentum in Adelaide for constitutional progress. By 1840, no other colonial capital had local government, which was probably an inducement to the Adelaide leaders to show the way. The sense of difference, and superiority, was pervasive. Gawler, ever the emotional liberal, was sympathetic to the idea. On 19 August 1840, the governor and his executive council passed the first colonial Municipal Council Act. Adelaide, not yet four years old, was deemed sufficiently moral, responsible, and substantial to have its own city council.

Responsible Government

What makes the difference between the British Empire today and the Roman Empire of the first century? It is neither civilization, intelligence, nor brute force, but righteousness. The British Constitution is founded upon the word of God.

John Blacket, 1911

The Members of the Council are elected annually, and, on the whole, they do their work very well.

William Harcus, 1876

THE FIRST CITY COUNCIL

In the old brave theoretical days of the 1830s, the colonization commissioners had requested that elective municipal institutions should be allowed in any town in their model province once it had achieved a population of 2,000. The Colonial Office agreed and Gawler had passed the first Municipal Council Act. The colonizers were feeling their way. As a later town clerk, Thomas Worsnop, puts it in his *History of the City of Adelaide* (1877): "The Act ... was ... in reality only an experimental Act, and much had to be learned—and something to be suffered—before municipal institutions took permanent root in South Australia."[1]

The council was to consist of nineteen common councilmen, one of whom should be mayor, and three aldermen. Only men "of full age" could vote, provided they had lived for at least six months in the province, and owned or rented a house, shop, business, or land in the city worth at least twenty pounds a year, and lived within eleven kilometres of it. Citizens who had received "public charitable relief" or had been convicted of a crime within the past two years were disqualified from voting. A councilman had to have personal property of the value of five hundred pounds, or own or occupy a city house worth fifty pounds a year. The council was empowered to levy rates and tolls, build a gaol, and look after a slaughterhouse and a market. There were curious provisos about quorum voting.

All the omens were bad for the young council. Sturt had written earlier: "I hope to see it work, for it will take a good deal off the hands of the government but I confess I have my misgivings." Fisher had written to John Rundle complaining of autocratic rule from Government House, and some of the commissioners feared that local government, competing with the governor and council, might mean a return to the evils of double government. However the limited experiment was sanctioned, with the hope that it would prepare the colonists for eventual self-government, and help spread the financial burden of the administration.

However the council was unfortunate in having the self-opinionated and ruthless Grey to deal with; and doubly unfortunate in that it had to try to find its feet during a period when both confidence and capital were at the lowest ebb. Yet the first attempt at local government was gallantly made.

On 31 October 1840 the election of the first council took place. The *Register* of that date noted with approval: "Adelaide has exhibited, during the last week, all the bustle and excitement which was to be expected from the first exercise of *popular representation* within the province—the first, we believe, that has been permitted within the Asiatic and Australasian possessions of the British crown." Gawler observed that the election had taken place with "moderation, order and discernment". The first council comprised almost all the prominent citizens who were not already members of the executive council. Some of them had taken part in the old Adelphi discussions. All of them were well endowed with both property and propriety. Fisher was elected the first mayor; Stevenson, Smillie, a Scots lawyer, and A.H. Davis, a Nonconformist merchant, became aldermen; and the councilmen included worthies like Nathaniel Hailes, the auctioneer, and Thomas Wilson, a prominent lawyer.

The council had no resources beyond a loan of 250 pounds and a potential rates income. The city's population was less than 8,000 and there were fewer than 2,000 houses. Ratable property was valued at 80,000 pounds, promising a revenue of 1,333 pounds at an assessment of 4d in the pound—if it could be collected. Nevertheless, the corporation began with confidence, committing itself to paying 1,000 pounds in salaries to the mayor, the city engineer, Kingston, the treasurer, Morphett, and others. At its first meeting on 4 November 1840, the council prepared a loyal address to the governor: "Regarding Representative Government as one of the most invaluable privileges of British subjects, we rejoice in the early concession to us of some of its advantages." They clearly hoped for more to come, but in the meantime promised to: "... exert ourselves to the utmost for the advancement of the prosperity of this city, the maintenance of peace and good order, the preservation of morals, and the promotion of that union which gives strength and efficiency to every effort at political, social and moral improvement."

Gawler answered with similar rhetoric. In fact, the council had little beyond rhetoric with which to advance Adelaide's morality and prosperity. A chronic shortage of money was to be their bane. Against a torrid background of financial insecurity and general public indifference to the corporation and reluctance to pay rates, their good intentions came to little. News of Gawler's recall in May 1841 upset them, but, perhaps with an inkling of Grey's autocratic nature, they passed a resolution promising to avoid political discussions, since such debates in English corporations "have uniformly tended to lower their character". Even this assurance of docility did not help them into the new governor's favour.

In the meantime, the council busied itself so far as it could. Acre 203 had been set aside for the use of a corporation in the original city plan. Gawler now benevolently sold it to them for twelve shillings. Such generosity was later criticized by the Colonial Office. Plans were drawn up for appropriate buildings but as there was no money they had to be shelved. The council had to confine its dignity to a single hired room in Hindley Street. It moved the market, built a slaughterhouse on the parklands where Bonython Park now stands, cleared a few stumps from the city streets, and agreed upon a city seal depicting two clasped hands. Even this modest activity got it into debt. At the end of a year, Fisher resigned as mayor, expatiating on the "novel and peculiar" circumstances of the first corporation and lamenting that he was passing on to his successor an enterprise deep in debt. He was succeeded by the solicitor Thomas Wilson after a long wrangle over whether or not Fisher had the right to resign. Most of the councillors were glad to follow Fisher into retirement. Only six remained after the next elections in a council dominated by more proletarian representatives. The *Southern Australian* sorrowed over this decline in respectability, for the new council had "a smack of too much radicalism to suit our taste".

Nothing went well for the aldermen and councillors. There was a muffled scandal when it was discovered that council officers were deducting their salaries from council income. A new rate of 9d in the pound was widely resented. Gawler's bills had been dishonoured in London, immigration stopped, and the harsh economies of Governor Grey (some of whose bills were also dishonoured in London) were resented. Simply put, South Australia had run out of credit. "Everything", wrote Worsnop, "was at the lowest ebb possible."[2] Businesses were ruined, shops closed down, and some recent immigrants speedily emigrated—to the east, to New Zealand, or back home. At least 6,000 people were out of work. Angry public meetings blackguarded the governor—who remained icily self-righteous through it all—and complained about prices.

In such a situation, the citizens were little disposed either to pay rates, or to sympathize with the council in its losing struggle with the governor. "The levy of the first City rate was not a popular act," wrote Worsnop with his usual conciliar understatement. "It was collected with difficulty, and in little less than a year 132 distress warrants were issued to recover arrears."[3] Rates were even less popular in the remaining months of the corporation's existence. Slaughterhouse fees—their non-payment that is—were a constant trial to the council. Those few councillors who did attend meetings fretted about the appalling state of the streets and the rickety bridge over the Torrens, but there was hardly any money to do anything about them.

To Grey, the council was premature. Relations between council and governor began frigidly and quickly slid into enmity. It was an unequal contest, for Grey had prestige, authority, and the Colonial Office on his side, whereas the council had little self-confidence and less popular support. When elections became due in October 1842 only 135 citizens bothered to enrol, so no vote was taken. Grey imposed a series of tolls to raise money, including harbour dues and a customs act. The council organized an indignant public meeting at the Queen's Theatre to protest about these "heavy additional taxes" at a time of "universal distress". Grey ignored this, whereupon the council raised the battlecry of the American revolutionaries—no taxation without representation in the Legislative Council. They couched their protest in much more respectful and circumlocutory language, but the governor was quick to note that the municipal council wished to set "all the principles" of the British constitution "at defiance".

Infuriated, these least subversive of gentlemen debated appeals to the Colonial Office, to the Supreme Court and the governor to amend the Municipal Act "to give it full efficiency". They were wasting their time. The governor either ignored or insulted them. The council had one moment of glory at least. Grey refused to improve the Torrens bridge unless public subscription raised 150 pounds of the 300 pounds estimated cost. So abominable was the name Grey to many Adelaide ears that the money was raised by private initiative—"without", as Worsnop puts it, "any interference on the part of the Government".[4] The bridge was completed more cheaply, using stone and timber from the parklands, and on 17 June 1843 Mayor Wilson broke a bottle of wine on the "City Bridge", congratulated a large crowd on their public spirit, then led them to a festive luncheon at the Tasmanian Hotel.

COLLAPSE

By then the first corporation was nearing extinction. Grey reported to the colonial secretary, Lord Stanley, that the council was unnecessary and inefficient. Respectable people would not stand, he claimed, or if they did, they were not elected. The council floundered amid accumulated debts of 1,670 pounds. Stanley agreed that the council should be wound up, and Grey eagerly did the winding.

In Pascoe's words: "Indignity followed indignity". There were: "no funds, and the furniture owned by the Corporation was 'seized for rent and publicly offered for sale' ... Mayor Wilson and Alderman Peacock waited upon the Governor and asked him what he intended to do. Governor Grey informed them that he was 'expecting despatches which would contain a disallowance of the Municipal Act'."[5] A meeting of the council was called in August, and although there was no quorum, a legal opinion was given that the corporation was now "legally defunct". The relics of the council gathered together the following month to frame an appeal to the governor to allow an election for a new council. This was their last gasp. Grey ignored the memorial and the landlord repossessed the council meeting room. There was no public outcry at this undignified collapse of at least partly democratic local government. By late 1843, the citizens had suffered the worst effects of the depression but it would take the province years to recover anything like the "first fine, careless rapture" of its original self-confidence. In the meantime, they were more concerned with survival than democracy.[6]

"Adelaide", declares Pascoe, "was now in the position of a country village." Grey, who was happy to leave the council idea defunct for the remainder of his governorship, was now undisputably supreme. An act "for the Better Government of South Australia" passed by parliament in July 1842 had abolished the Colonization Commissioners and divided rule. Grey was now responsible only to the colonial secretary, and Grey, as Gawler's downfall had shown, was a past master at the art of writing persuasive despatches.

GREY'S UNPOPULARITY

The act also authorized the governor to set up a nominated Legislative Council and open its deliberations to the public. Grey did so, but did not abandon a jot of his absolutism. He was imperturbable under attacks from the press, public protests, even the invasion of Government House grounds by hostile crowds. He told Angas by letter that he never read the newspaper attacks on him. On refusing a public petition to reduce taxation he wrote to Stanley that he was "prepared, most good-humouredly, to undergo the customary amount of odium". Odium was certainly heaped on him as he slashed expenditure all round, descending to economies like denying mustard to newly arrived immigrants at the depot, or stopping the mail service (one carrier) to North Adelaide. The citizens remembered the open-handed charm of Governor Gawler, whose expenditure at one time was five times greater than revenue, and united in blaming this remote, unbending young man for everything. One newspaper suggested that he should be burned in effigy; and the readers of the *Southern Star* were advised to "think upon Grey and let thy soul dispair". The *Register* quoted the Bible sardonically: "Woe unto thee, O Land, when thy King is a child."

Grey blandly ignored all this, just as he ignored a large public meeting at the Queen's Theatre on 16 March 1843 which expressed a "total want of confidence in the administration of Captain Grey". He stayed in absolute control of South Australia until November 1845 when he departed to govern New Zealand and, inevitably, soon collided head-on with public opinion there.

By late 1845, however, most Adelaide people were sorry to see Grey go. Good luck (mainly in the form of copper discoveries and good harvests), hard work, and what Grey called his own "fixity of purpose" had by then restored the province to solvency and confidence.

COPPER

The land came to the aid of the city in its time of tribulation. South Australia, although it was to be the poorest of the Australian colonies in its yield of gold, was generous in other minerals. Lucky strikes upcountry were to pull Adelaide back more than once from the brink of economic ruin. Menge had emerged from the bush on a number of occasions to declare through public lectures at the mechanics' institute that the province was rich in minerals.

In 1841, Adelaide was cheered in its time of crisis by the news of the discovery at Glen Osmond by two Cornishmen "in the humbler walks of life" of a lode of silver lead. Within ten years the mine was worked out, much to owner Osmond Gilles's profit.[7] The yield was comparatively modest, but the find was a useful fillip to Adelaide's confidence at a time when it was most needed, and stimulated a number of similar ventures in the Mount Lofty Ranges where prospectors found several lodes—usually small and difficult to work, but still payable—of galena, copper, and even gold. The stone chimney stack of the old mine still stands on the foothills just beyond the housing developments and hard by the teeming South Eastern Freeway as it begins to climb the hills. There, too, is the preserved toll house of the old mining village, semi-trailers roaring by on either side and sometimes crashing into it. They are the first memorials of "the rush that never ended".

Then copper came into its own. In 1842, the pastoralist F.S. Dutton, rounding up sheep, found rock outcrops coated with what seemed like "a beautiful green moss" on his property near Kapunda. The son of his neighbour, Captain Bagot, had found similar stones while picking wild flowers. Two years later, after prayers and a learned address by Menge, the Kapunda copper mine was opened. Twenty men dug 7,000 pounds worth of soft carbonate of copper from the earth before the end of the year.

The Kapunda mine produced about 800,000 pounds worth of copper before it closed in 1886. At last Adelaide seemed to offer something more than Wakefield's theories, city speculation, and gruelling work on a farm or sheep run. Amateur prospectors roamed the hills with their eyes on the ground. In 1845 the "Monster Mine" of Burra was found, a huge "bubble of copper" first seen by a shepherd on a hillside. Governor Grey presided over the necessary survey negotiations whereby "the Snobs", a syndicate composed mainly of Adelaide shopkeepers, put up capital of 12,320 pounds which in four years brought in an income of 172,480 pounds. Over 200 pounds was often paid for a 5 pounds share. The fortunate Snobs had at least 600 per cent profit from their investment.

The rise to financial glory of the Snobs who formed the South Australian Mining Association of Burra gives a graphic example of the astonishing opportunities that Australia could offer the lucky and hopeful ordinary man. The dominant element in the Snobs, eighteen out of eighty-six subscribers, were in Pike's words "shop keeping nobodies",[8] pretty well down the Adelaide social scale and never seen, until the copper boom, at Government House receptions. True, there were ten subscribers called gentlemen, among whom the canny Kingston was prominent, but there were also ten artisans and the group was mainly plebeian. John Graham, a director of the association by virtue of his 2,075 pounds investment, had been an upholsterer, publican, and shopkeeper. The Burra turned him into a plutocrat, worth about 200,000 pounds when he died after a long and lavish retirement at Heidelberg, Germany. William Paxton, a city chemist, and William Peacock, a radical and Nonconformist tanner, were others rocketed to opulence by the prodigal riches of the Burra, although old Adelaide hands like George Kingston and John Brown also prudently bought shares and shared in the shower of wealth. "Soon", writes Pike in his *Paradise of Dissent* (1957), "almost all the really rich were Burra proprietors. Their wealth challenged the social superiority assumed by the pastoralists."[9]

Of course many of the Snobs had taken a great risk and had scraped together their savings to buy shares at a time of economic uncertainty. In the early Adelaide tradition of fervid speculation they deserved their luck and it probably pleased observers like Angas to see that Providence had enriched the pious, or, at least, the humble.

Many Adelaide people resented the airs of the Burra nabobs, who turned out to be penny pinchers over payment to the miners. One satirist summed it up in verse in the *Register* of 25 September, 1848:

> I'll sing you a song by a youthful pate
> Of the Burra Burra shareholders who had a fine estate
> Which to them came by luck, not aim, most wondrous to relate,
> And little men unknown till then right suddenly grew great
> As Burra Burra proprietors, lords of the Monster Mine.

It is worth adding that for every lord of a monster mine there were hundreds of disappointed speculators in this era of "coppermania".

As imported Cornish miners burrowed into the Burra hillside, digging lumps of gorgeous green malachite and red copper oxide from the earth, Adelaide basked in the profitable glow. By 1850 there were fifty-nine copper and silver lead mines active in South Australia but none approached in opulence the fabulous Monster Mine. Henry Ayers, secretary of the Burra company, claimed that between 1845 and 1848 "you might safely say all South Australia was indirectly employed by the Burra mine". Immigration increased ninefold, South Australia became for a while the most prosperous of the Australian colonies, Adelaide bloomed again—and all thanks to the providential accumulation of copper ore beneath the hot hills of the Burra. Very few of the Adelaide tourists who now visit the sleepy little town of Burra, living on the memories of copper glories, realize how indebted the city is to the village.

THE LAND

Meanwhile, there had been less spectacular but more solid progress on the land. The soil round Adelaide and in the well watered regions beyond the hills like Mount Barker was fertile and comparatively easy to clear. At first the cost of imported farm equipment and stock was high, but the industrious settlers soon made the province self-sufficient in agriculture, and then a notable exporter of meat, wool, wine, fruit, and especially wheat. The hard working German immigrants, such as Captain Hahn's contingent which settled at Hahndorf, were important here. Francis Dutton commented on their frugality in his *South Australia and its Mines* (1846):

> Now see how differently the German labourer in the colony acts; the necessity of every farthing he spends, is seriously weighed, before he parts with it, you never see a German in a public house drinking spirits; he will come into the town many miles afoot, carrying, perhaps, a heavy load of vegetables, or what not, for the market; after he has sold his goods, he will take a lump of bread out of his pocket, brought with him from home, of his housewife's own baking, and his day's profit must have been very good to induce him to buy even a glass of ale to wash down his frugal dinner; more frequently it is a draught of spring water ... [10]

There might have been more Germanic revelry, of course, had German immigrants come from Bavaria, but the toilers who built their huts and churches at Klemzig, Hahndorf[11] and, later, Lobethal, Blumberg (Birdwood), Gruenthal (Verdun), and throughout the Barossa Valley were dour northerners, their natural toughness disciplined further by uncompromising Lutheranism. These Germans were to remain ploughing their fields while more fickle British immigrants deserted their jobs and farms wholesale for the Victorian diggings in the early 1850s. A series of excellent harvests on the freshly turned soil helped Adelaide survive the grim years of the 1840s. During 1842, for instance, when the depression was at its worst, the wheat crop was prodigal and Grey encouraged colonial officials to help bring in the grain. Good weather and steady agricultural expansion encouraged him to ask for more immigrants from the Colonial Office to mitigate the shortage of rural labour. John Ridley, although some give the credit to J.W. Bull, invented his famous reaping machine to reap the harvest more efficiently, and also set up a steam mill at Hindmarsh. Adelaide began to stage agricultural shows on the parklands. Good wheat growing areas developed at Mount Barker, Willunga, the Gawler Plains, and all round the city. Local growers carried their bags of grain to the windmill on West Terrace. In 1838 only 8 hectares were sown to wheat; by 1843 this had increased to 9,300 hectares, and by 1850 to almost 17,000 hectares. South Australia was becoming "the granary of Australia" and Adelaide, as Trollope called it, the "farinaceous city". *The South Australian* pointed out that when Grey arrived in 1841 the annual export of wheat had been worth only a little over 1,000 pounds. During 1845, the year of his departure, the figure had risen to almost 25,000 pounds.

The controversial governor had thus presided over a remarkable change in Adelaide's fortunes. When he came, the bubble had burst and there was gloomy talk of abandoning the city. As he himself reported in 1842: "In North and South Adelaide out of 1,915 houses, 642 are totally deserted; and out of this latter number 216 are neglected and falling into decay. Had this return been extended as to have embraced the villages of Hindmarsh, Thebarton, Bowden, Islington, etc., all lying in the municipality of Adelaide, the results shown would have been much more striking."[12] Yet when he left for New Zealand, "everything", in Blacket's words, "was full of life and promise". Adelaide had learned to love the man it once hated, especially when he abolished his port charges. A public meeting of notables was held at the Supreme Court to thank the governor on his departure. A fulsome address was presented, as was becoming an established ritual, thanking him for his "able, zealous and diligent administration of public affairs". Thanks to Grey, it seemed, "the Province of South Australia is at last fulfilling the fond predictions of its founders and friends" and would become "one of the brightest gems in the Imperial diadem of Britain". Even the *Register*, which had bitterly assailed Grey during the depression, observed: "For the talent of promptly meeting financial difficulties, for the firmness that will soon make a set of imbeciles or encroaching officials feel that they have at length a master mind to deal with, we give Captain Grey credit, as well as for legislative capacity and cool determination."

The *Register* was probably nearer the truth than the public address. So far as the fond predictions of the founders and friends were concerned, Grey had certainly cut down public spending and now ruled a prosperous and progressive province. However, corn would have grown and copper would have been found under any governor. So too would Eyre have pushed his explorations into the northern interior and along the terrible coast of the Bight.

Grey had certainly been hostile to the democratic intentions of the founding fathers. Compared with some of the governors of New South Wales, which was far from being a model, theoretical province, Grey had been at least as autocratic as Macquarie or Gipps, and had none of the liberal learnings of Bourke. He had nominated his friends to the non-official positions on the Legislative Council and expected complete obedience from them. He had treated the struggling City Council shabbily, and had allowed it to perish without any expressions of regret.

Perhaps the rule of a man like Grey was beneficial during this period for the young province. He had been busy, honest, and firm. He had retrenched and consolidated, so that those who survived the depression were at least more realistic about South Australia. He had pruned the young shoot severely, but it was now growing again.

GOLD

The goldrush of 1851 had a double-edged effect on Adelaide. It paralyzed business as the province's labour—between 17,000 and 20,000 men—swarmed eastwards to the Victorian and New South Wales fields. But it also pushed up the price of wheat to 15s and 6d a bushel, so that those farmers who remained prospered by supplying the diggers.

South Australia, so well endowed with copper and iron, had no rich gold deposits, although prospectors searched for years to come and there were small rushes to a few places such as Echunga. The *Observer* in 1851 had warned of "the disastrous consequences" if the province, so soon after it had found its economic feet again, were to be emptied of able bodied men. For a period, indeed, the situation was critical. There were only three active men left in the town of Gawler. The Burra mine was forced to close as the Cornish miners decamped to try to enrich themselves rather than the "Snobs". "In Adelaide windows are bricked up", wrote a Mrs. Evans, "and outside is written 'gone to the diggings'."[13] Bull wrote: "... the exodus tempted from their homes nearly the whole of the male population. In rural districts, the wives, daughters and younger boys had to take upon themselves what work they could do. Even in the towns and suburbs, on seeing a man, children would call out to their mothers, 'Look here, mother, there is a man'."[14]

However when lucky diggers began to return with their bags of gold the innate Adelaide business acumen reasserted itself. Inspector Tolmer suggested to the governor that Adelaide diggers would prefer to send their wealth back home on a reliable escort rather than entrust it to Babylonian Melbourne or bring it back themselves through bushranger country. Sir Henry Young agreed and passed a Bullion Act, whereby gold could be minted into coins and ease Adelaide's currency shortage. Tolmer dashed off through the scrub with a "strong spring cart" and a police escort to Mount Alexander in Victoria where, in Bull's words, "the escort party was met by the Adelaide diggers most warmly". Tolmer convinced the diggers that their interests would be best served by entrusting their gold to him, for the prosperity of their families and distant Adelaide. He also offered seventy-two shillings an ounce for assayed gold—at least twelve shillings better than the Melbourne price. There was, thought Bull, "some soreness at the dividing the great stream of gold which had commenced to flow to Melbourne". Eight days and 544 bone jolting kilometres later, the intrepid inspector was back in Adelaide with 21,000 pounds worth of notes and gold dust, deposited by 318 diggers. The gold escort continued for some time and Adelaide benefited pleasantly at a remove. The thought of diverting some opulence away from booming, vulgar Melbourne must have added to the citizens' pleasure. Hodder wrote: "Almost everybody dabbled in it, and a walk through the streets of Adelaide left the impression that the City was transformed into El Dorado, shop windows being placarded all along the line of streets, 'Gold Bought', 'Cash for Gold' ... and so forth."[15] Finally, most of the South Australian diggers, as might be expected from good Methodists, returned to the province when the gold ran out and invested their wealth in farms and shops.

Tolmer,[16] incidentally, whose career saw more downs that ups hereafter, received only a testimonial. George Tinline, manager of the South Australian Bank, who had first suggested the special assay, received a plaque and a substantial reward.

GOVERNOR ROBE

Grey's successor in Government House, Major Robe (1845–48) had all Grey's fondness for autocracy but none of his intelligence. "The poor Governor", wrote Harcus, "lived in hot water during the whole of his administration" and was "very weary" of Adelaide by the time he was recalled. Robe was a limited military man, hospitable in private—he and his officers brought hunting pink to chase foxes over the Adelaide Plains—but haughty in public. A Tory high churchman, he offended the influential Nonconformists by advocating state aid to religion, and particularly to the Anglican Church. And he offended Nonconformists and Anglicans alike by imposing a royalty of one fifteenth on all minerals taken from land alienated from the crown. This seemed outrageous to a city doing well from copper.

The governor was imperturbable. When a deputation of notables presented him with a memorial opposing state aid to religion he observed coldly, "I have no remarks to make, gentlemen", and dismissed them. Even Grey had not been as high handed as this. When Messrs. Morphett, O'Halloran, Bagot, and Davenport stalked out of the Legislative Council because of their opposition to mineral royalties, Robe merely lectured them on insubordination at the next meeting.

Robe, who in effect did little of lasting benefit for South Australia other than give his name to a pleasant fishing port on Guichen Bay, applied for a transfer to the military service. On 2 August 1848 he took leave, characteristically, of the Legislative Council by declaring: "In relinquishing the duties which have devolved upon me ... I look to my sovereign alone for any expression of approbation." He certainly got little approbation from Adelaide, and little enough from his sovereign. Robe was promoted to lieutenant-colonel and departed for Mauritius to serve his queen, presumably without further trouble from Nonconformists, as deputy quartermaster-general. Meanwhile, in a letter to Earl Grey on 2 June 1847, Angas had made a creditable effort to persuade the colonial secretary "to restore Colonel Gawler to South Australia". Angas thought that "great injustice had been done to that upright and sensible officer" and that "he would be sure to meet with a popular reception, the more so were he to be bearer of a Constitution founded upon simple, practical and liberal principles."

Gawler was warmly remembered after the acerbities of Grey and Robe. The province was tired of authoritarian rule from Government House. However, Gawler was doomed to remain in the idleness of semi-disgrace. Nonetheless, Angas and the Adelaide progressives were delighted with the next governor, Sir Henry Fox Young, who occupied Government House from August 1848 to December, 1854. At last, Whitehall had appointed a liberal civilian to preside over this most liberal and unmilitary of cities. In Young, Hodder wrote, "the colonists found an ideal Governor and a man after their own hearts". And it was straight to the Adelaide mercentile heart that Young went from the onset, by abolishing the mineral royalty.

SELF-GOVERNMENT

The despotic power of the governors was about to wane; and it was just as well that the flexible Young presided over the proconsular sunset. Now that Adelaide was prosperous again after the turbulence of the depression, its citizens felt that they had the time, energy, and numbers to press for more democracy.

Citizens had shown their resentment of the high handedness of the Grey and Robe regimes by packing the Queen's Theatre for protest meetings, signing petitions for their recall, avidly reading the polemics of the Adelaide press—always a scourge for the backs of haughty governors in the first decades—and even by rioting on two occasions in the hallowed grounds of Government House itself. Grey and Robe had both treated the Legislative Council rather like a military platoon, expecting it to obey the commander without question. Both had been contemptuous of the idea of municipal government.

It was time for constitutional change, and even if Adelaide had not wanted it, the Mother of Parliaments had decided that the time had come to tidy up its somewhat bothersome Australian colonies and untie them from the apron strings. In 1850, after consultation with the colonies, the British Parliament passed the Australian Colonies Government Act. South Australia, like other Australian colonies, was now to have wider representation—in her case a Legislative Council trebled in size from eight to twenty-four members. Sixteen of these were to be elected and eight—four officials and four non-officials—were to be nominated by the governor.

The despatch containing the new constitution arrived next year on the ship *Ascendant* amid scenes crying out for the pen of Gilbert and the music of Sullivan. There were the Adelaide notables ready to receive their Magna Carta. There too was that tireless champion of South Australia, George Fife Angas, who had come out on the *Ascendant* to live in the province he had laboured for. Angas had asked to be allowed to convey the act personally to Adelaide but was refused. Instead, Whitehall sent a clerk to the ship with the document. Unable to find the captain, he had given it to the steward, who, with pleasant irreverence, had dropped it into a dirty linen bag. Anchored in Adelaide, the red faced captain and the indignant officials searched the *Ascendant* for five days before the act was found amid the captain's washing. The press had a field day.

It had more fun describing the elections for the enlarged Legislative Council. Only adult males could vote in the sixteen electoral districts. Electors had to own property worth at least 100 pounds, or pay 10 pounds a year for rent, pastoral lease, or licence. As for the candidates, each had to own property worth at least 7,000 pounds, or pay 100 pounds a year in rent. It was an advance on what had gone on before, but this was certainly Property at the polls. As the electors milled round the booths, there were excitements, rows, even some broken heads. This was a Dickensian Eatanswill type election, for there was no secret ballot and the voters had to have their preferences recorded in a book. As if by divine right, the established Adelaide notables were elected: men like Sturt, Dutton, Bagot, Morphett, Finniss, Elder, and Kingston—names that were to occur again and again in the annals of Adelaide prestige and profitable public employment.

"The Council was a gathering of highly competent men", declared Pascoe at the turn of the century, in that style of reverential self-congratulation until recently prevalent in municipal history writing. "No finer band of legislators could have been desired."

STATE AID TO RELIGION

Certainly, the council acted decisively by settling that hornet's nest question stirred by Robe—state aid to religion. The council abolished it. In future churches would maintain themselves by voluntary contributions. Adelaide was the first city in the Empire to realize that Dissenting dream of cutting the financial nexus between the state and established church. The legislators supported Young in his moves to build railway lines to the port and to Gawler, and to improve the harbour at Port Adelaide.

NEW CONSTITUTION

Their main concern, once the religious controversy abated, was to achieve fresh constitutional reforms. The Australian Colonies Government Act had encouraged the colonial legislatures to make proposals for further changes. The South Australian Council was foremost, perhaps inevitably, and drew up a new constitution, accepted by the British Parliament in 1856. By this, South Australia achieved responsible government. The *Register* rejoiced that the province was ridding itself of "the incubus of nomineeism" and declared: "We are laying the foundations of a new political and social state. We are deciding whether public opinion shall be taken as the source of legislative authority, or whether the people are yet to be held in the leading strings of imperial domination."

These were radical words, but Adelaide in this vivid formative era *was* radical, in conception and implementation. This radicalism, moreover, was to persist.

Henceforth, South Australia would have its own parliament. It was to be bicameral, and both chambers were to be elective. The upper house, the Legislative Council, was to comprise eighteen members elected for twelve years by the whole province as one constituency. Electors qualified by the possession of land worth at least fifty pounds or certain other forms of property. The lower house, the House of Assembly, was to have thirty-six members representing districts, triennial elections, and full adult male suffrage with no property qualifications whatsoever. An even more progressive feature of the new constitution was the agreement that the ballot should be secret: the colourful humbug of the hustings, the rival gangs of paid bully boys, and the disorder round the open voting booths, which persisted for years elsewhere, were banished from Adelaide.

Furthermore, the absolutism of the governors was abolished. No longer could a Grey or a Robe act like a minor Louis XIV. All ministers were to be chosen from elected legislators and laws could be passed by parliament alone. Some able governors were still to exercise considerable influence, but their role had diminished to that of a benign social and constitutional figurehead. The reigning governor, Sir Richard MacDonnell, a progressive like Young, seemed quite happy at this stripping away of power.

The new constitution received the royal assent and was proclaimed by MacDonnell on 24 June 1856. Finniss was transmuted from colonial secretary to first premier. The crown vested in the new parliament all the unsold and unappropriated land in the province. Government departments were formed and a peaceful election of the first parliament was held on 9 March 1857. Veteran office holders like Bagot, Fisher, Davenport, O'Halloran, and Morphett were elevated to the Legislative Council. They were joined there by the redoubtable Angas and by rising men like Henry Ayers. The membership of the House of Assembly included inevitable names like Dutton, Hanson, Neale, Finniss (for Adelaide), and Kingston (for Burra and Clare).

A thousand strong crowd on North Terrace watched the parliament assemble.

South Australia, with a population of 100,000 or so, had taken on a heavy burden, for all these legislators, the burgeoning bureaucracy, and the attendant pomp and circumstance had to be paid for. The London *Times*, which had always taken an interest in the curious evolution of the Wakefield city, commented with Olympian indulgence:

> It must be confessed that it is rather an odd position for a new community of rising tradesmen, farmers, cattle breeders, mechanics, with a sprinkling of doctors and attorneys, to find that it is suddenly called upon to find Prime Ministers, Cabinets, a Ministerial side, an Opposition side, and all the apparatus of a Parliamentary Government—to awake one fine morning and discover that this is no longer a colony, but a nation, saddled with all the rules and traditions of the political life of the mother country.[17]

It must have seemed decidedly odd, probably funny, to the *Times* readers in teeming London. After all, it was only a few years ago that the news from Adelaide had been bleak—discontented immigrants, depression, the sour aftermath of a land boom, ruin and debt. Indeed, Adelaide was just about to suffer from another of its bouts of economic dismay. Yet neither the readers nor the editor of the *Times* knew their Adelaide. True, for all its grandiloquent new constitution it was a good deal smaller than Birmingham or Manchester or Liverpool. It was only twenty-one years old and had suffered some quite spectacular misfortunes. There was no army or navy, no university, no peerage, and but a handful of police.

But the Adelaide leaders were changed by colonial circumstance, the Wakefield doctrines as further interpreted by sages like Angas, and by the emerging Adelaide ethos. They had already shown their radicalism by such measures as abolishing state aid to religion, the secret ballot, and triennial elections. These were liberals and Nonconformists with growing self-confidence and plenty of space for manoeuvre and experiment.

REVIVAL OF THE CITY COUNCIL

The same democratic urges which had brought about the new constitution were strong for the revival of municipal government. Memories of Grey's hostility to the first city council still rankled. The depression had almost submerged the council idea, but the fatal and final push had come from Government House.

Since then, despite the growing prosperity and pretensions of Adelaide, the city's public services suffered badly from maladministration and lack of money. The Torrens, source of most of the drinking water, was foully polluted. Many children and adults were "Called to God", as the old gravestones in the parklands cemetery put it, long before their time thanks to dysentery, cholera, diphtheria, and other diseases. "Nightsoil" and rubbish were tipped wherever convenient to the tipper. Pubs stayed open until midnight and beyond, seven days a week, and were crowded with prostitutes, Chinese, lucky diggers, Aborigines learning about civilization, and prodigiously thirsty bushmen in their leggings and straw hats who, in the words of E. Lloyd in his *Visit to the Antipodes* (1846), "reminded you of the pictures of Spanish bull-fighters" were it not for their "enormous whips".

The ponderous wheels of the drays and the plunging hooves of bullocks and horses churned the mud of the streets into slime in which lady shoppers lost their shoes, drunks fell and, so the legend had it, trusting visitors to Adelaide vanished without trace. Lloyd tells a famous anecdote about the main street of Adelaide in the 1840s:

> There was a story told about the state of King William Street in winter. It is stated that

there was a man one day passing along the side of the street when he saw what he imagined to be a hat lying on top of the mud in the middle of the road. He picked his way carefully to the spot and was about to lift it up, when a voice below told him to leave it alone as it belonged to him; upon which the man replied by asking the invisible person why he did not come out. The person then stated that he would do so with much pleasure but that his horse was below him.[18]

When Dr. William Ullathorne, the Roman Catholic vicar-general for Australia visited Adelaide in 1839 he recorded some interesting impressions:

Like the Etruscan cities of old, it had been regularly laid out from the first in a square. The straight streets were (many of them) only marked out by rough roads and chippings on trees; the houses were here and there not brought into line.

As for the condition of the roads in winter:

I puzzled my friends in Sydney by telling them that the streets in Adelaide were fitter for the study of astronomy than for commerce. The fact was that miles of newly marked out streets were unmade, and after heavy Australian rain were full of pools of water ... in which the brilliant stars of the Southern Hemisphere were reflected.[19]

The *Register* of 11 August 1848 observed that a drunk had been fined for attempting to swim the liquid mud of Hindley Street from one end to the other, and that a bullock had drowned in the quagmire of Wakefield Street near the site of the Town Hall itself.

The governor set up a Central Road Board in 1849 but for a long time to come roads were bad and transport slow and hazardous. In 1848 the *Observer* called Adelaide "a filthy City" and attacked people who allowed their cellars to fill with "foetid water", had open cesspools, piled up dungheaps and butcher's offal, and left their pavements dirty "and in fact do everything in their power to provide employment for the doctors and the undertakers". Adelaide's "greasy thoroughfares" stank in the rain.

On 7 February 1849, a poorly attended public meeting asked for a revived corporation entitled "the Chairman, Councillors, and Citizens of Adelaide". Young preferred to set up a "City Commission", composed of five of his nominees. The commissioners were to be paid and empowered to levy rates and generally look after municipal matters. Altogether the commission expended over 33,000 pounds during their two and a half years' existence and brought about some improvements. However, the commission was no more than a temporary expedient. The exodus to the goldfields, the run on coin and banknotes, and the general paralysis of the city's economy in 1851–52, made administration difficult for the commissioners. Worsnop recalled: "The drain upon the population had seriously deteriorated all house property—in fact, property of every description, so that no assessment could with justice be levied upon the comparatively few tenements which still retained their occupants ... Ruin confronted everyone and every interest in the place."[20]

However, as already described, good times came back again with the return of the diggers, the gold escort, and the price of wheat spiralling. With Adelaide booming, Governor Young abolished the City Commission and on 1 June 1852 the City Corporation, after being extinct for nine years, emerged like the Phoenix from the ashes of its old tribulations.

The new corporation was composed of four aldermen and twelve councillors. The mayor (the durable Fisher assumed the mayoralty yet again) was elected by them. Adelaide was divided into four wards named after the governors—Hindmarsh, Gawler, Grey, and Robe. Every male householder who had property in the city or within eleven kilometres of it had the vote. Any councillor who refused to accept office, or resigned, would be fined.

Worsnop comments wryly: "The Mayor ... should be a *fit* person; also the Aldermen were required to be *fit* persons—but *fitness* was not an essential" for the councillors.[21] This did not mean, of course, that the mayor and aldermen had to be able to jog athletically round the parklands, but that they were morally impeccable. When elected, one councillor, being "no scholar", had to "make his mark" in lieu of a signature.

The mayor and corporation repaired to the Blenheim Hotel for their deliberations while a building was erected on the Town Acre bought by the first council for twelve shillings. During the period 1852–57 from the revival of the City Council to the meeting of the first parliament, the city fathers had the usual problems over rates, grants from the Legislative Council, and intestinal disagreements. Fisher, five times mayor, after threatening to resign several times in a way that had become traditional, finally did resign. But he soon ascended the Legislative Council so that, in the diplomatic words of Worsnop, "the public did not lose the benefit of his judgement and long experience". In 1854 the powers of the corporation were extended to give it more control over street cleaning and improvement, and the erection of buildings, but it was still restricted in many ways until 1861. The value of assessments increased from 148,504 pounds in 1855 to 189,514 pounds in 1857.

VICTORIA SQUARE

The corporation took control of the city squares, spending, in 1854, over 1,000 pounds on Victoria Square. This plunged it into costly and tedious litigation with Bishop Augustus Short who claimed that the Victoria Square acre had been intended for an Anglican cathedral in Light's city plan. This document had gone up in flames with many other records during the government hut fire of 1839, but Robe, stout Anglican that he was, had conveyed an acre of Victoria Square to the bishop in 1848. Short in 1855 demanded the restitution of this Church of England acre in the heart of the city. The corporation, perhaps because of a compound of self-esteem and the Nonconformist spirit, refused. The parties went expensively to law, but the upshot was that the bishop placed his cathedral beyond the Torrens and the whole square remained "for the use and recreation of the citizens".

In 1855, too, the corporation passed an act to reserve 16 hectares at the eastern end of North Terrace for a botanic garden. In 1856 the knell was sounded on the water-carts from the turbid Torrens (the charges varied from 1s. 6d. to 3s. per 50 gallons depending on the distance from the river) with the passing of the Waterworks Act which eventually resulted in a reservoir in the upper Torrens Gorge.

In 1851, a railway line was opened between the city and Port Adelaide. Two years later, however, the road between the port and the city was still rough, as the immigrant C.H. Barton found in December 1853. He wrote home:

> I then bundled into a cart driven tandem made to hold nine but on this occasion containing thirteen; we were five on the front seat with the driver, and the whole affair on two wheels. They race all the way, sometimes four abreast, as the road is very wide but full of holes, only a rough mud-causeway over a huge marsh. Three colonial lasses chaffed me quite blue, as I was out of spirits with being alone in a strange land, but I managed to give 'em as good back, and by the time we were galloping into Hindley Street we had a full chorus of "Cheer! Boys! Cheer!"[22]

An electric telegraph line was opened in 1855 from Adelaide to Melbourne. In the early 1850s, municipal councils were formed in the growing suburbs of Kensington, Norwood, Port Adelaide, Glenelg, and Gawler.

CONCLUSIONS

By 1857, then, Adelaide had come of age. It had attained self-government both through parliament and municipal council. Tutelage and control from Government House had ended. In fact, with reforms like triennial parliaments, manhood suffrage, and the secret ballot, South Australians had achieved, with little if any of the attendant dogma and suffering, many of the aims for which the British Chartists had so bitterly and fruitlessly struggled.

The province had survived many vicissitudes. It had endured the blunders of Hindmarsh, the muddles of the commissioners, the greed of the land speculators (and there were few Adelaideans, even the most honoured, who had not speculated feverishly for quick profits), bad harvests, and economic depressions. The number of city public houses—for, despite the prayers of Angas, Adelaideans were always mighty drinkers—can be seen as an economic barometer here. In 1840, a good year, there were 63 inns for a city population of 6,657—that is one tavern for every 105 citizens. By 1843, during the depression, the number of pubs dwindled to 32. Adelaide had sustained these and other misfortunes.

On the other hand, it had had remarkable luck. Geography and climate were on its side, along with happy historical accidents like the casual appointment of Colonel Light as the first surveyor-general. It was good luck that South Australia had attracted the interest of Wakefield in his Newgate Gaol and the active interest of able men like Torrens, Gouger, and Sturt.

Adelaide was above all fortunate, perhaps, in having the affection of George Fife Angas. Pascoe in his obsequious biographies of distinguished South Australians in *Adelaide and Vicinity* hails Angas as "Father, Founder and Faithful Friend of Adelaide". For once the hyperbole seems justified. Angas was a titan among philanthropists, and numbered among his achievements the annexation of New Zealand by Britain, the emancipation of slaves on the Mosquito Coast, and the foundation of the British and Foreign Sailors' Society. He was also a religious activist and a successful financier and merchant with interests all over the world. Yet he found time to give particular attention to South Australia, and chose to emigrate there himself in 1850. The hand of Angas was strongest in such matters as the formation of the South Australian Company, the selection of free immigrants, the settlement of the German Lutherans in the province and in moves towards constitutional reform. Angas had considerable influence in Whitehall and wrote long letters to colonial secretaries full of good advice and godly exhortation. He had used all his influence to oppose the pro-Anglican policies of Robe, and believed that "the Bible truth should be taught unfettered and without State aid". At the very beginning of the theorizing about South Australia, Angas had drawn up the following prescriptions for the province:

1. The exclusion of convicts.
2. The concentration of the settlers.
3. The taking out of young persons of capital and intelligence, and especially men of piety.
4. The emigration of young couples of good character.
5. Free trade, free government and freedom in matters of religion.

By 1857, with Angas comfortably settled on his wide Barossa fief at Angaston, Adelaide had gone a substantial way towards all these ideals.

Fortune had smiled on early Adelaide in many other ways. The times were peaceful, and no hostile foreign power interfered with the evolution of the settlement. There were alarums and excursions about Russians and even the Mahdi later but

Adelaide developed right through the nineteenth century under the Pax Britannica. Even the dreaded ex-convicts from the eastern colonies, when they reached the province in the form of the raffish Tiersmen of Mount Lofty, were generally peaceful. Indeed, they were a great help to the unhandy settlers and showed them how to adapt themselves to Australian conditions. The founders' aversion to transportation was beneficial in that it saved Adelaide from the social tensions and debasements of convictism. There was no Captain Thunderbolt or Kelly Gang in South Australia, nor, of course, was there much locally-dug gold for them to rob.

Perhaps the necessities of the time brought forth the men: explorers like Sturt and Eyre and inventors like Bull and Ridley. The province's mineral wealth came to the aid of the city with the galena in the hills, the copper deposits at Kapunda, and the Monster Mine at the Burra. The citizens were lucky to find ample local supplies of fine stone, brick clay, and limestone with which to build their permanent homes. And if the shortage of building timber and infestations of white ants seemed disappointing at the time, with hindsight we can say they were blessings in disguise for they forced the citizens to use lovely bluestone and freestone from the ranges. Finally, the sufficient rainfall, the fertile soil with which gardeners like Stevenson could work wonders, and the abundant, mellowing sunshine must have soothed over many pioneering difficulties. The people of early Adelaide could, and did, grumble and protest and pine for "home", but there was manifest a feeling that South Australia was indeed a lucky country.

The idiosyncrasies of Adelaide had not diminished by 1857. They had become almost institutionalized. Most of the Wakefieldian dreams had not been realized. For instance, Adelaide had not become an idyllic community of country squires, respectful yeomen, and even more respectful peasants. Dual control had been a costly and rancorous failure. However, immigration had been planned to a certain extent; there was a remarkably strong leavening of pious, industrious, and independent minded Nonconformists in the population; and Adelaide already preened herself as the moral, civic, and constitutional model of a new community.

"'You are proud,' Caroline Chisholm wrote to the *Register* in 1849, 'and have reason to be, of your city, but I am almost weary of this Adelaide, Adelaide ... '" By 1857 this civic pride, sense of difference, of superiority had become even more full blown. The citizens formed a defensive and self-satisfied front, like a herd of musk oxen on the tundra, against the inferiorities of the rest of Australia. Pike observes: "Adelaide might exploit her neighbours' markets and gold, but she refused to share their origins and ambitions ... Her people refused to admit that South Australia was ever a colony; it was an outlying English province with its own peculiar foundations, its own national song, its own commemoration day. Its parochialism was almost exclusive."[23]

The city's growth was organic and, on the whole, cosily compact and thus has lent itself reasonably well to a roughly chronological approach. Town and country developments, economic and social, religious and constitutional affairs have all been closely intermingled, the intimate happenings of a pioneers' village growing into a country town merging into a provincial community of 100,000 souls.

By 1857, Adelaide had the substance and self-fulfilment of responsible government. The province, after all, contained 109,917 people, most of these living in or near the capital. About 100,000 hectares were under cultivation. Goods to the value of 1,744,184 pounds had been exported. Were there not 70 flourmills, 226 manufactories, 167 day schools, 192 Sunday schools, and 300 churches and chapels with, in Pascoe's words, "accommodation for 50,000 persons"?[24] Not to mention mechanics' institutes, theatres, newspapers, and a Botanic Garden?

At the Proclamation Day anniversary celebration in 1857 the colonists could happily sing a song specially written for the occasion by H.S. Scarfe, entitled "The Pioneers":

> Fill, fill each sparkling glass, boys,
> And drain your bumpers dry,
> And listen while I sing, boys,
> Of days and deeds gone by,
> And while we call to mind the past—its hopes, its doubts, its fears,
> Let's ne'er forget the honour due to brave old pioneers.
>
> They left their much-loved England
> And braved the ocean's foam,
> Here, for themselves and children,
> To found a freeman's home.
> Now near the same old tree we meet, o'er which, with joyous cheers,
> The British flag was first unfurled by loyal pioneers.
>
> That little band of heroes,
> How manfully they plied
> The axe, the plough, the harrow,
> And labour'd side by side,
> For us they cleared, they ploughed, they sowed; a garden now appears,
> Where first they found a wilderness—those hardy pioneers.
>
> Like wave on wave advancing
> Crowds followed them ere long;
> The once small band now musters
> Some hundred thousand strong;
> Who've carried on through weal and woe, for one-and-twenty years
> The work so nobly then begun by gallant pioneers.

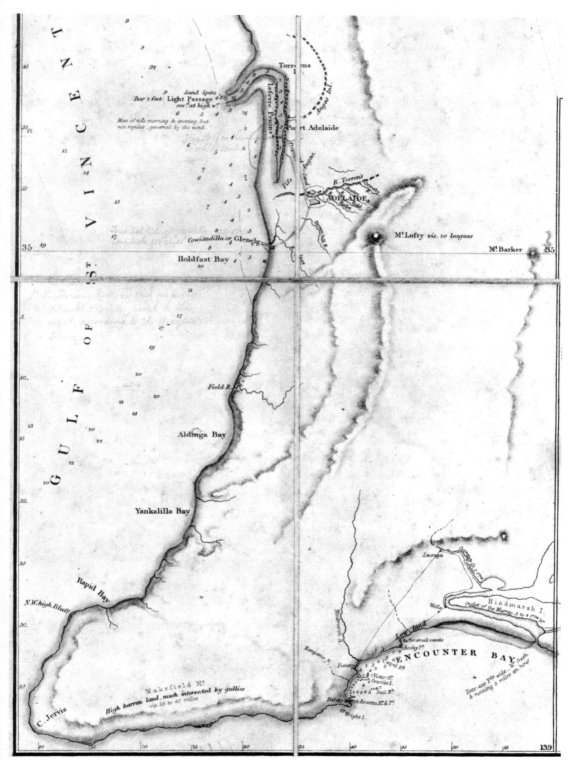

1. Map of the coastline near Adelaide, first published by John Arrowsmith on 5 February 1839. This is part of a complete map of the South Australian coast, drawn from the surveys of Captain Flinders and Colonel Light, first surveyor general of South Australia. An attempt was made to remove the site of Adelaide to the dangerous Murray Mouth area of Encounter Bay but this was strongly resisted by Light. From a facsimile map issued by the Libraries Board of South Australia.

2. Light's plan for the city of Adelaide, with its gardens and squares, acre allotments, and far-sighted belt of encircling parklands, as surveyed in early 1837. Comparison with the next illustration—an aerial photograph almost one hundred and fifty years later—shows how faithfully Light's plan has been followed. From a facsimile of John Arrowsmith's 1839 map issued by the Libraries Board of South Australia.

Aerial view of Adelaide, 1972. Light's city is now besieged by suburbia beyond the moat of the parklands. Since 1837 the klands have suffered serious encroachment, including roads, the railway, a race course, and buildings between North Terrace the Torrens.

4. Portrait of the young William Light, artist unknown, in the Adelaide Town Hall Archives. His Eurasian ancestry is more apparent here than in the later more idealized portraits.

5. The brig *Rapid* which, with the *Cygnet*, brought Colonel Light and his small surveying team to South Australia in 1836. This watercolour shows the *Rapid* anchored in Rapid Bay.

Westerly	Wednesday 4th Septr 1839. Modte and fine. extremely ill, at night fine
Westerly	Thursday 5 Modte and fine - exceedingly unwell. fine all day. at night Modte and fine
Westerly	Friday 6. Modte and Cloudy. very unwell all day — at night fine
Westerly	Saturday 7 Modte and Cloudy at noon Showery. very ill all day Showery all the afternoon at night Showery. very ill
Westerly	Sunday 8th Modte & Cloudy with Slight Showers at times at noon very fine fine all the rest. at Modte and fine. very ill all day

6. Some of the last entries in Light's diary for September 1839. He died of tuberculosis a month later on 6 October 1839.

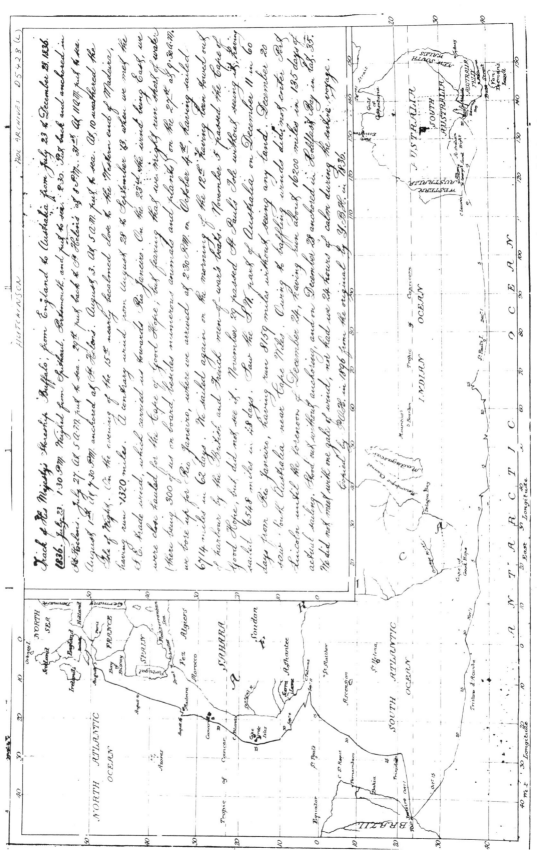

7. Lieutenant Bingham Hutchinson's sketch of the route from England to South Australia of His Majesty's storeship *Buffalo*, with a summary of the long but uneventful passage of the first settlers. Photograph by courtesy of the South Australian Archives.

8. H.M.S. *Buffalo*, South Australia's *Mayflower*, which brought Governor Hindmarsh and most of the first colonists to Adelaide. Inscribed "The Ugly Old Tub" this is the pen and ink drawing by Lieutenant Hutchinson who sailed in her with the founding fathers from Portsmouth in July 1836. Hutchinson soon after arrival led the first ascent of Mount Lofty. Photograph by courtesy of the South Australian Archives.

9. John Hindmarsh, South Australia's first governor. Bold and resourceful as a naval captain he was disastrous as governor. Hindmarsh was probably well-meaning, but his meddling almost ruined early Adelaide—which he proposed to move, first to Port Lincoln, then to the Murray Mouth area. He later governed Heligoland and was knighted.

10. Pencil sketch of the tent and rush hut of Robert Gouger, first colonial secretary, at Glenelg, Holdfast Bay, in 1836. Outside the tent the Proclamation of 28 December 1836 was read, and marines from the *Buffalo* fired a salute. Then Governor Hindmarsh and the notables retired inside to enjoy speeches, a little wine, and "a cold collation".

11. A view of Adelaide in 1836 during the "hutting period" when the first settlers lived in tents and huts.

12. Sketch of the landing place, by the mouth of the Patawalonga Creek, at Holdfast Bay in 1837.

13. Adelaide's christening certificate—a letter of 13 July 1837 giving King William IV's permission to the colonists to name their new city after Queen Adelaide. (Wakefield had intended to name it Wellington, for the Iron Duke had worked for the passing of the South Australia Act.) Addressed to Captain Hindmarsh, R.N., the letter from St. James' Palace reads:

My dear sir,

I have not delayed to submit to the King your wish to give to the principal town or capital of South Australia the name of Her Majesty viz. the Queen and I beg to acquaint you that His Majesty received the communication very kindly and desired that the capital might be named *Adelaide*.

Believe me to be my dear sir

Yours very faithfully

(secretary's signature)

14. George Stevenson, first editor of the *Register*, who grew powerful under Hindmarsh. A radical and able Scot of shady background, Stevenson provoked fierce controversies. He plotted against Light, who called him a "Paragon of blackguards". However he was a good journalist and the best gardener in early Adelaide.

15. Drawing of the first Government House, Adelaide, around 1837 by Mary Hindmarsh, daughter of the first governor. Even by the standards of early Adelaide, the first Government House was poorly designed and constructed. Centipedes fell from the thatch onto the heads of the governor's guests.

16. George Fife Angas, first chairman of the South Australian Company and perhaps the most influential single personality in the foundation and early development of Adelaide. A titan among philanthropists, this godly Northumbrian merchant put up his own money and encouraged others to invest in Adelaide. He greatly influenced the assisted immigration programme and brought out the first German Lutheran settlers. Angas came to South Australia himself in 1850 and lived on his wide Barossa fief near Angaston.

17. The first Congregational Church, on North Terrace, in 1837. Angas urged Congregationalists, Baptist, Methodists, and other Dissenters or Nonconformists to emigrate to Adelaide—the "Paradise of Dissent".

18. George Gawler, South Australia's second governor. This melancholy photograph was taken long after his recall, in semi disgrace, from Adelaide.

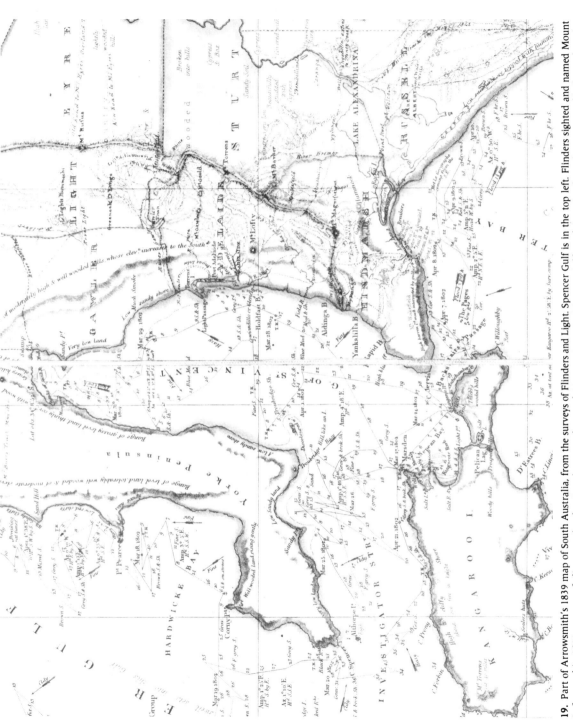

19. Part of Arrowsmith's 1839 map of South Australia, from the surveys of Flinders and Light. Spencer Gulf is in the top left. Flinders sighted and named Mount Lofty on his 1802 voyage of discovery in the *Investigator*, and named Nepean Bay, St. Vincent Gulf, Yorke Peninsula and Spencer Gulf after Admiralty notables. He reported that the coastal plains round the gulfs seemed good colonizing prospects. Nepean Bay, Kangaroo Island was the site of a whaling sta-

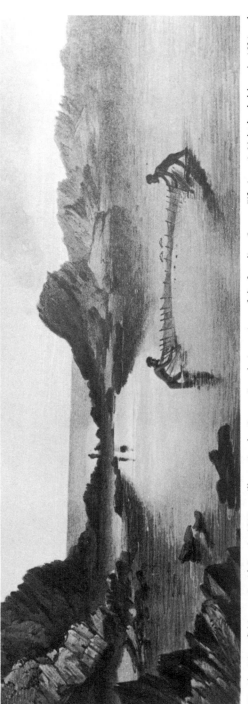

20. Aborigines fishing at Rapid Bay in 1845, an illustration by George French Angas (son of the founding George Fife Angas). Light landed here in 1836 and liked the Rapid Bay tribe, but considered the Kaurna, the Adelaide tribe, the "least interesting people" he had ever seen.

21. Aborigines on the south coast, about 1845, an illustration by George French Angas.

22. Sir George Strickland Kingston, who had been Light's deputy, then supplanter. Light thought him "a vulgar, over bearing upstart" but, unlike the colonel, Kingston lived on to succeed as architect, engineer, legislator, and speculator in Adelaide. His son, C.C. Kingston, was a notable premier of South Australia.

23. North Terrace in 1845, an illustration by George French Angas. On the left is an early bridge over the erratic Torrens and in the background Mount Lofty dominates the ranges or "Tiers". North Terrace is now Adelaide's most imposing boulevard (see illustration 128).

24. An early cartoon of Osmond Gilles, the province's first treasurer. A rich and bibulous republican, Gilles was in the thick of all the early quarrels, but did very well indeed out of land jobbing and investment.

25. Cartoon of George Morphett, another founding father who survived the early upheavals to progress to land ownership, political prominence, and a knighthood. Morphettville Racecourse commemorates his enthusiasm for racing.

26. Cartoon of James Hurtle Fisher, resident commissioner and first mayor of Adelaide. A "wily attorney" in Judge Jeffcott's opinion, Fisher prospered and acquired a coat of arms and a knighthood.

27. The Old Colonists' Festival Dinner, held at the rear of the City Bridge Hotel, Morphett Street, on 27 March 1851 to commemorate the first sale of city land in 1837. A lively sketch by S.T. Gill.

28. The Adelaide plains and Gulf St. Vincent as seen from Mount Lofty in 1845, an illustration by George French Angas.

29. Alexander Tolmer, the dashing but ill-starred inspector who, by his own account, was a mighty scourge of bushrangers and malefactors and the founder of trotting races in Adelaide. He led Adelaide's first mounted police and the gold escort, but died in poverty.

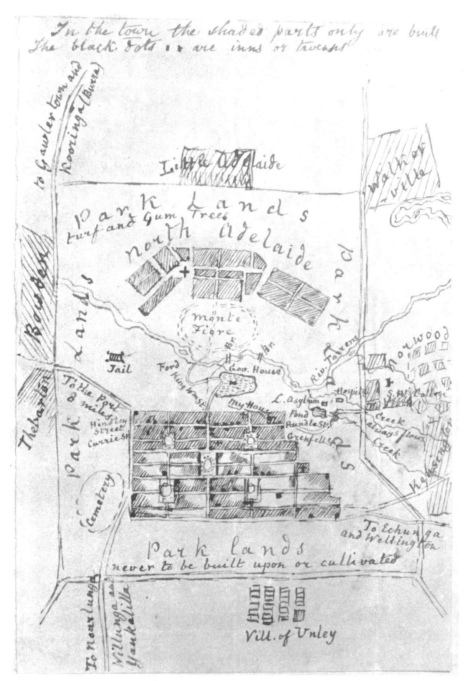

30. Map of the city of Adelaide around 1853, from the diary of C.H. Barton, detailing points of interest including inns or taverns. He thought Adelaide had "far too many" pubs.

2

ADELAIDE 1859-1970: A BRIEF CHRONICLE

Introduction

Essentially lower middle-class, Nonconformist and Radical in its origin, South Australia might well claim the title of the New England of the Antipodes. Even to the present day, it preserves signs and tokens of the principles on which it was founded; its progress having been the gradual and healthy growth of a pastoral and agricultural colony, undisturbed by the forced marches of gold mining. *R.E.N. Twopeny, 1882*

As I entered Adelaide, a gentleman in the train said to me with a wave of his hand: "My dear sir, the finest city on earth, and I have travelled a good deal."

Sydney Morning Herald *correspondent, 1907*

The foundation and settling-in periods, described in the first part, were complex enough, but there was a certain coherence about them. Adelaide was a small community, a pioneer township. Its citizens were united by common problems and challenges. Setbacks like the depression of the early 1840s were suffered by all. The discomforts of the immigrant voyage and the adjustment to a frontier society were common experiences. In general the community was ruled autocratically by the governor and his officials. Opportunities for personal advancement to the ownership of land or business were there for many settlers, given a certain amount of money, luck, and industry. The city's isolation meant that its citizens had to find their own way, with occasional references to a remote and idealized Mother Country.

After the formative 1850s, however, which saw considerable growth and constitutional progress, Adelaide becomes steadily more complex. Given that it is hard enough to generalize about its foundation period, with all the common denominators, then it is well nigh impossible to generalize about its years of growth to maturity. Obviously, Adelaide's population grew dramatically, from an estimated 546 in 1836 to about 850,000 in 1975. Its physical structure developed. Its economy diversified. Its problems, attitudes, opportunities, and preoccupations changed both with growth and general national development. I attempt to describe the evolution of some aspects of Adelaide life in the third part. In this one, I shall briefly mention some of the significant events in Adelaide's history in chronological sequence.

THE LATE 1850s

The 1850s had ended in a blaze of legislative glory with the opening of the first South Australian Parliament, the revival of the City Council and the enactment of Torrens's Real Property Act. This act, which created a simplified, cheap and efficient land titles registration system, was another remarkable South Australian invention. R.R. Torrens had worked for Lloyds of London and adapted the principles of the famous shipping register to his titles system. It was bitterly opposed by lawyers who fought for the old muddled but profitable—for them—deeds and conveyancing system, but it was extremely successsful. The Torrens titles system was copied in all the Australian colonies and many times overseas; most recently, perhaps, in Singapore. On other fronts, the paddleboat era on the Murray began with the race between W.R. Randell's *Mary Ann* and Francis Cadell's *Lady Augusta* in 1853. A year later, Australia's first railway, using horses to pull the trucks, was opened between Goolwa and Port Elliot, and south coast merchants had hopes of massive entrepôt trade at the mouth of the Murray River system.

In 1859, the province revealed more of its secret wealth when copper was discovered at Wallaroo on Yorke's Peninsula. Two years later even larger deposits of copper were found at nearby Moonta. Imported Cornish miners set up their "Little Cornwall" on the peninsula and the province, drought-stricken and economically depressed at the time, received help when it badly needed it. A retired Scots sea captain, Walter Hughes, enriched himself even more than the Burra Snobs had done thanks to the copper beneath his Wallaroo sheep pastures. His friends and compatriots in the firm of Elder, Smith helped financially and profited too. Hughes was lucky twice over in that he got the lion's share of the Moonta discoveries, despite the curious fact that his representative arrived second to make the claim in the Lands Office, yet was first to be attended to by the clerk. The Moonta-Wallaroo copper mines produced over 12,000,000 tons of copper worth more than 20,000,000 pounds before they finally closed in 1923. They thus eclipsed the Monster Mine and, like the Burra, provided Adelaide with substantial spin-off wealth over many years. In 1860, Hills water at last came to the citizens as welcome relief from the turbid liquid of the lower Torrens when the Thorndon Park reservoir was completed, connected by a main to the city.

During the summer of 1859, a ferocious bushfire burned its way down the Mount Lofty Ranges from Cox's Creek to the Hindmarsh Valley. Some farmers fled from their homes with only their clothes and a few possessions. The citizens collected 4,250 pounds for their relief. Also during 1859 a fine new pier was opened at Glenelg, Carl Linger and Mrs. C.J. Carleton won prizes for their "Song of Australia" at the Gawler Institute, and the *Admella*, a steamship plying between Adelaide and Melbourne, foundered off the Victorian coast in a protracted agony which took the lives of eighty passengers.

John McDouall Stuart, backed by pastoralists looking for new sheep runs, had begun his epic attempts to cross the continent from south to north. Stuart had one picturesque Adelaide rival. Inspector Tolmer, falling foul of the authorities (unforgiveably, his biography is not numbered among those of far less notable, if more respectable, Adelaideans in Pascoe's *Adelaide and Vicinity*,) made one more vain leap for immortality. As Hodder drily puts it: "Mr. Tolmer started to cross the continent, but soon returned."[1]

The 1860s

At the beginning of the 1860s, the population of Adelaide and its suburbs numbered about 18,500. By 1871 it had grown to 27,209 out of a total population for the province of 185,626.

January 1860 began with searing heat. To quote Hodder again: "Thermometer 158 degrees in the sun. Fruit literally roasted on the trees. Birds took shelter in the houses of settlers. Heavy rains followed. Influenza and bronchitis largely prevalent."[1] One wonders, almost reverently, at the stoicism of the citizens as they sat, in monstrous Victorian clothes, among their roasting oranges; first baked, then waterlogged. Undeterred, a crowd of 7,000 in May watched the first public review of the Adelaide Volunteers, South Australia's rejoinder to the remote threat of the Crimean War. The City Council imposed for the first time an annual tax on dogs, since "the enormous increase of curs of all colours, sizes and breeds had become a serious nuisance".[2]

During 1862, Stuart at last reached Chambers Bay, named after one of his Adelaide backers, on the northern coast of Australia. Adelaide feted the unstoppable little Scot on his return. He was rewarded with 3,000 pounds. Stuart had found more than 200,000 square kilometres of new grazing country west of Lake Torrens and Lake Eyre. Two years later, the province was made responsible for the administration of the vastnesses of the Northern Territory. It was to prove a costly incubus.

By 1861, Hindley Street was no longer the commercial centre. Business now centred on the corners of King William and Rundle streets. Banks like the Bank of Australasia, the Stock Exchange, insurance offices, and the offices of mining companies, architects, and lawyers lined King William Street, while Victoria Square then as now was overlooked by government offices, the post office, and the police court. Doctors were already prominent on North Terrace, churches on Wakefield Street, and counting houses and warehouses along Currie and Grenfell streets. Of the 283 hectares of South Adelaide, 194 had been built upon. North Adelaide's pleasant slopes were already notable for the villas of the rich, as was South Terrace. By then Adelaide had 53 kilometres of macadamized roads, lit by oil lamps.

In July 1862, the body of the Reverend Stow, Adelaide's first Congregational minister, was followed to its grave by a procession almost a kilometre long. Death was beginning to thin out the founders. James Chambers, the first man to drive a bullock team from Port Adelaide to the city, died about the same time. Charles Mann, the first advocate general, Robert Thomas, first printer of the *Register*, Bishop Murphy, the first Roman Catholic Bishop of Adelaide, Judge Jeffcott, drowned in the Murray mouth, and of course Colonel Light himself were among the many founders who had already gone.

The City Council took pride in three pieces of municipal progress during the 1860s: a proper Town Hall, an improved water supply, and gas lighting. The council had had a poor run during the first few years of responsible government. As Pascoe puts it: "The affairs of the City Council were not in an agreeable condition ... Councilmen quarrelled among themselves and such criticisms were passed on them that it was got to be considered by certain of them that it was discreditable to hold a seat in the Chamber. It is said that slights were put upon the Council by Parliament and that heartburnings were the consequence."[3]

THE TOWN HALL[4]

But less heartburning and more "cordiality and facility" occurred as the council's debt was reduced and "discursive discussion" gave way to "solid business". The council had one major aim: to erect a Town Hall such as had never been seen in the Southern Hemisphere, and when Mr. T. English became mayor in 1862 he pushed ahead with the project. The council stoutly borrowed the money for the hall: 16,000 pounds was estimated but 20,000 pounds was the final cost. Edmund William Wright, an architect who had been mayor himself in 1859, won the competition for the design. The foundation stone was laid by Governor Daly on St. George's Day, 1863, before what Worsnop called "an immense assemblage" of people in King William Street. Between the speeches, the onlookers were "well amused" by the band of the City Rifles playing "The Song of Australia" and "Goodbye, Sweetheart, Goodbye". The governor surmised that the building would be "a great ornament to the City" and used for his work a trowel, (still preserved in the Town Hall) surmounted with a crown, "of the purest silver, with a handle of polished sheoak". Despite the protests of penny pinchers—400 of whom signed a memorial stating that 5,000 pounds was quite enough for any Town Hall—the corporation pressed on with the building, and the Adelaide Town Hall was completed and opened by June 1866. A banquet for 800 diners followed.

Wright, strongly influenced by his Italian experiences, was an architect of talent, and Worsnop happily quoted impressed observers on the "beauty and elegancy" of "the largest municipal building south of the equator". The Town Hall had a frontage of 22 metres, and the Albert Tower stood 44 metres above the pavement. There was a huge and magnificent main chamber, a fine sweeping staircase made by G.L. Bonython, "enrichments of the Corinthian Order", pillars, porticos, and embellishments that were "triumphs of the decorative art".

At the opening, the corporation expressed its pride with gas illuminations all over the front of the Town Hall. Victoria and Albert's initials were prominent, and many other "brilliant devices". And for the final touch, as the citizenry watched the arrival of the "most influential men in the Province" for the banquet, the eight Albert Bells in the Albert Tower pealed through their twenty changes. "The chiming", Worsnop assures us, "was distinctly heard at times at the further end of North Adelaide". Later, in 1877, a large organ was imported from England at the cost of 2,000 pounds and installed in the Town Hall. When first played, it "created a sensation".

The corporation's pride in its new headquarters has been justified. The Italianate glories of the Town Hall, its spaciousness and dignity, have worn well and are probably more appreciated today than they were last century. The old building is still big enough, and noble enough (it makes the nearby modern tower of the State Administration Centre look parvenu), to represent modern Adelaide. For all their faction fights, the city councils of the 1860s had a confident vision.

As for the water supply, the Thorndon Reservoir on the upper Torrens was completed in 1861 and water flowed through the mains to public baths and fountains. In 1867, the city's streets and shops were lit by gas for the first time.

PRINCE ALFRED'S VISIT[5]

Adelaide civic pride reached an unparalleled zenith in the 1860s not because of gas or water supply, or even the new Town Hall, but because of the visit in 1867 of Prince Alfred, Duke of Edinburgh, the second son of Queen Victoria herself. An amiable, if dull, young man, Prince Alfred had been wandering round the Mediterranean in the Royal Naval steam frigate *Galatea* when the queen despatched him to inspect British colonists in the Southern Hemisphere. The *Galatea* accordingly sailed south into the blue. Adelaide was as much thrilled by the intimation that South Australia would be the first colony visited—one, indeed, in the eye for Melbourne—as it was dismayed by the lack of news from the wandering duke as to when exactly he would arrive. Triumphal arches were feverishly erected, enormous speeches prepared, addresses of welcome composed. "Beachrangers" watched the horizon along the Gulf, welcoming cannon were primed, and a huge heap of firewood was piled on top of Mount Lofty. There were some embarrassing false alarms before the *Galatea* slid quietly into Holdfast Bay at dawn on 3 October with no one to welcome her. A group of curious clerks spotted her first. A blushing Adelaide rushed to make amends, and a choir on the Glenelg sands began singing "God Save Our Gracious Prince".

Thirty-five thousand South Australians massed at Glenelg or in the city to receive Prince Alfred. Here, at last, was recognition from the highest source of Adelaide's progress and respectability! From Moonta miner to flustered councilman, all were determined to prove to the duke that the Wakefield system had worked, and that Adelaide was ten times more loyal to the crown than any Home city. The *Times*, with its usual Olympian tone when discussing things colonial, had observed: "Colonial life is sad and dull, and the excitement of a royal progress will be all the more welcome for that." Hodder ecstatically recorded:

> Never had Adelaide seen so great a show. Magnificent triumphal arches, miles of bunting, forests of evergreens, acres of red and gold cloth; merry peals ringing from the Albert Tower; the booming of cannon; the tramp of volunteers, joined by the members of friendly societies, the Corporations of Adelaide and other municipalities, and the German Club; the clangour of bands of music, the thrilling voices of 4,000 children singing the National Anthem; but, more impressive than all, the ringing cheers and the waving of handkerchiefs, as the first member of the Royal House of England passed along on Australian soil. At night there was a general illumination—a display of electric and magnesium lights and fireworks.[6]

Prince Alfred declined "a monumental list of engagements", but his time in Adelaide was extraordinarily crowded. He attended a Government House levee. He laid the foundation stone of Prince Alfred College and the new Post Office. He reviewed the volunteers. He inspected the Botanic Gardens, where the director was "amazed" at the princely knowledge of the specimens. He was on display at a ball in the Town Hall at which over a thousand colonists crammed into the ballroom. At special banquets he gallantly sampled wallaby pie, Murray cod, and an omelette made of emu eggs. He endured interminable speeches and passed on to his equerries innumerable addresses of loyalty.

He listened to a lantern lit *Liedertafel* sung by 500 German settlers in Victoria Square and addressed the crowd in German. At a Town Hall banquet, the mayor, after a somewhat excessive speech, invited him to down a "loving cup" full of local wine and presented him with a vellum Declaration of Loyalty encased in a "silver casket inscribed with views of Adelaide". The mayor announced at the beginning of his oration that he was going to open his heart to the prince, causing the Melbourne *Punch* to comment: "The Mayor of Adelaide is planning to indulge in rather a curious piece of surgery". Other municipal leaders pressed their declarations on the duke. Gawler's mayor handed over yet another silver casket decorated with a golden replica of Ridley's Reaper.

Everywhere there were craning necks, cheers, deal arches covered with flowers, gas illuminations which providentially did not burn down the city, and energetic curiosity and loyalty. Over 5,000 citizens tramped round the *Galatea*. All this heat, noise, and exuberant patriotism was overwhelming. Lord Newry, an equerry, later remarked that "the colonists have a hazy notion of protocol and procedure". The *Pall Mall Gazette* said that "loyalty never went to such excesses at home". The *Times* was cutting: "Novelty does not excuse the sheer vulgarity of much of the decorations."

What these lofty English commentators did not realize was that the crown, like so many things English, seemed infinitely dearer from colonial distances. The Australian colonies were in transports over Prince Alfred's visit—and this, incidentally, was the beginning of the tradition of royal progresses to outposts of empire. In England, the Widow of Windsor was unpopular and still waited the blandishments of Disraeli to show herself to her people. But to the Adelaide, Melbourne, and Sydney crowds Prince Alfred represented a recognition of respectability, a link with Home, and a fine opportunity for pomp and circumstance in cities hitherto starved of such things. He eased a sense of loneliness. He symbolized history and a ritualistic mystery. And so the necessarily materialistic settlers of a "new" country flung their hats and parasols into the air and cheered and cheered.

The duke seemed to like Adelaide. He showed a lively interest in the Horticultural and Agricultural Society's Show in the parklands and permitted the prefix "Royal" to be used. He drank some colonial wine at Gawler and allowed that he was "agreeably surprised ... I did not know that wines of such quality are made in the colony ... the wine I've tasted is remarkably like a Muscatel or a Madeira". He shot and fished at Lake Alexandrina, where his hosts were splendidly put down by Aborigines when asked to put on a corroboree with their women dancing naked. "What for we do it, more than white women?" Prince Alfred blazed away during a moonlit possum shooting expedition in the Hills. The animals must have been tied to the trees by the organizers for a companion reported: "the Prince proved himself a good sportsman by shooting 52 possums, of which he had 43 skinned, and left the rest among the trees." Finally, Prince Alfred gratified Adelaide's respectability by stating in a letter to the press: "I have noticed in Adelaide, an absence of the poor and rowdy class, so numerous elsewhere." Delighted, the *Advertiser* responded: "We should attempt to obtain British approval to a Federal Union of these colonies under the popular leadership of the young Prince now among us."

Away sailed the *Galatea*, carrying the duke to further junketings in the eastern colonies. More crowds, gas illuminations, and enough declarations of loyalty to sink the ship, had they been kept. One wonders what the duke did with them all. Prince Alfred had his moments of fun, as when he shot scores of rabbits at the estate of Alfred Austin in Victoria, the respected importer of rabbits into Australia. However, what he had called "the poor and rowdy class" were more prevalent in the east, as any Adelaide burgher might have warned him. A mammoth barbecue for the poor in Melbourne turned into a riot. Then, to cap it all, came the news that the duke had been shot through the ribs by a Fenian, O'Farrell, in Sydney. The news was, according to Worsnop, the cause of "the wildest excitement throughout the City and Province", and a "monster meeting" was held at the Town Hall "to adopt addresses of condolence to Her Most Gracious Majesty". The duke, who soon recovered, wrote to assure Adelaide that the attempted assassination had not "shaken my confidence in the loyalty in this colony". This must have smoothed colonists palpitating at the thought of what England would think of Australia now. O'Farrell was hanged.

The 1870s

Probably exhausted by all this imperial sentiment, Adelaide then returned to its normal preoccupations: the state of the harvest, productivity at the mines, the chronic sniping between City Council and Parliament, gossip, gardening, and fishing from the new jetty at Glenelg. In 1868, the council discovered that a man holding "the highest office under the Corporation" had for years been embezzling money—at least 1,500 pounds—from the corporation's funds. He went to gaol. The indefatigable Thomas Worsnop became town clerk. He remained in this office until 1898.

"At the beginning of March 1870", Worsnop writes in his admirable *History of the City of Adelaide*, "there was a scene of an unwonted occurrence. There was a riot.[1] Unwonted indeed, up until then, in the peaceable city but none the less there were police charges and bloody heads before the government offices in Victoria Square. The season had been bad and men were out of work. The commissioner of works offered a crowd of unemployed men jobs retrenching the grounds of the "Lunatic Asylum", at 1s. 10d. a rod. At this, the men began "to hustle him about". Then they attacked the Treasury until the mounted police came up and started to lay about them with truncheons and the flats of their swords. Six men were gaoled.

During the 1870s, one of its most prosperous decades, Adelaide still had much of the coltish expansionism of youth, still had explorations of the huge hinterland and events like the completion of the transcontinental telegraph line to excite the citizens. But Adelaide was already running along well established grooves. The look and the feel of the city was well recorded during this decade, notably by the distinguished and prolific English novelist, Anthony Trollope, and by a local justice of the peace, William Harcus, whose *South Australia: Its History, Resources and Production*, was published in 1876. The reasonable objectivity of Harcus's work separates it from the gaseous self-congratulation of most of the many nineteenth century books written about Adelaide.

TROLLOPE'S VISIT[2]

Trollope liked Adelaide, as is clear from his letters published in the Liverpool *Mercury* in 1875 and in passages in his massive *Australia and New Zealand*. He declared: "Adelaide is one of the pleasantest towns among the colonies, well built, well adorned and surrounded by gardens. I have seen no new town which has a greater look of general prosperity". He praised the vision of the founders, the setting, the width of the streets, the gardens, the atmosphere. He extolled the beauties of the Botanic Gardens. As an old post office man, and the putative inventor of the pillar box, Trollope was delighted by the grandiloquence of the new Post Office building in King William Street. He was pleased that the importance of postal services was here fittingly recognized in a country that depended so much upon them. He paid tribute to Light's plan, but found the gridiron at times monotonous, and wished for the winding streets of Europe. But in general he showered praise upon the grateful Adelaideans, and rounded it off by observing that Strathalbyn, a mainly Scottish settlement on the River Angas beyond the Hills, was one of the two prettiest and cleanest townships he had seen in Australia.

It is easy to understand the fondness of the creator of Barchester for the Adelaide appearance and lifestyle. Adelaide was in many ways the most Trollopean of cities and, conversely, Trollope the most Adelaidean of novelists. It is not hard to imagine clerics like Archdeacon Grantly and the Warden pottering in the shade of Bishop Short's new cathedral. Only the rooks were missing. Adelaide and district had strong Barsetshire undertones.

WILLIAM HARCUS

Harcus provides the customary flattering descriptions of the Town Hall, the Post Office building, the elegant houses of doctors on North Terrace, and the government buildings. But he is not afraid to criticize some buildings, especially Nonconformist churches, if they seemed "somewhat vulgar in style".[3] Harcus writes of Port Adelaide, which had begun as "a very unwholesome and unsavoury spot", but now, built upon silt dredged from the swamp, was a thriving port exporting wheat, copper, wool, tallow, meat, and mimosa bark. A railway now connected Port Adelaide with the city.

> Alongside the wharfs, three or four deep, lie every year magnificent vessels, whose crowded tapering masts look like a forest ... Very many colonists go "Home", as the old country is still called ... The friendly terms on which the colonists are with many of these shipmasters makes a voyage home on one of their handsome ships something like a pleasure trip.[4]

Harcus describes the new villages and municipalities developing beyond the parklands—Glenelg, Norwood, Mitcham, Kensington, Gawler, and others.

> Many of the suburban gardens are rich and beautiful, and vineyards and orangeries abound. When the fruit trees are in bloom, or covered with the ripening fruit, they present a scene of rare beauty while the air is fragrant with the mingled odours of "Araby the blest".[5]

Prosperous new towns were beginning to grow along the Gulf or in the pastoral interior: Gladstone, Jamestown, Port Augusta, and Port Pirie, with its "splendid steam flour mill".

But Harcus's most fervent praise was for the Adelaide Botanic Garden, which had really come into bloom under the direction of Dr. Schomburgk.

> But the glory of Adelaide, and the pride of her citizens, is our beautiful Botanic Garden which, under the magic wand of the accomplished Director, Dr. Richard Schomburgk, has grown into a thing of beauty which will be a joy for ever. We are a quiet, undemonstrative people, not much given to what Mr. Anthony Trollope called "Australian blowing", but we do boast of our gardens; and if this be a weakness, it is one in which we are encouraged, if not justified, by all visitors who come to see them. They who have seen all the Botanic Gardens in the other Colonies without a moment's doubt or hesitation give the palm to ours ... When H.R.H. the Duke of Edinburgh was in Adelaide, he visited the Garden again and again, and always with increasing delight.[6]

Harcus was even proud of Adelaide's Destitute Asylum and two "Lunatic Asylums", one on North Terrace, the other, with its "striking building regarded from an architectural point of view", beyond the south parklands.

In 1870 the Strangways Ministry enacted a bill to establish a transcontinental telegraph between Adelaide via Port Augusta to Port Darwin. In August 1872, the post-master general, Charles Todd, completed the link after herculean labours in the Centre and Northern Territory, and "South Australians", in Pascoe's words, "were drawn closer to the motherland". The queen knighted the premier, Henry Ayers, in honour of the occasion. The stations along the line constituted useful bases for explorers like Forrest, Giles, and Warburton as they probed the immense deserts to the north and west of Adelaide. In 1877, a telegraphic link between Adelaide and Perth was completed. In January 1870, the mayor opened the new city market near Victoria Square. The administration of markets and the slaughterhouse, and especially the collection of fees was and remained a chronic problem for the council.

OLD COLONISTS

In December 1872, Adelaide was invaded by a plague of locusts. "Happily", records Hodder, "the Botanic Garden escaped their ravages". That same month, to quote Hodder again "The largest number of old South Australian colonists ever assembled at the same time met at a banquet given by Mr. Emmanuel Solomon in the Town Hall, Adelaide". The distinction of being an Old Colonist, especially if one had come out of the *Buffalo*, or before about 1840, without an assisted passage, was already being jealously guarded and proclaimed in Adelaide. As the city solidified and grew, and as the founders died out, the survivors of the Hindmarsh, Gawler, and Grey eras looked back through rose tinted spectacles on the days when men were men.

Later, in the mid 1890s, Mark Twain made a boisterous tour of Australia compiling a number of sketches published in his book *Following the Equator*. While in Adelaide, he attended a commemoration banquet, probably in the Town Hall. With his sentimentality at full throttle, Twain made some amusing and penetrating observations on the old settlers at their honoured place at the table:

> There were six of them. These Old Settlers had all been present at the Original Reading of the Proclamation, in 1836. They showed signs of the blightings and blastings of time, in their outward aspect, but they were young within; young and cheerful, and ready to talk, and talk all you wanted, in their turn, and out of it. They were down for six speeches and made 42 ... They have splendid grit, the Old Settlers, splendid staying power. But they do not hear well, and when they see the mayor going through motions which they recognize as the introducing of a speaker, they think they are the one, and they all get up together, and begin to respond in the most animated way; and the more the mayor gesticulates, and shouts "Sit down! Sit down!" the more they take it for applause, and the more excited and reminiscent and enthusiastic they get ... And finally when ushers come and plead, and beg, and gently and reverently crowd then down into their seats, they say, "Oh I'm not tired—I could bang along a week!" and they sit there looking simple and childlike, and gentle, and proud of their oratory, and wholly unconscious of what is going on at the other end of the room. And so one of the great dignitaries gets a chance, and begins his carefully-prepared speech, impressively and with solemnity—
>
> "When we, now great and prosperous and powerful, bow our heads in reverent wonder in the contemplation of those sublimities of energy, of wisdom, of forethought, of—"
>
> Up come the immortal six again, in a body, with a joyous "Hey! I've thought of another one!" and at it they go with might and main, hearing not a whisper of the pandemonium that salutes them, but taking all the visible violences as applause, as before, and hammering joyously away till the imploring ushers pray them into their seats again. And a pity too; for those lovely old boys did so enjoy living their heroic youth over, in these days of their honoured antiquity ...

It was a stirring spectacle; stirring in more ways than one, for it was amazingly funny, and at the same time deeply pathetic; for they had seen so much, these time-worn veterans, and had suffered so much; and had built so strongly and well, and laid the foundations of their commonwealth so deep, in liberty and tolerance and had lived to see the structure rise to such state and dignity and hear themselves so praised for their honourable work.[7]

GROWTH OF SPORT

The 1870s were good years for sport in South Australia. Adelaide, which had begun with dingo hunting, possum catching, fishing, wildfowling, and primitive cricket was becoming a distinctly sports conscious capital. Horse racing, which had always been popular, advanced further with the formation in 1873 of the South Australian Jockey Club. The patron was, inevitably, the governor; and the president, just as inevitably, that enthusiastic equestrian, now president of the council, Sir John Morphett.

Shooters benefited from a new Game Law passed that year. Rabbits, which had been sedulously introduced to the province by misguided devotees of Home sports, had become a menace and were giving the settlers notice of the havoc they could cause. Protection was now removed from rabbits, and the battle between rabbit hordes and shooters and trappers began.

Cricket had appeared early in Adelaide's history thanks to the enthusiasm of cricketing publicans. The game now became more recognizable and formalized as new clubs formed in the suburbs. During 1874, for example, the master himself, W.G. Grace brought his All England cricket team to the South Australian Cricketing Association at the Adelaide Oval. Grace's team won by thirty-six runs. Later that year, the first of a series of "intercolonial matches" were held at the oval: Victoria defeated South Australia.

THE UNIVERSITY

It was also a good decade for education. In 1874 an Act of Incorporation was passed to found the University of Adelaide. The foundation stone of the present Mitchell Building by North Terrace was laid four years later. The academy was made possible by a gift of 20,000 pounds by William Hughes, who had become enormously rich from Yorke Peninsula copper. Hughes, characteristically of Adelaide, had intended to found a theological seminary for Nonconformist ministers. Thomas Elder donated another 20,000 pounds and other Adelaide magnates gave substantial sums.[8] In 1874 "model schools" were established in Adelaide and soon afterwards the Christian Brothers opened their college. New institutes, as at Burra and Riverton, were founded.

SHIPWRECKS

Adelaide continued to be upset by shipwrecks as Encounter Bay, the rugged coast of Kangaroo Island, and even the waters of the Gulf itself, during winter storms, took their toll. For instance, in August 1874 the graceful passenger barque, *The City of Adelaide*, was blown ashore on Kirkaldy Beach near Port Adelaide. This ship was one of the fastest on the run between Adelaide and London and was well known and loved in South Australia. She was a familiar sight running before the wind up the Gulf. The *City of Adelaide* is now a hulk under another name moored at Leith, Scotland. Perhaps before it is too late, she may still be restored to her former glory and brought back to Adelaide, which owes so much to the sailing ships.

Also in 1874, the schooner *Triumph* went down with all hands off Glenelg. In February 1875, the steamship *Gothenburg*, bound for the Northern Territory, sank in Flinders Passage with the loss of 112 lives, including a number of judges. There were many such wrecks.

POLITICS AND PROSPERITY

While the province prospered from grain, wool, and copper, and the surveying staff was increased so that 60,000 hectares of new land was made available to farmers each month, the South Australian Parliament in these years had a chaotic existence. "Ministries", in Pascoe's words, "appeared and disappeared with the rapidity of scenes in a cinematograph". Baker, Reynolds, Waterhouse, Dutton, Ayers, Blyth, Hart, Boucaut, who had remarkably expansive ideas, and Strangways succeeded each other as premier in smart succession. There were many able men in politics, but there was also much rancour and the absence of disciplined parties made for political musical chairs. Anyway, as the province was well established and productive, all the political wrangling "seemed", to quote Pascoe again, "to make little difference".

The city fathers took pride in such innovations as gas street lighting, the rise of the urban population to about 40,000, and the extension of the tramway to Unley and Mitcham.

The industrious Worsnop wrote proudly of a prominent Adelaide feature still notable today—the evening throngs, window shopping, or "ardently in pursuit of pleasure" in gas-lit Rundle and Hindley streets: "The whole of Rundle Street, half Hindley Street, and the northern portion of King William Street ... are crowded with a busy throng, the footways being occupied by a dense moving mass. The quantity of light afforded by the multitude of gas jets with which the shops are ornamented is sufficient to distinguish the features of relatives and friends, and give the streets an agreeable and cheerful aspect".

MAYOR SMITH

However, everything was not "agreeable" in Adelaide civic affairs. Edwin Smith, an active and progressive mayor, was open about the city's problems when he began the tradition of an annual mayoral report in 1879–80. For instance, Adelaide was strikingly unhealthy, with the highest infant mortality rate in all the Australasian colonies. The death rate for the year in the city was 188 for every 1,000 babies born, as compared with 126 in the country. Mayor Smith declared: "The causes at work are, in my opinion, the usual sanitary disadvantages of populous towns and especially the impure atmosphere arising from our defective drainage, our foul-smelling water tables, and the enormous accumulation within the limited area of the city of night soil."[9] Two Health Acts had already been passed, but epidemics of diseases like cholera were still frequent. In 1879 work began on a waterborne sewerage system and by 1881 sewage was being admitted to the sewage farm at Islington in the northern suburbs. Adelaide was the first Australian city to have such a system. The city remained progressive in this regard. By 1975 Adelaide was the first Australian city to be making substantial use of sewage farm effluent water for irrigation, as in the Bolivar region.

As for the Adelaide water, infamous to this day, some improvement was to come with the opening of the Happy Valley Reservoir in 1896.

But to return to Mayor Smith's report: his worries included flying dust from the unpaved streets (council was experimenting with asphalt for the footways), whether or not to close the West Terrace cemetery, the hazards of the level crossing at Morphett Street, the gunpowder magazine on the parklands, money, fees—and crime. The city's courts, reported the mayor, were punishing nightcartmen who failed to keep their wagons watertight five shillings, with ten shillings costs. Cab and wagon drivers were being fined for rounding corners or crossing street intersections faster than walking pace, or for smoking, or being asleep, while holding the reins. Some were fined for "furious" driving in the city, and three delinquents for driving prostitutes in an open vehicle. Citizens caught washing in the city's fountains were fined five shillings.

Turning to the bright side, Mayor Smith was eloquent on Adelaide's growth. He rejoiced, strangely to modern ears, in "the augumentation of traffic in the streets", because it signified "the expansion of trade and population". Adelaide was changing in a way bewildering to the surviving pioneers: "The old dwellings and workshops of the early days are vanishing rapidly, and the new generation springing up will know little of the habitations and scenes which from historical associations are dear to the few of the pioneers still left, so rapidly does the present become the past." Smith reported that the Parklands had produced large quantities of profitable limestone and had provided grazing for 541 cows, 82 horses, and 41 sheep. Known as "the Father of Gaslighting" in Adelaide, he also took pride in his plan to create the Torrens Lake, completed in 1881. There had been a number of attempts earlier to dam the Torrens, all frustrated by winter floods. However Smith's plan was realized. He forecast: "For more than a mile along the course of the river there will be a depth of 12 feet and over, and as the banks are a good distance apart—from 200 to 300 feet in many places—there will be a splendid course for boat races and swimming matches and a very ornamental sheet of water to add to the pleasure of those who stroll along the banks."

Mayor Smith went on to urge the formation of a national art museum—the National Gallery on North Terrace was opened in 1881—and mused: "Through its educational power some South Australian Michaelangelo may eventually arise who will advocate, elucidate and describe critically, yet pleasantly, the progress and essential influences of art in the antipodes." No Michaelangelo was to emerge, but a Hans Heysen, certainly. Smith was a model city father. A prosperous brewer, he had been mayor of Kensington and Norwood, and went on to a distinguished parliamentary career and a knighthood. Twopeny declared of the achievements of Smith's mayoralty—the Torrens Lake, the gas lights, and the tidied up parklands and squares: "I do not know that I ever saw so much done entirely at the initiative and by the energy and persistence of a single man." Adelaide's appreciation of Smith was such that he succeeded Sir Henry Ayers as the president of the Savings Bank. Smith was to organize the Adelaide Jubilee International Exhibition of 1887, and spend his money, patronage, and time on the Adelaide Hunt Club, cricket, rowing, bowling, chess, and tennis. He crowned his career, in nineteenth century Adelaide eyes, by donating in 1894 the bronze statue of Queen Victoria which now, much dulled by pollution, gestures at the traffic surging across the midriff of Victoria Square.

Mayor Smith concluded his 1879–80 report by saying: "I can scarcely imagine any higher satisfaction or nobler pride than that which the pioneer colonist must feel when contemplating this beautiful city which has risen before his eyes, since its inception some forty-four years ago. Then it was a dense forest, now it is a prosperous city, holding within its embrace 40,000 souls."

1880-1900

Legislative advances during these twenty years included an act to authorize payment to members of parliament in 1887, the establishment of a totalizator the following year, the provision of free and standard education to the compulsory age (six to thirteen years)[1] in 1892, the establishment in 1894 of boards of conciliation for industrial arbitration, and enfranchisement of women the same year. The first and last measures were notable constitutional firsts for South Australia, showing that the old reformist current in Adelaide's history was still strong. As is shown in the section "Adelaide Respectability, Virtue, and Vice", the campaign for women's right to vote was fought mainly by a powerful female temperance pressure group, and when ladies began to use their electoral strength, in 1896, Adelaide's era of moral stuffiness started simultaneously.

Generally, the '80s and '90s were decades of slow and genteel growth for Adelaide, a time of consolidation, and Light's city suffered fewer of the alarums and excursions of the earlier years. The population of the metropolitan area grew steadily to over 162,000, a little less than half of the total for the province, and most of the population growth took place in the suburbs rather than within the parklands. The year 1881 saw the opening of the Art Gallery by Prince Albert Victor, an exhibition, and the opening of the Torrens Lake. A crowd of about 40,000 people watched an official procession of boats containing Governor Sir William Jervois and city fathers sail up the lake to a marquee where they energetically "drank toasts and made speeches suitable to the occasion". Adelaide loved pomp, hunting, congratulatory speeches about progress, and gala days.

DEFENCE

Adelaide now had a Fire Brigades Board, established in 1882, but, despite the Pax Britannica, was often agitated about defence. There were the mounted police, the Volunteers, and the Rifles, whose ceremonial parades were a familiar city entertainment. Their rifle practice at the butts on the South Park Lands was a familiar hazard for people from Unley and Mitcham visiting the city.

Adelaide had had a dread of Russian invasion ever since the Crimean War and had nervous seizures whenever a Russian ship steamed enigmatically into the Gulf. Forts were built at Glanville and Largs and a military road constructed from Semaphore to Glenelg. (The Glanville Fort was recently restored with National Estate money.) What Hodder hopefully hailed as "the nucleus of the South Australian navy", the little 1,000 tonne gunboat *Protector*, arrived from England in 1884 and was duly inspected by various mayors and corporations. She cost 65,000 pounds. Her size was disappointing to the dignitaries, but her powerful Whitworth guns, one of which is preserved at Port

Adelaide, were reassuring. War news from Europe in 1885 upset Adelaide again. The city bestirred itself to provide what Hodder, hopefully again, I suspect, called "... two thousand disciplined men under arms and three thousand auxiliaries ... in case of an emergency. An experimental call to arms one night in April resulted in the assembly of a considerable proportion of this force in a very short time."[2]

Fortunately, Adelaide's defences were never put to the test during this period and the traditional peace of the province endured. The *Protector* was to remain no more than a nucleus. She never fired a shell in anger and arrived too late to be of any assistance when sent to help quell the Boxer Rebellion in China. Her hulk, sadly, for Adelaide was always unsentimental about her ships, is now a Queensland breakwater, at Heron Island. (Similarly, the last of the ketches, the *Annie Watt*, now disintegrates on a vacant lot in Semaphore.)

A real call to arms came in 1899, with the outbreak of the Boer War. South Australia, like the other colonies, mustered and shipped out her volunteers in what seemed then a noble crusade to defend the Empire and help the Mother Country. The soldiers marched smartly down King William Street between aisles of cheering citizens. "The presence", observed the *Register* of 31 October 1899, "in the streets of Adelaide of the valiant, well set up volunteers—the first all Australian contingent to proceed to a battlefield—was indeed a thrilling spectacle." The vigorous equestrian statue near the gates of Government House is the main memorial of a conflict to which the province sent about 1,500 men, 59 of whom were killed. Adelaide had been blooded.

FIFTY YEARS OF PROGRESS

In 1887, Adelaide celebrated its Jubilee. To celebrate it staged an International Exhibition housed in an enormous exhibition building. This exuberant mass of domed Victorian Gothic loomed over North Terrace until 1961. Exhibits, all testifying to the province's success, ranged from Northern Territory gold to Pilsener beer.

Sir Samuel Davenport, the "Squire of Beaumont", pre-eminent among successful Old Colonists, penned a remarkable introduction to H.J. Scott's *South Australia in 1887-88*. Remarkable in that his prose glowed with imperial sentiment at its zenith, with open satisfaction at the achievement in Adelaide of so many nineteenth century English aspirations. Adelaide in its jubilee year signified success to Davenport: success in commerce, population growth, productivity and progress in general. He congratulated the citizens for such virtues as "intelligence, energy and perseverance, hardy daring and untiring labours, sterling character and unflinching bravery". As a result, they had "effected that great conquest of a savage land ... Forests have been reduced to smiling wheatfields, marshes to garden grounds—hills to terraced fruit grounds and vineyards". As indisputable evidence for progress, Davenport pointed out that from 1836 to 1886 the province's population had grown from almost nothing to over 300,000, and the value of its imports, exports, and banking deposits had all increased to nearly 5,000,000 pounds each. He contrasted the 1880s with the situation in 1836: "The kangaroo and the emu fed over the glades of the Adelaide Plains. ... Here peace and silence were undisturbed except by the hunting aborigines, whose 'coo-ees' in the daytime were heard from the hills, and the doleful cries of howling dingoes at night."

Scott industriously compiled official details to show how Adelaide had progressed from this "wildest state of nature". For instance, Adelaide now had waterworks, deep drainage, a well established mayor and corporation, government departments, a museum, a university, and an array of churches. The province had 1,950 kilometres of railway track and 136 institutes affiliated to the Public Library. While Adelaide was still very much Trollope's "Farinaceous City", mainly dependent upon cereals, wool, wine, fruit, and minerals for its livelihood, several manufacturing industries had developed in the city, ranging from ship building to the manufacture of boots, candles, and confectionery. The Adelaideans were illuminated by gas at night, drank water piped from the Thorndon Park Reservoir, and could travel by horse drawn trams round their city to contemplate such marvels as the Torrens Lake or the City Bridge.

All this and more was undeniable progress to Davenport and other leading citizens, and by any standards it represented substantial achievement. Of course, there was a seamy side to jubilee Adelaide—dirt, disease, high infant mortality, crime, corruption, and pollution; and of course such matters were never mentioned in books written by Adelaide people to congratulate Adelaide people. This progress was scarcely beneficial to Davenport's "hunting aborigines", or to the deforested hillsides and polluted waterways. But Adelaide, in the 1880s, rarely bothered its collective head about such matters. The queen was on her throne and the future seemed bright. There was plenty of money to be made, and plenty of churches in which to thank God for it. The Empire was snug and impregnable. Like one of its ornate city trams, Adelaide proceeded, with some dignity and occasional mishaps, along the prescribed route to its terminus of respectability.

DEPRESSION

The 1890s were a sterner decade. A severe commercial depression settled on all the Australian colonies, depriving them of their economic innocence. The hectic era of land booms and strident expansionism exploded like a huge balloon all over the continent. Employers and the new trade unions locked horns in a series of strikes beginning with the great maritime strike of 1891. Practically all the financial institutions in Melbourne, for instance, went bankrupt. Many Australians, in a land that had quickly acquired a reputation for easy plenty, actually starved; and many more endured bleak hardship. By 1893, most of the private Sydney banks had closed their doors. People lived from hand to mouth and economic misery was not confined to the working class. Several ruined businessmen committed suicide rather than face families raised on the assumption of material wealth, and Sir Charles Lowe, later a Supreme Court Justice in Victoria, recalled later that he and his family survived mainly on rabbits caught in the bush.

As the historian Brian Fitzpatrick put it, the depression was "like the ending of childhood—never glad confident morning again."[3] The self confidence of colonial Australia, an exuberant assurance commented on by Trollope and other visitors, took a drubbing from which it never completely recovered. There was one sure indication of the loss of social momentum: the birthrate fell sharply. During the 1880s, on average, every thousand Australian married women gave birth to 320 children. By the 1900s, this figure had fallen to 235. The large families of the mid-Victorian period had gone for ever. Similarly, immigration declined to a trickle. The collapse of laissez-faire capitalism wrought a substantial change in the national character. Michael Cannon writes:

> With all his faults, all his hypocrises and extravagances, the man of the high Victorian age had a colour and dash about him. He knew how to enjoy his brief mortal span; how to risk everything in the adventure of living and growing.
> Compare him with the Edwardian man of only 20 years later. All the dazzle had departed;

all that was left was a soured, phlegmatic individual, bound by an increasingly rigid social philosophy which froze Australia into a mould for the following half century.[4]

Adelaide suffered the general malaise in the early 1890s. In 1891 10,000 unionists demonstrated in sympathy with the striking seamen and dock workers. Other groups, like the shearers, went on strike. The value of South Australia's exports fell from 6,186,000 pounds in 1891 to 3,487,000 pounds in 1898. The great firm of Elder, Smith and Co. made its first and only loss in trading in 1893. During that year, the *Register* reported many "insolvencies" and strikes. Drought and poor harvests since 1884 added to the gloom. A number of banks, including the Bank of South Australia, ceased operations. "The ruin", says Pascoe, "was wide and deep." Many South Australian families left the province for Western Australia to try to improve their fortunes.

Yet Adelaide did not suffer as keenly as the bigger cities of the east. It was smaller, had not endured the backlash of goldrushes and land booms, and had, moreover, a sober folk memory of its own ruinous depression of the 1840s. As it had not leaped so rashly as Melbourne or Sydney, so it did not fall so far. Then there was the ingrained Nonconformist acumen of Adelaide. The Bank of Adelaide remained open throughout the crisis. Finally, the discovery of the silver and lead of Broken Hill—for Adelaide was to benefit from the spin-off prosperity even though it was over the border—indicated that once more mineral wealth would help the city in a time of stress.

Still, the depression had been a terrible experience for a young and vulnerable city. Adelaide greeted the twentieth century with much of the old mid-Victorian stuffing knocked out of her. There were noticeably fewer speeches from politicians and city fathers about triumphant progress and limitless opportunities. Wakefield's utopia was flawed: indeed, some idealistic South Australians forsook it for communal villages by the Murray or joined William Lane in his doomed attempt to build an ideal "New Australia" in Paraguay. As with the other Australian cities, some of the "dazzle had departed". The foundation dreams of the Morphetts and the Angases had been shown by circumstance and exploration to have definite limitations. The agricultural frontiers of the province had now gone as far as they could. Indeed, they had over-extended themselves beyond Goyder's Line of 254 millimetre rainfall and hundreds of farming families had been worn down by a losing battle against drought, exhausted soil, rabbit infestations, and unstable prices. The trade unions had been damaged and embittered by the strikes. They began to turn for redress to political action and in 1892 the first labour member was elected to the South Australian Parliament. The *Register* of 8 May 1893 reported that "a large crowd" assembled at the rotunda in Elder Park to listen to "several of the recently returned Labour representatives". "Mr. Coneybeer said that after the brilliant victory the party had achieved, and the many demonstrations they had had he could hardly find breath to again express his joy and thanks at the results". Similarly, the employers had been shaken, and tended towards combinations, monopolies, and cartelism.

The South Australian government had weathered the depression, with only one year of deficit, but only at the price of harsh retrenchment and economy. It soldiered on while thousands of South Australians rushed to Western Australia to dig for gold, and all the staple industries of the province, with the main exceptions of copper and wine, declined.

1900-1945

During this period Adelaide was involved in three wars on behalf of Britain: the South African War, Great War, to which holocaust the state sent 28,000 men, and then it followed the Union Jack into the Second World War. Adelaide rejoiced in more royal visits and a post war boom in the 1920s, staggered before droughts, such as the regular "old man" of a drought in 1914, endured a bitter depression in the early 1930s, then picked up economically with strong government leadership. Industrial diversification and the encouragement of secondary industries reduced the state's dependence upon the old primary industries. The census of 1933 showed that the population had risen to 580,949—a slower rise than the national rate—for South Australia had its economic limitations.

With federation—and South Australian politicians played a prominent part in this—Adelaide was no longer the capital of a province, but of a state owing some allegiance to the federal government. However, sentiment and the quickly established tradition of interstate jealousies and particularism meant that the city's sense of difference endured largely unimpaired.

Notable events included the introduction of electric lighting in 1900 and early shop closing the following year. The Adelaide High School was opened in 1908 and electric trams, which gradually replaced the horse-drawn trams, began running in 1909. During 1919, the first *Lord* Mayor was elected. In 1920 the Prince of Wales visited Adelaide amid scenes of exuberant loyalty, with thousands of school children forming patriotic patterns on the oval. In 1936 the centenary year was celebrated in style and the foundation stone of Parliament House laid. During 1937 Mount Bold Reservoir, which almost doubled Adelaide's water supply, was completed and the South Australian Housing Trust established. Trolley buses began their run. Early in 1939, the state suffered its worst recorded heatwave and a series of bushfires. A record high temperature of 47.6 degrees Celsius was recorded in Adelaide.

WOWSERS

A browse through the newspapers of the period reveals more on the preoccupation and attitudes of Adelaideans then. These forty-five years were the heyday of the wowsers, spearheaded by the Woman's Christian Temperance Union described in detail in the third part. The *Register* reported, favourably it would seem, on one of their meddlesome displays in support of the early closing referendum in its issue of 4 April 1910:

> The temperance workers were early afoot on Saturday ... A valiant effort was made to gather the fruit of an extensive canvass of the city which had been going on for some time ... various devices were resorted to to attract attention and influence public opinion, chief

of which were white ribbon favours and card shield badges bearing the mottoes: "For the sake of the boys, vote in the top square" ... Considerable interest was taken in the young crusaders, who doubtless made a powerful appeal to many a parent's heart.

The white ribboners prevailed and Adelaide drinkers were cramped by restrictions. "Recent Sabbath visits by the police", reported the *Register* of 6 July 1910, "to various city and suburban hotels have resulted in a batch of prosecutions before the Adelaide Police Court lately." In 1925 the W.C.T.U. was campaigning to close the hotels at noon on Saturdays. A correspondent to the *Register* of 11 August 1925, spoke up for the long suffering and oppressed majority:

> The Premier told the Rev. D.C. Harris he would not close the hotels at noon on Saturdays, as requested by the reverend gentleman and his party. The Premier did quite right, and voiced the opinion of a large majority of the State. There are hundreds of men who all the week take no stimulants until they have ended their week's work. They go home, clean, have their dinner, then retire to have a glass or two of beer ... The W.C.T.U. ought to be satisfied. They have 6 o'clock closing, and all have settled down to it. Why bring the matter up again?

Under the heading of "Temperance Workers Celebrate", the *Advertiser* of 2 July 1932 reported on further wowserish endeavours:

> In celebration of the signing of the first local abstinence pledge by seven men of Preston on September 1 1832, the Prohibition League is conducting a two day Centenary Fair in the Adelaide Town Hall ... The president (Mrs. F.W. Dinnis) said that the purpose of the fete was to raise funds to prosecute the fight for Saturday 10 o'clock closing of liquor bars.

The annual convention of the W.C.T.U. at Willard Hall in 1945 included reports by "lounge combers"—pairs of temperance ladies who made "authorised visits" to report on "what they had seen". The *Advertiser* of 14 September 1945 reported that there were thirty of these moral vigilantes, some of whom reported on "demoralising scenes". The convention clamoured for the abolition of hotel lounges and drink waitresses. However, a Victorian visitor "admitted that she had not seen anything 'very dreadful'".

Despite the prayers and interference of the temperance crusaders and their like, sin still managed to exist in early twentieth century Adelaide. For instance, the *Advertiser* of 5 May 1931 solemnly reported on a bookmaker caught in the act: "Entering a locked bedroom at the Hotel Grenfell through a verandah window on Saturday, Mounted Constable Garrihy found a man sitting by a telephone. He arrested the man for betting." The unfortunate bookmaker was fined fifty-six pounds, five shillings. Delinquents could still be flogged, but the punishment was rarely given. The *Advertiser* of 10 October 1932 reported: "Before Mr. Justice Napier ... ordered ... the two men found guilty of the Gouger Street hold up in August to be whipped, that form of punishment had not been administered for three years."

Adelaideans of this period could be radical enough, despite our common assumption that the pre-war city was stifled by conformity. There was a move, fortunately frustrated, to demolish the Town Hall and replace it with some modern excrescence. There was even a proposal in 1933 to move Queen Victoria's statue as a traffic hazard, and the question of removing the governor from Government House on North Terrace was seriously debated in the City Council and the government in 1924. The *Register* of 7 July 1925 reported under the heading "Discussion in Council":

> The Government wanted the whole of the Domain. Both Liberal and Labor Governments desired the removal of the Governor's residence. The late A.H. Peake, when Liberal Premier, had been prepared to take the whole of the domain as a national memorial, and the present Labor Government was prepared to do the same.

Cr. Lundie: "What rates do they pay?"

Cr. Bruce: "They don't pay any ... the question is whether it is proper to use Government House for another purpose."

Cr. Lundie: "We want it for workshops."

[It was thought that a soldiers' memorial could be established there].

Cr. Edwards said: "The only people its removal would inconvenience would be the few gentlemen who attended the levees, when they dug out hideous hats, and paid their respects to His Majesty the King. Then they were in a hurry to get back to their offices. From the social aspect, what could be more pleasant than to have Government House at Fullarton, where the nobility could pay their calls, hidden from the vulgar public eye.

Councillor Lundie, a Labor man, went further to argue for the removal of all the public buildings from North Terrace. "It should all be park." In the end the council voted by a substantial majority to leave Government House where it was. Popular feeling would probably have been against banishing the governor to Fullarton or anywhere else. Many correspondents protested against the idea in the press. One wrote: "As all the old landmarks are so rapidly disappearing from Adelaide, I wish also to raise my voice in protest against the proposed removal of Government House. The absence of the flag from the position it has held for so long would simply be a disaster." "Old Traditions" wrote to the *Register* on 3 July 1925 to argue that Government House on North Terrace "helps to inculcate a deep-seated spirit of loyalty" among passers-by "who are not fortunate enough to visit the homeland".

Meanwhile the Adelaideans, royalist and republican, employed and unemployed, enjoyed their traditional recreations, prominent among which were window shopping and eating. The *Advertiser* of 5 October 1932 recalled when there was a traffic jam in Rundle Street as the citizens peered at the "masterpiece" of a window dresser possessed of "the latest American ideas". The masterpiece "was a little Japanese lady standing in a bower of wistaria ... contrived from handkerchiefs". As for eating, the *Register* of 1 August 1925 declared, with some emotion: "*Special Afternoon Teas.* Visitors to our State have frequently been heard to remark 'Ellis Cafes are something for Adelaide to be proud of, as they compare very favourably with those of either Melbourne or Sydney.'" These cafes, "around which the social life of Adelaide so largely centres", were about to revolutionize the urban scene with their "delicious home made cakes, cinnamon and savoury toast, hot scones etc." If Ellis Cafes are to be believed, Adelaide's cinnamon toast-based social life in the 1920s would have gratified Founder Angas, if not Founder Light.

Even during the depression of the early 1930s, when over 25,000 men were on relief and the City Council had to enact by-laws on the erection of "humpies" by the Torrens, there was evening entertainment for those with money to buy tickets. For instance, during 1931, the citizens could listen to Peter Dawson in "Armed to the Teeth". The *Advertiser* of 4 May 1931 remarked on this favourite local son: "Still almost as brilliant as a raconteur, a purveyor of joviality, clever quips and good natured banter as a singer, Mr. Peter Dawson is returning 'armed to the teeth' with songs. He has not changed much since he was here in 1919. That boyishness Adelaide knew, when he was a member of St. Andrew's Church choir (Wakefield Street), is still there." Or people could go to "Uproarious Comedy" at the Majestic where Winnie Lightner's "tomboy style of comedy" was on display in "The Life of the Party". Charlie Chaplin's "City Lights" was screened at the Wondergraph; the Adelaide Repertory Company put on Galsworthy's "The Show" and the Commercial Travellers' Association had its fifth annual ball at the Railway Dining Hall.

And, through all the vicissitudes of the period, old Adelaide occasionally broke up into transports of decorous gaiety, as at the Armistice of 1918, and every New Year's Eve. The *Register News-Pictorial* wrote a breezy piece about the junketing round the Town Hall on 1 January 1931—the end of a bad year and the beginning of a worse one: "'Happy New Year,' said the Lord Mayor. 'Hurrah!' yelled a thousand or so voices in something like unison, from the throng that gathered at the Town Hall, then 'Happy New Year!' Then the clock chimed and across the way pink and green rockets were let off from a roof top and coloured fireworks and flares made a brilliant scene." The "furthermost squatter" was linked by radio with the Town Hall as "hooters roared, squeakers wheezed and streamers were thrown". Rundle Street was crammed with "jesters" and "young men and their maids" walked about and sat down when they were tired. "Some fancy dresses appeared, to make it the gayer." The "courageous sentiment" of the revellers was: "It was a bad year, 1930. We must see through the next."

THE SECOND WORLD WAR

The Second World War brought considerable industrial stimulus and diversification to Adelaide, worries over defence (trenches were dug in Victoria Square), servicemen training at Woodside Camp, munitions factories, and General Douglas MacArthur in Adelaide railway station en route from Darwin to Melbourne. Voluntary enlistments in South Australia exceeded 70,000, including many women. Dazed survivors from the debacle at Singapore were temporarily accommodated in the stately rooms of the South Australian Hotel. Ship building at Whyalla was expanded. Italian and German prisoners of war from the Middle East were interned near Barmera. Adelaideans were subjected to blackouts and encouraged to collect scrap metal and dig slit trenches. Petrol, meat, sugar, butter, and tea were rationed. There were rumours of Japanese landings on the Coorong at one stage but in fact the state and city remained unviolated. South Australia was remote from the areas of conflict, and the only local enemy action appears to have been a Japanese submarine shelling of a merchant ship off the south-east coast.

Adelaide received the news of the end of the war with a huge collective sigh of relief and another outburst of restrained frolickings in King William Street. The *Advertiser* of 11 August 1945 remarked how "the City streets resounded with the cheers and laughter of thousands of people", and went on:

> More than 1,000 people—girls in evening dress, servicemen and civilians—joined hands in King William Street and sang "Auld Lang Syne", then, with their numbers increasing every minute, they formed themselves into a cheering procession, led by three sailors, and marched along King William Street, Rundle Street, Grenfell Street, and back to the centre of the city ... At 1 a.m. a long crocodile of cheering, singing servicemen and civilians was still moving slowly up and down King William Street ... Girls on the Adelaide Telephone Exchange reported that from the moment radio stations broadcast the first news of the Japanese willingness to surrender, the switchboard had become "just one mass of light".

With the war giving the final touches, Adelaide had greatly changed from the sober little agricultural service centre of a city which had ambled into the twentieth century. Suburbs, many of them containing industrial areas, had submerged the paddocks beyond the parklands for many miles in a surge that was to grow more powerful in the postwar years.

The city's industrial and commercial infrastructure was now much more varied and complex. Premier Playford later described how this transformation had come about: "On the Governmental side, it has been achieved by encouragement and assistance to industry, development of our resources and improvement of living standards. On the production side, it has been accomplished by wise management and a contented labour force whose record of industrial stability is unequalled elsewhere in the Commonwealth." The changes must have seemed radical enough to any citizen living through these years. But they seem minor when compared with the changes that were to come in the hectic postwar period, when the population of Adelaide and district, so slow to grow hitherto, was to more than double.

POSTWAR IMMIGRATION

The federal government was badly rattled by the Japanese menace to its empty northern and interior spaces during the Second World War. Elements of xenophobia, racism, and sheer concern for Anglo Saxon survival were contained by the popular concept of "the Yellow Peril". Moreover, Australia believed that she needed more settlers for economic growth. The result was the extraordinary assisted immigration scheme, zealously begun by Arthur Calwell in 1947, which from that year to March 1973 brought 1,907,298 free or assisted immigrants to Australia. Of this total, 1,061,026 came from the British Isles, but the remainder, an increasing proportion of non-British settlers, hailed from the countries that had free or assisted passage agreements with Australia. These countries included Italy, Greece, the Netherlands, and Turkey. Approximately 215,000 assisted immigrants of all nationalities came to South Australia. There were, too, many thousands of immigrants who paid their passage.

Adelaide, resolutely re-aligned away from primary production to secondary industry by Playford, welcomed these new settlers. The city's ingrained Britishness probably made it more attractive to British immigrants who soon made an Old Country enclave of the new city of Elizabeth in the north and at Christies Beach, another Housing Trust development, in the south. Italian and Greek settlers may have been predisposed to settle in South Australia because of climatic familiarity. At all events, they settled in large numbers, especially in older inner suburbs like Norwood and Unley where drab little decayed villas and small shops were revolutionized by Mediterranean *brio*. Adelaide's tradition of industrial stability, comparatively cheap land prices, and the cheap rented houses built by the Housing Trust were further inducements to immigrants to choose South Australia. Moreover, there were, for several years, plenty of jobs for immigrants.

The years from 1945 to 1969 cover a period of remarkable growth and change in Adelaide's history. Most obviously, it grew in all directions, save where steep slopes, salt bush, or the sea inhibited the developer. The keynote was industrial growth in an economic climate that was generally buoyant and confident. The pipeline which carried Murray water from Morgan to Whyalla was completed in 1944, and the pipeline from Mannum to Adelaide in 1954. Full scale production of the Holden car began in 1948, and work on the Woomera rocket range started the same year. Private firms took over the munitions factories for the products of peace, especially electrical goods. Rationing of certain goods persisted for a while but came to an end in 1950 when rationing of petrol, butter, and tea ceased. The airport at West Beach was opened in 1955: curiously the government preferred the suburban name to that of distinguished local aviators, such as Sir Ross Smith, The State Electricity Trust was established in 1946.

The city landscape changed markedly as old buildings in the busy parts of the city were annihilated to make way for clinically functional high-rise towers. The T. &. G. Insurance building was the first of the series of angular towers which has turned the northern end of King William Street into a windy canyon. As Rundle Street and its peers went modern, much of the rest of the city proper was neglected. It declined in population and became down at heel, while retaining a seedy charm. The growth was in the suburbs beyond the parklands, where industrial expansion coupled with heavy immigration from overseas and population drift from the rural areas spurred land devouring leaps by suburbia. The Playford government's policy of allowing bank loans only on new houses resulted in the lamentable decay of the old villas in the city and inner suburbs. While parts of the city's heartland died as residential areas, energy was concentrated on the mobile frontiers of development. As a result, Adelaide's natural environment, especially the hill slopes, coastline, and southern vales, suffered more destruction and aesthetic ruin in these few years than they had in all the previous period of settlement. Urban ugliness, as pioneered by Sydney and Melbourne, appeared extensively in Adelaide for the first time.

Meanwhile, in the country, storage silos for wheat had changed the face of the wheat industry. In 1962, exports of bulk wheat exceeded exports of bagged wheat for the first time. There were prosperous times for vignerons and cattlemen, and even some good years for the wool and lamb industries. However, labour-saving machinery coupled with the attractions of Playford's industrialized Adelaide took much of the life out of many country townships.

The city had changed substantially. That mordant observer, Donald Horne remarked in *The Lucky Country* (1964): "Adelaide has moved into the technological age. Despite the tradition of conservatism it is a go-ahead place where industries migrate. Much of it is now noisy, dirty and confused; people now work there who may not have heard of the old families, and the new class of managers and experts provides a new social force."[1] A snap judgement, perhaps. Horne should have been more specific about Adelaide's "tradition of conservatism", because in constitutional and political matters it had often shown the way to the other capitals. But on the whole it was a fair summary of the new appearance of a city reshaped by a dominating premier. Adelaide had lost much of its grace and cosiness. It had become more similar to Melbourne and Sydney and Brisbane. Its rulers had decided, reasonably according to their lights, that progress meant more people, more products, more machines. To achieve this, against severe geographical handicaps, they had provided an improved water and electricity supply, mass produced housing, and stable government. The eccentric, pietistic town that had jogged for years on the sheep's back or the wheat dray was now a marker pin on the map for multinational corporations like General Motors Holden and Chrysler. All round this new, strident Adelaide, vineyards, market gardens, and almond orchards vanished beneath rented or heavily mortgaged homes for the labour force.

Amid all the helter skelter of change, however, the strong personality of the old Adelaide soon influenced the newcomers. By Australian standards, the city remained markedly sedate. The entrenched hostility to "immorality" still restricted drinking hours. When the Festival of Arts was first held in 1960, some visitors were dismayed by the curbs on liquor and the paucity of good restaurants. The Totalizator Agency Board was not established until 1967. There was no motel in the city until the 1960s. And Adelaide was still conspicuously loyal to the crown. When Queen Elizabeth II came to Adelaide in 1954, the first reigning monarch to visit South Australia, the city went into transports of loyalty recalling the flag-waving extremes which accompanied the earlier visits of Prince Alfred and the Prince of Wales. *The Advertiser* of 20 March 1954 used prose almost identical to the florid declamations on Prince Alfred of the *Register* of 1867:

> Yesterday was the people's day in Adelaide, when a crowd of 300,000 streamed into the city to express their loyalty to the Queen and the Duke of Edinburgh during the Royal Progress. The Queen had captured the hearts of South Australians, the Premier, Mr. Playford, said last night … During the Royal Progress it was a flag-waving, friendly crowd, which at times restrained its cheering in awe of the Queen's graciousness and the significance of her position … New Australians as well as the old provided many touching scenes of loyalty, particularly in Hindley Street.

"More than 800 of Adelaide's leading citizens" attended a reception at Government House, 150,000 of the led citizens watched a fireworks display in Victoria Square. The fountain in Torrens Lake was turned on at the precise moment the queen alighted from her plane at Parafield. A team of three artists, six carpenters, two painters, and a seamstress spent eight weeks making the loyal decorations on the South Australian, Gresham, Strathmore, and Berkeley hotels.

There was even a popular song written, "Here's to Royalty", for the *Sunday Advertiser* and broadcast over 5AD. Yet some people were still discontented. "Six Years' Service" of Unley Park wrote to the *Advertiser* of 19 March 1954: "Her Majesty is in Adelaide and I wonder how many people have paused to think how the Cheer Up Society have been overlooked. We gladly slaved to entertain and give meals to the soldiers and airmen of the Empire and our allies during the whole war period—now it seems we are overlooked."

THE PLAYFORD ERA

Much of this post war period was for Adelaide the Playford era. The plain spoken cherry orchardist from the Hills was the city's father figure for almost three decades. The Protestant work ethic incarnate, he epitomized the old Adelaide verities. Son of a long established family that had been prominent in politics and the church, thrifty, parochial, prudent, and morally conservative, Playford stood foursquare against interstate delinquencies such as ten o'clock closing of hotels, lotteries, and the T.A.B. He was sceptical about the value of universities and the arts. "In every sense Sir Thomas Playford is Mr. South Australia", remarked the perceptive Jeanne MacKenzie in her *Australian Paradox* (1962). By this she meant that he exemplified the stuffiness that occasionally made Adelaide the laughing stock of interstate libertarians.

Mrs. MacKenzie quoted an Adelaide journalist, Cliff Eager, who wrote in the *Adelaide Mail*:

> You just can't judge Adelaide and many Adelaide people by the standards of the rest of Australia. You have to accept it as a community that was set in a provincial, self satisfied mould a very long time ago. The ordinary process of industry, speculations, cynicism and dispute, the freedom of thinking, the right to raise hell if you don't agree with something … only partly exists there. The order of life is established there, as it has been for many years … Worth is gauged by the careful, moderate expression of an opinion that conforms and does not disturb or by possession of no independent opinions at all.[2]

All this Mrs. MacKenzie, like many other observers, lays at Sir Thomas's door. Or perhaps a better inference is that Playford spoke and acted accurately for the majority of Adelaideans of his time—even though he was often kept in power by the weighted votes of country voters, small farmers, most of them, with whom his political views chimed in unison.

The Playford voters would not sense the embarrassing undertones of the ludicrous "Ern Malley" trial at the end of which Max Harris was fined for publishing obscene verse. Or the police raid on a wine tasting at the first Adelaide Festival. Or the complexities of the Stuart trial; or Tom Lehrer declaiming that "South Australia has the best government of the 18th Century" from the Festival stage after five of his songs had been banned as "salacious by any standards" by Sir Thomas's chief secretary. To urban and rustic conservatives, the protests of the liberals were but thorns crackling under the pot. And when intellectual visitors like Mrs. MacKenzie criticized Adelaide for "stuffiness, traditionalism and ancestor worship", this could be dismissed as the whingeing of inferior outsiders.

Philistinism and pharisaism—Playford and the Adelaide he ruled could certainly be accused of these and more from one viewpoint. However, from that same viewpoint, the Adelaide social tradition *was* strongly philistine and pharisaic. But this is only half the story. Playford, who ruled with something of the autocracy of Governor Grey, just as potently represented the businesslike dash and legislative audacity that was also part of the Adelaide tradition. Some of his measures, such as heavy state involvement in attracting and controlling industry, and founding Elizabeth and the South Australian Electricity Trust, would be seen as authoritarian socialism in any social context other than Adelaide's. One Adelaide veteran tells me that. Labor men of the time, such as Frank Walsh, confessed that they could never have hoped to achieve such socialistic measures as the nationalization of the state's electricity. Yet much radical change was brought about by this nominally conservative premier. Other examples were his introduction of price controls and strict control of the allocation of building materials. Playford seems to have been not so much a party man as an individualistic, pragmatic, regional potentate whose first loyalty was to his state and city. Through firm direction he industrialized South Australia out of its old role as a mendicant state dependent on federal charity in bad farm seasons to a reasonably prosperous community with an enviable record of industrial peace and expansion. In short, a wowser strong on business efficiency and probity, and as such Playford was the archetype of the man old Adelaide warmly respected. Playford declared with justice in his last policy speech:

> When my Government first took office South Australia was a rurally based economy. We saw the need to develop secondary industries which would provide plenty of jobs and export earnings during seasonal downturns in the agricultural and pastoral industries. Our policy has been to keep taxation and other costs well below those in the eastern States. We succeeded so well that we have turned South Australia from the mainland State with proportionately the lowest number of factory workers to the one with the second highest number. Great industries were attracted here, thrived, and have remained the root and branch of our well being ever since.

Yet the old order was changing by the end of this period. Playford's adamantine opposition to relaxation on drinking and gambling almost certainly eroded popular support for the Liberal Country League. Labor came back to government in 1965 after thirty-two years in the wilderness. When Dunstan succeeded Walsh as premier, he struck at the roots of Adelaide wowserism with such measures as allowing lotteries and the T.A.B. and permitting pubs, for so long scourged by the Woman's Christian Temperance Union, to stay open until 10 p.m. A strong indication of the changing mood of Adelaide was that when the Liberal Country League returned to power in 1968, it too, was reformist, as in such measures as the relaxation of the abortion laws and a more equitable electoral redistribution.

31. Adelaide's first railway station, built in 1856.

32. Rundle Street about 1860. Twenty years earlier the streets had been likened to ploughed fields. Note the tethering posts and the now famous name, Chappell & Co., on number 54.

33. North Terrace in 1864, showing Scots Church which, with its splendid weathercock, still stands.

34. King William Street in 1865.

35. Adelaide from the Torrens River at Southwark about 1865. The river—mud holes in summer and flooded in winter—was a pol[l?] eyesore. It was not until the 1880s that Mayor Smith created the Torrens Lake. Note the water cart in the foreground: for many years ditch was Adelaide's water supply.

36. Aborigines encamped on the south parklands in 1865. Citizens complained to the *Register* in the early days about Aborigines cutting d[o?] parkland trees, and the editor, Stevenson, deplored their "beastly corrobories". The last member of the Adelaide Kaurna tribe died a few y[ears] after this photograph was taken.

37. A typical pioneer's bark and slab hut in the nineteenth century—the hard and often dreary and squalid reality of life for many in the bush. In front of the hut is a bullock team, the only early transport for heavy goods, and behind are ring-barked trees. From a postcard in the possession of Mrs. Sadie Pritchard.

38. Adelaide Town Hall just after its completion in 1866, with the old market in the background. The Town Hall was designed by Edmund Wright, a former mayor, who admired Italian buildings. It got the corporation into debt but has always been a source of pride to Adelaideans.

39. Government House from King William Street in 1867. One outraged lady wrote to the *Register* to complain of the language used by bullock drivers like the character in the foreground of this sketch.

40. City ball to honour the visit of Prince Alfred, Duke of Edinburgh, in 1867. This illustration of the grand occasion is somewhat idealized—by all accounts the ball was a hot and fearsome crush. The much feted Prince proceeded to Sydney where he was shot by O'Farrell, an Irishman. Prince Alfred recovered; O'Farrell was hanged.

41. The Railway Hotel, North Terrace, in 1873—humble ancestor of the huge hotels now in that area.

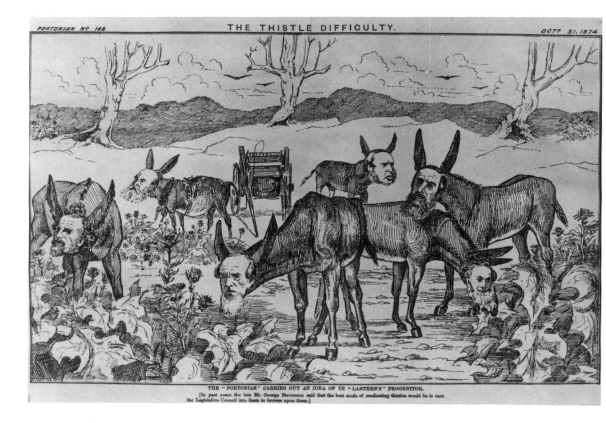

THE "PORTONIAN" CARRIES OUT AN IDEA OF YE "LANTERN'S" PROGENITOR.

[In past years the late Mr. George Stevenson said that the best mode of eradicating thistles would be to turn the Legislative Council into them to browse upon them.]

THE CITY PIGS.

42, 43. Two satirical cartoons from the *Portonian* of 1874 which portray the city fathers and legislators most disagreeably. "The City Pigs" makes no bones about Adelaide's pollution problems.

44. Striking aerial view of Adelaide from *The Illustrated Sydney News* of July 1876. The open plains beyond the parklands are now densely settled (see illustration 117 for a similar view one hundred years later).

45. Rundle Street in the 1870s. It was never expected that this narrow street (now a mall) should become Adelaide's main shopping street. The trams were drawn by two horses and drivers could be fined for exceeding 10 m.p.h. or for carrying prostitutes.

46. Thomas Worsnop, an energetic nineteenth century town clerk. He published his *History of the City of Adelaide* in 1878.

47. South Australian Aborigines about 1880. Their degeneration to fringe dweller status is already marked, and they wear cast off clothes and government issue blankets.

48. North Terrace, from East Terrace, about 1880. The large building centre was the School of Mines, now the South Australian Institute of Technology. Beyond it are the Mitchell building of the recently founded university and the museum building.

49. Sir Samuel Davenport, a pioneer who made good as landowner, farmer, and legislator, stands proudly before his mansion, Beaumont House, in 1880. He lived there from 1856 to 1906.

50. Sir Edwin Smith, an active Adelaide businessman and philanthropist. As mayor in the early 1880s, Smith had the Torrens Lake created and cleaned up the neglected squares and parklands.

51. The Royal Agricultural Show on the parklands near Frome Road in 1884. At least until the Second World War Adelaide's prosperity depended heavily on primary production. At shows such as this inventions like Ridley's Reaper and the stump jump plough were exhibited and admired.

52. Crowds in Jetty Road, Glenelg in the early 1890s with the train from Adelaide on the right. Like the English, Adelaideans did enjoy the seaside even if they were forbidden to bathe (it was considered immoral) until just before the turn of the century.

53. The Adelaide-Melbourne express steams its way through the Adelaide Hills, around 1900. The first express from Melbourne arrived in Adelaide in 1887, crossing the Mount Lofty Ranges via nine tunnels, two viaducts (shown in this photograph), and a newly constructed bridge over the Murray River. From a postcard in the possession of Mrs. Sadie Pritchard.

54. A wood burning paddle steamer on the Murray, around 1900. The Murray never became a second Mississippi, nor Adelaide a second New Orleans, as some of the founders had hoped, but there was an important and colourful era of steamer trade on the great river. From a postcard in the possession of Mrs. Sadie Pritchard.

55. The unveiling of Queen Victoria's statue in Victoria Square in 1894. Sir Edwin Smith, a former mayor, donated the statue.

56. The draped statue of Queen Victoria in Victoria Square on the day of her funeral in 1901. Adelaide, the most Victorian of cities, deeply mourned her passing.

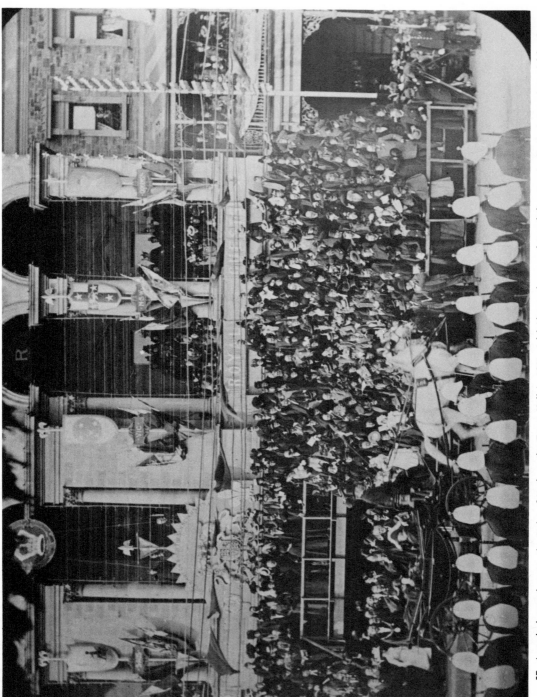

57. A packed crowd greets the Duke of York at the Town Hall in 1901. Adelaideans always welcomed the opportunity to express imperial loyalty.

58. King William Street looking north from the Post Office Tower in the early 1900s. The traffic pace is leisurely and the Town Hall firmly dominates the scene.

59. Looking south across Victoria Square from the Post Office Tower in the early 1900s. At the edge of the square stand the classic facades of the law buildings, and beyond the parklands spread village-like settlements towards Unley and Mitcham.

60. Departure of the Bushman's Corps for the Boer War from Adelaide Railway Station in 1900. Fifty-nine of them were killed. Next to the station is the Legislative Council Chamber and in the background the new Parliament House, which was finally completed in 1939.

61. The unveiling of the war memorial on the corner of North Terrace and King William Street on 6 June 1904. This was for the Boer War: Adelaide had been "blooded".

62. Lord Kitchener inspects Boer War veterans on the Government House lawns in 1910.

63. Workmen laying tram tracks and erecting poles in Victoria Square for the electrification of the tram system in 1908.

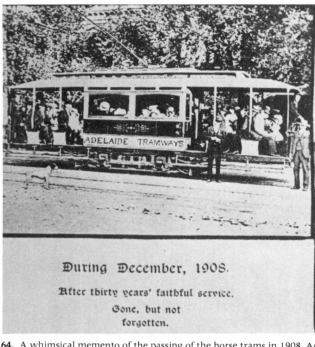

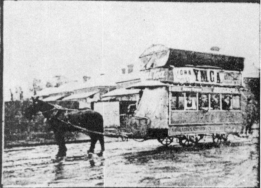

In Affectionate Remembrance

OF THE

ADELAIDE HORSE CARS

Which succumbed to an
electric shock.

During December, 1908.

After thirty years' faithful service.
Gone, but not
forgotten.

64. A whimsical memento of the passing of the horse trams in 1908. According to one critic, it was not uncommon for tram horses to be severely flogged, or even to founder between the shafts. Their supplanters, the electric trams, are now a receding memory.

65. Excited straw hatted cyclists ride convoy to Adelaide's first electric tram. From a postcard in the possession of Mrs. Sadie Pritchard.

66. North Terrace about 1910 with Scots Church on the left. Adelaide was still a city of warehouses and dominant churches.

67. Once more the necks crane, the plumes flutter and bunting dangles over King William Street for a royal visitor. This is the presentation of addresses to the Prince of Wales at the Town Hall, July 1920. The Prince Alfred Hotel, on the right, is a loyal reminder of Adelaide's first royal visit by Prince Alfred, the Duke of Edinburgh, in 1867.

68. The Bee-Hive corner in the 1920s. This building still stands at the hub of commercial Adelaide but is dwarfed by the towering high-rise up King William Street.

69. A busy King William Street in the 1920s with cars and trucks jostling with trams and pedestrians.

70. Official opening of Parliament House, home of the Legislative Assembly, in 1939. The building, in an uncompleted state, had been used for some years. Note the much older Legislative Council building beyond.

71. Folk dancers representing (from left) the Latvian, Polish, and Dutch communities at the 1972 Adelaide Festival of Arts. Since 1945 non-British migrants have had a growing and welcome influence on the Adelaide lifestyle. Photograph by courtesy of the Adelaide *Advertiser*.

72. South Australia's premier Sir Thomas Playford in 1958 speaking to the parliament he dominated for twenty-six years. Photograph by courtesy of the Adelaide *Advertiser*.

3

MOSAIC OF
A COMMUNITY

Commerce and Industry

"Look Johnny! This is how much we took today!"
Otto Peters to John Martin on the opening day of John Martin's, 1866

Trade follows the flag was a respected maxim of the British Empire. The founders of Adelaide, typical of their country, class, and period, were such unabashed commercialists that trade actually preceded the flag in South Australia. The whalers of the South Australian Company were already operating from Nepean Bay, Kangaroo Island before Hindmarsh proclaimed the new province at Holdfast Bay.

It was axiomatic to the Wakefieldians and to other British colonizers that for a settlement to succeed it must set up a sound economic base. As soon as possible, a proper colony should work its way free of financial dependence upon the Mother Country, then delight the old lady by sending her raw materials to fuel her industrial revolution. The founders of South Australia took pains, through pamphleteering, planning, and the proclamations of the Colonization Commissioners, to show that their province would be different, economically and otherwise. Its probity and respectability would be embedded in good business. Angas's South Australian Company, soon involved in shipping, farming, banking, building, fishing, and general commerce as well as whaling, was the mentor and facilitator of early Adelaide.

Stephens declared in his *Land of Promise* in 1839: "There never was a colony which within the same time had assumed one-tenth part of the outward signs of an independent community ... trusting to its own resources."[1] This confident statement was made a few months before Adelaide was almost ruined by a serious economic crisis brought about by speculation, inexperience, and some maladministration. Yet the city did survive, and prosper, just as it was to survive later depressions. This indicated a certain acumen and solidity which brought the shrewder commercialists through the buffetings of droughts and unstable world markets, and allowed them to thrive in kinder days.

From the first and right up to the present day, Adelaide has been the commercial queen bee of the province. Adelaide was proclaimed and occupied as a city well before it had a sound commercial base, and even before agriculture and grazing were properly established in the surrounding rural areas. There was a marked tendency here, as in all the major Australian towns, for immigrants, many of them city-bred, to stay in or near the urban centres if they possibly could. Trollope in the early 1870s was one of the many visitors who commented on this, and he singled out Adelaide as the worst example of a comparatively overcrowded city sitting on the edge of a vast and almost uninhabited colony. The acute over-urbanization of Australia, even more excessive today despite the official talk about decentralization, was apparent from the beginning.

THE RURAL INDUSTRIES

It was only when the hardier and more ambitious souls moved out into the bush with their flocks and ploughs that Adelaide became secure. Right up to quite recent times, the city was able to exist only because of rural industries, notably mining and wheat farming, often carried on hundreds of kilometres from Rundle Street. Yet the city remained and remains overweeningly dominant over the countryside which underpins its economy. It never crossed the minds of the Burra "Snobs" actually to live in Burra. They made their stately way from their city mansions to the hot little mining town once a year to partake of directors' port and patronize the miners who crawled in unimaginable depths with candles stuck in mud on their helmets to dig out copper. Similarly, the great pastoral families rarely lived on their remote properties, but enjoyed their incomes in Adelaide. Yet basically, it was the isolated miners, shepherds, cockatoo farmers, and agricultural labourers who made possible the banks, insurance offices, and shops of the city.

The Wakefieldians had expected that their new province would depend mainly upon the farming and pastoral industries. Angas encouraged the South Australian Company to import sound Devon bulls and heifers, and Saxon-Merino, Southdown, and Leicester sheep. McLaren built the new wharf named after him and a road across the swamps so that Port Adelaide could replace Port Misery. Stock were shipped in from Van Diemen's Land, or overlanded from New South Wales by way of the Coorong or the Murray Valley.

The first export of wool, a small clip valued at 770 pounds, was shipped out in 1838. Only three years later, in 1841, South Australian wool exports were valued at 36,225 pounds. The pastoral industry grew rapidly, although there were setbacks in drought periods. By 1932, there were over seven million sheep in the state. By 1972, the value of wool exports exceeded $150 million, and of beef, lamb, and mutton, over $37 million.

South Australia had even richer potential for grain crops, especially wheat. The repeal of the British Corn Laws in 1846 was an encouragement and by 1853 breadstuff exports were the province's leading export, valued at 257,144 pounds. In 1972, South Australia exported almost $80 million worth of wheat and $25 million worth of barley.

Colonel Light had foreseen that the province would grow and export "all the produce of Portugal". Light himself, Stevenson, and Hindmarsh were keen gardeners and proved that Mediteranean fruits like olives, oranges, and grapes could thrive in Adelaide. A large variety of fruit crops is now grown in South Australia, the main types being citrus, peaches and apricots, especially in the irrigation settlements of the Upper Murray, and apples in the Adelaide Hills.

As for wine, the state now contains roughly 44 per cent of Australia's vineyards and produces over 60 per cent of the commonwealth's wine. The origins of the wine industry are described elsewhere in this book: the principal production areas are now Adelaide and Southern Vales, Langhorne Creek, Coonawarra, the Barossa Valley, the Upper Murray, and the Clare-Watervale areas. Good, locally grown wine and the culture that surrounds its production add an agreeable, claret-coloured tincture to the Adelaide sense of difference.

From the opening of the Wheal Gawler Mine at Glen Osmond in 1842 onwards, mineral discoveries and mining were always important primary industries, at times the salvation of the city.

THE CITY

Thus Adelaide grew prosperous and filled out its grid iron pattern beside the Torrens by milking, administering, and financing the far flung industries of the interior. While some of its citizens were involved in primary industries like farming in the early decades, the growing metropolis soon concentrated on secondary and tertiary industries, administration, and the retail trade.

Building, naturally, was the first major Adelaide industry. Gouger was advised before leaving on the *Africaine* that the most suitable dwelling for the pioneers would be "a weatherboard house of four rooms, with a loft, constructed of framing, without ceiling or internal linings on account of the harbouring of vermin, a tin-plate roof, perhaps varnished, or otherwise slate, which could be erected for 80 pounds or 100 pounds". Houses like this were brought out and assembled in the city by some of the richer pioneers, but most settlers had to put up with the expedients of the "hutting" period. Necessity, and the survey delays, stimulated a mushroom building boom and the parklands were soon pocked by clay pits and brick and lime kilns. By 1838 there were an estimated 620 dwellings in and around the city.

In 1839 both the Royal Agricultural Society and the Adelaide Chamber of Commerce were formed, and an exchange two years later. Trading was largely carried on through auction marts. J.F. Bennett in his *South Australia* (1843), stated that Adelaide was already recognizable as a city, with the usual professional people and tradesmen, shops and warehouses, land agents, printers, distilleries, breweries, public houses, and so on, and five steam mills for grinding wheat.

The city was almost floored by the depression of the early 1840s, picked up with good harvests and the copper boom, and was unpleasantly checked by drought and speculation in crown lands in 1865. The satirical weekly *Pasquin* summed it up:

> Again to flourish and again to fail,
> Again to whitewash and again to jail,
> Again to idle and again to sail,
> Again returning with the homeward mail,
> The vicious circle made from head to tail.

Still, there had been solid and continuing growth. A.A. Simpson summarized the Adelaide commercial scene in 1867 in the *Centenary History of South Australia*:

> By that time the colony contained the Aerated Bread Company's bakery; 7 manufacturers of agricultural implements; bone-dust works; 4 candle and soap makers; 4 chaff and corn cutters worked by steam; 14 coach manufacturers; 10 cordial manufacturers; 3 dye works; 3 hat manufacturers; ice works; 3 jam manufacturers; an olive oil manufactory; 6 organ and pianoforte makers; 5 breweries; 8 foundries; 18 printing presses, 9 sawmills (steam); and a tannery. There were also 151 wholesale stores ... 184 offices of professional men and companies; 137 builders; timber, iron, stone and livery stable yards, and 1,118 retail shops of all kinds.[2]

This was modest progress, but some of the more thoughtful Adelaide businessmen were beginning to concern themselves with diversification. The province had dangerous economic limitations. Its survival depended too much upon copper, wool, and wheat with their attendant hazards of unstable prices and demand and drought. It had very little gold and, apparently, no coal. This was much the driest of the Australian colonies. Even in the Adelaide area, water supply had become a worry. There was a feeling that local products and manufactured goods needed more respect and support, not least from the South Australian government.

CHAMBER OF MANUFACTURERS[3]

The result was the formation of the South Australian Chamber of Manufacturers, the first of its kind in Australia, in 1869. The formation meeting consisted of a group of shopkeepers sitting on soap boxes in a disused grocer's shop on the corner of King William and Rundle streets. One of them was J.A. Holden, saddler and ironmonger, whose name is preserved by the major allegedly Australian car. This led to an inaugural meeting at the Town Hall, the election of Samuel Davenport as president, and agreement on ambitious aims:

> To promote the development of South Australian produce and manufactures—
>
> By the collection and diffusion of information relative thereto.
> By affording a medium of communication with private persons and public bodies on all matters which the Chamber may consider of importance.
> By considering any proposed new industry with a view to giving practical suggestions and assistance.[4]

The chamber soon became a gadfly, pressure lobby, and innovator. Its aims and activities bespeak the Adelaide spirit. Of course there was profit in it for the members, but many of them were energetic in commercial good works for the general benefit of the province. Davenport, later knighted, a man of multitudinous interests and enthusiasms, legislator, farmer, orchardist, viticulturist, philanthropist, summed up the colonial Adelaide dream when he declared, as he often did: "The key to happiness lies in industry, moderation and modesty".[5]

Fired by sentiments like these, the chamber became a ubiquitous urger and initiator on practically all commercial and industrial fronts. There seems to have been no end to its interests. It campaigned, often successfully, for diversification of crops and fruits as with Smyrna figs, flax, mustard, chicory, almonds, sugar beet, and olives. It introduced the more docile Ligurian bee. It made possible the establishment of a tweed, flannel, and woollen manufacturing industry at Hahndorf and, later, Lobethal. It encouraged exotic activities like ostrich farming, sericulture (a failure), and the profitable breeding of horses for the Indian Army in the north of the state. It encouraged the wine industry. It coaxed and encouraged various ministries in such matters as improving drainage and water supply, setting up technical education classes, and offering bonuses to industrial innovators. It fought most vigorously to stop the government favouring intercolonial and foreign manufacturers, but to encourage local men to tender for contracts. Even the iron gates for the Botanic Garden had been ordered from Melbourne. By 1876 there were 397 factories in the province, employing over 6,000 workers. The major activities here were mining and smelting, machinery making, and clothing manufacture.

Increasing protection by tariffs, improved communications and transport, help from the commonwealth government after 1901 and, especially, the stimulus of the Great War which reduced British imports and stopped imports from Germany altogether—these and other factors stimulated South Australia's industry to more growth and diversification. The Port Pirie smelters were established in 1889 to smelt the zinc-lead ores from Broken Hill, and to refine gold and silver. By 1933, after severe setbacks during the Depression, South Australia had 1,710 factories, employing 26,348 people with an output worth about 21 million pounds. The production of industrial metals, railway rolling stock, machinery, furniture, housing, printing, clothing, and food constituted the main industries.

However, South Australia was still essentially a primary producing state. The

Liberal Country League had been elected to government in 1933, led at first by Richard Butler and from 1938 by Thomas (later Sir Thomas) Playford. This politically conservative dominance was to last for thirty-two years, yet on the industrial front it was to be extraordinarily radical, almost socialist. The paradox is only explicable in the context of the Adelaide tradition of progressive legislation. In 1936 a group of imaginative public servants, industrialists, and politicians, among whom J.W. Wainwright, the auditor general, was prominent, recognized that South Australia depended too heavily upon primary products. There was serious unemployment and a real fear that the state might lose some of the secondary industries, notably motor body building, it already possessed. It was decided that the answer to these and allied problems was a vigorous policy of state intervention and involvement. This policy still continues. It has brought about an industrial revolution in South Australia within a short period of time and has greatly reduced the state's dependence upon primary production. The Second World War, which brought, among other things, ammunition works to Hendon, Finsbury, and Penfield, ship building to Whyalla, and more clothing factories, helped this process. The fruits of this industrialization policy, with government usually in the role of facilitator and often initiator, include the Housing and Electricity Trusts, reduced company taxation and wharfage charges, the Torrens Island Power Station, the Port Stanvac Oil Refinery, the new city of Elizabeth, and the introduction of natural gas as a fuel. There has been extensive development and diversification in secondary industry. Adelaide is no longer the "farinaceous city". Indeed, at the time of writing, the wheat, meat, wool, fruits, and dairying industries are all struggling with high costs and declining markets. Even the wine industry is uncomfortable.

Adelaide depends more for its prosperity, and even more for its jobs, upon the "consumer durables" industries—motor vehicles, electrical and household appliances. What is bad for Chrysler, at Tonsley Park, and General Motors Holden, at Woodville and Elizabeth, is decidedly bad for Adelaide. The largest single industry in South Australia, and one of the main contributors to industrial growth since 1945, is the motor vehicle industry. At the time of writing, one in five Adelaide workers were employed by the this and related industries, and there was hope that a multi national consortium would set up a factory for four cylinder motor engines in the city.

THE RETAIL TRADE

Adelaide began as very much a town of trade and shops. The pioneers were so obsessed with speculation, buying, selling, jobbing, and haggling that the resultant collapse of the early 1840s almost brought the whole enterprise down round their ears. Adelaide still is the shopping centre for South Australia. Shrewd investment and profitable business were always at the core of Adelaide respectability. Thus as the family businesses grew, boomed during the good years, and survived the recessions which swept away their weaker brethren, then the great traders assumed the influence wielded in their localities by the merchants of the Hanseatic League, or the Rialto in Venice. A cosy nexus joined Rundle Street to the Adelaide Club, the City Council, the governor's levees, and Parliament House.

Of course it took many years and some luck before *dignitas* and *gravitas* were accorded to counter and till. Like the energetic original David Jones in Sydney, the foundation John Martin and Henry Miller of Miller Anderson's began in a humble way. In the 1880s, Twopeny was condescending about Adelaide's shops, although he thought "Steiner and Wendt's silver-ware and jewellery shops have a style of their own which does them immense credit". He remarked that most of the goods sold were British made, that the retailers preferred variety to specialization, and that "in the second rate shops there is often an unnecessary assertion of the shopman's equality with the customer, and a great indifference as to whether he buys or not".[6]

John Martin's, a massive presence on both Rundle Street and North Terrace, famed for its annual Christmas pageant, which began in 1933 and now comprises more than 50 floats and 1,000 marchers, still determinedly loyal to the crown and flying the Union Jack, is perhaps the most essentially Adelaidean of the great retail enterprises. "The Big Store" began as Peters and Martin on 24 October 1866 on premises at 94 Rundle Street. It offered general drapery, clothing, gloves, ribbons, and fabrics "Terms CASH", and trusted "by assiduous attention to business, with small profits, to merit a fair share of patronage". In a full page article on the store in the *Advertiser* of 12 July 1933, someone wrote of John Martin and Otto Peters during the opening day:

> One can imagine these two men, with their high ideals and bold ambitions in their tiny office … in the infant city of Adelaide, penning the words "to inform their friends" … that "by assiduous attention to business" they hoped "to merit a fair share of their patronage". A correspondent in 1866 wrote in to say of the opening:

> My father was the first customer, as he arrived soon after the doors were opened. In the evening, my father again went to the store and arrived just as Mr. Peters had emptied the contents of a Cash Box on the counter, with the jubilant remark, "Look Johnny, this is how much we took today!"

Peters and Martin were certainly assiduous and successful. The partnership was dissolved in 1871 and eventually, in 1889, became a limited company, popularly known as "Johnny's". As early as 1886, it was taking up 27 single column inches for advertisements in the *Advertiser* each week. By 1933 it was taking up 700 inches. It pioneered the wholesale bargain and the big plate glass windows trimmed "in an artistic manner".

The *Illustrated Adelaide News* of October 1880 wrote of the store: "Inside, what with the hurry and bustle of assistants, the eager pushing of customers, and the almost endless heaps of every description of Drapery and Fancy Goods, one could almost imagine it would be impossible to keep order and system in the management of such an extensive concern." In 1875, John Martin's employed 16 male and 16 female assistants, two "Cash Boys", a shopwalker, a clerk and a manager, as well as Bosun the watchdog and a horse drawn delivery van. By 1933, the store had 1,300 staff and 28 delivery vans.

Miller Anderson's, Harris Scarfe's, and Cox Foy's are other prominent Adelaide retailers with long histories. Miller Anderson's, now in Hindley Street, began as Miller and Gale in 1839, a bare three years after proclamation. Henry Miller, one of the founders, placed a large advertisement in the *Register* in 1853, pledging himself to "do for his customers all that capital, perseverance, economy and civility combined can accomplish". He was in "the grocery and drapery line", sold goods "direct from London", and added in a postscript: "Henry Miller will have great pleasure in showing and telling any person the price of any of his articles —a system which he prefers to ticketing, as is well known that ticketed goods are but baits for the unwary." Shop assistants worked long hours. As a concession, Miller Anderson's in November 1878 decided to close at 4 p.m. on Saturdays. Harris Scarfe's began in 1851 and Cox Foy's, originally Foy and Gibson, in 1866.

Rigby's, still Adelaide based and one of the largest Australian-owned publishers in the country, began as W.C. Rigby's bookshop and newsagency in Hindley Street in 1859. Rigby's did well, absorbed Cole's Book Arcade and published many thousands of school books for the state's schools.

Banks and insurance firms have always done extraordinarily well in prudent Adelaide, where the emphasis upon personal savings has usually been higher than in other Australian cities. For example, the Savings Bank of South Australia began in 1848—its first deposit was 29 pounds made by a shepherd; and there was competition from other banks like the Bank of Adelaide, the English, Scottish and Australian Bank, and the Union Bank, of which the busy George Fife Angas was one of the first directors. The T. and G. Mutual Life Assurance Company, still strong in Adelaide, reflected the local leaning to temperance: the T in its title denotes Temperance.

W. Menz and Co., biscuit and confectionery makers, began in Adelaide in 1850, Motteram and Sons, another biscuit manufacturer, in 1875, and in 1903 the firm of Waltons began making their locally celebrated Betty Brown Sweets. Leaver's hats were for many years a feature of the city's commerce. William Leaver founded the firm in Leigh Street in 1849. He later moved to King William Street. The *Advertiser* of 12 July 1933, reminisced:

> Old residents of Adelaide will remember the enormous John Bull type of hat made of tin suspended over the footpath in front of the works ... When Mr. Leaver arrived he brought with him machinery for making hats from animal fur, but owing to lack of material, most of the plant was never used. It was not until 1908 that hats were manufactured in Adelaide from rabbit fur. In the early days it was the fashion for hats to be made to order, but now fur-felt machine made hats are worn by 90 per cent of men.

Another dominant commercial presence, now gone, was that of James Marshall and Company ("of Adelaide and London") of Rundle Street. Myers later took over the store. The *Register* of 26 August 1910 gushed:

> *Spring Millinery.* Last spring it was written of James Marshall and Co.'s millinery department that it was like a gorgeous garden. That was a fitting description of the rare beauties of the models. Well, this year Marshalls are presenting a pageant unequalled in the splendid history of the firm ... What trained skill, what studied ingenuity, what superb delicacy are lavished on ladies' hats!

The press was clearly anxious to keep its advertisers happy. Marshalls placed innumerable full page advertisements, as did other now vanished Rundle Street traders, like Charles Birks and Co., Craven and Armstrong, and Hall and Savage.

Immigration, Working and Living Conditions

I seem to have fallen on my legs. Here am I, the very first day that I set foot on Australian land, engaged at two pounds a week.
C.H. Barton, 1853

The workingman is a great power everywhere in Australia, but South Australia is his paradise. He has a hard time in this world, and has earned a paradise.
Mark Twain

Some cautious generalizations can be made about Adelaide's people for most of the city's history. They have tended to be predominantly young, which is typical of any immigrants' city. There were also originally somewhat more men than women, although planned immigration ensured that, compared with the other colonies, South Australia's population was better balanced.

The great majority of South Australians have always lived in or near Adelaide. From foundation to statehood and up to the 1930s most—well over 90 per cent—South Australians were British or Irish born, or Australian born of British ancestors. Some non-British European immigrants arrived in the 1930s and very many more during the great postwar drive for migrants beginning in 1947. Adelaide—that is, the whole metropolitan area—more than doubled in size from 1947 to the present day and a substantial number of the newcomers were Greeks, Italians, Yugoslavs, Dutch, Poles, Germans. The 1966 census shows that of a total state population of 1,091,875, no less than 245,948 were born in overseas countries. In other words, almost a quarter of South Australians were immigrants.

During the foundation period, the majority of Adelaide people had been born in the British Isles. Later the proportion of Australian born people in Adelaide rose to an average of about 90 per cent, until the postwar immigration programme, which has only recently eased, increased the immigrant component again.[1]

The general image of early Adelaide is of an almost entirely British population, sober and respectable, hailing mainly from southern England. The reality was rather more variegated and raffish. The Adelaide citizenry in 1840 represented quite an ethnic mix as described by Governor Grey in his letter of 16 January 1845:

> The European population are collected from almost all parts of the world. They were wholly unacquainted with one another previously to their arrival here— you meet Scotsmen in kilts and plaids—Irish women without their bonnets and blue cloaks thrown over their heads—Germans in their national costume and very picturesque they are (we have about a thousand Germans here who have abandoned their country on account of religious persecution), Chinese with their wide trousers, Indians in different costumes, Natives with kangaroo skin cloaks, Frenchmen, Runaway Convicts who have come overland, with large beards and a bush appearance, Catholic priests (and now a Catholic

Bishop), English country dandies, all mixed in our streets—all accustomed to different laws and usages, all ignorant of one another, of the country into which they have come, of its seasons, of its soils and their different degress of productiveness (indeed, until lately of those that would grow here), never accustomed to act in unison, having no common interest, ignorant of the nature of the Government under which they have come to live, of the personal character and capacity of their Governor who had arrived from the other extremity of the earth to govern them they did not know how—Such was the nature of the society into which I was thrown—moreover when I arrived great distress prevailed.[2]

Grey may have exaggerated, for he would probably have been at pains to show that his autocratic rule was justified by thus emphasizing the backwardness of the Adelaide citizens. However, it seems that early Adelaide fell considerably short of Wakefield's dream of a community of Anglo Saxon squires, merchants, and artisans. At all events, much of Grey's Tower of Babel moved on to the goldfields in the early 1850s and the bourgeois British norms of Adelaide reasserted themselves .

EARLY IMMIGRATION

The Colonization Commissioners, before they were discredited and abolished, recklessly poured emigrants into Adelaide before the city was planned and before the country surveys were made. During 1839 alone, they shipped 5,230 assisted immigrants to Adelaide, all guaranteed jobs or maintenance, to the little settlement of tents and huts, thus forcing Gawler into heavy expenditure, the abandonment of the self-supporting principle, and his eventual disgrace. Assisted immigration ceased during the ensuing depression, was revived on a smaller scale by Grey when conditions improved, and was later expanded as the province found prosperity. Money from landsales—and these boomed during the copper mining furore—was used in the Wakefield tradition to assist immigration with the Act for the Sales of Waste Lands of 1842. By 1845, land sales had contributed 32,000 pounds to the Emigration Fund and South Australia was assured of a generally consistent and adequate supply of assisted immigrants for most of the colonial period.

This did not stop the grumbles, of course, especially when labour was scarce for mining or agriculture. During Robe's period of office, would-be employers gathered together 2,000 pounds to ship in cheap Chinese labour from Hong Kong. The governor did not agree, preferring his equally unsuccessful scheme to settle superannuated militia men from all over the Empire in South Australia to give the province, no doubt, a ruddy military complexion.

South Australia was always well publicized by its friends in Britain, by men like Angas, Smillie, and Stephens who wrote glowing books and pamphlets, went on lecture tours, and stressed the morality, job opportunities, good weather, and general perfection of the province. Even ageing sahibs of the Raj were entreated to bring themselves and their capital to retirement in sunny and respectable Adelaide.

There was never much difficulty, even at the beginning, attracting middle-class ideologists and speculators like the Morphetts, the Elders, and the Hacks to South Australia, for reasons that have been stressed. The emphasis in the immigration campaign was upon the lower strata of society, upon the tradesmen, shopkeepers, miners, small farmers, servants, and labourers who were needed in large quantities before the newfound Adelaide aristocracy could relax in their bluestone mansions.

The authorities wanted "no idlers, no drunkards and no paupers". Angas wanted "pious people" and, on the whole was extraordinarily successful in getting them. He loaned 8,000 pounds to the Lutheran German refugees to enable them to settle in the province—and then, for he was a businessman too, provided them with land on his estates at 12 per cent interest so that they were bound to him as tenants for more than thirty years. (In retrospect, Angas has been criticized for his 12 per cent. In fact, this was a low interest rate by the standards of the time.)

Angas interviewed scores of British prospective emigrants himself and made sure that most of the emigration agents, like him, looked for sobriety, piety, and industry in the applicants. He badgered Evangelical ministers to send out the best of their flocks, wrote emigration propaganda for fairs on placards and generally was a supreme urger. Wherever Angas lived for long in England, as in Devonshire, sure enough number of hand picked immigrants would leave that area for Adelaide. Some idea of the influence of Angas and his supporters can be had from the tone of the "Regulations for Labourers wishing to emigrate to South Australia" of the Colonization Commissioners. Not only should the applicant be young and healthy but he "must be able to give satisfactory references" to prove that he is "honest, sober, industrious, and of general good character". He also had to have an acceptable testimonial from a minister, certified by "two respectable householders".

Pike's study of the commissioners' registers shows that assisted immigrants came from all over the British Isles, with the biggest number, 35 per cent, hailing from Sussex, the Home Counties, and London. Twenty per cent came from Gloucestershire, Wiltshire, Dorset, and Hampshire, and 15 per cent from Scotland. The rest originated in the other counties—only 5 per cent came from Northern England and Ireland. Most were townspeople, mainly Londoners, which made their first contacts with bush life all the more painful. Their urban origins also help explain the marked and continuing tendency of the settlers to huddle together in Adelaide rather than brave the rigours of the country.

Pike further shows that 56 per cent of the male immigrants described themselves as agricultural labourers, 20 per cent as building tradesmen, 12 per cent as tradesmen and artisans, 6 per cent as mechanics. Another 6 per cent were miscellaneous, ranging from fishermen to gentlemen. As for the women in these pre-liberation times—apart from wives and mothers—64 per cent were domestic servants, 22 per cent were seamstresses, and a downtrodden 14 per cent were rural labourers.

One Wakefield principle that was generally realized in early Adelaide was that assisted immigrants should be young and that the sexes should be roughly equal in number. Between 1836 and 1840, for example, the commissioners sent out 3,942 men, 3,548 women, and 4,718 children. Of these adults, only 12 per cent were over the age of thirty. Among the "superior class" of settlers who paid their own way, there was a higher proportion of older people and of men, yet according to the census of 1840, out of 14,610 settlers, 7,000 were under twenty-one and only 170 men and 190 women were over the age of fifty.[3] The old history books with their photographs of grey bearded (hardly any photographs of women were used) veteran settlers give the inference that early Adelaide was a geriatric settlement. On the contrary, it was predominantly young. However, by the late nineteenth and early twentieth centuries, the authorities were worried by the increasing proportion of the aged in the city's population. The modern immigration programme has reversed this trend and Adelaide today is, as it was in the foundation period, a city of predominantly young people.

The general parity of numbers between the sexes must have pleased the founding fathers. They wanted none of the eastern colonies' hunt for women or the more dubious aspects of mateship in their province.

OPPORTUNITIES

The "superior class" of settlers could soon acquire land or businesses with reasonable luck. What of the assisted immigrants? Some of them were certainly not, in reality, the hard-working paragons the emigration authorities had looked for. Emigration agents were keen to attain their quota. Some applicants obviously had facile tongues, for a fair proportion of "no hopers" were deposited in Adelaide. "What am I to do with a trumpet maker?" protested Emigration Agent John Brown to Wakefield in a letter dated 10 April 1837. "What is the use of a gin-drinking, half-starved mechanic with vicious habits ... from some of the back settlements of London? ... I have one man on crutches and another with an ankle dislocated for years, both no doubt with medical certificates that they are able-bodied workmen."[4] Brown urged that more attention be paid "to moral and physical character".

Yet the impressions of most observers at this time and in later decades were that the Adelaide immigrants were generally more respectable than their counterparts in Sydney or Melbourne. A. McShane, surgeon, gave evidence in 1840 to a British parliamentary select committee on South Australia. When asked what occupations the assisted immigrants had he replied that they were "agriculturists, small farmers and mechanics generally, and female servants". There was "generally" plenty of work. As for wages, McShane said that labourers could get seven shillings a day, and artisans like stone cutters, masons, and carpenters from twelve to fifteen shillings a day. Were the settlers of a good class? "They were a good class, certainly," replied McShane. Would they go into the interior? Those who came from big cities "would rather hang about the town".

Some of the assisted immigrants did well for themselves. Seventy one-acre city blocks were bought by them when the city land was auctioned off in March 1837. These were often soon subdivided, often with enormous profit, when rampant speculation set it. By 1844, about fifty commissioners' immigrants had managed to purchase 80-acre country sections. After fifteen months in Adelaide, Jacob Pitman, carpenter and assisted immigrant, was able to write to his brother that his newfound wealth comprised "8 acres in Prospect Village, value 160 pounds; 4 acres in Payneham, value 60 pounds" as well as prime pieces of land in Walkerville, Grenfell, and Rundle Streets, not to mention a 40-acre farm "in Hindle Vale, 13 miles south of Adelaide" and his own dwelling. "You must remember", added the prudent Jacob, "that this land is worthless until stocked with labour and capital ... when it will return 1000 per cent."[5]

However, Pitman was obviously shrewder, and luckier, than most immigrants. Thousands broke their hearts in South Australia: homesick, unlucky, feckless, or disorientated. Probably the majority of settlers experienced ups and downs of fortune before achieving a modest stability. In a long letter to his step-brother in England, a Magill market gardener, Henry Grinham or Greenham—"I am sometimes called one, sometimes the other"—describes his colonial adventures between 1837 and 1850. Grinham's history is perhaps typical of that of many settlers of the period. While "out of a situation" in Maidstone, Kent in 1837, young Grinham heard that a convict ship bound for Van Diemen's Land was short of hands. "I thought I would try the country," decided Grinham, a sentiment shared by many footloose young Englishmen at the time.

So he worked his way out to Hobart, where "I was robbed of the suit of mourning I bought when my mother died. It cost me 7 guineas and was as good as new". Next, Grinham hired himself out to a grazier sailing for Port Phillip "which was just being colonized". He thought the infant Melbourne was very pleasant—"Its appearance was like a nobleman's park"—although "At the time I arrived, Melbourne could boast of but one brick house, two weatherboard, with a few sod huts and more tents. There were only seven white women in the colony." At this stage, at least, Adelaide could look down on Melbourne. It had Light's plan, a Government House of sorts, and several buildings, including Osmond Gilles's coveted cottage with a weathervane on top.

Working at a station forty kilometres upcountry from Melbourne, Grinham injured himself with an axe. "I was near losing my great toe." His master sent him to look after the home station. He was alone for three months, except for Aborigines, whom he placated with "damaged tobacco". Grinham expressed the typical settler's contempt for the natives. He expected that his step-brother in England had heard that Aborigines stole because they were starving: "It is no such thing. I never was in any part of the country where they could not get a belly full of the garbage they used to live on before the country was settled, in an hour. Neither are they the innocent, harmless creatures they are sometimes represented—revenge is their darling passion." Grinham spent a number of years as shepherd and sheep farmer. "At best a squatter's life is a kind of half savage life, not fit for a married person with a family." Drought, or a fall in the market or bad luck ruined him often. When this happened, "I took my gun and dog, mounted my horse, and off up the country again to try my luck."

Finally, in the late 1840s, Grinham settled by the source of Third Creek in the hills above Adelaide, where he bought 19 hectares and cleared land for fruit growing.

> I had grapes this year 1 inch in diameter, and plenty of them. I had more than a bushel of apples off one tree that had been planted less than four years. I sold them at 6d a pound—cherries at 1/6d a pound. Gooseberries and raspberries bear as well here in the hills as in England. I have about 300 trees planted—small ones … I grow a great many vegetables between my trees at present, which sell very well—cabbage from 1s to 3s a dozen—cauliflowers about 4s a dozen—potatoes from 4s to 14s per cwt … I keep a team of eight bullocks with which to draw timber from the hills to town for hire.
> With this and what I make out of my garden, I manage to pay my way.[6]

The good opportunities Adelaide offered to imported labourers to stop working for wages and set themselves up as auctioneers, shopkeepers, publicans, and small farmers tended to worsen the labour shortage at times. Wakefield himself protested that the authorities made it too easy "for the labouring classes" to become "market gardeners and cattle rearers". But then, like all organizers of people, his best laid schemes often went agley thanks to human nature. It was this labour shortage that made Grey think of importing convict labour, to encourage unhandy civil servants to help bring the harvest in when enough farm labourers could not be found.

Mineowners had to make vigorous efforts to attract sufficient Cornish and Welsh miners to Burra, Kapunda and Moonta. The goldrush caused an acute labour shortage in the province. All these factors tended to make the Adelaide labourers choosy about the work they did and militant on wages. It also made them less respectful than the middle classes would have hoped, as newcomers like Bull soon found as they got no touched hats and precious few "sirs" on arrival at Port Adelaide.

DEPRESSION AND INDUSTRIAL UNREST

Of course, times were not always good for working class settlers in Adelaide. They suffered even worse than the bourgeoisie during the depression of the 1840s when both work and rations were scarce. Those caught up in speculation soon lost their savings and were destitute. There were other grim times, notably in the 1890s and during the bleak depression of the 1930s when 200 factories closed down, one out of three trade unionists in Adelaide was out of work, and some of the unemployed camped in hessian tents along the Torrens.

Some journalists then as now were eager to sensationalize industrial unrest and to moralize about it. Under the heading of "The Mooch About Brigade", the *Register* of 14 January 1910 stated:

> Despite the fact that the notice board at the Labour Bureau bears a requisition for 100 labourers in connection with the reclamation works on the River Murray, there were scores of able-bodied men passing the time away in the gutter on Thursday. The pay offered is 7/6 a day, or piece work may be undertaken. When asked by a reporter why the job was distasteful to them, several of the unemployed said that they did not like working in water, and that the "tucker" was not good enough.

On 16 March of that year, the *Register* reported with obvious pleasure that the strike of brick layers and masons must soon end because the manufacturers had decided not to supply any more bricks to building sites while the strike lasted. "This means that even those men who are now receiving the 12/- a day demanded by the general body of unionists will be thrown into enforced idleness."

"17 Injured in Battle Between Police and Communist Rioters", blared the *Register News Pictorial*, where the editor seemed to equate protesters with Bolsheviks, on 10 January 1931. "Fierce Conflict Outside Treasury Buildings. Iron Bars, Stones and Pick-handles used ... Policeman's Jaw Fractured, Many Heads Broken." This must have chilled the elderly ladies of Unley Park and Medindie as they sensed Leninism stalking the streets of Adelaide. They were reassured to read further: "Premier sees Fight from Office Window". The struggle surging round the corner of King William and Flinders streets was described as "one of the most serious riots in the State's history". It was "organized by Communists" to protest against the removal of beef from the unemployed's rations. The rioters carried placards saying "Class against Class" and "Down with Imperialism". The police drew their batons. The unemployed threw stones, or bottles and glasses obtained from the Windsor Castle Hotel. The mounted troopers rode up and some of the crowd took refuge in the Post Office. When all was quiet again, Premier Hill "declared that the riot was organized by the Communists".

In the worst days of the depression, some of the unemployed wretchedly encamped on the Exhibition Grounds or near the City Bridge felt themselves driven to political extremes. But red flags and Marxist placards outside the Treasury Building were exceptions to the rule. The rule was that the great majority of Adelaide workers were usually too comfortable to respond to any abstract ideology of the left, beyond using it during times of stress as a bogeyman to extract higher wages from employers.

During 1931, as an emergency measure, the government reduced the basic wage by 10 per cent. This provoked anger, even among policemen. The *Advertiser* reported on 31 January of that year: "'I am amazed that the Secretary of the Police Association should indict his own comrades by concluding that a wage reduction on the same scale as that applied to all members of the Public Service would lead the police to adopt one of the slogans of the Communists, namely the "Go Slow",' said the Chief Secretary, Mr. Whitford, yesterday." The price of bread was cut by a halfpenny: to 4d delivered and 3½d sold over the counter. Gas company workers had to take off one week in five. The federal government granted the state 45,000 pounds to pay for "relief work". Rations were not provided to any single man who earned two guineas or more a week. The weekly rations comprised 4 loaves of bread, 3½ lbs. of meat, sugar, jam or honey, oatmeal, rice or sago, tea, raisins, and soap. The City Council allotted a 4,834 pound grant to employ men to dig ditches and improve footpaths.

Conditions were even worse for many rural workers at the time, for the state was enduring another bad drought. The *Advertiser* organized an "Outback Relief" scheme and reported on 1 May 1931: "Parcels of warm clothing and boots arrived in hundreds yesterday, and all baskets at the city depots had to be emptied several times during the day. Most of them might have told a story, for there were scores of indications that genuine sacrifice and goodwill had gone to the making." The establishment of Kuitpo Colony, now a centre for alcoholics in the depths of the Kuitpo Forest in the Hills, was one measure taken by a hard pressed but inventive government to ease the unemployment situation. The *Advertiser* stated on 3 June 1931:

> Whoever said the days of the colonists were over had not visited "Forsyth's Foresight" at Kuitpo, where sixty single men, eager to find work when none was to be obtained, were given a chance to see whether they had in them some of the iron possessed by the colonists who made the State. They had proved it in twenty different ways. They were turned out on virgin country, heavily timbered ... and in a few months they are as near an approach to a self-supporting colony as is possible with the 500 acres they possess.

Voluntary groups like the Lend a Hand Club, which made clothes "for destitute families", were active during the depression.

Yet on the whole the Adelaide working man was lucky. Even when the city was teetering on the brink of collapse under Gawler and Grey, the immigrants were guaranteed rations by the authorities and some semblance of a job. Australia generally soon became notable for the prosperity of its workers. They achieved good wages, benefits from friendly societies, political representation, and well established trade unions far in advance of their British counterparts. The Adelaide workers shared in this general prosperity: indeed, they were often better off than workers in the other colonies. For example, South Australia was the first to give legal recognition to trade unions, in 1876. In 1894 C.C. Kingston improved industrial relations with a new system of compulsory arbitration.

Again, the savage depression of the 1890s, which closed several banks and burst the biggest of the Australian booms, does not seem to have affected Adelaide as severely as it hit Melbourne or Sydney. Adelaide never had real slums, unlike the other capitals. The strong tradition that the working man should have a decent home was later institutionalized by such developments as the well-planned new suburb, Colonel Light Gardens, which was completed in 1927, and the establishment of the Housing Trust in 1936, which provided good modest homes at a standard rental of twelve and sixpence a week.

As the following extract from the *Register* of 21 August 1925 indicates, the Adelaide workers were certainly not in awe of politicians:

> "Don't you affect that autocratic manner with us! I have 300 or 400 men here who intend to see you now", said Mr. J. Nolan, leader of an unemployment demonstration which invaded a meeting of the Executive Council on Thursday morning, to the Premier (Hon J. Gunn), when the latter ordered them to leave the premises. *Mr. Gunn:* "I have made a promise that I will see you at 12 o'clock." *Mr. Nolan:* "You promised us jobs before this and you have not fulfilled your promise. We cannot rely on you."

Eventually, the premier managed to persuade them to go off to the Destitute Board "for provisions", and locked the door, allowing the cabinet, no doubt deeply shaken by these home truths, to continue its deliberations.

The state government's radical policy of intervening to establish new secondary industries, begun in the 1930s and continued after the war, brought thousands of new workers to Adelaide, attracted by safe jobs and cheap, convenient housing.

Again, there was very little industrial or political violence in Adelaide. The workers there achieved their aims—essentially, a fair share of the good life—with no Peterloo, no Tony Pandy, and very little of the bitter unrest which accompanied, say, the Chartist movement in Britain and some of the industrial conflicts in the other states. Blows were exchanged in the old open elections, but this represented high spirits more than anything else.

The depression of the 1930s was an unusually pinched and bitter time in Adelaide and left a legacy of apathy and ruin. At least the experience stimulated the state government to take active steps to prevent the recurrence of a similar economic breakdown—and at least the sufferings were usually less acute than elsewhere. There was far more rioting, protest marches, and police charges during the anti-Vietnam War demonstrations in the late 1960s and early 1970s—and these were held in times of prosperity and full employment.

STANDARD OF LIVING

For most of its existence, Adelaide was a local centre of government imposed on what was essentially a largish market town servicing a huge rural hinterland. The province's economy was based mainly upon primary production—the wheat, mining, pastoral, fishing, market gardening, and wine industries. Thus the country districts from the 1840s offered opportunities for men of capital to buy or lease land or to finance mining and farming. These industries provided steady and expanding job opportunities for rural workers and miners and the immigration authorities were always anxious to attract suitable labour for the land. When the primary industries slumped, as they often did due to drought or falling markets, then Adelaide suffered. When they prospered, Adelaide smiled.

In the city itself there were usually good opportunities for the "superior class" of immigrants in the professions. Lawyers, doctors, and land agents have always done particularly well in Adelaide, and still do. Obviously, there were excellent prospects in this prayerful town for clergymen. Middle class newcomers with drive, connections, money, and a little luck were soon welcomed to the upper echelons of society. People of humbler origin might scale the steps of respectability by means of a period of industrious shop keeping or, as in the case of John Graham and the other Burra Snobs, by means of inspired speculation.

Surgeon McShane had told the Select Committee in 1840 that Adelaide labourers could expect seven shillings a day and skilled tradesmen from twelve to fifteen shillings a day. This was about twice as high as the current rates in England.

That observant young Oxford graduate, C.H. Barton, who was surprised by the high rate of pay on his first day at Port Adelaide, wrote home to his sister: "I was ferried across the harbour by an old Oxonian who had been a commoner of Christ Church and said his present place was worth more than a studentship. He would not take anything from me when he heard I was a fellow collegian."[7] The Rev. Blacket, ever on the watch for good points about Adelaide, wrote:

> A lady coming up from Port Adelaide in 1840 was complaining of the high price of commodities in the new settlement. A gentleman began to question her as to the evils of which she complained. "My good woman, what price do you pay for meat?" "Oh, sir, it's verra dear. We pay about 10d a pund for't." "And what would you pay for such meat in Glasgow?" "Oh, we wadna pay mair than 5d" "What wages had your husband in Glasgow?" "He used to get twa and twenty shillings a week." "And, pray, what does he make here?" "Oh, sir, he disna mak aboon 13s a day just noo." (£3. 18s a week.)[8]

Some immigrants, then as now, tended to whinge. In good times we hear of legs of lamb being sold for 6d each in Gawler. The Select Committee on South Australia concluded from written evidence that in 1840 tea in Adelaide cost 4s. a pound, bread was 4d a loaf, 7s bought enough vegetables for two persons for a week, milk was 4d a pint, fresh butter was about 2s 6d a pound, and meat was about 1s a pound.

South Australia, after development, has always been lavish in its production of foodstuffs and the Adelaide citizens have usually eaten and drunk well and cheaply. Harcus in 1876 described the abundance of wheat, meat, vegetables, and fruit available and went on: "All these ... which are luxuries to the poor,—and even to a large section of the middle class—in England, are, during the season, the daily food of the poorest in South Australia ... It would do an Englishman's heart good to look upon the breakfast table of a South Australian of moderate means, groaning under the weight of the most luscious fruits."[9] The situation is much the same today, despite inflation, as any recent visitor to England, where severe prices are charged for poor quality exotic fruits, would testify.

Throughout colonial times, then, immigrants usually found plenty of work for wages in or round Adelaide and good opportunities to prosper, given reasonable luck, through private enterprise. Food and accommodation were usually cheap and plentiful. Even during droughts and depression, there was usually more than sufficient to eat. Supply generally exceeded demand in labour, and the workers benefited accordingly. Solidly built cottages of brick or stone could be bought in suburbs like Prospect in the 1870s and 1880s for about 300 pounds. Comparatively, these were much more within the reach of workers than the $30,000 average cost new house of the mid 1970s.

By 1908, as J.D. Gordon's *Handbook of South Australia* shows, some diversification had taken place of the state's industries and the range of job opportunities had widened. Rural workers could expect about £1 a week plus their keep and there was a constant demand for them. However the new industries of Adelaide offered opportunities for industrial workers including fitters, turners, boilermakers, machinists, patternmakers, and the like. To take a few examples, for a forty-eight hour week, cabinetmakers could earn up to £3 12s, machinists up to £3, and general hands up to 50s. Masons and bricklayers could earn 1s 4½d an hour, carpenters 1s 3d, and builders' labourers 1s.

As for the cost of living, in 1908 bread in Adelaide cost 3d a loaf, eggs were 8d a dozen, milk was 4d a quart, rump steak was 8d a pound, bacon 9½d a pound, sugar 2½d a pound, and butter 1s 1d a pound. According to Gordon, accommodation was comparatively cheap, too. The rent for a four-room house within three and a half kilometres of the General Post office was 9s a week, a seven-room house 20s a week. The penny sections on the trams made it cheap for workers to travel round Adelaide.[10]

A Scottish emigration agent, John Wright, enthused about the living and working conditions of Adelaide workers in 1913 and the City Council, it its year book for that year, quoted him with palpable pleasure. After praising the city's plan, beauty, and economic activity, Wright lauded the "wonderful facilities furnished by the city for the enjoyment, sport, health and relaxation of even the poorest citizen". Adelaide was, he thought, "the paradise of the working classes" and he carried home to Scotland "the most delightful memories of one of the most beautiful spots on earth".

WOMEN

Thus far jobs mainly for male immigrants have been discussed. What of the women settlers—usually roughly equal in numbers to men in the immigration programme? The wives, of course, were scarcely ever considered for remunerative work. Like all Victorian British women, especially in colonial conditions, theirs was a life of explicit subordination and, in most cases, of very hard work. The wives of the successful business and professional men, of course, soon gravitated to comfort and tea on horsehair sofas while Irish female domestics toiled in the kitchens. Even these rich ladies had to rough it at first in the "hutting" period on the parklands or in a tent in the scrub while a farmhouse was being built. They were prolific letter writers, for they had plenty of spare time, and there are many letters recording the privations suffered by genteel females, some of whom were nothing like as good-humoured as the diarist Mrs. Thomas, wife of the government printer. Some grumbled about the heat, the dust, the flies, the shops, losing their shoes in Rundle Street mud, homesickness, or having to sell family plate to pay increasingly uppish servants. The *Register* of 8 July 1843 wrote of the sufferings of one "fair correspondent" who frequently had to leave the footpath and "plunge ankle deep" into the mud of the roads to avoid "being gored or run over" by insolent bullock drivers and their beasts. The *Register* remarked that ladies on footpaths were also annoyed by "bakers' carts, butchers' horses and the German people's goat carts". However, these dependent ladies soon bloomed in Adelaide as the wealth began to flow in and solid bluestone walls protected them from the discomforts of colonial society.

The wage-earning immigrant woman had a much harder row to hoe. Governesses were always in demand, but had to be adaptable. When the penniless governess Clara Morison, in Catherine Spence's novel of that name, arrives in Adelaide in 1850, she is warned not to expect too much by Mr. Campbell the merchant. Campbell says:

> ... you must form no extravagant ideas of the remuneration of governesses here. They can get no more than they do at home, and often not so much. They are frequently called upon to assist in household work, and generally are made to act as nursemaids. The only point in which their situation is better than in Scotland is, that their term of service is not generally so long. There is more chance of promotion; but girls should be cautious in that matter, too; for I have seen some governesses make wretched marriages, from not knowing the man's character, and having no one to find out what he was for them.

Eventually, Clara is offered fifteen pounds a year by a hard-eyed Adelaide matron to live in and teach seven rowdy children.

Under the assisted immigration scheme no unmarried woman could be accepted unless she was young, capable of hard work, vaccinated against smallpox, and had a certificate of good character and was accompanied by a near relative. Single women could not be taken on the emigrant ships unless the numbers already accepted were greater than the number of single men on board—such was the commissioners' horror of licence on the high seas and immorality in Adelaide. As domestic servants, which was all that most of them could hope to become, they could expect from twelve to twenty pounds a year, living in, which was from half to a third less than a male servant received. If a girl married a farm worker, the two of them would receive from thirty to forty pounds a year.

It must have been a hard enough life in Adelaide for a poor, single woman: sweated labour, dust and heat to ruin her English complexion, unimaginably far from home. Yet colonial opportunities, as the middle classes often complained, soon broadened the horizons and increased the expectations of both men and women workers. At least they had escaped some of the rigidities of the English class system. In colonial Adelaide, Jack—or Jenny—might soon become as good as their masters given a bit of luck.

There was usually a shortage of "female domestics", so much so that the authorities turned a blind eye to the importation of shiploads of unmarried Catholic Irish women. During the first eight months of 1855, for instance, 2,800 immigrant women reached Adelaide, "of whom", as Hodder puts it, "2047 were Irish, or nearly treble the number of English and Scotch females". Several of these high-spirited girls, not one of whom in Hodder's opinion was "a really good domestic servant",[11] had to be lodged and fed at the government's expense in barracks. Appalled at the potential perils of popery and prostitution, the city fathers petitioned the home authorities to stop sending out Irishwomen. Sir Richard MacDonnell later amused an audience at the Royal Colonial Institute by telling them how as governor he once had to cope with over 4,000 unemployed females:

> I did what I could for them; built them barracks, offered to pay their fare, and all expenses to any employers willing to take them off my hands, for I was sorry to have to add that they were occasionally very unruly. Now, as women in a state of rebellion are not so easily dealt with as men, I might mention that by a happy thought they were on one occasion reduced to obedience by the cooling effects of water from a fire engine.[12]

The whole tone of this speech—the amused tolerance tinged with contempt of the ex-governor beguiling his predominantly male audience with his tale of hosing down wild Irish girls when they were "very unruly"—must make anyone concerned with equality between the sexes seethe. And it was against such attitudes that working women had to struggle in Adelaide as elsewhere. At least it can be said in mitigation that South Australia was the first of the states to bring in votes for women.

On the whole, though, Adelaide was as "male chauvinist" as they come: women do not figure at all in the photographs and biographies of distinguished citizens in books like Pascoe's. Women are mentioned in the old histories merely as adjuncts to their husbands. Clara Morison was expected to teach a little singing, music, and arithmetic as a temporary measure before merging into the conformity of married life. The wives of the Adelaide gentry presided over the servants and organized charity bazaars while their husbands played the stock market and relaxed at the Adelaide Club. The wives of the workers dug the garden and looked after the children while their husbands laboured then repaired to one of Adelaide's innumerable pubs. "Justice to All" wrote to the *Register* on January 1910 to protest about the working conditions of Adelaide waitresses. The correspondent claimed that some had to work from 8 a.m. to 11 p.m., and were allowed only twenty minutes for their meals. "Surely this beautiful city of the South should not tolerate this. Adelaide is far behind the times."

INDUSTRIAL REVOLUTION

Adelaide's industrial revolution, presided over by Sir Thomas Playford, and the heavy postwar immigration into the metropolitan area are described in other sections. According to the 1971 census, the percentage of people employed in such traditional industries as farming, fishing, and timber in the state's total employed population had fallen sharply in proportion to other activities—to a mere 9 per cent. There were more clerical workers—14.46 per cent—and a great many more craftsmen, process workers, and industrial labourers—33.32 per cent.

There is, of course, as in all capitals in this excessively bureaucratized country, a profusion of public servants. As for the private sector, one in five Adelaide workers depends upon the ramifications of the car industry. Since the war, Adelaide has had a good record of industrial stability, but growing militancy by some unions, encouraged by the uneasy fortunes of the consumer durables industries in the late 1960s and early 1970s, has damaged this record over recent years.

Still, although the Playford/Dunstan industrial revolution had, in part, turned a little sour by 1976, Stewart Cockburn, writing in the *Advertiser* of 27 April of that year in an analytical series called "Playford to Dunstan", was able to assemble some agreeable facts about jobs, and general social conditions in Adelaide. For example, savings bank deposits per head were higher than in any other state capital except Melbourne. Official statistics for 1975 showed that South Australia, with 9 per cent of the national workforce had lost less than 4 per cent of working days through industrial disputes. Housing and industrial land, building stone and cement were substantially cheaper than interstate. Five hundred million dollars had been spent on new plant and equipment by industrial firms in South Australia. Labour turnover was lower than in Sydney or Melbourne—although, of course, choice of jobs was more limited. Cockburn wrote:

> More blue collar workers drive their own cars to work in Adelaide than in any other capital city except Brisbane ... Adelaide has a higher percentage of owner-occupied dwellings than either Melbourne or Sydney, a higher percentage of homes with TV, more homes with mains sewerage, more solid or brick veneer houses, and more homes with two or more cars ... There is less pollution, less congestion and ... a generally lower adult crime rate than in the eastern States.

All this was true enough: Adelaide newspaper readers had enjoyed reading such pleasant comparisons between their city and the disreputable east since 1837.

Architecture and Town Planning

Adelaide is a charmingly attractive city—wisely planned and full
of amenity, unostentatious and refined, courteous and homely.
Sidney and Beatrice Webb, 1898

From 1836 to 1947, the population of South Australia, clustered most thickly in and around Adelaide, grew slowly and sedately (given the odd boom and decline) from a few hundred to almost 650,000 people. During the intervening years from 1947 to 1976, this figure has almost doubled, to about 1,300,000. About 70 per cent of these live in metropolitan or urban Adelaide, continuing and intensifying the Australian tendency towards increasing urbanization. Therefore Adelaide's physical growth from foundation to the end of the Second World War was steady rather than spectacular; whereas with the great postwar expansion the city and her suburbs were transformed.

George French Angas in his *South Australia Illustrated* (1846) wrote poetically of the appearance of Adelaide as viewed from the Mount Lofty Ranges " ... the plains stretched out beneath, with the City in the distance, sparkling in the midst of its cultivation, and the blue Gulf beyond, present an enchanting scene of surpassing loveliness." Angas, as a son of a founding father, may have exaggerated but Adelaide, even its present overblown condition, has always looked appealing from the hills. At night it is a riot of multicoloured lights twinkling against a velvet blue carpet. During the day, the steeples and highrise buildings of the city rise grandly above the olive green heads of the parkland eucalypts, and even the rawest outer suburbs are glossed by sunlight and the tufts of trees.

On the ground, and especially during the early shanty town days, Adelaide was not always idyllic. Settlers complained of heat, drought, loneliness, centipedes, snakes, dingoes and, particularly, the flies. "The bluebottle", observed James Stephens in 1839, "deposits living maggots; and if not narrowly watched by the guests at the dinner-table, it will lodge a score of them upon one morsel of food while *in transitu* from plate to mouth".[1] "Wire gauze", reported another pioneer, "is absolutely necessary, to prevent the fresh meat from *walking away*."[2] The Torrens was a cold flood in winter, a succession of turbid waterholes in summer, and badly polluted all the time. The city streets were notoriously bad—dust heaps in the summer and quagmires in the winter. In the dark, citizens kept tumbling into the open wells.

Necessarily, too, most of the early buildings in the makeshift city were gimcrack and temporary. The settlers lived, worked, and even worshipped in tents, mud huts, and wurleys. People were considered lucky if they had a prefabricated wooden shack, a Manning house,[3] imported from England—although even then termites caused devastation. Moreover, there was a shortage of good timber for building and the first settlers were unskilled in such trades. They had to rely for some time upon despised but handy ex-convict drifters from the east who showed them how to come to terms with Australian conditions. However, most of the colonists were energetic and patient. The shortage of timber and the abundance of termites were blessings in that they were obliged to make use of the excellent local stone, quarried from the hills, for their buildings. There were also limestone deposits on the plain, and good clay for bricks. Lime and clay were dug from the park lands until late in the nineteenth century. The large cellars of old houses in areas like St. Peter's and upper North Adelaide are in fact the cavities from which the limestone was dug to build the houses.

HOUSE STYLES

As time passed, humble, then comfortable, and finally rather grand stone houses, churches, and warehouses appeared along the city streets. Gawler had shown the way with his relatively stately new Government House and some well-constructed public buildings. The stone mason's art, using the fine local bluestone, the honey-coloured stone of the ranges, and the slate of Willunga, began to flourish in Adelaide as the city prospered on copper, wheat, and wool.

The earliest dwellings were usually made of limestone with bricks used as quoins to contain the random rubble walls. The construction was simple: a central corridor, three or four rooms, and a sloping iron roof usually extending beyond the walls to form a verandah, for this Indian idea was obviously suited to sunny Adelaide. In a letter home dated 7 December 1853, the recently arrived immigrant C.H. Barton described what was probably the typical Adelaide home of a Mr. Allen:

> Their little cottage was in a strange, out-of-the-way street, hardly containing two houses consecutive, but the small garden in front was neatly laid out, and beautiful pinkflowered creepers of Australian growth were trailing over the verandah, whilst the inside was brimming with snug English comfort. The Parlour contained a neat little Broadwood, a trifle the worse for the late hot winds, and jingling accordingly; the mantel piece was garnished with elegant nick-nackeries, and I observed crochet books lying about the room. It is strange to find such luxuries at the Antipodes, and plenty of them, for there seemed to be pianofortes in half the houses in Adelaide ... The houses in Adelaide are all one-storied, seldom more than 3 in a row—the streets immensely wide, but full of great gaps, unfilled by buildings, and unpaved ... The shops are often very grand, especially the grocers' stores and the public houses, of which there are too many.[4]

About 1870, the theme of the symmetrical cottage or house was varied and elaborated on to produce the famous and distinctive Adelaide villa. A "villa front"— usually a pushed forward parlour, and often a bay window and "return verandah" with iron lace—a tiled floor, and a "bullnose" roof were added. The central corridor remained, as did the footing of bluestone and the "well type" iron roof, but the whole concept was enlarged and dignified. Until the early twentieth century these fine villas, usually on large blocks of at least a quarter of an acre, proliferated in North and South Adelaide and in inner suburbs such as Unley, Walkerville, and Kensington.

From about 1905 onwards, the popularity of the villa waned as local self-confidence and public taste degenerated in favour of a succession of increasingly inferior styles. These included the Queen Anne style, with its penchant towards leaded windows and tiled roofs, the bungalow deriving from Californian fashion, mock, or should it be mockery, Tudor, Spanish Mission, the austerity hutches of the war period and the spread of Housing Trust homes, and the superficial stylism of many modern homes. Such houses can be found in any Australian city. However, it is notable that even the humblest Adelaide houses were usually well built and had a sizable garden. There was and is a strong tradition of working class home ownership. Unlike most other capitals, Adelaide has never had significant slum areas.

THE ADELAIDE VILLA

It is in the city and inner suburban villas—they rarely survive more than about six kilometres from the city centre—that Adelaide's sense of difference in domestic architecture chiefly lies. Their long forgotten architects and builders deserve honour today, for they wrought something indigenous and unique. During the long rule of Premier Playford, who obliged lending institutions to provide finance only for new houses, many villas were neglected, fell into decay, were occupied by southern European immigrants and were generally considered unfashionable. (In fairness to Playford, it should be noted that damp-proof courses were not generally installed until about 1910. Many of the old homes suffered from salt damp and cracking). For the last ten years or so, the villas have come splendidly into their own again. Their handiness to the city, the spaciousness of lofty ceilings and big rooms, charming ornamentation, shady verandahs, solid construction, and large, citrus-dotted gardens are now treasured. I speak with feeling as one who has lived in a villa for six years. They are certainly prominent among Adelaide's contributions to civilized living.

PUBLIC BUILDINGS

Many of the features which make the villas so appealing to modern observers were also marked in Adelaide's best surviving public buildings. These include the lovely mellow stone, gables, verandahs, iron or slate roofs, and sense of spaciousness, permanence, and harmony with the environment. They can be seen in such fine old survivors from colonial times as Government House, the Legislative Council building, Ayers' House, and St. Peter's Cathedral. Local or specially commissioned British architects also provided Adelaide with distinguished buildings in other styles, such as the classical Police Courts and the Italianate Town Hall.

For long years, peaceful Adelaide grew slowly in stone. Light's spacious city took many years fully to materialise. Even in the 1870s, Harcus could observe that it was still largely "the skeleton of a city". Dozing in the heat under the hills, the city pushed up its churches and banks and warehouses in a gentle organic growth. Horses clopped through the dust of King William Street and the merchants set their prosperity against good or bad harvests, good or bad foreign markets. Mark Twain observed in 1895: "There was nothing to remind one of the humble capital of huts and sheds of the long-vanished day of the land boom. No, this was a modern city, with wide streets, compactly built; with fine homes everywhere, embowered in foliage and flowers, and with imposing masses of public buildings nobly grouped and architecturally beautiful. There was prosperity in the air; for another boom was on."[5]

For many years, the rosy-stoned Scots Church was the tallest building on North Terrace. Now it seems insignificant; dwarfed by department stores and office buildings. For many years, the gumtrees of the parklands out-topped the city buildings. Now the tall angular heads of motels and government offices soar above them. Adelaide is now more a city of skyscrapers than churches, and even taller buildings such as the King William Tower are planned or newly completed.

Rapid postwar expansion in Adelaide, as in other Australian cities, took place amid a welter of bad taste and expediency. Handsome old buildings were demolished and ferro concrete skyscrapers sprouted to their place. The towering A.M.P. building, for instance, grew over the bones of a fine old bank and helps destroy the human scale of part of North Terrace. The statues of the explorers Stuart and Sturt in Victoria Square now gaze at a wall of high buildings. Light from Montefiore Hill surveys some notable architectural eyesores. Just six years ago, when the tide was already flowing strongly for conservation, the city's noblest hotel, the South Australian, famous for its colonial charm and wide verandahs, was ripped down in the name of progress. One of Sir Reginald Ansett's Gateway Inns is being built on the site. The loss of the South was probably the last, if the worst, in Adelaide's catalogue of architectural self-mutilation. Now public and official opinion is reasonably zealous to preserve the still considerable remnants of the distinctive Victorian city.

Again, the example of brilliant town planning set by Light was generally not followed. Just before his last illness, he planned the northern town of Gawler, which is one of the state's most charming towns, and he had a hand in the design of Glenelg on the coast. Thereafter both city and suburbs suffered from bad planning or laissez-faire sprawl. Unrestricted industry and commerce were allowed to disfigure much of South and even North Adelaide, where O'Connell Street is almost as ugly as a Melbourne commercial thoroughfare. Many of the city acre blocks were honeycombed with alleyways and some jerry-built workers' terraces appeared. They are bearable now only for their picturesqueness or the mellowness of their stonework. Indeed, many city areas became thoroughly run down and seedy.

I have interviewed a number of senior Adelaideans on this matter of the decay of the residential city area and the inner suburbs. I was told that, until quite recent years, most people regarded old buildings as inferior and that one was stigmatized socially by living in the more modest of them. Moreover, most of the old villas built before about 1907 were badly affected by salt damp. With a few exceptions there were few really outstanding and durable buildings erected before the 1870s. Over and above this, there was a general feeling that history began and ended in England. Such attitudes permitted the demolition of Light's cottage in Thebarton and even led to a strong move in the late 1920s to pull down the Town Hall and build a new one in its place. This potential disaster was averted only narrowly, Sir Arthur Rymill, a former lord mayor, told me because of a group of councillors with mercifully longer vision. Eventually, this group brought about the restoration of the Town Hall's interior decoration from Edwardian drabness to its original beauty and exuberance. The Colonel Light and Queen Adelaide Rooms were named, superbly decorated, and lined with relevant paintings.

THE SUBURBS[6]

The suburbs developed rapidly in a radial sprawl from the central city area. Villages like Mitcham and Marion grew beside the main roads and creeks, usually as orchard and farming units. Hindmarsh and Norwood were working class suburbs from the onset and eventually became industrialized. In 1851, two reporters from the *Register* walked from Adelaide to Glenelg. They passed through paddocks of wheat and hay, passed tiny villages which are now huge suburbs, and noted that Glenelg had 80 houses, some of them fine "marine villas" and 250 inhabitants. By the 1890s there were agglomerations of houses, almost always on a gridiron street pattern, along highways like the Glenelg and Port roads and intensive settlements around new municipalities like Prospect, Campbelltown, and Unley. However, the strong rural flavour of the Adelaide Plains persisted until well into living memory. By the 1970s, suburbia had engulfed virtually all the open spaces within easy commuting distance of Adelaide on the plain. The farms have gone, some of them, like Paradise, passing on their names to a rash of houses. Most of the vineyards have disappeared and even the green swathe of the Penfolds vineyards on the foothills of Stonyfell is about to be developed. While pushing for thirty kilometres or more to the north and south, suburbia also surged high into the foothills, sprinkled the hills' face with bijou desirable residences, and even established some lamentable beach heads near the hills' crest before planning restrictions were imposed.

Amid this helter skelter of development, little thought was given to good planning and the reservation of open space as exemplified by Light. True, there are some delightful pockets of tasteful, well-preserved villas, as in Unley Park and Walkerville, one or two well-planned suburbs like Colonel Light Gardens, and some good examples of modern housing that harmonize with the environment. The rest is undistinguished at best, and offensive at worst—although the prolific Adelaide trees and flowers do much to mitigate both ugliness and monotony.

In sum, with a few exceptions, Adelaide suburbia is a solid mass of decent but unimaginative and repetitive brick housing, differing only from the suburban sprawl of Melbourne and Sydney in that, mercifully, it is much less extensive. The satellite city of Elizabeth, built by the Housing Trust and now mellowed by well-grown trees and shrubs, is a pleasant exception to this rule. The pity is the greater in that Adelaide's architectural and planning origins were so exciting and that good taste and good design persisted for so long in the city's history.

THE CITY PLAN

Yet in these matters too, Adelaide's sense of difference is remarkable. The wanderer in the city, the inner suburbs, and round the old village hearts of some of the outer suburbs soon becomes conscious of the distinctive Adelaide style of housing—the brush fences, the flowers, the sturdy, numerous, and now well cared for villas built of local stone. Again, the endemic radicalism of Adelaide has shown itself over recent years in strong government measures to establish environmental control and plan for the future. With the City of Adelaide Plan, accepted by council in 1975, the city will be divided into four functional districts. The central core district, the commercial heart of South Adelaide encompassing Victoria Square and Rundle Street, will contain the highest buildings and closely linked business and public activities. Here the emphasis will be upon easy, comfortable movement by pedestrians. In 1976 the western section of Rundle Street became the exhilarating Rundle Mall. The second "frame" district round the core will contain lower density activities of greater variety, and in smaller buildings. The third, residential, district, comprising all of North Adelaide and a large segment of South Adelaide will be further improved to attract more people back to live in the city proper. The fourth district will be the restored and more closely cherished parklands. The aims of the planners are to make Adelaide stronger economically and a more attractive place to live. More trees, pedestrian walkways, landscaping, and facilities for "leisure living" are promised, better historical and environmental conservation, improved public transport, and fewer cars. This will, it is hoped, reduce suburban growth.

MONARTO[7]

Determined that Adelaide should not lose its present humanity by growing much bigger, the Dunstan government in early 1972 projected the new city of Monarto on the Murray Plains on the far side of the ranges and about 65 kilometres from Adelaide. Monarto is to be "a lively, cosmopolitan place". The premier said that he did not want to build "a Versailles in the bush", but declared: "We have big plans for Monarto. I believe that in bringing them into being we shall stir men's blood, not only in Australia but well beyond our boundaries."

It was seen that by the year 2,000 Monarto could siphon off from 150,000 to 200,000 of Adelaide's increasing population and that the capital's numbers should be pegged at 1.3 million at most. Monarto was to be established at a cost of about $2,500 million, much of this to come from the federal government.

Since Monarto was announced the critics have severally attacked it, and with growing ferocity as the national economic climate worsens. The site for Monarto—on which over $20 million had been spent by late 1976—the proposed drainage system, the soil and bedrock, and the economic viability of the project have all been seriously criticized. More damaging, the original assumption that Adelaide was going to keep on growing at 3 per cent a year has not been substantiated; the growth rate is now less than 1 per cent. Since the Monarto decision, the Dunstan government has also become committed to a new city centre at Noarlunga. In 1975 the federal government granted only a mere $600,000 for Monarto for the budgetary period. In 1976, the Fraser Government gave nothing. Some public servants, scheduled for transfer to Monarto in a year or two, have protested bitterly against this "conscription". The conservationists worry that Monarto will eventually be joined to Adelaide by a corridor of development which will wreck the character of the central ranges. In March 1976, the chairman of the Monarto Commission resigned because there was apparently very little for him to do to justify his $30,000 a year salary. Local pony clubs meet over the quiet hectares of the projected city; and some of the land has been leased back to farmers.

Yet if Monarto proceeds it will exemplify exciting new forms of urban living, transportation, and energy use. The city plan, comprising a series of lakes, many natural bush reserves, and concentrated pockets of industrial, recreational, and shopping areas on the Canberra model, indicates that Monarto could be a highly agreeable place in which to live.

The Parklands, Squares, and Botanic Gardens

> The conception of this belt of verdure, on which none but public buildings may be erected, dividing the working part of the town from the residential part, has always seemed to me a masterpeice of wisdom in city planning, and hardly less admirable are the five open reserves in the city which serve as its lungs.
>
> *R.E.N. Twopeny, 1882*

THE PARKLANDS

The glory, and perhaps the most distinctive feature, of Adelaide is its parklands, 690 hectares of open space reserved in perpetuity for public use and encompassing Light's city with a swathe of green. Since the Municipal Corporations Act of 1849, the parklands have been under the "care, control and management" of the City Council, and their outer boundaries delimit the area administered by the council.

On 12 November 1877, Sir George Kingston, once Light's deputy surveyor-general (and usurper), wrote in the *Advertiser* that Light's original plan of 1837 showed the city: " ... surrounded on all sides by an area of vacant land which Colonel Light, in pursuance of his instructions ... described as Parks to be reserved from sale and dedicated as Park Lands for the use and recreation of the citizens, with the exception of nine blocks ... which were stated to be reserved out of the Park Lands for various Government buildings or other purposes." On a plan drawn and dated 7 February 1837 Light wrote: "The dark green round the town I proposed to the Resident Commissioner to be reserved as Parks Grounds." Light remained in office long enough only to sketch the parklands roughly in on his city plan. Yet his intentions and, indeed, those of the commissioners, seem to have been clear. The parklands were to be preserved. Whether this was because of visionary urban planning, or to keep a clear field of fire from the city in case of concerted Aboriginal attack (a real, if unfounded, fear in the early days), or a compound of both, does not really matter. The authorities, on the whole, shared Light's idealism sufficiently strongly to rebuff attempts to build on the parklands, even when South Australia seemed to have a superabundance of land and scarcely any settlers. The outer boundaries of the parklands were finally set at approximately 460 metres from the inner boundaries.

Gawler allocated 2,300 pounds to buy the parklands to make assurance doubly sure. The money, pleasantly, was never demanded by the Colonial Office: thus no money actually changed hands over the reservation of the parklands. However, government altruism, reflecting the attitudes of the time, had its blind spots and there were over the years substantial encroachments on the parklands, many of which are now regretted. The original reservation was actually 920 hectares: thus 230 hectares have been lost.

During the early years of settlement a large cemetery (13 hectares, later 24) and an immigration depot were established on the west parklands and many newly arrived immigrants set up their tents under the eucalypts. Governor Hindmarsh was concerned over squatters on the parklands who cut down trees and dug the ground for clay for their mud-walled huts. The Kaurna, members of the local Aboriginal tribe, often camped there. As early as 19 August 1840, "A Townsman" was moved to protest in a letter to the *Register* about a whole body of natives hewing and cutting away at the fine trees". The editor agreed that the "wholesale destruction" of trees by Aborigines was bad, doubtless forgetting that the settlers were cutting down trees all over South Australia. He went further to object to "the nuisance of their beastly corrobories [*sic*]" and hoped that they would take "their discordant orgies" elsewhere.

The *Register*, probably speaking for the majority of citizens, continued to grumble about natives on the parklands until progress and civilization had exterminated them. On 6 December 1845, for instance, the *Register* declared:

> The inhabitants of North Adelaide have much room to complain of the disturbances which the natives now nightly make with their hideous corrobories. About three hundred of these savages howl and bellow at the top of their voices, for five or six hours at a stretch, so as effectually to preclude rest and quiet in the neighbourhood.

And in similar vein on 4 April 1846:

> We would really entreat the attention of the policy to the proceedings of the natives on the Park Land in North Adelaide. Not only is the destruction of trees proceeding wholesale, but the inhabitants are nightly disturbed by the horrible howling in their beastly corrobories. Morning and evening both sides of the river are crowded by the savages, armed, too, with spears, and accompanied by troops of half-starved curs, frightening and often insulting every unprotected female they meet.

The parklands were first seen as a kind of general purposes no man's land. The first Adelaide hanging, a mammoth public entertainment, took place on them. Builders quarried for limestone and dug for brick clay. Marquees could be erected on them for public junketings, such as the special dinner held in "the Grand Pavilion on the Park Land" on 21 February 1846, to welcome that "gallant traveller" Captain Sturt home from his explorations. A few days later, over 1,500 people paid to enter the pavilion to inspect "the Great Annual Show of Grains and Fruits of Colonial Growth". Probably the first recorded game of football held in the province took place on the north parklands in April 1860.

Above all, the parklands were used for grazing, sometimes with controversial results. On 23 May 1846, indicating, incidentally, that the settlers still thought of May as spring despite geography, the *Register* observed: "Now that the Park Lands are beginning to put on their spring livery, they are becoming as usual covered with droves of stray cattle, goats and scabby sheep, notoriously belonging to persons who have no right to depasture on these lands at all". The *Register* went on to hope, in vain, that a continental style "town herd" might be set up, controlled by a civic herdsman.

After the collapse of the first City Council in 1843, the parklands deteriorated badly. They were stripped of trees, heaped with rubbish and offal, and were scarred by clay and lime pits and squatters' shacks. With the passing of the act to reconstitute the council in 1849, the parklands, like the city, came under the control of the City Commissioners. They acted with despatch, and within three weeks had passed by-laws to save the parklands from further ruin. Henceforth, written permission was required before any budding developer could dig building material from the reserves. The parklands were fenced with post and rail fences and workmen were sent to bury animal carcases and remove rubbish. An Aboriginal camp at what later became Elder Park was removed. Squatters were ordered to remove themselves and their dwellings from the parklands within six months. Two evicted for the general good in this way were the Rev. S.G. Klose and William Haines, who had homes on the north parklands.

There were still of course several illicit but official uses made of the parklands. For instance, a slaughterhouse had been established on the area later known as Bonython Park in 1840. This remained in operation, servicing the adjacent cattle market, until the opening of the metropolitan abattoirs in 1910.

For many years, citizens grazed their stock on the parklands: until quite recently there were gates marked "Cows Only", and horses still wander on sections of the northern belt. Tanners washed hides by the banks of the Torrens until public protest stopped them. The early agricultural shows, from the beginning a prominent feature of the Adelaide scene, were held on the parklands. The drag hunt rode across them under the critical gaze of city crowds, and people crossing the parklands from Unley to the city complained about errant bullets when the military volunteers practised at the parkland butts.

The government soon made heavy inroads, on the special reserves mentioned and beyond. The parkland strip between the Torrens and North Terrace was rapidly encumbered with a Government House, an institute and public library and, later, a university, an institute of technology, a hospital, botanic gardens, Parliament House, even the railway station. This provided a peculiarly happy juxtaposition of public buildings and Adelaide's prime boulevard, but it alienated a large piece of parklands. Further expanses were taken over for sport or public utility; notably for a high school, one of the loveliest cricket grounds in the world, a zoo, a racecourse, croquet lawns, playing fields, golf links, and the Adelaide Gaol. There have been incessant attempts over the decades to "beautify" the parklands in a way that grates on the present taste for indigenous beauty. The Conservator of Forests reported to the City Council in 1879, for instance, that "perhaps the worst feature" of the parklands were the numerous eucalypts. He went on: "The Gums as a rule are not very ornamental trees, and besides, those in the Parklands have a very unhealthy appearance". They should, he urged, "give place to others of a more suitable character". Similar urges about that time were behind the introduction of blackbirds, snapdragons, and foxes to make the Australian scene seem more civilized.

As a result of such attitudes, and with the best will in the world, the guardians of the parklands replaced many of the despised eucalypts with ashes, elms, and poplars and covered several hectares with imitations of British municipal parks, complete with statuary, childrens' playgrounds and herbaceous borders brilliant with impeccably British flowers.

Zealous Victorian "improvers" the councillors may have been, but they had an understanding that the parklands were precious, and well nigh unique. They honestly believed, just as most of their contemporaries believed, that tennis courts, imported trees, and meticulous gardens enhanced the amenities of the parklands. And they soon became proud of their extent. The mayor's *Annual Report* of 1878 pointed out that London had one acre of park to every 1,400 inhabitants, New York had one acre for 820, and Sydney had one acre for every 190 people. In beneficial contrast, Adelaide had one acre of parks for every 18 citizens. Council workmen "collected and stacked" the parklands hay. According to the *Register* of 6 January 1885, the cost of doing this that summer was 127 pounds. And when in 1896 the dumps of house refuse "on the various portions of the Park Lands" became "a grave danger to the public health", the council banned the dumping and set up a refuse incinerating works in Halifax Street. However, controlled dumping to fill old quarries continued.

As the suburbs spread beyond the parklands, especially after 1945 with the large increase in assisted immigration, this green belt became subject to new encroachments as wider roads were laid down, adding to the already substantial alienations caused by tramway and rail construction. Nowadays, most Adelaide people only notice the parklands as a fleeting impression of green as they hurtle in and out of the city in the rush hours. Even at that level, they provide a welcome awareness of nature amid the welter of metal and noise and the visual affronts of the suburban arterial roads. There was even a proposal accepted by one government but rejected by another, and by public opinion, to cut fresh roads through the grass in the interests of the freeways of the Metropolitan Adelaide Transport Scheme, the notorious MATS plan.

In the 1970s many Adelaide people cherish the parklands even more than their grandparents did. The suburbs extend for thirty kilometres beyond and Light's wise planning example of substantial reserves has not been followed. One city planner, Charles Reade, proposed concentric rings of parklands around the city in 1910, when there was still space and time, but his ideas were rejected. Accordingly, the present generation, activated by a new concern for the urban environment, guards the parklands jealously.

During 1974, a plan sponsored by the City Council by Urban Systems Corporation was submitted to the authorities, and this makes detailed proposals for the parklands which will probably be implemented. It points out that since foundation, approximately 260 hectares of parklands have been alienated and that this process should be reversed where possible. If the plan is implemented the Adelaide Gaol on the parklands, begun by Gawler, will become a "cultural centre" and at least nine roads "which destroy the continuity of the parklands and dissect them into a series of parks" will be closed and grassed over. A very large area of parkland will be turned into "forest parks" and people will be encouraged to take "fun rides" on horse-drawn vehicles. There will be cycle ways for cyclists at present abused by the traffic system and several sections at present alienated, such as Government House grounds and Thebarton Police Barracks, will be restored to "recreational use". Much of the railway station area will become a "major metropolitan recreation area".

The planners intend to replace many of the imported trees and shrubs by a sustained policy of planting native species of forty-seven varieties. At present, the parklands are pleasant enough. Parts of them, such as sporting areas and the sites used for visiting circuses, are heavily used, but for much of their extent you can walk alone for miles under ash trees and the surviving gums, with wagtails dodging about you and flocks of galahs wheeling across the sky with a flush of pink. To protect and encourage such birds, the council has forbidden the use of pesticide sprays on the parklands, and certain areas of grass are not mown, so that seed-eating birds may feed. Self-sown eucalypt seedlings are now allowed to grow to maturity.

Altogether, Adelaide's magnificent nature strip should be even more pleasant, and more popular, when the plan for parklands conservation and restoration is implemented.

THE SQUARES

Light planned six squares in North and South Adelaide, and these, too, are a distinctive feature of the city, although they have suffered far more from progress than the parklands. The great central Victoria Square has been riven by wide interesting roads. The Queen Empress herself stands helplessly over teeming processions of cars and trucks. The statues of the explorers Sturt and Stuart gaze, not at sweeping vistas, but at beetling government offices. There is a fine fountain, but with roaring traffic on all sides, Victoria Square is no place to relax. The same may be said for most of the other squares. They have been quartered by wide roads into dusty patches of grass and are dotted with municipal lavatories. Perhaps the pleasantest, Wellington Square in North Adelaide, was until recently under dire threat of bisection by a new arterial road.

However, the Urban Systems Corporation Plan intends to put all this right. For Victoria Square, for example, it proposes the closing, digging up, and landscaping of the present diagonal roads through the square. The east-west road would be lowered and covered with a landscaped, paved deck, and pedestrian bridges built over the north-south road. Equally radical proposals for Whitmore Square, to take another example, include facilities for open air eating, a children's cycling loop, an adventure playground, and a garden maze. In sum all the parks would be improved and restored to their original purpose of providing inner city retreats.

THE TORRENS

Named after Colonel Torrens of the Board of Commissioners, the original modest creek that bisects Adelaide was called Karra Wirri Parri (river of the redgum forest) by the Aborigines. Light was delighted by its "crystal water" and it was the lifeline of the young city as the supplier of water for the watercarts that traversed the streets. The carter used to filter the tea-coloured water through sponges to remove larger pollutants. The colonel left a strip of parkland on either side of the Torrens as it passed through his city, and from the beginning the river banks, eventually "beautified" with flowergardens and formal walks, were popular recreation areas. It was never a noble waterway, being but a string of waterholes in a dusty gulch in summer and a cold, turbid torrent in winter, but in 1881 the council dammed it to create the ornamental Torrens Lake.

Of course, like all rivers unlucky enough to run through Australian cities, the Torrens soon became grossly polluted. In 1974, the outspoken Sir Mark Oliphant, governor of South Australia, perhaps in this case with more passion than accuracy, likened Adelaide's river to a sewer, full of "unspeakable things". It has a particularly rough time in the suburbs on either side of the city, but within the city proper and the parklands, it is a pleasant prospect. There are ducks and pleasureboats, a sight-seeing craft called *Popeye*, and a splendid fountain in the middle of the lake which is illuminated at night. A stroll by the leafy, duck-flecked Torrens is one of the meditative pleasures offered by Adelaide.

There are plans, which may not be utopian, to restore strips of greenery and footpaths along the whole length of the Torrens from the hills to the sea.

THE BOTANIC GARDENS

Adelaide, given sufficient water, has always been a remarkable city for plants. Anthony Trollope was among many notable nineteenth century visitors who recorded his delight over the flowers, fruits, and trees that flourished there. The 18 hectares of the Botanic Gardens have always epitomized this floral excellence, and to this day remain perhaps the pleasantest spot in Adelaide. William Harcus in his *South Australia: Its History, Resources and Productions* (1876) declared:

... the glory of Adelaide, and the pride of her citizens, is our beautiful Botanic Garden, which, under the magic wand of Dr. Richard Schomburgk, has grown into a thing of beauty which will be a joy for ever. We are a quiet, undemonstrative people, not much given to what Mr. Anthony Trollope called "Australian blowing", but we do boast of our gardens; and if this be a weakness, it is one in which we are encouraged if not justified, by all the visitors who see them. They who have seen all the Botanic Gardens in the other Colonies without a moment's doubt or hesitation give the palm to ours".[1]

No doubt there was some municipal blowing in this and similar civic outbursts, but the Botanic Gardens, founded in 1854, have always been of high standard, and have reflected the local passion for, and success with, gardening.

The first editor of the *Register* and Hindmarsh's right-hand man, George Stevenson, was a keen gardener and often lectured his readers about the enormous potential of horticulture in Adelaide. Stevenson's garden in North Adelaide was considered for years to be the best in the city, and settlers followed his example. They found that they could grow flowers, fruits, and shrubs undreamed of in England. Roses would bloom here longer and in greater profusion. Geraniums never seemed to stop flowering. South Australian sunshine would make exotic fruits like oranges, grapes, olives, and peaches thrive.

The pleasances of the Botanic Gardens with the range of plants from massive Moreton Bay Figs to minute cacti are a sort of temple for South Australian gardeners who flock here for refreshment and ideas. They have always been popular: for instance, during the annual agricultural show they were thronged with rural visitors, and superintendents reported with pleasure that the country people were better behaved than the city folk. Of course, in this sabbatarian society, their gates were locked on Sundays.

A distinctive feature of Adelaide today is the exuberance of the city and suburban gardens—a collage of vivid ranks of scarlet cannas, geraniums tumbling over brush fences, aisles of jacarandahs, oranges, and lemons in practically every garden—and of this gardening religion, the Botanic Garden is the holy place.

The Churches

It is hoped that South Australia will become the headquarters
for the diffusion of Christianity in the Southern Hemisphere.

George Fife Angas, 1844

The Colony is ... rid of the incubus of an established Church and
delivered from the rapacity of a grasping priesthood.

Edward Stephens, 1839

By 1857, there were according to Pascoe 192 Sunday schools in South Australia and
about 300 churches and chapels. They offered, he claimed, "accommodation for
50,000 persons", that is, just a little less than half the population of the province at one
sitting.[1] Most of these churches were in or near Adelaide, or course. Thus statistics implied remarkable piety, even for the mid-nineteenth century, in Adelaide.

Prayers, hymns, sermons, and godly exhortations saluted the heavens each sab-
bath from the churches and meeting housing of Anglicans, the various divisions of
Methodism and Presbyterianism, from Roman Catholics, Unitarians, Baptists,
Congregationalists, Lutherans, and Quakers. As time passed, additional exhortations
rose to the Adelaide skies from denominations like the Bible Christians, the Welsh Free
Church, the Greek and Russian Orthodox, Muslims, Jews, and many others.

The religious ardour has dimmed in recent years, but probably not so much as in
other Australian capitals. For most of its history Adelaide has been renowned—or
notorious, depending upon your views—for religious zeal; and admired, or dreaded, for
its sabbatarianism.

Adelaide was a Victorian city, and the Victorian age, however much modern
critics assail it for pharasaism, was essentially a religious age. Moreover, in religious
observance as in other ways Adelaide, with its own peculiar emphases, tended to be
more Victorian than almost anywhere else. Thus the city acquired its soubriquet of
"City of the Churches". This might have been a gibe by less reverent easterners, but certainly the old photographs show that the numerous spires and towers of churches and
conventicles were dominant features of the urban vista. Similarly, the broad country
scene was speckled with little chapels, many of them now mute ruins of stone. The old
histories, guidebooks, memoirs, and studies of Adelaide invariably bulge with long sections on churches and churchmen, and faded photographs of heavily bearded
clergymen stare reproachfully at the modern reader.

Just as Adelaide was planned by the founders to be an exemplary colonial city in
cultural, constitutional, and economic matters, so it was planned to be extraordinarily
religious. Above all, Adelaide was to be a new Jerusalem for Dissent, in Hodder's
phrase, "a Paradise for Nonconformists".[2] "We appeal", wrote George Fife Angas in one
of his circulars, "to the Dissenters more particularly ... "[3]

Religion had not loomed large in the founding of the other Australian colonies. The authorities thought so little about it when they despatched the First Fleet of felons to Botany Bay that they forgot, until the very last moment, to appoint a chaplain to go with them. Sydney, Hobart, and Brisbane were established, not to save men's souls, but to provide "salutary terror", in agreeably remote spots, for convicts. Perth and Melbourne had been founded to please the land seeker, not the clergyman.

The founders of Adelaide pursed their lips over the sinfulness of other Australian settlements. They resolved, from the start, that Adelaide would be different.

Religious Dissent has often provided enthusiasm for colonization as the Pilgrim Fathers in America show. In the 1830s, some British Dissenters were weary of their grudgingly granted toleration and the many subtle discriminations made against Dissenters in Britain. Nonconformists, too, as men of independent minds, have often been successful in commerce—inventive and active. They have been busy round the roots of most British reforms.

So it is not surprising that many of Wakefield's supporters were, like Wakefield himself, Nonconformists, as were Angas's backers in the South Australian Company. There were, of course, many Anglicans, like Morphett, among the founders, but usually they were Evangelicals, people who were just as eager for reform and improvement as the Methodists and Baptists. The symbol of oppression to the Dissenters in England was the established church with all that it implied. The founders wanted no Anglican domination in Adelaide as was made clear by the *Morning Chronicle*'s report of 1 July 1834 on a meeting of intending emigrants at Exeter Hall, an important Evangelical meeting place in London. The chairman declared: "We do not contemplate anything that can partake of the character of an established church, convinced that what is called the voluntary principle will amply supply a sufficiency of means to give to everyone in our colony proper moral and religious instruction". Dissent and Evangelicalism had a strong, pervasive, and continuing influence upon the history of Adelaide. Although both Dissent and Nonconformity in a sense were abolished here. There was no denominational norm to dissent from or conform with.

ANGLICANS

The establishment of the various denominations during the early period was an intrinsic part of the foundation process.

Despite the stated hostility of many of the founders to the established church idea, the Colonial Office, suspicious of Dissent, had managed to insert a clause into the South Australian Act whereby the Privy Council could appoint colonial chaplains of the English and Scottish established churches. Glenelg quickly appointed the Rev. C.B. Howard, before Dissenters' protests brought about the excision of the clause. Howard sailed out on the *Buffalo*.

Despite his refusal on moral grounds to offer spiritual consolation to the dying Light, Howard appears to have been a kind, vigorous, and high principled man. His violin playing soothed frayed nerves on a *Buffalo* infested with Hindmarsh's dogs and stock. He took out with him a prefabricated wooden parsonage and church. He pushed the pieces of parsonage on a handtruck to the city site, but there were problems with his pre-packaged church, for we read of Howard and Gillies dragging a "huge sail" through the dust with ropes to provide a roof for worshippers.[4] Holy Trinity Church on North Terrace, named after Howard's *alma mater* in Dublin, was opened in July 1838. The oldest church in the archdiocese of Adelaide, Holy Trinity soon became the spiritual meeting place for the Anglican establishment. Here the governors, the red-coats (who marched down North Terrace behind a band), and the gentry prayed in the big pews. Here, too, in 1840 Bishop Augustus Short was enthroned as first Bishop of Adelaide. Holy Trinity was and is perhaps the most charming of the old Adelaide churches, but the bishop, sensitive about his dignity, did not rest until he had a proper cathedral. Holy Trinity, incidentally, has since followed a stern, low church Evangelical path, keeping the right to elect its own incumbents, most of whom latterly were trained at Sydney's Evangelical Moore College.

Howard worked hard in his vast dusty vineyard. He rode his horse Luther to Echunga, Encounter Bay, Mount Barker, the Lyndoch Valley, and many other outlying places to hold services, wrote a *South Australian Church Hymnbook* and made the time to be active on behalf of the Botanic Garden, Hospital Board, Aborigines, and Savings Bank. He died, desperately in debt, in 1843.

Only one other colonial chaplain was appointed for the Adelaide Dissenters eventually achieved victory in their fight with Governor Robe on state aid to religion. The voluntary principle was enshrined as part of the Adelaide way of life. South Australia was the first part of the British Empire to sever the cosy link between government and Anglicanism.

Similar Nonconformist urges strengthened the determination of the City Council to deny Bishop Short an acre in Victoria Square for an Anglican cathedral. The bishop accepted his reverse with good humour and busied himself on the creation of a St. Peter's Cathedral (personages as diverse as Gladstone and Queen Adelaide contributed to the building fund) on the northern side of the Torrens which would—and does—"present a noble vista to King William Street". St. Peter's is much better there than amid the clangour and exhaust fumes of Victoria Square. Its noble twin spires, fifty-one metres high, preside over parklands and river and one of the loveliest cricket grounds in the world.

We can also thank Bishop Short in that he prevailed over the mania for brick of the original architect, Sir Herbert Butterfield. Short insisted, quite rightly, upon stone. Butterfield withdrew. Short was equally determined that the other buttress of Adelaide Anglicanism, St. Peter's College, completed in 1851, should be stone Gothic. Captain William Allen, who helped found the boys' school with his Burra wealth, wanted the design to be Italianate but as usual Dr. Short had his way.

St. Peter's College and Cathedral (perhaps the bishop favoured this saint because he had attended St. Peter's College, Westminster) symbolize the definite social pre-eminence of Anglicanism in Adelaide. The roll call of notable South Australians who attended St. Peter's is virtually an Adelaide *Who's Who*: the current premier, the Hon. Don Dunstan, is an old boy of "Saint's". Government House has usually discreetly backed the Church of England and Anglicans have usually been predominant in places of power and privilege like the Adelaide Club, parliament, and the long-established Adelaide business houses. Anglicanism is and always has been the largest single denomination in South Australia. In the 1966 census 286,154 persons described themselves as Anglicans.

Yet the Church of England never achieved in Adelaide anything like the hegemony it enjoyed in England, or indeed, in the other Australian capitals. Anglicans were always outnumbered by the combined Nonconformist denominations attracted to this new city so philosophically favourable to religious Dissent.

PRESBYTERIANS

Scots, doughty colonizers everywhere, were markedly attracted by the opportunities of South Australia. The Highland-style names of many country properties with their glens, bens, lochs, and braes testify to this. They brought their own established church, the Presbyterian Kirk, with them, but like the Church of England it had to endure "disestablishmentarianism" in radical Adelaide. The Established, the Free, and the United Presbyterian churches united to form the Presbyterian Church of South Australia in 1865. Scots Church, founded in 1851, is the centre of Adelaide Presbyterianism. For many years its graceful spire was the tallest edifice on North Terrace. Presbyterianism was especially strong in South Australian agriculture and business, as represented by successful Scottish dynasties like the Elders and Barr Smiths. Scotch College and the Presbyterian Girls' College were founded as proper schools for the children of well-to-do Presbyterians. In the 1966 census there were 42,687 Presbyterians in South Australia.

ROMAN CATHOLICS

If the Adelaide founders had one blind spot in their enthusiasm for religious liberty, it was towards Roman Catholicism. For one thing, Dissent and Catholicism have never accorded well. For another, the founders wanted no truck with convictism. Most early Australian Catholics were Irish, and many Irish people in early Australia had been transported there, often for political reasons. Thus, until quite recent years, South Australian Roman Catholicism was never as well entrenched as that of, say, New South Wales or Victoria.

Catholicism first came to this most Protestant province with the overlanders from the east who stayed on in the hills as Tiersmen. Later, many Irish came out as assisted immigrants. So many Irish labourers settled in one section of North Adelaide that it became known as Irishtown.

Roman Catholicism thus began modestly in Adelaide until it was organized and given driving force by the outstanding and fiery priest, William Ullathorne, who visited them for two weeks in 1840. Ullathorne was rebuffed by two vehement anti-Catholics among the Adelaide magnates. McLaren denounced "popish practices", and Gawler, equating Catholics with Irish convicts, said he saw no reason for a priest to come to Adelaide as there were no convicts there. However, there is evidence that many other colonists were more tolerant. Colonel Torrens, an Irishman, was anxious to form "another Erin" in South Australia and encouraged Irish labourers to emigrate there.[5]

Francis Murphy became the first Roman Catholic Bishop of Adelaide in 1844 and St. Francis Xavier's Cathedral was founded hard by Victoria Square in 1851. Kingston supervised its early construction and later additions continued until 1926. The result is a curious architectural muddle and the cathedral suffers the indignity of not having a soaring spire on its main tower. One was projected for years, but St. Francis Xavier's still puts up with a funny little temporary cap.

Later prelates, notably Archbishop John O'Reily, strengthened Roman Catholics in Adelaide. O'Reily, for instance, established orders like the Marists, the Passionists, the Dominican and "Blue Nuns" in the city. Important Roman Catholic schools in Adelaide include Rostrevor College, St. Aloysius, and Blackfriars. By 1966 there were well over 200,000 Roman Catholics in South Australia, their numbers increasing quickly with immigration from Catholic areas of Europe.

Overall, one has the impression that Roman Catholicism has played rather an outsider role for most of Adelaide's history. The long list of biographies of distinguished citizens that accompany and almost dominate some of the earlier histories of Adelaide and its satellite municipalities contain very few Roman Catholics. Hodder somehow managed to write his long two volume *History of South Australia* (1893) with scarcely a reference to Roman Catholicism, although he wrote copiously and respectfully about Methodism, for instance. Hodder did remark that in 1843 Holy Trinity, heavily in debt, was almost taken over for Catholicism or a grocery store, "both dangers being imminent".[6] The situation has changed in recent times with, for example, a Catholic, the Hon. Des Corcoran, the deputy premier. Mr. John Roche, the lord mayor at the time of writing, is the first Catholic to have been elected to this position. But for most of Adelaide's existence the local eminence of a few Catholics like the Governor Sir Dominick Daly were exceptions to a discreet and unspoken but unrelenting rule.

JEWS

Like the Catholics, Adelaide's Jewish community probably suffered from some social discrimination in the early years. However, this was surmounted, the more easily because their numbers were always small—a mere twenty-five according to the 1844 census and rising to only 1,249 by the 1971 census—and because of their general success at achieving prosperity. The province's reformist and tolerant philosophy must have appealed to members of this most persecuted of faiths. Among South Australia's founders, for example, Colonel Torrens had been one of the advocates in the House of Commons of civil emancipation for the Jews.

Adelaide's Jewish pioneers included Jacob Montefiore, who led their congregational affairs as early as 1838; and Judah Moss Solomon who, in 1840, was first president of the Hebrew congregation. The Rundle Street synagogue was consecrated in 1850. The Hebrew Philanthropic Society was founded in 1852. Solomon, mayor of the city from 1869 to 1871, also began a strong tradition of civic involvement and eminence by Adelaide's Jewish community. It provided no less than four mayors and two lord mayors (most recently Alderman Bridgland); and it was a Jewish mayor, Sir Lewis Cohen, who, in 1911, first asked the British Parliament to grant a lord mayoralty for Adelaide. This was agreed to in 1919. Cohen, incidentally, set a record for mayoral election, having served for five annual terms as mayor and two as lord mayor. He was the grandfather of Lord Mayor Bridgland and Deputy Lord Mayor Alderman Lady Jacobs.

Thus, in both commercial and civic affairs, Adelaide's Jews were conspicuous out of all proportion to their numbers: the Adelaide ethos clearly accorded well with their traditional strengths.

THE NONCONFORMISTS

It was neither the Anglicans nor the Catholics but the Nonconformists, the Dissenters of the "Free Churches"—Methodists, Congregationalists, Baptists and the like—who were the most powerful single element in Adelaide's religious history. Together with their natural allies, the Presbyterians and Evangelical Anglicans, they tended to occupy the positions of influence and set the moral tone of the city. South Australia was planned as the Land of Canaan for British Dissenters tired of the social snubs and professional restrictions of the Old Country, burning, like Moses, to lead their people to spiritual bliss by the desert's edge.

Of all the free churches, it was the Methodists or Wesleyans who had the greatest impact upon Adelaide. In the 1966 census 227,483 persons described themselves as Methodists, only about 60,000 fewer than the Anglicans. Adelaide probably was and still is the most Methodist city in the world.

The Methodist lay preacher Samuel East came to Kangaroo Island in 1836 on the *Africaine* and he led the singing of Wesley's hymns under the gumtrees. On the mainland, Methodists gathered every Sunday by the Torrens near a straggle of huts named "Buffalo Row".

The first Methodist minister came to the province under providential if traumatic circumstances, for when, in 1838, the Rev. William Longbotton was sailing in the *Fanny* from Van Diemen's Land to Western Australia the brig foundered off the dunes beyond the Coorong. The local Aborigines, probably members of the same tribes which later attacked the survivors of the *Maria* sinking, helped the castaways and eventually Longbottom was enthusiastically received by the Adelaide Wesleyans and persuaded to stay.

Methodism flourished like the green bay tree throughout the province. Thus Harcus: "The Wesleyan Methodists are a large body, and the country districts owe much to them for the religious ordinances which they enjoy. In this work they are ably supported by the Primitive Methodists and Bible Christians, who have erected chapels in and supplied religious teaching to every little village and hamlet in the Province".[7] Methodism ensured that Burra and Moonta, for most of the Cornish miners were Wesleyans, were distinguished more for their hymn singing than the hard drinking and raffishness of the usual mining town.

The Congregationalists or Independents, Baptists, and Quakers were also numerous and influential in early Adelaide. The pioneer Congregationalist minister, Thomas Stow, after whom the pleasant Stow Church in Wakefield Street is named, arrived in 1839 and Governor Hindmarsh, seated on a box, attended his first service. Stow was helped by the ubiquitous Angas and funded by the London Mission Society, to whom he reported that he had cut the reeds and felled the timber for his chapel himself. "Centipedes crowded into our beds", wrote the minister. "The white ants ate up our furniture." The glare of the large tent, standing in the blaze of an Australian summer day, aggravated the opthalmia "to which all newcomers are liable".[8] Once acclimatized, however, Stow was an ardent colonist. He wrote to the Missionary Committee: "What a land is this to which you have sent me! The loveliness and glory of its plains and woods, its glens and hills! ... I cannot ... leave it out of my estimate of God's goodness to me".[9]

The first Adelaide Baptists were led by the excessively godly David McLaren, second manager of the South Australian Company. Harcus comments that the Congregationalists, Baptists, and Presbyterians "manage to attract the intelligent, practical and hard-headed men amongst us, and they come to the front in business and political organization". Indeed they did. Take, for instance, McLaren, a Calvinistic Baptist, and the Methodist Stephens brothers, all influential figures in early Adelaide and all shipped there by the busy Angas, himself a Baptist. Angas's South Australian Company was managed almost exclusively by Dissenters.

McLaren, after whom McLaren Vale is named, only responded to Angas's entreaties to accept the managership because of an appeal to Christian duty pleasantly coupled with an unusually high salary. Angas and McLaren made a compact to "hold the rope" in business and prayer, and both saw sometimes ruthless profiteering as perfectly compatible with Christian duty. Averse "to every species of recreation and merriment", McLaren was unpopular, but a good businessman and a vehement opponent of any attempt to give special treatment to Anglicanism in the province. He thought the best settlers for South Australia were Calvinistic Highlanders like himself, despised Angas's Lutheran settlers, and abominated Popery, and, therefore, the Irish. His idea of relaxation was to read theological treatises. Pike writes of this Adelaide John Knox:

> A revealing picture of the man shows him sombre in black, striding with disapproval through the worshippers assembling outside the Church of England and meeting a small group of natives returning from the river. Pointing to the Wesleyan chapel where he was about to preach, McLaren fell on his knees, lifting his hands and closing his eyes in a mime of prayer. He was overcome to see the aborigines nodding with delight and pointing heavenwards, thus proving that they were familiar with the idea of a deity on high. McLaren went on his way refreshed in spirit by the reflection that these black brands were already half plucked from the burning.[10]

The Aborigines always were polite.

The equally influential Stephens brothers, Samuel, John, and Edward, were all devout Wesleyans, sons of a Cornish minister. Samuel was the first manager of the South Australian Company and ended a stormy career by being thrown fatally from his horse on the hills above Glen Osmond. John Stephens fought the good fight for Wesley through the columns of the newspapers he edited in Adelaide—the *Observer* and, later, the *Register*. He bitterly attacked the demon drink in all its manifestations, but as a political radical as well as a Nonconformist, he was equally bitter in his attacks on any sign of backsliding or corruption among Adelaide leaders. Neither financial troubles (offended magnates withdrew their advertisements) nor any number of libel suits dampened the fire of his pen. Edward Stephens successfully managed the banking branch of the South Australian Company, was active in Nonconformist activities like the South Australian Bible Society, and eventually became a governor's nominee in the Legislative Council.

Angas cajoled, financed, or gave job opportunities to many more active Dissenters like these to draw them to South Australia and used his personal influence with the commissioners to ensure that at least a third of the settlers sent out by the Land Fund were industrious Nonconformists. Methodists, Baptists, Presbyterians, Congregationalists, Evangelical Anglicans, Bible Christians like the Rev. James Way, father of Sir Samuel Way, and Quakers like John Barton Hack who established a model property at Echunga—all these denominations had much in common. And where they differed, the circumstances in Adelaide and the enveloping social vision of the founders brought them together. United they opposed immorality—which included bathing in the sea at Glenelg for many years—alcohol, the sinful arts, and any attempt to reproduce in South Australia the social classes and religious hierarchy of England. United they stood for sabbatarianism, religious freedom, political progress, social reforms, sobriety, and good profitable business.

Angas, yet again, added to their ranks the German Lutherans, dissenters from religious conformity at home.

Much of the drive for constitutional progress in Adelaide, progress often far in advance of that made in comparable societies, derived from the local strength of Nonconformity. Since Wyclif and Cromwell, British Dissenters had been reformers and in the nineteenth century they were prominent in all movements for social and political change, including Chartism. Coupled with this radicalism went a suspicion of social pretensions and of government itself, as the governors and legislators of Adelaide soon learned.

It is not surprising that South Australia from the beginning was attractive to Nonconformists. Stephens in *The Land of Promise*, spoke of their hopes for the province in an article in the radical British newspaper *The Operative* of 5 February 1839. Stephens argued that Chartism would never prevail against the entrenched conservatism of England and went on: " ... emigration is *the* answer ... The Colony is never to be wrapped in Downing Street swaddling clothes ... It is managed by Commissioners ... and the Colony is a self-supporting one ... The Colony is likewise rid of the incubus of an established Church and delivered from the rapacity of an established priesthood".

Angas, that great facilitator, had written—and the sincerity of the man is palpable:

> My great object was, in the first instance, to provide a place of refuge for pious Dissenters of Great Britain, who could in their new home discharge their consciences before God in civil and religious duties without any disabilities. Then in the second place, to provide a place where the children of pious farmers might have farms on which to settle and provide bread for their families; and lastly, that I might be the humble instrument of laying the foundation of a good system of education and religious instruction for the poorer settlers.[11]

These were imperial sentiments, and although the reality was less noble than the dream, there is no doubt that for most Dissenters fleeing the snubs and discriminations of England, Adelaide was a "Paradise". Nor is there any doubt that the Nonconformist spirit, affected by local circumstances, was and to a certain extent still is the dominant feature of the Adelaide ethos and a significant contributor to its sense of difference. Certainly, during the last few years, the traditional pietism of Adelaide has crumbled away. The once fashionable Methodist chapel in Wellington Square is now a commercial television studio, for years the base of Ernie Sigley. Many other city churches and chapels are unused or have been taken over for various concerns. New religions have emerged. There is a mosque in South Adelaide (Muslims first came to South Australia in the form of Afghan and Indian camel drivers in the north) and the onion domes of a Russian Orthodox Church gleam over the south parklands. City gardeners are startled from their weekend calm by visitations by earnest missionaries for various millennarian sects. The chants and tinkling tambourines of Hare Krishna apostles rise over the din of Rundle Mall. The Salvation Army is well established and well liked in Adelaide: indeed the first Australian bridgehead of General Booth's followers was the inaugural Salvation Army open air meeting in the Botanic Park in 1880. Earlier still, in late 1845, the first Australian Churches of Christ group began with a meeting in Franklin Street, Adelaide, led by Thomas Magarey.

One last point. Recent commonwealth year books do not break up the religious statistics into states but the 1901 census revealed the peculiarity of South Australia's religious disposition. It showed that the South Australian percentage of Anglicans was 29 as opposed to the Australian average of 39 per cent, of Roman Catholics 14 as against 21, of the Nonconformist Methodist, Baptist, and Congregationalists 34.5 as opposed to 19, Lutherans 7 as opposed to 2. The proportions have not changed greatly since.

This explains a curious Adelaide phenomenon, particularly remarkable to an English visitor. The English social structure, especially in the nineteenth century, had the Anglicans firmly on top with the "chapel folk", the Nonconformists, most numerous in the lower middle and working classes. In Adelaide Methodists and kindred spirits permeated the establishment, the ruling class, from the beginning.

There is still a certain social cachet attached to Anglicanism and St. Peter's College, thanks to the strenuous if discreet efforts over the years of bishops and governors. Yet the Nonconformists have always been so strong and so successful that they occupy in force the upper regions of the social pyramid and have taken their values with them to the heights. Prince Alfred's College, the Methodist Ladies College (note the *ladies*), Scotch College, and the Presbyterian Girls' College have always seen themselves as socially equal—or almost equal—to the Anglican colleges. Thus Adelaide aristocracy became an odd hybrid of Methodism grafted onto Anglicanism, with a strong flavour of Presbyterianism, and this is reflected in the city's evolving mores.

Of course, explicit religious belief has waned in Adelaide, but not, perhaps, quite as much as elsewhere. And if Adelaide, in these swinging times, is a less raucous Babylon than Melbourne or Sydney or Brisbane, it is largely because of the inherited gravity and restraint of the old Dissenters, and of the foursquare religious traditions of the city.

Collectively, religious Dissent has indoctrinated Adelaide for most of its history. It should really have been called the city of the chapels, assuming the clear English distinction between church and chapel. On the bad, Pecksniffian side, this has meant stifling sabbatarianism, a narrow view of righteousness, stuffiness, parochialism, even hypocrisy. On the good side, Dissent has inculcated the city with a sense of decency, pragmatism, political and ethical concern, and social empiricism.

Education

It takes a very great deal of effort to make a little progress in educational affairs.

Alfred Williams, Director of Education, 1912

The reformers and Dissenters who created Adelaide were almost as concerned about education as they were about religion, looking upon both as inseparable parts of the same mystic entity. Angas, typically, defined the moral obligation when he stated at the formation of the South Australian School Society in London in 1836: "I consider it a duty, before even a tent be set up in the new province, to provide for education."

Similarly, the founders were anxious from the first to establish in the province mechanics' institutes, a British institution designed to placate and elevate the workers by means of respectable adult education. The commissioners decreed that if there were over 150 immigrants on any ship, a schoolmaster should be appointed to provide elementary education and moral lectures on the voyage. Like many of the commissioners' plans, this one does not appear to have succeeded, although there is evidence that respectable and religious tracts were handed hopefully round on the emigrant ships.

As in so many other matters, practice amid the stresses and uncertainties of early Adelaide differed greatly from theories refined in the Adelphi. A harshly utilitarian attitude to education soon developed, especially marked among politicians, so that many years later a philistine school inspector could declare: "What South Australia needs is rainfall, artificial manure and cheap labour ... education can wait."

The sectarianism of the new province was almost as much a hindrance to educational growth as commercial preoccupations. While in England, the Adelaide Dissenters had acquired such a pent-up dislike of Anglican dominance in both church and schools that they probably over-reacted in the heady religious freedom and equality proclaimed below Mount Lofty. Governor Robe, believing Anglicans to be "the most respectable members of the community", stirred up a bull ants' nest of controversy by his efforts to give state aid to religion and to church schools. After a tremendous amount of rancour, the Nonconformist advocates of "voluntaryism"—that is, financial self-sufficiency for churches and church schools—prevailed. State education when it came was secular and to this day any move towards a strong element of religious education, even of the most innocuous, "undenominational" kind, is a sure flashpoint of florid dissension in Adelaide.

Nonetheless, once the province had settled down, the youth of Adelaide were given educational opportunities generally superior to those available in British cities of comparable size. By 1844, there were fourteen schools in the city operating on the self-help principle. Clergymen like the Rev. Stow found that opening a school for the children of his flock supplemented a meagre income. In 1851 a Central Board of Education was established with public money and in 1875 John Hartley was appointed president of an expanded Council of Education, which quickly developed into the state Department of Education. Son of a Wesleyan minister, Hartley contained all the Adelaide virtues in his spare frame, and perhaps a modicum of the Adelaide vices. As Colin Thiele shows in his admirable history of the education department, *Grains of Mustard Seed*, Hartley observed "that strict code of morality, uprightness, integrity and service" extolled by most Adelaide pulpits. On the other hand, Premier Boucaut could criticize Hartley for "red tape, love of power, uniformity and doctrinairism". The *Bulletin and Lantern* of 21 May 1881 called him an "educational autocrat".

Hartley toiled unsparingly for over twenty years until, on his bicycle, he collided fatally with a horse and cart. A long procession of pupils and teachers followed his hearse to the North Road cemetery and six headmasters acted as pall bearers. Hartley and his inspectors had built up a vast, complex, and generally efficient system of primary schools rigidly centralized upon the director, and ruled "by regulation and circular" and the awful peregrinations of the inspectors and the Results Examination. Thiele shows that Hartley personally was imaginative and no friend to rote learning, but shortage of money, interference by politicians and sectarians, and the traditions of the Australian bureaucracy willy nilly helped create a rather inhuman administrative pyramid surmounted by what Thiele calls "the inflexible face of officialdom behind the administrator's desk".

Of course, education departments in the other colonies developed in much the same way, and South Australia's difficulties were worsened by its size and chronic poverty. When harvests were good, as in the 1880s, there was expansion, but generally Hartley and his successors, all grossly overworked, had to struggle along with inadequate budgets. During the 1930s depression, South Australian teachers, notoriously the worst paid in the commonwealth, endured a 15 per cent reduction in salary. Quality of schools ranged from tin or asbestos sheds in the mallee with a woman teacher on 90 pounds a year (she had to resign if she were disloyal enough to marry) to the big model schools, such as those in Grote and Flinders streets, and later the secondary schools. In 1876 a training college for teachers was established. This was transferred to the university in 1900. In 1892 the Education Act was amended so that education became free for most children. In 1905, a state secondary education system was instituted with the formation of the Adelaide High School and nine "district high schools".

As in the other states, the system seems to have been designed to process industrious and moral sons and daughters of Empire, strong on reading, writing, and arithmetic, and needlework for girls and drill for boys. "Drill strengthens the frame", vouchsafed one sage, "and cultivates a habit of ready obedience."

Meanwhile Catholic children attended Catholic schools, identical, if even more poverty-stricken, with the public schools, apart from religious teaching. The Lutherans set up their own schools. And of course independent colleges such as St. Peter's (Anglican, 1847) and Prince Alfred's (Methodist, 1869), later with counterparts for girls, were set up to carry on the traditions of Tom Brown's schooldays in the antipodes.

The University of Adelaide was founded in 1874 with donations from copper and land kings whose statuesque shapes, covered, like all Adelaide's statues, with verdigris and bird droppings, now preside over its front lawns. Characteristically, the first intention of the magnates was to found a theological seminary. Architecturally, the university ranges from the lively Gothic of the Mitchell building and the Elder Hall to 1970s functional, like the Wills building. It is cramped for space and the result is a pleasant and humane jumble of buildings, old and new, flights of steps, grottoes and recesses filled with greenery and agreeable surprises like a Japanese garden and a waterfall. Since Vice-Chancellor Badger's study overlooks this waterfall, it has been dubbed Badger's Leap by the students. The university has a good scholastic record and can take pride in alumni like Oliphant, Bragg, Florey, and Mawson. Its satellite, the Waite Agricultural Institute, was created by the wealthy landowner Peter Waite and has become a valuable centre for agricultural research and teaching.

Technical colleges, seminaries, an active Workers' Educational Association, a vigorous university department of adult education with its own radio station, VL5UV, Flinders University in the southern suburbs, and six colleges of advanced education now give Adelaide further educational substance, and its Department of Education, in this Dunstan period, is one of the most imaginative and liberal in the commonwealth.

Perhaps the most distinctive new educational phenomenon is the huge new Department of Further Education, created on the recommendation of the Karmel Report of 1972 and finally formalized with the passing of the Further Education Act in March 1976. Unique in Australia and influenced by modern British further education ideas, it has begun to develop the enormous potential for further education. With a budget for 1975–76 of nearly $40 million, a professional staff of well over one thousand and over 90,000 students, this department has shown the way to its counterparts in other states.

Culture

There is still a tag, prevalent in Adelaide—*Adelaide for Culture.*
Paul McGuire, 1939

The Adelaide pioneers were more interested in bettering their souls and their economic condition than anything else. However, some of them had always an interest in culture—respectable culture that is—and since 1960 at least, with the establishment of the biennial Adelaide Festival of Arts, culture has predominated over church in the municipal image.

Typically the Wakefieldians packed crates of books for the *Buffalo* to be used as a library in the projected Adelaide Mechanics' Institute. As early as 1834, a South Australian Literary Association was formed, based on the Adelphi Chambers in London, with the object of "diffusing useful knowledge among the colonists".

THE INSTITUTES[2]

Governor Gawler encouraged the opening of the Mechanics' Institute in 1839—a wooden hut on the site of the present railway station—and there and in the much more substantial stone building later erected on North Terrace the serious minded citizens gathered to borrow books and to hear "lectures on uplifting subjects by leading colonists". Johann Menge lectured on the wonders of geology to a crowd of notables before the first sod was turned over the Kapunda copper mine. The British mechanics' institutes had been founded at the turn of the century by a Quaker academic, George Birkbeck. His idea was that the "mechanics" of the Industrial Revolution should learn "useful knowledge" on the arts and sciences at these "peoples' seminaries" and so improve both their souls and their earning capacity. The institutes were to be controlled by the mechanics themselves.

Institutes under a variety of names, such as athenaeums and schools of arts, spread throughout colonial Australia like a cultural epidemic, and were especially popular in New South Wales and Victoria. However, in Adelaide the practice differed from British theory even more than in the other colonies. Adult education in the form of classes and lectures never really caught on, perhaps because the godly South Australians had quite enough lectures and classes in their churches. And from the start the Adelaide Institute, like its counterparts in the country towns, was inexorably controlled by the bourgeoisie.

The institutes (the demeaning, to respectable ears, prefix "mechanics" was soon dropped) developed and still survive mainly as libraries and meeting halls, and there is scarcely a South Australian town or suburb that does not possess one. Usually, they are pleasing Victorian buildings built of the honey-coloured local stone, but often down-at-heel these days.

In 1861 the Adelaide Mechanics' Institute combined with the South Australian Subscription Library to occupy a fine new building on North Terrace, and later cultural growths along that same boulevard included the Public Library, the National Gallery, and the Museum of Natural History. It was at the institute of the northern satellite town of Gawler in 1859 that "The Song of Australia" was judged to be the prizewinner for a national song contest. Characteristically nineteenth-century South Australian, with its highflown sentiment and regional pride, it fulfilled Agnas's hope that a regional ballad could be written which combined "solemnity with life".

Other learned societies soon grew from the same intellectual compost which nourished the institutes. The Adelaide Philosophical Society, which developed into the Royal Society of South Australia, was founded in 1853. A crop of similar societies covering interests from astronomy to zoology soon appeared.

CULTURAL BEGINNINGS

The Adelaide colonial newspapers advertised amusements and entertainments, some of which were of cultural dye. The *Register* of 4 April 1846, for example, declared: "We are glad to learn that something like excellent music is at last to be publicly heard in South Australia. Mr. Ravec, an accomplished violinist, just arrived from Singapore, proposes to favour the public with a display of musical powers, which, from what we have learnt of their extent, will indeed be a treat of the choicest kind. Mr. Jinberg, who has lately settled in Adelaide, is said to be a good pianist, and is to assist on the occasion." It was clearly something of a struggle, amid the roughness and uncertainty of the foundation period, to generate any substantial cultural activity. Under the heading of "The Fine Arts", the *Register* of 8 November 1845 reported: "By the help of Book Clubs, the kindness of unforgetful friends at home, and an abundant supply of newspapers, most of the colonists have contrived to keep tolerably forward their knowledge of the current literature and politics of the day. The 'fine arts' however,—painting especially—have as yet been beyond their reach." In the same paper, a Mr. Bennett had to rely on the "Patronage of the Lieutenant-Governor", when he advertised a concert of "vocal and instrumental music" at the Freemason's Tavern, tickets five shillings each.

The high-minded citizen found it hard to buy good books in Adelaide. Typical of the novels offered for sale by Platts of Hindley Street, all with "strongly-bound, gilt backs", were *The Female Bluebeard* by Eugene Sue, *The Log Cabin* by Mrs. Clavers, and *The Castle of Inchvally* by Mrs. Howard.

Two hundred people turned up to hear Mr. Bennett's concert, including "a large number of country gentlemen, with their families, and of the *haut ton* and respectability of the city". For several years, Adelaide's "*haut ton* and respectability" had to make do with portions of the classics leavening the farce and vaudeville at the popular theatres. For example, in October 1845 the Pavilion Theatre slotted the third act of "Othello" between "a variety of singing and dancing" and "a laughable farce".

The occasional artistic immigrant like Carl Linger gradually improved the cultural scene. Born in Berlin, where he studied music at the university, Linger arrived at Port Adelaide on the *Princess Louise* along with three hundred other German settlers who came to South Australia mainly for conscience's sake. In a letter to his mother, Linger wrote that "because the country generally is not very advanced culturally" he would forsake music for farming. His thirty-two hectare block near Gawler, on which he built a house for sixty pounds, broke his health and his heart, so he walked to Adelaide "with two shillings in my pocket". Within a few years, Linger was presiding over considerable musical activity in the city. He was conductor of Adelaide's first Philharmonic Orchestra, had formed the Adelaide Choral Society, founded the Adelaide *Liedertafel*, conducted the *Messiah*, and had written the stirring music for Caroline Carleton's "Song of Australia".

Yet, as in all the Australian capitals and, indeed, in all the British provincial cities, music, drama, painting, and literature had an uphill struggle in Adelaide until well into the twentieth century. There was no government money for the arts. Commerce prevailed, and commercial attitudes. The chronic economic depressions endured by Adelaide, the isolation, the newness of everything, the lack of a settled sense of folk culture among the settlers (the Germans were an exception here), the suspicions felt for drama and art by some influential ministers, the parochialism—all these militated against cultural growth.

It is remarkable, for instance, that when Anthony Trollope made an extended visit to Adelaide in 1872, no cultural or learned society made proper use of the opportunity. Here was, as Adelaide was very well aware, one of the most famous and popular of English novelists, one whose moral, amusing, and humane stories were appreciated by the citizens. Yet no group or individual invited Trollope to give lectures, or readings, or seminars. The press was extraordinarily interested in him, but there were no in-depth interviews or appreciations of his works printed. Trollope stayed with the Elders, made notes industriously for his travel book, toured the country towns, descended the deepest mine at Moonta, and made some informed criticisms of the wasteful nature of local wheat farming. (He felt, correctly, that there was insufficient attention paid to soil conservation and enrichment.) Trollope was treated as a Celebrity. His wanderings and inspections were reverently reported by the newspapers. But there was no genuine cultural communication between him and the Adelaideans. He may as well have been a visitor from another planet. Of course, the citizens waited impatiently for his book *Australia and New Zealand* to be published in England; and were finally relieved when he was kind and approving about Adelaide.

Twenty-six years later, in 1898, the cultural scene had not improved all that much according to two more distinguished visitors, the busy socialist intellectuals, Sidney and Beatrice Webb. The Webbs inspected the education system, which they praised, met Premier Kingston, Chief Justice Way ("a character"), the governor, and the mayor, "Charley Tucker ... extremely anxious to be deferential and polite, but extremely awkward ... he had by far the most enquiring mind we had met". The Webbs thought South Australia "perhaps the pleasantest of all the Australian colonies". But they were condescending about its "cultural attributes":

> Adelaide ... resembles more than any English town we know a German "Residenzstadt"— the capital of a little principality, with its parks and gardens, its little court society, its absence of conspicuous industrialism, and its general air of laying itself out quietly to enjoy a comfortable life. It lacks the charm of the German Residenzstadt in history, art (especially music and the theatre) and scholarship. On the other hand, it has the interest of democratic politics and an ever progressive mobility. It is to be hoped that it will gradually add some of the charms of the German city—music, for instance, by a municipal band, if not by a municipal opera house, might easily come; the little University might develop some scholarship; and there is already the nucleus of a public art gallery. Adelaide has, in fact, more chance than any other Australian city of becoming the Weimar or, more precisely, the Stuttgart of the Southern Hemisphere.[3]

I suspect that the Webbs, who usually overwhelmed their readers with facts and statistics, were guilty of superficial judgment here. With their admiration for German cities, they should have noted that people of German descent were prominent in Adelaide, not least in music. By 1898, Adelaide already had several brass bands and, thanks to the efforts of people like Linger, a quite thriving interest in music. Yet in general the Webbs' summary of Adelaide's characteristic is interesting; and their comparison of the city with Weimar and Stuttgart can be added to the other equations of Adelaide with Athens and Florence. The point, of course, that all these comparers overlooked, was that Adelaide is Adelaide.

THE ARTS

In literature, Adelaide prides itself on its connexions, sometimes a little strained, with writers like Adam Lindsay Gordon, C.J. Dennis, John Shaw Neilson, and the Jindyworobaks. Catherine Helen Spence with her Jane Austenish perceptions of a genteel Adelaide governess, *Clara Morrison* (1854), and Simpson Newland with his "Boys' Own Paper" style novel of colonial life, *Paving the Way* (1893), were perhaps more attuned to contemporary mores.

Adelaide has always been many sided, and resident writers like the poet, the late and much lamented, Ian Mudie, the biographer, poet and children's writer, Colin Thiele, and the elegant poet, biographer, publisher, and novelist, Geoffrey Dutton are as much an integral part of the Adelaide scene as insurance skyscrapers and *The Advertiser*. And it is somehow appropriate that the city of churches is also the home base of Max Harris, Australia's columnist gadfly. The avant garde poetry magazine *Angry Penguins* emanated from Adelaide and, with Harris its editor, was the victim in 1944 of Australia's most notable literary hoax—the Ern Malley poems. Produced by James McAuley and Harold Stewart, these verses were an attempt to imitate abstract contemporary poetry with "deliberately concocted nonsense".

Painting, music, and drama have usually found Adelaide a congenial setting. Colonel Light himself had a delicate skill with watercolour. The names of the early topographical landscapists S.T. Gill and George French Angas, and Sir Hans Heysen of a later period are outstanding. Adelaide now has several galleries and art societies. In 1975, bewildered crowds stood before Jackson Pollock's *Blue Poles* in the National Gallery, trying to relate more than a million dollars to the exuberant paint images before them. An annual event in the city is the exhibition of paintings by local artists for sale in the Elder Park by the Torrens.

R.E.N. Twopeny wrote in his *Town Life in Australia*: "'How on earth am I to get on in Adelaide?' said a musician of considerable merit to me, 'when, as you know, there is no one with whom I can provoke comparisons'. The very superiority of the man was fatal to his success."[4] Alleged colonial cultural inferiorities, pervaded by rose-tinted memories of London culture, always seemed acute to such wounded souls. However, since Governor Hindmarsh's daughters sang by the reedy banks of the Torrens, the citizens have been fond of music and singing, particularly when they had a religious flavour. In 1843, a combination of three flutes, one violin, violoncello, and piano was described as a "grand orchestra", and in 1859 an orchestra of twenty players accompanied a performance of the *Messiah*. Chamber music groups gradually appeared and in 1920 the South Australian State Orchestra was formed. The University Music Society, based on the Elder Conservatorium, was founded in 1954.

If Adelaide drama was provincial it was also popular. The first theatre, the Theatre Royal, was an annexe to the Adelaide Tavern and the first real theatre, the

Queen's Theatre, which seated a thousand people, was opened in 1841 and ruled the theatrical roost until 1868. Music hall acts and vaudeville were popular in many Adelaide inns, but the entrenched Grundyism of the establishment imposed irritating restrictions on all forms of drama for many years. However, in recent decades Adelaide's thespians have had reason to take pride in an increasing number of well-equipped theatres and substantially more official and popular support.

Adelaide's cultural claims began to have more credence interstate, then internationally, after 1960 when the first Adelaide Festival of Arts was held, and became a biennial event. Henceforth, the festival would be the crown, the focus, and the grand stimulus for the state's culture. As well, it would be a source of waxing municipal pride, for it brought prestige to a smallish provincial city and, moreover, a pleasant access of business for the merchants and hoteliers of the Festival City. With the festival an established, successful fact, (opened on one occasion, moreover, by the Queen Mother), city fathers and loyalists began seriously talking once more of their city as "the Athens of the South".

However the festival, which lasts for three weeks every second March, has had it critics and its crises of identity. One Board of Governors rejected Alan Seymour's play, *One Day of the Year* (since become immensely popular and a set text in many schools) as unsuitable because it seemed to criticize the R.S.L. Another play, *The Ham Funeral* by Nobel prize winning novelist Patrick White was rejected by the 1962 festival committee amid stormy controversy. But in general the festival has succeeded extraordinarily well, becoming an immanent and influential feature of Adelaide's lifestyle. It comprises a Writers' Week,—a unique rally of the literary clans in Australia—ballet, opera, drama, music, art displays, seminars, exhibitions, folk dancing, craft, and many other cultural activities in one exhausting whirligig. It brings illustrious performers, orchestras, dance troupes, artists, and writers to Adelaide from overseas and at the local level it provokes a city-wide rash of exhibitions, concerts, and other cultural activity. It is also one of those rare occasions when non-British immigrant groups in the city can give an inkling of their native cultures. The display of folk dancing in Elder Park by troupes of Greeks, Austrians, Italians, Croats, Hungarians, and other nationalities is one of the most genuinely popular festival events.

Of course, Adelaide's festival is variously criticized as elitist, expensive, of being too broad, too narrow and so on. But in general the citizens have taken the festival to their cautious but loyal hearts, and they reject any suggestion that their festival should lower its standards to compete with the forced junketing of Melbourne's Moomba or Sydney's Waratah or Brisbane's Warana.

In 1972, the elegant keystone to the festival edifice was slipped into place when the Adelaide Festival Theatre, between Parliament House and the Torrens Lake, was opened. It is impossible to approach it without a feeling of excitement. This remarkable building, which also houses a drama complex, was built with none of the fuss, expense, or ballyhoo of Sydney's Opera House and is declared by many to be, in its quiet Adelaide way, much superior.

The Festival Theatre, now two festivals old, has gained many superlatives in description since it was opened. A long encomium by Andrew Porter, the theatre and dance critic of the *New York Times* and the *Financial Times*, was published with palpable pleasure by *The Advertiser* on 23 March 1974. Mr. Porter spoke of festival facilities in cities like Bayreuth, the English and Canadian Stratfords, Salzburg and Edinburgh, and went on: "But when you put everything together—looks; facilities for performance and for the performers; convenience for the audience; setting; climate; and that elusive quality, the 'feel' of the whole place—well, then, Adelaide, I think, comes out on top. I simply can't fault it. It is one of the world's great theatres." This most welcome critic praised the "rich and exciting mix" of the whole festival, the Town Hall, the Art Gallery, "the beaches and mountains and sun"; above all, he praised Light's city: "Adelaide is a jewel, and should be spoiled no more." Always sensitive to the Adelaide image, the citizenry must have purred as they read all this. *Newsweek* of 29 March 1976, commenting on the 1976 Festival, which brought sixteen hundred writers, artists, and performers to the city, concluded: "The role that the Adelaide Festival plays in the cultural life of Australia is immense."

The festival—pantheon of Adelaide's, and indeed Australia's, culture—is now solidly based in a city which has always given more than the usual honour to culture, asserting once again in the second half of the twentieth century the city's sense of difference.

It was the City Council which took a vigorous initiative with both the Festival of Arts and the Festival Theatre. A triumvirate composed of Lord Mayor Hargrave, Sir Lloyd Dumas of the *Advertiser*, and Professor John Bishop of the University of Adelaide led the movement for the first festival, with strong backing from the Council. As early as 1954, the Council was considering the establishment of a Festival Hall—the original idea was for a concert hall—in Victoria Square. Later civic dignitaries, such as former Lord Mayors Sir Arthur Rymill and Sir James Irwin, persisted with the idea with such effect that a Festival Hall Act was passed in 1964 during the term of the Playford government. The plan then was to build the hall on Montefiore Hill where a Bonython mansion, Carclew (now a children's drama centre), was acquired. The state government promised to provide $800,000 and the Council made itself responsible for raising $1.2 million. However, the Council knew its Adelaide. The government stipulated that the community should put up $100,000 for a festival building. In fact, $160,000 was raised by the Council's public appeal. (The surplus was spent on works of art, now in the Festival Theatre.) The federal government contributed $200,000.

In 1965 a significant change took place. Within the Adelaide City Council and within the community generally a conviction was developing that a concert hall was the wrong building for the festival city and that Carclew was the wrong site. The Council sought the views of anyone who wished to express them, including the leaders of ballet, opera, music, drama, within both state-subsidised and commercial spheres. The firm view emerged that the "hall" should become a 2,000 seat multi-purpose theatre capable of producing symphony orchestra concerts, opera, ballet, musical comedy, but not drama. Premier Dunstan had assumed office by this time and it was with his encouragement the Council determined that the theatre would be built. In this exploratory period the concept of a three-theatre complex was first put forward.

Next came a series of discussions on a new site and, during the time of Premier Hall's government, the location by the Torrens was chosen (Hall having remarked how well London's Festival Theatre looked by the Thames). Multi-purpose theatres were relatively new and to a degree experimental, so Town Clerk Russell Arland, the principal architect, Colin Hassell, and the acoustic consultant, Michael Price, toured world theatres to ensure that the latest overseas experience was applied. Then the Council went ahead and built the lovely Festival Theatre with greatly expanded state government financial asssistance. Premier Dunstan, when he returned to the helm of state affairs, maintained a continued interest and gave the Council the encouragement it needed.

In 1974 a Festival Centre Trust was formed by the government and assumed responsibility for the operation of the theatre and the construction of the Playhouse, the Space, the Amphitheatre and the car park adjoining, to complete the whole complex.

Many observers say it was the congenial and effective relationship developed during the planning and construction of the Festival Theatre that formed the basis of the cooperation between the state government and the Adelaide City Council on many other important city projects, the City of Adelaide Plan being probably the most important. This pioneering work in Adelaide's modern cultural life by the city fathers needs to be stressed, if only because admiring interstate and international articles on Dunstan's Adelaide imply that he alone, a magical compound of gourmet cook, poet, actor and politician, turned a sobersided city into a cultural dynamo with one wave of his charismatic wand. Dunstan certainly stimulated and amplified this artistic efflorescence during his second premiership. For instance, his government's generous commitment made possible the expansion of the Festival Theatre into the present exciting complex of Theatre, Space, and Amphitheatre. But the patient spadework had been done and the imaginative first decisions made by the City Council—in the direct Adelaide tradition of honouring the arts.

Adelaide Respectability, Virtue and Vice

The traditional adjectives to apply to Adelaide are parochial,
decorous, conservative, gracious, provincially aristocratic.
John Gunther, 1972

Where is the core of the British Empire? In the Adelaide Club ...
Here ... you will find the England of Kipling, or even of Dickens.
Boyd Neel, 1960

Traditionally, Adelaide society was characterized by what Pike has called a "nobly depressing rectitude". This rectitude had been deliberately imported, lock stock and barrel along with churches, ministers, the Protestant ethic, and copious quantities of good books by the founding fathers. It was expected that Adelaide should be pious, industrious, and grave; and so, on the whole it turned out. Here was a Mediterranean setting, but it was no Mediterranean community which developed on the dusty plain by the warm blue gulf. Rather it was a Nonconformist throng of Britons transposed from the fogs and chapels of Manchester, London, and Glasgow to the startling stars and wide expanses of South Australia. The Adelaideans clung with an almost doctrinaire fervour to their Britishness, to the attitudes, customs, snobberies, and even the stifling clothes of "home".

Most notably, they had brought with them a vehement particle of British Dissenting religion. This developed in isolation—just as Puritanism became the dominant force in colonial Massachusetts—to set the moral tone of Adelaide. Thus the Adelaide sabbath, with all that this implied, became an extreme example of Victorian sabbatarianism. Implicit in this were temperance, a stress on outward pietism, a hostility to "immorality", and a yearning for Adelaide-style respectability. The city was founded specifically to be different from other Australian cities. There were to be no convicts, no military, no paupers, no rum currency. Instead there were to be the Reverend Stow, that godly businessman David McLaren, articulate Methodism in the form of *Register* editor John Stephens, and the many disciples and agents of George Fife Angas. There was to be good planning, good government and, above all, religion. And to the early citizens and their descendants for many years, religion was synonymous with morality and a special, joyless reverence for the sabbath.

That tragic figure, William Light, was out of place in Adelaide. In his earlier years, the colonel had been a dashing romantic, wanderer, man of action, and dreamer. He was a Regency gentleman of the better type. This Peninsular War veteran, this Mediterranean rover may have had a premonition, when he came to South Australia with his mistress, that a rising tide of respectability would soon engulf him. It is perhaps as well for the colonel's reputation that he died as soon as he did, and in such Byronic circumstances, after giving the citizens their city. For, paradoxically, Light, once respectably dead, soon became Adelaide's legend—although Maria Gandy was never mentioned. Adelaide was to be thoroughly Victorian in sentiment and attitude even in advance of England.

Its formative era, peopled by picturesque characters like Inspector Tolmer, was short lived. There were no convicts, bushrangers, goldrushes, or profligate land boomers to prolong it. It soon solidified into a respectability that was to hold Adelaide in an alabaster grip until well into the twentieth century. And this respectability was not typified by adventurers like Light or Eyre or Sturt. It was epitomized by more limited, more sober, and more financially successful men like Fisher, Kingston, Gilles, and Edward Stephens. Later, the bold commercial dash of merchants like the Elders and Barr Smiths was counterbalanced at home by God-fearing respectability.

Twopeny observed in 1882:

> In Adelaide middle class respectability is too strong for larrikinism, and reports a far healthier social and moral tone than obtains in either Melbourne or Sydney; but for these advantages the little town pays the small but disagreeable price of Philistinism. Want of culture, Phariseeism and narrow mindedness find a more congenial home there than anywhere else in Australia, but to my mind these are a cheap price to pay for the piety and real goodness which they cloak.[1]

The Evangelical Governor Gawler, who forbade dancing at Government House, spoke for the burgeoning respectability of Adelaide in 1840 at a pavilion next to Fordham's Hotel where two hundred leading citizens gathered to commemorate the foundation three years before. The *Register* of 11 January 1840 reported Gawler in full moralizing flight: "I heartily wish that some of the Colonization Commissioners might drop down in the midst of the respectable meeting now assembled. It would give them an idea which they cannot now have of the prosperity and progress of South Australia." The colonists cheered loudly, as unaware as the governor that the province was on the point of encountering economic storms. Gawler passed on to safer ground to praise the local "kind of government which has not been tried elsewhere" and went on: "let us keep a high tone of society—let us bring our sable brethren into a comfortable state—and there will not be such a colony in the world as our colony". Adelaide achieved the desired high tone, but the sable brethren suffered much the same as elsewhere in Australia.

Gawler next approached a problem which must have agonized Adelaide teetotallers over the years: the fact that the province had a superb capacity for wine growing. However, he managed to harness even this fact to his chariot as he declared: "Ardent spirits are truly the root of all evil. They are the origin of more than two thirds of the crime which occurs in the British Colonies, and it is a vice for which there is no excuse in a country like this ... Look at Spain, Portugal and the South of France, and you have nothing of the kind there ... Let us follow their example and be strictly a wine-drinking community." This last sentiment must have jarred some of his xenophobic audience. They would certainly have agreed with the governor that "ardent spirits", especially gin and rum, did the Devil's work wherever English was spoken but I doubt if they shared Gawler's enthusiasm for the morality of Catholic Mediterranean Europeans. "Look at ... the south of France" indeed. Yet many of them had already invested in wine growing. Wine was a more genteel drink than rum, surely. So for those who could stretch a point of dogma and partake of wine, or at least sell it, no doubt it seemed quite respectable to increase Adelaide's prosperity by profiting on the vine.

Once it had defined its moral code, Adelaide society tried to settle down into the social pyramid form common to all British communities. There was, after all, a governor to represent the Crown. The Crown, in Britain, symbolized peers and squirearchy, middle class and lower orders, all in an ancient system, "the rich man, in his castle", as the Anglican hymn puts it, "the poor man at his gate/God made them high and lowly/And ordered their estate."

Not surprisingly, such old world ideas never caught on completely in Adelaide. The social pyramid was somewhat flattened. For one thing, Adelaide was mainly Nonconformist and the Nonconformists had never been considered upper class in England. The sterner Adelaide Dissenters were long sceptical of the Adelaide Government House set and its pretensions. Unlike Sydney or Melbourne, Adelaide never contained a significant number of army officers and veterans to form a ready made upper class. Land distribution in South Australia, mainly in thirty-two hectare blocks, favoured the small farmer rather than the squatter who, in the eastern colonies, soon acquired vast properties and squirearchical pretensions. Perhaps the counterparts to these were most marked in the mid north of South Australia, where thirty or so pastoral dynasties managed to parcel up about two thirds of the best land among themselves.

Morphett, rather like Wentworth in New South Wales, and just as unsuccessfully, sought in 1849 to create a Torrens side peerage with his proposal for an upper legislative chamber composed of big land owners like himself adorned with hereditary titles. The idea appears to have been taken seriously only by a very few, but it was a splendid opportunity for Stevenson to use the *Register* as a cudgel. The notion of South Australian titles was to Stevenson "fudge in its purest absurdity" and Morphett "an indifferently shingled legislator". He suggested that the Land Sale Book should become the local peerage record. The *Adelaide Times* was equally humorous about the city's "flunkeyhood" being elevated to an ermined "North Terrace clackocracy".[2] Adelaide preferred its lords British.

However, as soon as they comfortably could do so, some men strove to climb the rungs of the makeshift colonial social ladder. One way of doing this was to own broad acres. Davenport, who had a fine property at Macclesfield, wrote to his father in 1844: "You might have a pretty park of 500 acres, a good, roomy healthy house in it for 400 pounds, your tenants would supply you with meat, bread and garden produce and all other country luxuries—good horses, fruit and trees you could amuse yourself with ... The Governor would put J.P. after your name and doubtless make you an Honourable member of Council."[3] Davenport was to do even better than this. He went on to parliamentary eminence. a knighthood, great wealth, and fame as "Squire of Beaumont".

Another way was to bring over, or make, so much money in the city that the governor would notice you, and invite you to Government House. The old Dissenters had urged the authorities to send Adelaide a governor who was "not a soldier, sailor or place hunter", but eventually they too fell under the spell of Government House eclat. Poor Hindmarsh in his insect-infested hut had never been able to stage grand occasions. Gawler, despite his pious opposition to dancing and cards, put on a few levees and receptions, to which some of the city gentry came in court dress and wearing swords. Robe went further. He extended his active patronage to hunting and racing. In 1847 the Adelaide Hunt Club had its first run, indulged in by 130 sportsmen, and by 1850 there were a good number of regular race meetings. At such gatherings, the new colonial aristocracy would flutter its wings. Robe pleased the ladies, too, by his encouragement of music and dancing. He held balls at Government House to mark the queen's birthday and the new year. There was ferocious competition among the fair for the honour of partnering the bachelor governor. The *Register* of 3 January 1846 reported:

> His Excellency the Governor celebrated the ninth anniversary of the establishment of the colony on Wednesday last by a grand ball and supper. The company, which was unprecedentedly numerous, began to arrive about ten o'clock, and the dancing, which commenced soon after that hour, was continued with great spirit till dawn of the next morning. The supper-rooms were thrown open at one o'clock, and his Excellency's guests had every reason to be pleased with their reception and entertainment.

But Robe was not liked for his mineral royalties and attempts to provide state aid to religion. Sir Henry Young, amiable, civilian, diplomatic and married, filled the role of social arbiter nicely. Young agonized his guests by requiring London-style etiquette and dress at his receptions much to the amusement of Adelaide plebeians. Pike quotes a humorous and widely circulated bill of the time:

> We understand that His Excellency Sir Henry Young ... has been pleased to authorise -x- to affix the letters S.N.O.B. after those of J.P. in the description of his identity and permission to use the arms of the celebrated family of Snobs of that Ilk, namely, a scutcheon of pretense ... with a nose proper at the extremity of which a human hand with the thumb and finger extended as taking a sight *vert*.[4]

Social snobbery soon became strong in Adelaide as it was in all the allegedly classless Australian colonies. Once the humbly born Dissenting founding fathers settled down and became mellowed by affluence, they, and particularly their wives, tended to covet some at least of the privileges of wealth they had criticized in England. No city could have adored a royal prince more lavishly than Adelaide did in 1867, when it feted the Duke of Edinburgh with gas illuminations and endless addresses of loyalty. Adelaide may have rejected Morphett's idea of an hereditary aristocracy and chuckled at "Squire" Fisher's pride in his new coat of arms, but the realities of privilege and social gradations were there in strength. The obsequious tone of public addresses to visiting royalty and titled governors does not accord well with the foundation principles of well-nigh republican democracy.

And while South Australia was better known for wheat farms than sheep runs, for thirty-two hectare blocks than vast properties, something like a land-owning squirearchical class did emerge. As J.B. Hirst has shown in his *Adelaide and the Country, 1870–1917* most of the big landowners tended to live in the city, appointing managers for their estates. However one or two, like W.T. Mortlock, resembled English squires in the bush. Mortlock's Martindale Hall near Clare, now owned by Adelaide Univeristy and used memorably in the film *Picnic at Hanging Rock*, was a fair copy of an English stately home. To this demesne the Adelaide Hunt Club, horses, hounds, and all, travelled by special train.

For the first years of settlement, the Adelaide class system was confused. During the "hutting" period the colonists were more concerned with survival than social distinctions. Writing as "A Colonist of 1839" on "Some Social Aspects of South Australian Life" in the *Register*, Catherine Spence was nostalgic about the free and easy, communal atmosphere of the foundation period:

> In the early days of a free colony we see something of that Utopia where man learns the usefulness, the dignity and the blessedness of labour, where work is paid for according to its hardness and its disagreeableness, and not after the standard of overcrowded countries where bread is dear and human life and strength is cheap ... Perhaps never in any human society did circumstances realize the ideas of the community of labour and equality of the sexes so fully as in South Australia in the early days .

But grandees like the Mortlocks and Sir Sidney Kidman, of whom it was said that he could walk from Adelaide to Darwin on land that he owned or leased, were exceptions to the generally egalitarian rule that prevailed over rural South Australia. Most of the cultivated land was owned by small farmers. Pike observes:

> The 16,350 independent farmers of 1900 employed fewer than 16,000 paid labourers ... Owners might do any work without being downgraded. There was little to separate master and servant even when success came. Prosperity and age brought farmers to town but did not alter their practice of social equality. To them and their hospitable wives worth was measured in sincerity, not wealth. Their thrift, perseverance and lack of pretension were middle class virtues already enthroned in Adelaide.[5]

It was in the city that the pinnacles of influence existed, and these were rapidly occupied by "old colonists" and scions of Old Adelaide Families. As we have seen, names like Morphett, Fisher, Dutton, Elder, Barr Smith, Kingston, and Davenport crop up again and again on prestigious, governor-backed committees, the City Council and Parliament. Old colonists showed their gentility and moral worth by patronizing societies like the Mechanics' Institute and various scientific or philosophical bodies. They were sociable at the South Australian Club, which emerged from the ashes of the 1840s depression as the Adelaide Club. Since 1863 this club has represented Adelaide masculine gentility on North Terrace.

Yet even as social stratification settled on Adelaide, the sense of difference remained strong. Gentility in Adelaide was never synonymous with blue blood and high living. Knighthoods were freely showered by governors among Adelaide notables, and respectfully accepted, but baronetcies and peerages were not. Society never completely closed the mahogany doors upon the rest of Adelaide. Burra copper propelled "nobodies" like the shopkeeper Graham and the chemist Paxton to the top of the social tree, but nothing but continuing moral worth would keep their descendants there. Pike points out that only twenty-five Adelaide families were mentioned in Burke's *Colonial Gentry* of 1891, and very few of the "old colonists" wanted to probe their ancestry beyond the arrival of the *Buffalo*.[6] To be fair, the same could be said of most of the adventurers who "came over with the Conqueror" to found a new English aristocracy. They too were mainly *arriviste*: magnates in the new land, nobodies at home.

It was respectability, rather than any inherited virtues, that counted in Adelaide society, and even the poor could aim at this. To be sure, it was a very great thing in Adelaide to be a "pioneer"—descendant of a man or woman involved in the Adelphi discussions and who sailed south on the *Africaine* or the *Buffalo*. There is a similar veneration in the United States for alleged or real descendants of *Mayflower* passengers. It was almost as fine to be an "old colonist", a scion of a (preferably self-paying) settler who came to Adelaide before the gold rush. There was always a good deal of old colonist cliquism controlling politics, banking, insurance and commerce, and fostered by some independent schools.

Yet overt and recognized respectability could bring almost as much honour to an Adelaidean whose grandfather never dined with Hindmarsh or commiserated with Colonel Light. Comparative newcomers, like Sir Langdon Bonython who rose from obscurity to wealth and influence on *The Advertiser* could scale the social Mount Lofty in their own lifetime. Adelaide-style respectability carried its obligations. It is remarkable, for example, how so many successful businessmen, almost as a matter of course, gave away to worthy causes large portions of their income. George Fife Angas, often in financial straits because of his philanthropy, is one striking example. The Elders and Barr Smiths who gave large sums to the University of Adelaide, and Peter Waite, another self-made man, who donated most of his private fortune and the very mansion he had built for himself to form the Waite Institute, followed this tradition. Of course, it was a feature of British Victorian private enterprise for captains of industry to give generously to good works. Cynics could regard this as their passports to salvation. Yet in Adelaide this idea that the acquisition of riches is good but to give them away is at least as good was especially strong. The city's churches, educational institutions, parks, charities, and even the conservation movement flourished because of it. And it still survives in the flag sellers who lie in wait along North Terrace every morning. To take one recent example, it was an Adelaide philanthropist, the late Kenneth Stirling, who gave $100,000 in 1972 to make possible Adelaide University's radio station. Government money had been refused.

Respectability then, rather than ancient lineage or conspicuous consumption, was paramount in Adelaide society. For a long time, the city fathers looked askance at the professions and the public service, seeing more virtue in high-level trade and self-reliance. To quote the admirable Pike again: "A man was judged respectable not by the destination he had arrived at, but according to the road he had travelled; and the five roads to respectability in Adelaide were early arrival, thrift, temperance and its illegitimate offspring abstinence, piety and the ownership of land."[7] Mind you, while it seems true that a poor but respectable shopkeeper might be thought well of, Pike's five roads seem to have been more clearly recognized when they led to wealth and social status. This, in Adelaide, usually meant productive investments in local banks and insurance companies, children at the right schools and membership of the right clubs, attendance at approved churches, intermarriage with the right families, broad acres and the possession of an imposing villa in the right parts of North Adelaide, East Terrace, the inner suburbs, or the Adelaide Hills. In current terms, Adelaide aristocracy was essentially White Anglo Saxon Protestantism on parade.

Hugh Stretton remarks in his *Ideas for Australian Cities* (1970): "It was easy to mock the respectable society of the old Adelaide oligarchy. They did tend to marry each other's money, meet at the Club, cultivate tennis and bougainvillea, attend chamber concerts and 'preserve standards' in quaintly Victorian ways. But they had other qualities, which were eventually to converge in sparking their industrial revolution."[8] Many mordant and witty observers often found it easy to mock them, at church, at the hunt, at the Stock Exchange and elsewhere. Their shady-hatted ladies clung gamely to gloves and calling cards long after they had become extinct in England. Pike quotes two critics of Adelaide's parvenu social pretensions in the 1840s. One claimed there were no real gentry in the province: "The only noblemen I am aware of are a few—a very few— of nature's noblemen." Another complained of "the impertinent attempts of every low butcher and baker to set up for a gentleman".

Such comments could be brushed off by the oligarchs as the buzzings of envious blowflies. However one satirical thrust, at least, went in up to the hilt for it was aimed from within the ranks of the aristocracy itself. In 1905 a small red pamphlet with a thistle on the cover and entitled *Arcadian Adelaide*[9] was issued by a Twin Street printer. It was written by a personable and well educated lady "Thistle Anderson" who, scorning to hide behind a pen name, had her real name, Mrs. Herbert Fisher, also printed on the cover. She had, too, an impeccable North Adelaide address. Detesting Adelaide as she did, Thistle Anderson had hit upon the novel idea of writing a hostile pamphlet on the city and its people and paying for its publication.

To this modern reader at least, *Arcadian Adelaide* seems an unbalanced and at times hysterical diatribe. She loathed everything about Adelaide, accusing the citizens of snobbery, dullness, small-mindedness, even cruelty to horses. She called the city, so touchy about its civic dignity, "the Village". "Their ideas are, for the most part", she wrote of her gentlefolk acquaintances, "about as broad as Blondin's wire, and their cardinal virtues are Religious Belief and Conventionality". (Blondin was a tightrope performer.) She dipped her pen in acid to observe, further, "May a merciful God forgive Adelaide her wine ..." The unkindest cut of all was that she thought one of a few good things about Adelaide was that one could buy a railway ticket to Melbourne there.

Even granted the strong Adelaide tradition of journalistic satire and invective, *Arcadian Adelaide* was extraordinary. And the fact that many of her arrows found their mark is proved by the fury of the protests. One Adelaide defender, John Norton, went to the trouble of printing a *Reply*, price one penny, which was an incoherent jumble of passionate abuse concluding with a chauvinistic order to Thistle to "Quit books for babies".

Thistle Anderson's broadside was a rare event, for Adelaide's blanket respectability tended to emasculate homegrown social comment in the late nineteenth and early twentieth centuries. Her scalpel-job on Adelaide society slashed in a wide arc from the pretentious display of the *nouveau riche* through a not so oblique reference to illegitimacy and on to an attack on the old families:

> Let us glance at local society. In a street I know, on one corner, Rags, a cheap but successful draper, has reared a red and white edifice ... Further up, an inferior edition of the share market assumes the pretensions of a Grand Duke ... The main industry ... is child-bearing and Adelaide, both married and unmarried, does her best to help the birth rate along. Motherhood *may* be the noblest mission of woman, but I question whether the Almighty Himself would approve of the perpetuation of some of the Village's "family trees".

However, oblivious, or at least outwardly oblivious, to such onslaughts from persons they would have deemed either envious, ill-conditioned, or mad, the Old Adelaide Families marched in serried ranks down the years exercising a prevailing and only recently diminished influence over commerce, the press, the pulpit, Parliament, culture, and just about everything else that mattered.

The respectability which was their lodestar had a number of elements. One was thrift. Adelaide set up its banks early and South Australians, right to the present day, have generally surpassed their neighbours in the zeal to save or invest in building societies and insurance. The rich, most of them, practised thrift themselves and warmly urged the lower orders to be thrifty. They were even more ardent, if not quite so exemplary, in advocating temperance as another straight and narrow path to respectability that all could follow.

TEMPERANCE AND THE DEMON DRINK

The first settlers were understandably thirsty. Old colonists recalled the heaps of bottles round the Glenelg tents after the first Proclamation Day. The bottle eased loneliness and assuaged the mighty Australian thirst. Beer and spirits could be bought at a high price at a shanty on the Holdfast Bay sand dunes as the settlers waded ashore. Taverns and grog shanties, some rough, some comfortable, all popular, sprouted all over Adelaide and by crossroads in the bush. Splendid Adelaide pubs like the Richmond, the Rob Roy Hotel, the Royal Oak, the Kentish Arms (whose licensee in 1848 was John Cocker, "the first cricket champion of South Australia"), the Elephant and Castle, and the Stag can trace their ancestry back to the companionable hostelries of the 1830s and 1840s. Some of the names have changed but the popularity and atmosphere remain.

The urge for beer and good company is part of the British way, of course, but in early Adelaide, with no theatres and most other facilities lacking, many of the citizens regarded the pubs as a home from home. They were, in effect, community centres where news was passed round, advice given, and entertainment provided, all to be washed down with home-brewed ales and Bengal rum. William Teasdale of the British Hotel soon made his tavern well known for "vaudeville and gaiety" in North Adelaide, and he brought the settlers together from their scattered huts and tents for such spectaculars as his "English Festivities" in 1838. The advertisement read: "A bower will be erected at the British Tavern on 26th December by R.N. Watts when a good band will be provided and every accommodation for those who delight in the harmony and dance. Everything will be studied for comfort, respectability and good order. Dancing to commence at 3 p.m. to be continued for three days. Admission 2/6." Later, in 1850, this same hotel organized the first intercolonial cricket match, at which a Perth team defeated an Adelaide team on the parkland opposite the pub. The game was followed by several hours of drinking, singing, and speeches. Breweries quickly appeared, to prosper mightily.

When the young immigrant C.H. Barton arrived in Adelaide in 1853, he encountered almost Bacchanalian scenes. He wrote to his sister on 7 December: "There I was, wandering about the queer, dusty town, with its broad streets strewn with dust and floating straws, the colonials standing laughing, talking and singing in the cool evening air, the atmosphere redolent with cigars, brandy nobblers, raspberry spiders and other Australian luxuries." Barton observed "the sharp company in white Panama hats that thronged all the bars", and thought "there were far too many taverns".[10]

As if the popular and numerous pubs, the beer and spirits, were not bad enough for the temperance element in Adelaide respectability, it was further dismayed by South Australia's suitability for wine growing. Morphett wrote to the commissioners in 1837: "The climate appears to have such a resemblance to Syria and the other countries of the Mediterranean that I have sanguine hopes that we might be able to raise such valuable products as wine, olive oil, figs, maize, flax, rice, indigo and tobacco." Morphett was quite right about the wine, at least. Other early settlers, including officials of the South Australian Company, recognized the similarity between the soils and climate of the province and those of the vineyard areas of Europe. They planted cuttings near the Torrens and in North Adelaide. In 1838, John Reynell planted vines from John Macarthur in New South Wales on the warm slopes of Reynella, thus inaugurating the magnificent era of Southern Vales wine growing. The Hamiltons were equally early. About the same time a small band of Austrian Jesuits planted vines, a few of which are still bearing fruit today and were the ancestors of some Barossa varieties, on the beautiful uplands round their settlement at Seven Hills in the mid north. More vine cuttings were brought in from Cape Colony. From the mid 1840s, the South Australian wine industry really took hold. Vignerons like the Penfolds, the Hardys, the Seppelts, and the Gramps established vineyards along the seaward-facing slopes of the Mount Lofty Ranges, and the Barossa Valley, where the German settlers nurtured their vine cuttings and drew upon ancient European skills, began to reveal its superlative potential in grapes and wine. Famous vineyards like McLaren Vale and Orlando were established, new areas like the Clare and Coonawarra regions were developed, and by 1971 nearly 26,000 hectares of South Australia, most of them near Adelaide, were producing wine grapes. For a long time the South Australian vignerons, struggling to find acceptance in Europe and especially in Britain, were dismissed as colonial producers of strong, rough, or over sweet wine but it has now been recognised in Australia, and even in London, that the best South Australian wine bears comparison with the best wine from any part of the world.

Thus, the abundance of cheap, easily available wine in the province was always a source of anxiety to the defenders of Adelaide's respectability. They were consoled to some extent by the thought that good wine is a gentleman's drink (cheap wine was another matter—the wine bars certainly were not respectable) and that its production brought in money. Gawler, as we have seen, urged the colonists to drink only wine if they had to indulge while avoiding "ardent spirits".

But if wine caused anxiety to the respectable, beer and spirits—especially, no doubt, Barton's brandy nobblers and raspberry spiders—were gall and wormwood. The *Register* of 13 September 1845 vainly urged its more alcoholic readers to take to ginger beer, the which "cooling and grateful beverage" was available from Mr. Lyons, Rundle Street. Throughout Adelaide's social history, there has been a vigorous running fight between the temperance lady and the publican, the wowser and the brewer, the abstainer and the possessor of the famous Australian thirst.

From 1915 to 1967 Adelaide's drinking habits were distorted by six o'clock closing and the infamous "6 o'clock swill". During this period wowserish respectability prevailed and Adelaide acquired its teetotal, stuffy, and rather hypocritical image. However, it is a little too easy for us in this morally relaxed age to dismiss the old temperance advocates as mere busybodies. Certainly there was among them a strong element of unctuous clergymen strikingly like Dickens's Rev. Stiggins and Rev. Chadband, of grim, black clad women, often adorned with widow's caps, who strove to replace the working man's schooner with a cup of tea. Ladies of whom the acidulous Thistle Anderson wrote: "The outward semblance of the Adelaide female is intense respectability, and of course, being homely to look upon, and exceedingly badly clothed, she has no temptation to err from the path of strict propriety."

Yet we should remember that Adelaide, despite its churches, was for most of its history almost as disposed to drunken street brawls, heavy drinking, and alcoholism as Melbourne or Sydney or even London. There was a pub every few yards down the main streets, and these stayed open to midnight and beyond for many years. Drink was cheap, money usually plentiful, and wild Tiersmen, farmworkers on holiday, and shearers with their cheques converged on the only city for hundreds of miles to paint the town red. Even many of the "old colonists" loved their drink, but usually took care to get drunk only within their clubs or mansions. And despite the vehement efforts of the temperance people, Adelaide streets at night could be bacchanalian until well into the twentieth century. "Sherlock Holmes", a fearless investigator on the staff of the *Register* wrote the following piece on 18 January 1910:

> Larrikinism in Adelaide. For many years, Adelaide has had the reputation of being a sober, quiet, and generally speaking law-abiding city of respectable, well-disposed people. That enviable reputation, however, cannot apply now, judging by the scenes to be nightly witnessed in the main city streets of mobs of drunken men and youths staggering about and interfering with people, especially girls and young women, and all the while using foul language ... On Saturday night, Rundle, King William, and Hindley Streets, and North Terrace, were overrun with the foul-mouthed, disorderly and intoxicated element, who ran amok; many of them were stylishly-dressed. On North Terrace, their conduct was scandalous in the way of insulting remarks to passers-by—catching hold of and pushing women and girls about, jostling, and a general desire to greatly interfere with the peace of strangers to them who were on the terrace. Rundle Street was practically in the same state of siege. There is far too much congregating at corners; also near buildings, and in the streets.

As early as 1837, Judge Jeffcott had complained about "the alarming extent of the vice of drunkenness" in Adelaide. Hindmarsh agreed, but was obliged to license public houses to bring in revenue. Gawler forced the taverns to close at 10 p.m. and banned, or tried to ban, cock fighting, gambling, and home brewing. Grey was even harder on Adelaide's Barrie McKenzies. Under his regime, drunks could be fined five shillings with the option of a night in gaol, double on Sundays. Later governors were less severe, but by then the forces of temperance and its extreme wing, abstinence, were becoming strong.

A Methodist preacher formed a Total Abstinence (the idea of abstinence was, inevitably, American) Society in Hindmarsh in 1839. On 13 April 1844 the *Observer* reported a "Teetotal tea-meeting" at the National School Room , Light Square where "the principles of teetotalism were warmly and ably advocated by the Rev. T. Reynolds." The *Register* of 25 October 1845 advertised a meeting of the Adelaide Total Abstinence Society: "A public meeting will be held in Trinity Church School room ... when the principles of the Society will be advocated by several gentlemen." By 1850 there were said to be over a thousand total abstainers in Adelaide, and three hundred in Methodist Burra. Most Adelaide citizens regarded the teetotallers with good humoured tolerance. When they became too vehement they could always be ejected from festive company and their publicity bills torn down. Temperance when it was no more than a sensible restraint over strong drink accorded well with the city's morality, but total abstinence seemed fanatic and unBritish. Several Nonconformist churches in Adelaide maintained their "wet vestries" for most of the nineteenth century.

There was a definite swing towards teetotalism during the later decades of that century. During the 1890s, under the heading Temperance News, the press reported many meetings of groups like the Ebenezer Lodge or the Sons and Daughters of Temperance. The abstainers had proselytized well and had indoctrinated young people through the Sunday schools. Adelaide Methodism was generally hostile to alcohol in any form and several ministers of other denominations joined the movement.

THE WOMAN'S CHRISTIAN TEMPERANCE UNION

Finally, temperance found its driving force when it fused with the ancestral women's liberation movement. For when the Woman's Christian Temperance Union was formed in Adelaide in 1886—an offshoot of an American organization founded in 1874—it rapidly became the spearhead of Adelaide temperance and the scourge of Adelaide drinkers. The ladies of the W.C.T.U., the White Ribboners who sang "Hold High the Torch", were a formidable, pertinacious, and well-nigh unstoppable pressure group. Miss Isabel McCorkindale, a prolific writer on temperance and purity, edited a chronicle of the local branch entitled *Torch-Bearers: The Woman's Christian Temperance Union of South Australia, 1886–1948*,[11] and this makes fascinating and, for some readers, blood-chilling reading. Led by Methodist activists like Frances Willard, after whom Willard Hall in South Adelaide is named, and Elizabeth Webb Nicholls, the temperance ladies formed a shieldwall of starch against the devil, as made manifest in bottled beer. With typical Adelaide paradox, however, the W.C.T.U. was almost as politically radical as it was morally conservative.

The White Ribboners were suffragettes to the marrow. They supported the Women's Suffrage League, founded in Adelaide in 1888, and they fought manfully or womanfully for the vote with much quicker success than their British sisters. When the act granting the franchise to women was passed by the South Australian Parliament in 1894, a Mrs. C. Proud made it clear that this had been achieved in the teeth of male hostility. "It has been won," Mrs. Proud told the temperance ladies, "in spite of the bitterest opposition, and with hardly any help from the daily press. Our great morning journal opposed the suffrage."

Of course resemblance between the White Ribboners and the modern women's liberation movement is scarcely more than skin deep. The women's liberationists today, or their leaders at least, are usually morally permissive, whereas the W.C.T.U. ladies and their supporters were often moral reactionaries. Some of them may have fought for votes for women as a good thing in itself, but the impression is that to the majority of them the franchise was a means to an end. That end was to use their new electoral power to harry drinkers, brewers, and gamblers through the legislature. This they proceeded relentlessly to do, for the iron age of Adelaide puritanism begins with the election of 1896, at which South Australian women voted for the first time. Mrs. Webb Nicholls rejoiced: "I say unhesitatingly that the results were in favour of morality and temperance to a greater degree than in any other election". One parliamentarian grumbled: "The Government is a Government of promises, and all that is needed, is a few old women to get up a deputation and they will obtain a promise from the Government."

Certainly most of them were old, and they were not very numerous, but the women of W.C.T.U. had an extraordinarily strong influence upon the Adelaide lifestyle for the next four or five decades. They afford a graphic example of the power that a pressure group, albeit small and oligarchic, can wield if it is resolute, ruthless, and adept at using publicity. They had a few male allies in clergymen like the Rev. J.C. Kirby, but they were essentially a militant feminist body. Their power base was strong— some of the churches, notably the Methodist churches—and their respectability, which often extended to the ultimate of Government House approval, was impeccable. The powerful folk memory of Adelaide wowserism was on their side. Their foes, or victims, were all who liked to drink for reasonably long hours. They were against publicans, vignerons, and brewers, as well as gamblers, prostitutes (and their far more numerous patrons), liberated literature, and sin in the widest possible sense of the word. There is no doubt that Adelaide liked the bottle. Thistle Anderson observed that one of the most frequently heard statements in Adelaide was "come and have a drink". The victims were far more numerous than their persecutors. Yet the White Ribboners triumphed. They were never to achieve their highest aim of abstinence but they managed to make life uncomfortable for everyone they considered to be sinful.

Among their triumphs were the formation of the Social Purity League, and the badgering of the Education Department into endorsing nonsense called "scientific temperance instruction" in schools. The W.C.T.U. made many "solemn protests against the traffic in liquor, vice and opium". Another example of their self appointed omniscience was their protest "... against the giving of beer to prisoners, as in many cases it was the cause of their downfall. The Union promised to give something better in its place—fruit, cake, eggs, milk, tea, coffee and cheese being among the gifts." The imagination boggles at what the convicts thought of this piece of White Ribboner logic.

The electoral influence of the temperance forces was at its height during the Great War period. They had already succeeded in restricting the gamblers and the pubs, as with the Licensing Act of 1908. But their glory was the referendum of 1915 which achieved a small majority for the six o'clock closing of hotels. "Vote 6 o'clock" glowed in gaslight from the balconies of Willard Hall in Wakefield Street every evening during the referendum campaign. When the government considered repealing this ridiculous law in 1938, the W.C.T.U. rallied its supporters brilliantly. The Town Hall was engaged for a protest meeting and a procession of 4,000 temperance enthusiasts marched six abreast from the city bridge up King William Street. Bands of gimlet-eyed White Ribboners sat in the public gallery through the night while repeal was debated, and the members were cowed. When repeal was defeated by one vote, the ladies trooped out to the entrance steps and sang the Doxology.

Incidentally, there was a male counterpart to the White Ribboners. This was the White Star Society to which, according to the *Register*, the Rev. Kirby lectured in the Stow Lecture Hall in January 1885. The White Star men bound themselves to "live manly lives" and aim for "moral improvement". They never amounted to much.

The glacial period of Adelaide wowserism persisted right up to the 1960s, although a thaw set in during the 1950s and the great melting began during the premiership of Steele Hall and, especially, Don Dunstan. Pietistic morality prevailed from the onset of Adelaide's history to well within living, and even recent, memory. Adelaide was essentially a *Victorian* (The Queen, *not* the State!) city and historians like T.L. Jarman have pointed out that much of the Victorian attitude was the apotheosis of Methodism. Adelaide was always powerful on Methodism. The shades of John Wesley would have found happy haunts in the Methodist churches in most city streets and in every country settlement of any size.

SABBATARIANISM

Many of the founding fathers were Evangelicals or Dissenters, and some of them were recent converts, with all the zeal of conversion. The linchpin of Evangelicalism was strict Sabbath observance. Adelaide had always been strong on Sabbath observance. In the "hutting" period, the settlers were more free and easy, but there were holy men loud in criticism of sinful enjoyment even then.

One pietist wrote to the *South Australian* on 30 June 1848: "For miles around Walkerville wherever a bird small or great presents itself, the deadly weapon is pointed. This is most disconcerting to the Christian who wends his way with solemn mien, invited by the church bell, to the House of God ... The strong arm of the law should arrest and awe those who care not to remember the Sabbath day to keep it holy." But the people of "solemn mien" triumphed over the pointers of "deadly weapons" and their like. The Adelaide Sabbath became a fearful thing, and the very memory of it still distresses some senior citizens. Black, sweltering clothes, no beer, no laughter (except among sinners), bone-numbing pews, hymns and moral exhortations, padlocks on the swings in the playgrounds, locked gates at the Botanic Gardens and libraries, no shopping, "solemn miens" in droves. Even the trains were reduced to a moral minimum, and the godly would not even go to meet a steamer if it arrived on the Sabbath. It must have been Hell, not Heaven.

Yet while this W.C.T.U. type wowserism covered the surface, there was always a fairly strong undercurrent of the Old Adam, hedonism and interest in innocent pleasure. The godly could ban swimming, as they did in Glenelg for many hot years (when it was allowed, the wretched, overdressed citizens were only permitted to immerse themselves in separate cages for ladies and gentlemen), but the pleasure seekers no doubt swam, picnicked, and read "light" literature, kissed, cuddled, swore, and even gambled and drank on the Sabbath. The minister and his consorts could not be everywhere.

There was moreover always a regard for civil liberties which were woefully encroached upon by official respectability. Pike quotes Charles Mann's remarks to Governor Gawler in 1840, when that Evangelical was considering laws against the profanation of the Sabbath: "The expediency of Sabbath legislation ... as a means of

promoting morality is undoubted ... But personal freedom is a right, and every individual, accountable for his own morality, is entitled if it so pleases him, to be a
drunkard or a Sabbath breaker."[12]

SIN

This was well said, although one could disagree with Mann's belief in the
"expediency" of coercive moral legislation. In the case of Adelaide there is no doubt at
all that sin always flourished, although it was largely driven underground. Thistle
Anderson remarked that Adelaide had more brothels and opium dens than the much
larger Melbourne. Such statements are hard to assess, but the occasional gamey comment in the morally censored Adelaide press indicates that prostitution, drunkenness,
drug taking, and assorted crimes from murder to larceny were always well represented
in Adelaide.

Recent studies like *The Other Victorians* show that Anglo Saxons have always tended
to be mighty sinners in private when official respectability has obliged them—if they
wished to do well in trade, politics, and social life—to be excessively blue-nosed moral
in public.

There was, of course, a lusty and seamy side to Adelaide. The official historians,
obsessed with progress, politicians, and respectability, never mention it but, fortunately
for the truth, the newspapers did. Prostitutes always seem to have prospered in
Adelaide. Even in 1842, when most of the citizens were struggling to survive the
economic depression, harlots were so well patronized that a petition was presented to
Gawler objecting to "the large number of females who are living by a life of prostitution in the City ... out of all proportion to the respectable population". On 22 July 1843,
one outraged moralist felt compelled to write to the *Register*.

> ... to direct the attention of the authorities to a house of the worst description which ex-
> ists in the neighbourhood of Light-Square, and which, by the sale of contraband articles,
> must be very injurious to the interests of the fair-trading licensed victualler, as well as ut-
> terly subversive of the morals of the community. The house is kept by a notorious
> character named "Black George", who, besides pandering to the worst passions of both
> sexes, is known to harbour the few villains who infest the town, and to connive at their es-
> cape ...

We cannot doubt that Adelaide always had its share of Black Georges, brothels,
thieves' kitchens, and houses "of the worst description". On 5 May 1893, the *Register*
matter of factly reported under the heading of Public Health: "the Sanitary Inspector
reported that brothels in Knox-street were still occupied by the people complained of,
they having been unable to obtain other premises". Prostitutes appear to have operated
round the taverns of Hindley Street, which were allowed to stay open until 11.30 p.m.
to accommodate the patrons of nearby theatres. "A Midnight Rambler", an ancestral
moral exposure style reporter of the *Register*, investigated these pubs in 1879 and concluded: "Adelaide life is many-sided, and one of its darker sides has of late become so
black as to cast its sombre shadow over the whole." This rambler was suitably appalled
to find that the "saddling enclosure" of the Theatre Royal Hotel was nothing less than a
"hotbed of evil", where "wanton women" lured "young swells" to perdition.

Even more titillating to respectable Adelaide than such sensational reports—of
which there were many in the press—was a lecture on "Dissolute Adelaide" delivered
by the Rev. A. Turnbull "to a large audience" in the Christian Crusaders' Hall in

January 1885. According to the *Register* of the eighth of that month, this dauntless, and curious, clergyman "disguised himself, so that he might better discover the real state of things in the haunts of vice". One wonders how the Rev. Turnbull disguised himself, how far he went in his investigations, and how the Christian Crusaders, who were "orderly throughout", took his revelations.

Larrikinism was always a marked feature of Adelaide life. There were rival "pushes" as in Melbourne and Sydney, and the press frequently declaimed against minor mayhem in the city and suburbs ranging from the damage inflicted on Colonel Light's monument to brawls on election nights. This extract from the *Register* of 31 July 1893 under the heading "A Larrikin 'Push'" is typical:

> A correspondent writes: "The latest phase of larrikinism appears to be the stealing of milk-jugs left by persons on the doorsteps or window sills. Several jugs were stolen in the west of the city on Saturday night. Peaceful citizens were aroused from their slumbers by stones being thrown at their houses, the opening and closing of garden gates, etc. An application of the 'cat' would have a salutary effect upon these evildoers, whom, now that attention is called to the fact, the police will no doubt keep a more vigilant eye upon."

"Disgusted" wrote to the *Register* of 13 January 1910 observing:

> It is impossible for a lady to walk through the leading thoroughfares of the city without being insulted by blackguards ... even in the suburbs "presumed gentlemen" have been known to insult ladies who may happen to be alone.

The W.C.T.U., the Temperance Alliance, and their kind never succeeded in legislating Adelaideans away from their horse races, bottles, and other alleged sins. But they certainly did succeed in discrediting such relaxations. As late as the early 1950s there was not one motel in Adelaide.The indignities of the six o'clock swill prevailed. Max Harris was indicted and fined two pounds for publishing the allegedly immoral symbolism of the phantom Ern Malley.

Highly moral men and women, who could be grossly immoral in the broader sense in their mercantile "mark ups" and land jobbing, ruled the respectable roost. I.I. Kavan in the *Australian Quarterly* of June 1960 lamented that the brave new Festival of Arts was spoiled by: " ... the archaic laws and customs which prevail in South Australia. The dead Sundays, the 6 o'clock closing time on weekdays, the comparatively poor gastronomic achievements and notable shortage of good hotels, restaurants and night clubs, makes the visitor's life at the Festival difficult, and, at times, tedious." This was the same year the festival governors rejected Alan Seymour's play, "The One Day of the Year" because they thought it to be critical of the R.S.L. and the memory of dead soldiers.

THE PERMISSIVE AGE

Other times, other customs. Morality in Adelaide has swung in a huge pendulum arc from restrictive to permissive. Some would say excessive. Premier Dunstan, who first came to national attention through the white shorts in which he scampered up the steps of Parliament House when he was attorney general in the Walsh government, is now firmly at the helm. A Trudeau-like figure, Dunstan has broken the old mould of South Australian premiers—sober, respectable, moral—as exemplified by leaders like Sir Thomas Playford (son of a Dissenting clergyman) and Walsh.

His immediate predecessor, now Senator Hall, began the process with his youth, sharp dressing and, occasionally, radical legislation. But Dunstan, who has appeared reading favourite passages from Shakespeare and Yeats on television, who is as much at home presiding over the vision of Monarto as reading verses to children at the zoo, is something startlingly different for Adelaide and, indeed, for the nation as a whole. The dreary Bolte, Reece, Askin style of elderly partisan premierships offered a drab background to Mr. Dunstan's highly literate and dashing mode of running a state. He is a Labor man, too, with a relatively docile cabinet and trade union movement, yet his dazzling suits, well dressed hair, and snappy cravats set him off vividly against the wide-trousered, school of hard knocks image of Labor leadership. Perhaps a phenomenon like Dunstan, or, indeed, Senator Hall, is only possible in Adelaide.

There is no doubt the Dunstan government has swept up and dumped most traces of puritanism left by the Hall government. Under Premier Hall, South Australia moved to make abortion legal in special cases, the first state to do so in Australia. The iniquitous licensing laws had been liberalized before this.

Permissive or (to use a less pejorative phrase) Florentine attitudes under Dunstan have relaxed censorship and increased the colour and variety of Adelaide's night life. The sex spectacular "Oh Calcutta" was very nearly staged in Adelaide recently until it was pipped on legal technicalities by a rearguard morality pressure group based on Holy Trinity Church. The permissives prevailed, however, in such matters as encouraging the growth of better restaurants, serving wine unstintedly, more relaxed drinking laws (pubs may soon be allowed to open on the Sabbath itself!), and the staging of a vast quantity of permissive drama. Adelaide cinemas screen films as avant-garde, as pornographic as any in Australia. Massage parlours pop up like erotic mushrooms from the ground which Angas hoped would be "blessed" due to the importation of "pious people".

The ancestral wowsers will be turning most agitatedly in their graves over Mr. Dunstan's *pronunciamento* that nudes can frolic in the waves at Maslin's beach, thirty kilometres south of Adelaide. The premier is also pondering the question of exposing remote beaches in national park areas to the cultural shock of nude humanity.

Adelaide swings as lustily, and with a good deal more style, than hedonistic Sydney or sunburned Perth. And yet, and yet ... The W.C.T.U. and kindred bodies still exist. Adelaide is still most richly endowed with reasonably active churches. The traditions of generations cannot entirely be annihilated by a spate of permissive legislation.

The old Adelaide worship of respectability, the old Dissenting conscience, had their sturdy virtues. Among them were an expectation of probity in public and business life, a regard for thrift, honesty, reliability, and the better side of gentility. The people who set aside the parklands, created the beautiful freestone Adelaide villas, preserved the walks along the Torrens, patronized the arts with substantial loyalty, and guarded (perhaps better than we permissives have done) the vistas of North Terrace and North Adelaide—these people were by no means Philistine.

It is fashionable now to mock the mores of Victorian Adelaide. There is some justification for this, but it will not be substantiated until we have shown beyond doubt that we are putting something more civilized in their place. This still has fully to be demonstrated.

If Adelaide is a more agreeable place to live in than congested Melbourne or raucous Sydney, it may well be partly because of the heritage of dignity and restraint that comes from the old Dissenting traditions.

Popular Amusements

> If a vote were taken from the whole of the theatre-going public in South Australia as to which they preferred out of drama, comedy, farce, grand opera, vaudeville, pictures or musical comedy, it is probable that the poll would result in the big majority for musical comedy.
>
> The Register, *13 June 1925*

While the Adelaide gentry were riding to hounds, attending Town Hall or Government House receptions, or enduring the opera, how did the ordinary citizens amuse themselves? Some became ardent participants or spectators in games like football and cricket, and the Adelaide race meetings were "Republics" where miners and shop assistants could place their bets, cheer the horses, and even shake hands with the notables.

But what could the average Adelaide worker and his wife do with themselves during leisure time, which was substantial by comparison with that in England? They could potter in their gardens for, as Trollope and other visitors had noted, Adelaide was a city of gardens. They could boat on the Torrens lake, or stroll in the parklands, the squares, or the Botanic Gardens. They could sun themselves on the long broad metropolitan beaches and as time went on and Adelaide puritanism came to terms with the Adelaide summer, they were actually permitted to bathe. Swimming in the murky waters of the Torrens was allowed earlier—so much so that one of the *Register's* many querulous correspondents wrote on 30 December 1843: "A correspondent complains of the military and others daily bathing above the higher bridge. He says that the principal bathing pool is sometimes crowded, and for the remainder of the day the effects are not only palpable, but extremely unpleasant, if not positively prejudicial to the citizens who are obliged to drink the accumulated impurities ... " Or they could wander around the commercial centre and window shop, or drink themselves merry in the pubs and gather in noisy crowds in Rundle and Hindley Streets to annoy the respectable.

The rich had plenty of "refined amusements". Apart from their various sports such as hunting, racing, polo, croquet and golf, there were the complex rituals of society at leisure. The rich entertained each other at elaborate country house parties in their summer season mansions in the hills, such as Auchendarroch at Mount Barker or Shurdington at Mount Lofty, or in stately homes on the plains like Davenport's Beaumont House. Skill at cards and dancing was a *sine qua non*. Mr. Wivell, "Professor of Dancing etc.", who offered instruction in the "New Waltz, Gavottes, Minuets" at his Acadamie de Danse in Rundle Street in 1885 was typical of many dancing teachers who advertised in the press. The Adelaide aristocracy had an insatiable appetite for balls, assemblies, parties, and receptions, especially when they were held at Government House or the Town Hall. This florid description in the *Register* of 22 April 1910 of a "Mayoral Garden Party" held at Victoria Park shows how grandiloquent such occasions could be—and also demonstrates the bland superiority felt by Adelaide about things Asian.

> The Mayor and Mayoress supported by their daughter (Mrs. H. Bridgland) received the first of the guests at 2.30 p.m., and during the next hour and a quarter there was a procession of electric cars, motor cars, taxis and horse cabs and carriages to the main entrance, and an incessant stream of guests down the carpeted walk ... Apart from the Cabinet Ministers, politicians, clergymen, military officers, professional men, and prominent citizens, who, with members of their families, numbered considerably over 2,000, interest was lent to the occasion by the presence of officers and cadets from the Japanese warships ... The proceedings throughout went with a merry swing. The visitors from the land of the Rising Sun experienced the warmth of a real Australian welcome, and the ladies particularly saw to it that the "little brown men" were not left to themselves. A pretty compliment was paid to them in the course of Messrs. Wilkinson & Co.'s display of fireworks, when sandwiched between advertising devices, rockets threw out strings of national flags surmounted by that of Japan. The Adelaide City Brass Band was in attendance.

Brass bands and fireworks were also enjoyed by the working class who, if they had less leisure than the wealthy, still had quite a lot, and made the most of it. Copies of colonial newspapers show that there were shoals of clubs, societies, interest groups, and other bodies formed for the amusement or edification of their members. Temperance groups were numerous and, like the Wesleyan societies, were powerful on lectures and tea parties. According to the *Register* of 11 June 1885, "A very pleasing entertainment was given by the members of the Parkside Temperance Lifeboat Crew to the inmates of the Lunatic Asylum". On 1 January of that year, the Adelaide Working Men's Club offered "sports to suit everybody" at the Exhibition Grounds. "Choice selections" were played by brass bands and "working men, wives and families" were urged "to rally up and make our first anniversary a success". Friendly societies like the Oddfellows were established by the early 1840s and advertised their regular dinners, meetings, and entertainments.

Mr. Richards of King William Street advertised "a grand display of fireworks" in front of the Freemason's Tavern, Pirie Street in the *Register* of 21 February 1846. To remind freeloaders that fireworks cost money, Mr. Richards begged "to state that, for want of an enclosure, he is obliged to give his display publicly, and therefore trusts to the generosity of those who may do him the honour of witnessing it for remuneration. A collection will be made."

For those who were not members of societies, there were always the Adelaide hotels for hospitality and amusement. The Adelaidean seeking entertainment could drink, play billiards, or enjoy "free and easy concerts". And it was in the pubs especially that popular theatre and the music hall were born. One of Adelaide's earliest theatres, the Pavilion, began as an adjunct to the Southern Cross Hotel. The *Register* of 6 September 1845 contained the following advertisement:

> Pavilion Theatre, Currie Street (Entrance in Rosina Street). Mr. Handeman begs most respectfully to announce to the Inhabitants of Adelaide that he has completed, by the advice of his friends, fitting up the "Southern Cross" as a theatre, and trusts that the entertainments produced will be opened on Monday evening next, on which occasion the performance will commence with "The Married Bachelor", after which a Variety of Singing, the whole to conclude with the farce of "A Tinker, a Tailor, a Soldier, and a Sailor" ... Admission: Boxes 2s 6d, Pit 1s 6d.

The colonists loved farce. A companionable atmosphere, plenty of beer, sawdust and footlights and side-splitting antics on the stage were just what a man in the pit wanted after a hard day colonizing South Australia. Mr. Handeman tried a few more cultural productions but he knew how his bread was buttered and balanced them with humour and vaudeville. For instance, the Pavilion on 25 October 1845 advertised the third act of "Othello", but was careful to soften the culture with "a variety of singing and dancing" and "the Laughable Farce of 'The Mayor of Garratt'".

The one and sixpennies in the pit liked to marvel at extraordinary phenomena too. Mr. De Pree, "The Wizard of the South", a necromancer, appeared in Adelaide for "Positively four nights only" in August 1845, offered "universal satisfaction" and challenged "any person south of the Equator to compete with him for one hundred guineas". Earlier still, the *Adelaide Observer* of 23 December 1843 was complimentary about the opening performance at the Olympic Theatre, which consisted of "the celebrated burletta of 'The Wreck'", a farce called "The Two Thomsons", and an "original epilogue" by Mr. Crosby "in the costume of a pirate captain".

Twopeny was succinctly informative about the popular theatre as it had developed in 1882: "The colonial taste in theatrical matters follows the English pretty closely. Opera-bouffe and Gilbert and Sullivan are preferred to everything else. Next in popularity is the 'New Babylon' type of play. Low comedy also draws well." Twopeny was scornful about the average theatre in Australia. He disliked the adjacent bars, which brought in "the beer money" and formed "a rendezvous for all the bad characters in the town". He remarked that while Melbourne had only four theatres and Sydney two, little Adelaide had two theatres and a number of concert halls. He thought that Adelaide's Theatre Royal in Hindley Street was rivalled only by Melbourne's Bijou Theatre.

George Seth Coppin, "Father of the Australian Theatre", English strolling player and comedian, settled in Adelaide in 1846 when he was twenty-seven, and wrought a theatrical explosion in the colonies. Coppin rebuilt the old Queen's Theatre, renaming it the Royal Victoria Theatre, and a theatre at Port Adelaide. In 1849, he opened the Coppin's Royal Exchange in Hindley Street and, a jovial host, carved at the head of the table for his guests. As a comic character actor, Coppin made Adelaide laugh in roles such as Mould the bailiff in the farce, "Not Such a Fool as he Looks". And as actor manager and entrepreneur, Coppin arranged for visiting English celebrities to perform in Adelaide while on their way to the eastern colonies. Gustavus Brooke, the Irish tragedian, and Edwin Booth, the American Shakespearian (and brother of President Lincoln's assassin), were among the hundreds of theatrical notables attracted to Australia by Coppin and the free-spending gold diggers. The most remarkable, and un-Adelaidean, was the notorious Lola Montez, former mistress of Franz Liszt and King Ludwig of Bavaria. Lola, an Irish girl really, agitated the non-Methodist elements in Adelaide with her famous Spider Dance. Passing on to Melbourne, she drove the diggers wild, and called on one critical newspaper editor with a whip.

In 1875, James Cassius Williamson and his wife, Maggie Moore, had a tumultuous reception from Adelaide audiences with their play "Struck Oil!" They later toured the province with the play, which was popular for many years. Williamson proved to be an even better businessman than Coppin, took over the Theatre Royal, and presented the first authorized version of "H.M.S. Pinafore" in Adelaide in 1879. His company was to dominate Adelaide, as it has Australian, theatre right up to recent years, latterly through Her Majesty's Theatre.

Long gone Adelaide theatres can be briefly recalled by the browser in the files of the colonial press. For example, the *Register* of 30 April 1860 described the debut of the San Francisco Minstrels at the Victoria Theatre, watched by "a very numerous and respectable audience". "Mackay's Latest Burlesque, as delivered by him at the St. James Theatre, London", was advertised on 19 May of that year. During 1893, to take some random examples, Adelaideans were invited to see "the wonderfully gorgeous Pantomine" offered by the Lilliputian Opera Co. at the Theatre Royal; "the novel series of entertainments" known as "the Continentals"; the "first class comedy 'Uncles and Aunts'"; the city organist playing the organ in the Town Hall; and the Battle of Waterloo on Cyclorama. Entertainments during 1893 also included "Professor Woodroffe's Glass-blowing" which "continues to be well patronised"; the Adelaide Harmonic Society's presentation of "The Lily of Killarney", and Worth's Paragon Specialitie Company at the Bijou. "We are informed", pronounced the *Register* of 8 August 1893, "that 1,500 persons visited the tattooed man ... at the Cyclorama Buildings. Signor Signaro, the fire-eater and bamboo-climber, is now an additional attraction."

By 1910 the new electric trams had helped Adelaide night life. The *Register* of 7 May 1910, observed:

> The electric trams, besides making Adelaide a real city, have revolutionized the entertainment business in it. Only a few years ago it was difficult to keep one theatre open throughout the year. Now there are places of amusement on every side, and they are patronized by many thousands in the course of a week. In the days of the horse cars, people living a couple of miles out in the suburbs were content to stay at home, smoke the pipe of peace, and read a book rather than be rattled back to town in over-crowded, dimly-lit conveyances to see a show, and to thank their lucky stars if standing room were available in the last car to the terminus ... All that, however, is now happily changed. People are hurried in from their homes in beautifully appointed and brilliantly lit electric cars, and as a result the show business is booming. The increase of houses of amusement has been as astonishing as the variety of the entertainments provided is bewildering.

During that year, tram-borne amusement seekers had remarkable choice in entertainment. There was the Pianola Hall in Rundle Street. At the Tivoli Theatre they could watch the Wille Brothers, clad in purple tights, performing feats "undreamt of in the equilibrists' world". In May, special trains carried people out to Cheltenham Racecourse to watch the Bleriot monoplane make its "first Australian public fight". Films, beginning to compete with the theatre, were offered by the Lyceum Pictures at the Empire Theatre, Grote Street ("a fine pictorial adaption of Helen Jackson's famous novel 'Ramona'") and at the Arcadia Picture Palace where "the pictures are excellent and absolutely flickerless".

In May, 1910, the citizens were invited to watch a certain Sacco Homan fast for forty-three days in a glass case in Hindley Street. Watched by "a large crowd", Mr. Homan when released, appeared to the *Register* to be "lean and limp", but he had a whiskey and soda "which made him shudder" and repaired to the Central Hall where "a vaudeville entertainment completed the programme".

In Victoria Square, people were urged to enter "the cosy and warm Trocadero Canvas Theatre" where they could watch "fifteen beautiful and varied films of animated pictures" including the western "The Mexican's Revenge" and "Nick Carter in Danger". Or they could go to the Town Hall to hear Mr. Edward Reeves read passages from Dicken's "The Cricket on the Hearth", or recite "Enoch Arden", "one of Tennyson's most pathetic stories".

J.C. Williamsons offered the pantomine "Aladdin" at the Theatre Royal in May 1910 and the Royal Agricultural and Horticultural Society held its spring show at the Jubilee Exhibition Grounds. The Caledonian Society, which occasionally presented "A Nicht Wi' Burns", had a ball in the Town Hall. The Amalgamated Society of Carpenters and Joiners enjoyed a "smoke social" in the Trades Hall and there was a "building trades picnic". The *Register* of 2 April 1910 urged its readers to visit the Zoological Gardens on Saturdays, which was a "free day", to see the children "inspecting the birds and beasts, riding on the elephant and the Bactrian camel, and generally having a jolly good time".

In January 1910, the *Register* advertised a "Viceroy Tea Balloon Carnival" at the Jubilee Oval under the auspices of the Beebe Balloon Company. "There will be a race mid-air between Zahn Rinaldo, the Austrian aeronaut, and Albert Eastwood, the daring Australian balloonist. They will leave the Jubilee Oval attached to a monster balloon, and, from a great height, will with the aid of six parachutes race to earth." The amusement industry could occasionally be daring, even in Adelaide.

On 20 August 1910, the Theatre Royal began a season of "The Bad Girl of the Family", described by the *Register* as "the sensational bedroom drama that has caused such a controversy in London". At the Tivoli Theatre in January of that year, patrons could hear "a number of the latest English songs and dances" while watching Mr. Harry Rickard's Vaudeville Company—"not a dull moment from beginning to end". Meanwhile, "The Squatter's Daughter" at the Theatre Royal that month was "drawing like a porous plaster". As a change, there was "Jiu Jitsu Wrestling" at the Jubilee Exhibition Building in August 1910, and even a jiu jitsu school for ladies in Franklin Street.

However, Adelaide wowserism was still on the watch. The *Register* of 13 July 1910 printed a reaction to the heavyweight boxing match between the first Negro world champion, Jack Johnson (who had earlier defeated Tommy Burns in Sydney), and the ex-champion Jim Jeffries:

> Mr. Smeaton M.P. introduced to the Premier (Mr. Verran) a deputation organized in connection with the Social Reform Bureau asking that the exhibition of the Johnson-Jeffries fight at the moving pictures should be prohibited. Mr. Smeaton M.P. said that they did not want to decry or repress the healthy means of enjoyment provided by the cinematograph, but he had seen certain pictures that bordered on the undesirable. They believed that it was proposed to flood the world with views of the Johnson-Jeffries fight. That would be bad for the community, for there was nothing elevating or educational in such a show.

A later correspondent saw through the cant of the Social Reform Bureau by suggesting that it would not have objected had the winner not been black and his victim white.

Circuses on the parklands were always popular and visitors like the famous tightrope walker Blondin astonished the citizenry. Processions and sports to celebrate St. Patrick's Day were always conducted with what the *Register* called "characteristic fervour".

"The climate of Adelaide", stated the *Register* on 10 February 1922, "is declared to be eminently suitable for the production of photo plays". Influenced by this, and "a desire to give Adelaide girls their chance to screen", the Greater Wondergraph Company began to make "a local moving picture". That year there was still farces galore, such as "The Pommy Bride", "set at an outback station", at the King's Theatre. The English Pierrots offered "a cheery night's entertainment" at Austral Gardens. The revue "Mary's Lamb" at the Majestic was "full of enjoyable, humorous situations".

By 1925, Adelaide dancers were able to rotate to the music of Joe Aronson and his Synco Symphonists at the Floating Palais on the Torrens. This idea was emulated by a London company which built a floating palais on the Thames. Also in 1925, the miniature railway was opened at the zoo and the Majestic Theatre stiffened its usual offerings of revue and vaudeville with moving pictures, some of which would scarcely be considered entertaining by modern audiences. However, the *Register* of 7 May 1925, thought one film about "the mode of manufacture of steel hawsers for suspension bridge building" was "very interesting". Band concerts, as at the rotunda in Elder Park, were always well attended, as were the various brass band rallies of the Salvation Army.

In such ways, and in a myriad others from playing euchre to cheering visiting royalty, Adelaideans amused themselves. Despite the efforts of "respectability" to stamp it out, "two up" schools were common for many years. The *Register* of 26 January 1925 reported under the heading "'Two up' in the City" on an episode in Adelaide that would have looked well in "The Sentimental Bloke": "During the afternoon of January 7, Plainclothes Constables J.W. Regan and J. Walters visited a lane in the West End of the city, and noticed a group of about fifty men, formed in a ring, and a man in the centre apparently tossing pennies into the air. They rushed into the group and arrested four men. One of them struggled and escaped." At the magistrates' court later, the ring leader ingeniously claimed that he had been tossing three, not two pennies into the air and was playing "three up" (which presumably was not illegal) not "two up". His solicitor observed that "he was astonished at the dissimilarity between the two games". But the magistrate would have none of it.

Indeed, two up was so well entrenched in Adelaide that in July 1925 a school developed among "the crowd of labourers waiting outside the Government Labour Bureau". One of those ubiquitous plain clothes policemen swooped and thirteen sportsmen were charged in the Police Court.

Another popular diversion was to listen to the Botanic Park orators on Sunday afternoons. The *Register* on 10 February 1922 reported:

> A stroll through the Botanic Park on Sunday afternoons is quite worthwhile. Several leather-throated orators had much to say when I visited it recently. One, who called himself a Rationalist, told the crowd not to listen to what other people said, but to think for themselves. He did not seem to object to folk listening to what he said. A little further on a Socialist was holding forth. Much of what he said led nowhere.

The pattern has not changed all that much. In the 1840s, the citizens would visit the "umbrageous Parklands" by the Torrens to see the agricultural show, and their descendants flock to the Royal Show every September. The colonists watched the parades of the Volunteers; their descendants watch John Martins' Christmas Pageant. Brass bands and friendly societies, work picnics, and sociable pubs were popular and still are.

However, theatres like the Pavilion, the Empire, the Olympic, and the Majestic are but fitful memories at best, and musical comedy, melodrama and farce have withered before the television and the cinema—although, these nostalgic days, the Olde King's Music Hall company keeps the flag flying. It is hard to imagine what Mr. Smeaton M.P. and the Social Reform Bureau of 1910, who deemed that scenes in the film of the Johnson-Jeffries fight "bordered on the undesirable", would think of the R certificate erotica and violence on most Adelaide film screens today. The picturesque little Theatre Royal in Hindley Street, with all its memories, was wrecked to make way for a peculiarly unlovely car park. The Wizard of the South, Blondin, Coppin, Sacce Homan the Starving Man, and Joe Aronson and his Synco Symphonists have given way to rock groups, pop idols, and bingo. But then—*plus ca change c'est plus la meme chose*. Adelaideans, like the British everywhere during the period, loved a good vulgar belly laugh and modern Adelaide has nurtured the televised Ernie Sigley Show, which occasionally packs them in at the glamorous Festival Theatre itself.

Sport

The more ample reward attaching to labour out here leaves the colonist more leisure. And this leisure he devotes to working at play.

R.E.N. Twopeny

The international distinction of Australian sportsmen and women in such sports as cricket, tennis, and swimming stems from deep historical roots. In all the Australian colonies, visitors were struck by the antipodean passion for sport. The perceptive Twopeny, for instance, in the 1880s noted that Australians had far more public holidays, at least twelve a year, than the English. He went on: "Saturday is always a half holiday. Nine till five are the accepted hours for the clerk; half-past nine till six for the shop assistant. The eight-hour system is generally accepted in all classes of manual labour ... In all trades and professions the hours and work of the subordinates are much less than in England."[1] Then the Australians had "fine and temperate weather" and a rural fondness for outdoor sports. Twopeny concluded that "this may fairly claim to be the most sporting country in the world. In Australia alone, of all countries, can any sport be called national in the sense that the whole nation, from the oldest greybeard to the youngest child, takes an interest in it." Of the Australians, Trollope declared: "Cricket, athletics, rowing matches, flat racing, and steeple-chasing are dear to them".[2]

All these sporting enthusiasms were at least as well marked in Adelaide as elsewhere. Solid one-piece cherrywood and willow cricket bats came out on the *Buffalo*, and perhaps footballs too. The settlers brought their fowling pieces with them and as soon as possible they were banging away at the bewildered wild life. They pulled fish out of the sea and the creeks, marvelling at their abundance. They were wretched without their horses. The first voyages were severe on horses, and the founding fathers had to pay high prices for small Timor ponies. But gradually horses arrived with the overlanders, or were shipped in from Van Diemen's Land, and the new colonial gentry could feel themselves again.

Fresh from the restrictions of Britain—the bad weather, the long working hours, the strictly guarded game preserves—the first Adelaideans must have felt ecstatic about the sporting potential of their new home. There were the parklands for cricket and racing. The bush was full of animals and birds, owned by no one. In those pre-conservation days, it was axiomatic for most Englishmen, if they saw a wild animal, to shoot or trap it, or chase it with hounds. And then to eat it, or at least skin it. If it had no value either as food or trophy, then it ought to be got rid of to make way for sheep.

CRICKET

Of the genuinely popular sports, cricket was outstanding from the beginning. Twopeny summed it up: "Cricket must, I suppose, take the first place amongst Australian sports, because all ages and all classes are interested in it and not to be interested in it amounts to a social crime ... of the game itself there is no end."[3]

Cricket and Adelaide have always accorded very well together. In the imagination of cricket lovers, illustrious names like Giffen, Richardson, Bradman, and the Chappell brothers are interwoven with that of Adelaide. There can be no other cricket ground in the world that more agreeably sets off the game and reflects its traditional spirit than does the Adelaide Oval. As they talk of it over the radio, itinerant test match commentators reveal that is has a special place in their esteem. To lie on the Adelaide Oval's warm, grassy slope and watch Ian Chappell bat against England, to see the seagulls fleck the green turf, sense the rustling of the Moreton Bay figtrees in the breeze, and let the gaze wander over the cathedral, the trees and the everpresent hills—this is a setting in which to really enjoy cricket.

When the *Buffalo* sailed for South Australia, cricket was a popular and well established game in England, and, indeed, in the other Australian colonies. A game according to the rules of the day—four ball overs and twenty-four inch stumps—is recorded in Sydney as early as 1803. Both the *Register* and the *South Australian* reported the formation of the London Tavern (Currie Street) Cricket Club on 12 November 1838 and that subsequently two members were willing to play any two gentlemen a game of "single wicket" for a twenty guineas stake. John Bristow, publican of the Great Tom of Lincoln Inn, Thebarton, advertised perhaps the earliest recorded Adelaide game in the *Register* of 19 October 1839.

CRICKET

A grand match will be played on Monday, October 28, on the Thebarton Cricket Ground between Eleven Gentlemen of the Royal Victoria Independent Club, and Eleven Gentlemen of Adelaide, for Twenty-two Guineas a-side. Wickets to be pitched at ten o'clock. Refreshments will be provided, and everything done that can add to the pleasure of the public.

Mr. Bristow's advertisement is interesting on a number of counts. It shows that cricket was already being played in Adelaide less than two years after proclamation. There was a cricket ground at Thebarton at least. No doubt cricket had been played from the earliest days of settlement to help reduce the tedium of waiting for the land surveys to be completed. The connexion between cricket—a festive, sociable game in its preprofessional days—and the pubs was clearly strong. The early Adelaide inns were lively community centres well to the fore in such matters as music, drama, sport, and organized entertainment. Indeed, Mr. Bristow, carrying on the honourable tradition of Hambledon's Bat and Ball Inn in England, arranged for foot races, juggling, and even a competition to climb the greasy pole to beguile the crowd in the intervals of his grand 1839 match.

As A.G. Moyes, the well-known South Australian cricketer and cricket writer, has shown in his *Australian Cricket: A History*, the Adelaide inns continued to foster the sport. The London Tavern and the Kentish Arms were outstanding here. John Cocker, the proprietor of the Kentish Arms, had played for Kent against All England. When he arrived in Adelaide in 1846, he formed the Kent and Sussex Club, that had a ground on the parklands near the end of Stanley Street, to play the already formed Adelaide Club, which had a ground by the Torrens Bridge. The Adelaide Club members were known as "the Toffs" for only "Gentlemen members" were invited. Under arm bowling prevailed, and Cocker was very good at it, but one of his fellow players, Tom Botten, inaugurated effective round arm bowling in the province. Mr. Justice Bundey was another cricketing pioneer. He formed the Union Club and vainly urged the Adelaide businessmen to give their employees time off to play cricket. The North Adelaide Club was popularly known as the Pigs and Whistles, for they had their meetings in a pub of that name.

And it was in an inn, the Prince Alfred Hotel, that the formative meeting of the South Australian Cricket Association was held on 31 May 1871. Constituent clubs included the Kent, South Australian, Norwood, and Stepney Clubs. A major aim was to establish a "Central Cricket Ground, similar to those existing at present in the sister colonies", and the initiative here was taken by the South Australian Club and its secretary, H. Yorke Sparks. The Adelaide Corporation granted five hectares of parkland which were, in Sparks's words, "to be grassed, levelled, and surrounded by a belt of trees, shrubs, etc., so as to render it both serviceable and ornamental, and a place of pleasant resort". Patrons of "other manly sports" could also use it. Such was the genesis of the Adelaide Oval. (Earlier, in 1850, the City Commissioners had granted the use of two hectares in this area to be the Adelaide Cricket Club: this had been subsequently used by the South Australian Club.) There was a long wrangle with the City Council over fees and regulations but these and other difficulties were overcome and the first game was played on the Oval in 1873.

The name Oval, incidentally, was proposed by a Surrey enthusiast and accepted. The Adelaide Oval was modelled on the famous Kennington Oval, and the use of the pleasant term oval for sportsgrounds throughout South Australia and elsewhere stems from this.

Of course, the Adelaide Oval took many years to mature. Early curators like G.W. Gooden struggled against rough ground, thistles, and poor soil. Zealous supporters— among them Sir Edwin Smith and H. Yorke Sparks—helped. Moyes writes of Sparks: "Mr. Sparks bought 150 old iron posts at an auction sale and offered them to the Association at cost price ... The energetic Sparks then had the posts screwed into the ground, bought some chain for 17 pounds, gave it to the Association, which could not afford to pay for it, and then he and his brother threaded it through the iron posts, thus originating the term 'a hit to the chains'."[4] And gradually the Oval settled down: stands were built, the turf improved, the trees grew, and it eventually became indeed, to use Sparks's words, "a place of pleasant resort".

The seal of approval was placed on the Oval a year after its opening. In the summer of 1874 an English Eleven captained by Dr. W.G. Grace himself played the South Australians on the Oval. The overgrown ground was rapidly prepared by an enormous flock of sheep. Grace and his men had had a rough time getting there. They suffered sea sickness on their journey from Melbourne and then were mortified by the condition of the pitch at Kadina. Grace wrote that "the whole area was covered with small stones". Worse was to follow, for they had a wretched time on their all-night drive from Kadina to Adelaide. "In the dark we lost the track and began driving out in the bush until, at last, as we had taken seven hours to cover 35 miles, we thought it wiser to wait until daylight before proceeding on our journey. We reached Adelaide in the afternoon, stiff and tired, but the 22 of South Australia did not take advantage of it as they lost their first eight wickets for ten runs and were out for 63."[5] Six thousand spectators paid 2/6 each to watch the great doctor play, and many more non-paying spectators watched from the slopes of Montefiore Hill. Alexander Crooks leaned over Mr. Sparks's chain to catch Grace out after a big hit. The doctor objected that he had been caught behind the boundary, but the umpire would have none of it.

Thereafter, cricket in South Australia went from strength to strength. In the 1880s, illustrious local cricketers like A.H. Jarvis, George Giffen, and J.J. Lyons showed their prowess on the Oval. During the 1891–92 season Lord Sheffield brought out an English Eleven to play a series of tests, one of which was played at the Adelaide Oval. There were photographs of the two teams—the Australians in bowlers, the English in straw hats—sitting warily amid the palms and cacti of the Botanic Gardens. When the

Sheffield Shield was instituted in 1893, South Australia had a strong side, and won the shield the following season.

In those days, the Adelaide pitch, now notoriously placid, was fast and dangerous. Moyes writes: "The Adelaide pitch was well-grassed, cut short, then shaved close. It shone like glass and played like greased lightning, so that few bowlers could turn the ball on it."[6] With time, other great cricketing names emerged: Joe Darling, Clem Hill, Ernest Jones, Clarrie Grimmett, Victor Richardson, Sir Donald Bradman and, most recently, Ashley Mallett and Ian and Greg Chappell. Of Jones, a man of the people, legend has it that when as a member of the Australian team he attended a Buckingham Palace garden party, he was asked if he had been to St. Peter's College. Jones replied that he had been there often, driving the dirt cart. St. Peter's rival, Prince Alfred's, has the distinction of having produced four captains of the Australian cricket team: Darling, Hill, and Ian and Greg Chappell.

As cricket throve on the Oval, it was also keenly played on the suburban ovals, the parklands, and throughout the state. Moyes recalls: "I remember well in my own early days in Adelaide the pitches on which we used to play as lads—hard earth with matting which was carried laboriously either by hand or stretched along between handle bars and seat of a bicycle, then placed in position and pegged down. We thought nothing of it, since all youngsters, and the older ones also had to do this unless they were privileged to play in a senior team, or the first eleven of one of the two big Public Schools."[7]

FOOTBALL

Adelaide is now one of the most vehement of the Australian Rules Football cities. Modern Saturday Adelaide is as ardently devoted to football as the old Sunday Adelaide was to religion. In Adelaide of a winter Saturday, anyone uninterested in or hostile to Australian Rules is a misfit. The game is played and worshipped in the Adelaide Oval, Football Park, and several suburban and country ovals. The evening television screen and the *Sunday Mail* next morning are besotted with marks, inquests, replays, and controversies raging round the oval leather ball. At certain hours the city roads are packed with football fans' cars, usually dangerously driven for their occupants are either exhilarated or enraged by the result. There is no refuge for the anti-football person even in the recesses of the Botanic Gardens, the parklands, or the Belair Recreation Park, for usually an afficionado will be nearby with a loud transistor.

A Rules game on the Adelaide Oval has a special atmosphere of its own—and one quite different from the Oval's summertime cricket guise. It is usually dank and chill, or raining. Lowering clouds hang over the hills' face. The wind blows pie papers and drink cans down the terraces and players slither and thud in the muddy grass. The seagulls, inveterate spectators and meddlers in the cricket, are usually absent. But the cold-nosed, foot-stamping spectators, huddled among the bare Moreton Bay figs from the rain, love it all. This is an essential part of their Adelaide.

In view of the current football fervour, it seems odd that the origins of the game in Adelaide's history are rather obscure. Hodder, Pascoe, and most of the other early historians do not mention football, although it was obviously a popular game by the 1860s at least. Yet they do make references to cricket. On closer reflection, the oddity is explained: football was not so *respectable*.

To the Pascoe-style chroniclers cricket was agreeably gentlemanly. It brought notables like Grace and even the occasional peer from Home, where the game was revered. Similarly, hunting, racing, sculling, archery, shooting, tennis, croquet, and so on were irreproachably bourgeois, at least, and often basked in Government House patronage. But football, like cock-fighting and boxing, was proletarian and to a Pascoe or a Blacket, this was a larrikin business. As authorities like Morris Marples in his *History of Football* (London, 1954) have shown, in its native England, football had violent and confused origins in early folk history. A prime excuse for riots and mass brawls, it was for centuries either ignored or persecuted by the establishment. Then one wing became respectable as Rugby football for public schoolboys in the mid nineteenth century, and the other was codified and became accepted as Association Football at the turn of the century.

But what could the Adelaide gentry make of Australian Rules, a volatile compound of Rugby, Gaelic football, and vigorous native elements that was invented in the dubious city of Melbourne? There were no clear English precedents to guide them. Twopeny observed in 1883: "Of course there are numbers of people in the upper and middle classes who still have a holy horror of football as a dangerous game."[8] So the notables tended to ignore the growth of football in Adelaide: until it became too well entrenched to overlook any more.

We cannot doubt that Adelaide youths kicked round a leather ball, or some object approximating to one, from the earliest days of settlement. There was a strong folk tradition of football, with ad hoc rules, in Britain. Later immigrants, reflecting trends at Home, must have increased the interest and encouraged the move towards organization. One of the earliest references to a more formal football activity comes in the *Register* of 27 April 1860 which recorded:

> During the last few days active preparations have been made by a number of gentlemen for organizing a Foot Ball Club, and their efforts appear to have been eminently successful, as many as forty two having consented to join. On Thursday evening, a meeting was held at the Globe Inn, Rundle Street, for the purposes of completing the necessary arrangements ... There were about sixteen gentlemen present. A draft copy of rules and regulations for the guidance of the Club was submitted to the meeting, and, after a few emendations, approved of and passed.

A pioneering game was held on the north parklands the following Saturday watched by "a considerable muster both of members and spectators". The game lasted for nearly three hours, and "the most active side" won by "one or two more goals than their opponents".

From this modest beginning, the footy passion quickly grew and spread. The *Register* reported at length on a later game in its issue of 28 May 1860:

> A grand match between the members of the recently-established Adelaide Football Club living north, and those living south of the River Torrens took place last Saturday afternoon on the North Park Lands. The weather, fortunately, proved most auspicious for the occasion, and a day more adapted to give verve and vigour to the limbs could not possibly be desired. There was an exceedingly large number of spectators, among whom were noticed His Excellency the Governor the Hon. W. Younghusband ... and many other gentlemen, besides a considerable number of ladies who graced the scene with their presence. Messrs. Cussen and John Acraman were chosen captains, the former of the North Adelaideans, who were distinguished by wearing blue colours, and the latter of the South Adelaideans, attired in pink. The game commenced shortly after 2 o'clock, when there were upwards of forty competitors, and as the afternoon progressed the number increased to nearly seventy. One hour and a half elapsed ere the first goal was made. It was obtained by the pinks, both sides having displayed a great deal of spirit and energy in the play; during the course of which those concomitants to the game—injured shins, awkward tumbles and

other ludicrous mishaps—frequently occurred, and apparently formed no small item in the amusement of the assembled company. A brief intermission having taken place, the struggle recommenced, and after three quarters' of an hour of hard play the second goal was made by the blues ... Schroeder's band was engaged, and during the afternoon several pieces were well executed.

The growth and interest continued so that next month, on 11 June, the *Register* could report:

> Adelaide Football Club. The healthful and invigorating exercise of football is becoming popular here. The above club, which has only been established a few weeks, now numbers upwards of a hundred members, including two members of the Legislative Council, one (the Speaker) of the House of Assembly, several merchants, lawyers and other gentlemen. On Saturday last, a game between the old and present Collegians against the other members of the Club was played on the North Park Lands ... The strength of the two parties of combatants appeared to be equal, for not one goal was made in more than three hours play ... During the afternoon there were a great many of those mishaps designated in common parlance "spills", but their occurrence injured no one, and they proved a constant source of amusement to the beholders.

The elements of the game as it later developed in Adelaide were already discernible: the "combatant" spirit, the "spills", the territorial allegiances, the varying coloured guernseys, and the excited and amused armchair heroes watching from the touchline. But these disorganized melees between large numbers of "combatants", where three hours strife could not "make" one goal, obviously needed reform and regulation. In 1878 a conference of leading Australian teams was held which agreed upon the first set of rules. One important new rule was that players could run with the ball only if it were bounced every five or six yards. Restrictions were placed on numbers in teams. Gradually, Australian Rules football as it is revered in Adelaide took final shape. By 1879, clubs had formed in many rural and suburban centres. The city scene was dominated by three clubs—Norwood, Port Adelaide, and South Adelaide—until the turn of the century. Football gear was striking—woollen hats and guernseys, tight trousers, vivid stockings, and highly polished lace-up boots that extended well up the leg.

R.C. Casble, McLean and Co. of Rundle Street advertised in the *Register* of 22 May 1885: "To All Footballers. First shipment just arrived, in all the club colours. Football Ribbons, knickers etc." By this time there were regular and plentiful references to football in the papers. In the same number, for instance, there was a report of a match between the new Hotham Club and South Adelaide and an advertisement for a forthcoming game at the Adelaide Oval between Old Scholars of St. Peter's and Prince Alfred's. Just as Rugby football was fostered and made respectable at the English public schools, so, from the start, the Adelaide academies nurtured Australian Rules.

Aboriginal talent at football was patronizingly recognized by the *Register* of 3 June 1885 when it reported a match at the Oval between a team of local players and a team "chosen from the aboriginals now on a visit to Adelaide". "Some surprise was manifested by a number of spectators at the form exhibited by the 'darkies'".

By the 1890s, terms and concepts like "premiers" and "premiership" had emerged. The game had become so popular that local fervour almost matched that of Melbourne. There the admirable Twopeny, who actually played the game "a couple of score of times", felt obliged to conclude, despite the fact that he was "an Old Marlburian", that of Rugby, Association, and Victorian football, "the Victorian game is by far the most scientific, the most amusing to both players and onlookers, and altogether the best". Twopeny gave evidence of the Melbourne addiction to this homegrow game: "Some measure of popularity of the game may be gathered from the fact that the member who has sat in the last three parliaments for the most important working-man's constituency, owes his seat entirely to his prowess on behalf of the local football club."[9] He estimated that "some 10,000 people ... pay their sixpences to see the Melbourne and Carlton Clubs play of an afternoon" and declared: "A good football match in Melbourne is one of the sights of the world".

Considering the difference in the size of the cities, Adelaide was just as keen: for instance, the *Register* of 10 July 1893 reported that between four and five thousand people watched a match at the Adelaide Oval between Port Adelaide and South Adelaide, a game "that delighted the heart of everyone". With spectator enthusiasm and club rivalry, of course, there came increasing violence. A letter from an indignant fan printed in the *Register* of 7 June 1893 shows that football had in some ways degenerated from that original merry conflict on the north parklands which had so entertained the governor and his ladies. The writer bemoaned "loss of interest" in football caused by "discreditable scenes both on and off the field", and went on:

> Respectable people will not countenance such proceedings. The disturbance that took place at the conclusion of last Saturday's match was perhaps the worst that we have had inflicted upon us. Briefly, the facts are these: As soon as the umpire and players started to leave the field, the spectators surrounded them from all quarters. One hoodlum in the crowd, who had lost his temper and probably his money as well, made a rush at the umpire, and while they were engaged, a mean, contemptible ruffian kicked the umpire on the side of the knee, completely laming him. What a manly action! The police cannot be blamed in the matter. As soon as they saw what had happened, they acted with decision and quickly stopped the disturbance. But why did they not make any arrests?
> I am, Sir, AN OLD PLAYER.

Next month, the "central umpires ... resigned as a body" to protest against "their treatment this season".

Little changes under the sun. Elderly fans who currently deplore violence in football (beercans, which were used as missiles, have recently been banned from Adelaide ovals) need to be gently reminded that the good old days could be just as rough.

By 1896, perhaps partly because of the depression, Adelaide football reached its nadir. One match at the Adelaide Oval between Norwood and Port Adelaide attracted a wretched gate of three pounds. North Adelaide and West Torrens Clubs were called by the *Advertiser* "subsidized encumbrances" to the dominant South Adelaide, Port Adelaide, and Norwood clubs. The introduction of an electorate system which brought in West Adelaide in 1898 and the doughty Sturt a few years later started an upswing in the game's fortunes. A holiday match between Norwood and Port in 1908 brought 26,000 people and 570 pounds to the turnstiles. Max Lamshed writes in his *South Australian Story*: "It was a hard, bullocking game in those days, with the equivalent of 50 points an outstanding score and 35 points often a winning one. In 'The Advertiser' reports of 1908 are named such giants as Aldersey, Geddes, Chamberlain, Hansen, McKenzie, Treadrea, Jessop, Dewar, Pope and Londrigan."[10]

Since this revival, Australian Rules has massively entrenched itself in the city's affections. The league premiership (Woodville and Central Districts have been added to the veteran clubs) is a regular winter's bone of contention, as is the annual premiers' and state clash with the Victorian high priests of the game. Enormous crowds muster for major games. Almost 60,000 fans crammed themselves into the Adelaide Oval for the 1957 final. An enterprising local confectioner markets iced lollies in football colours, and football prowess helps careers as diverse as car sales and television stardom. A colossal new Football Park has been built out at West Lakes on the confident assumption that Adelaide will continue to cleave to Australian Rules.

The game is an integral part of the bush ethos, too, and the leather ball is punted high from rural pitches against a backdrop of gum trees and vast skies from Port Mac-Donnell to Streaky Bay, from Yorktown to Oodnadatta.

SOCCER

There has, it is true, been a little disquiet of late among the ranks of the faithful over the growing local popularity of Association Football, or soccer. This English game had its supporters in Adelaide at least by the 1890s, for the *Register* of 25 July 1893 mentioned a game between "the Adelaide Rowing Club and the Association Eleven". By then, local loyalties were, of course, firmly committed to Australian Rules which, in its pace and fluidity, has much in common with soccer. Accordingly, soccer's tremendous growth in popular appeal during the twentieth century in Britain, the Continent, and South America was not reflected in Adelaide. Greeks, Italians, Yugoslavs, and Britons emigrating to Adelaide after 1947 brought their enthusiasm for soccer with them, but with Australian Rules so deeply rooted, the game became a minority, New Australian affair. This alienation from local customs, in Adelaide and elsewhere, was epitomized by exotic names for clubs such as Azzuri, Hellas, Beograd, and Juventus. Until quite recently, to attend an Adelaide soccer match at, say, Olympic Park, was to experience an hour and a half of Mediterranean colour and passion. This, too, is changing under the influence of the World Soccer Cup and the potent proselytysing for the game by British television's superb soccer programmes. There is now much more indigenous interest in soccer. Visiting teams like Glasgow Rangers and Sunderland are appreciated by Adelaide crowds.

RACING

> There is hardly a town to be called a town which has not its racecourse, and there are many racecourses where there are no towns.
>
> *Anthony Trollope, 1872*

For months the founding fathers were frustrated by the scarcity of horses in the province. Few horses survived the rigours of the first ships' passage. The settlers had to await the arrival of Australian-bred "Walers" (tough New South Wales horses) that came from Van Diemen's Land, or with the overlanders. Before these arrived, ponies were ordered from Timor. Of a consignment of 119, only 9 were still alive when the ship reached Adelaide on 22 April 1838. Hodder estimated the cost as 500 pounds each.

The Adelaide region was ideal for horses, and once they came they flourished and the lines were carefully improved by the settlers. A good horse was essential to Adelaidean mobility and self-respect. The pride which used to express itself in the maintenance of a handsome horse, whether for riding or draught work, is now lavished upon that much inferior creation, the motor car. But in colonial times the horse, from the noble Clydesdale to the graceful thoroughbred, ruled supreme in transport, farm work and, indeed, in sport. Twopeny remarked: "Nearly everyone born in the colonies learns to ride as a boy, and not to be able to ride is to write yourself down a duffer. Horseflesh is so marvellously cheap, that it is not taken so much care of as at home. In outward appearance, the Australian horse has not so much to recommend him as a rule, but his powers of endurance rival those of the fabled Arabian. A grass-fed horse has been known to go as much as 100 miles in a day."[11]

South Australians were well able from experience to appreciate Adam Lindsay Gordon's riding exploits in the province, such as his famous leap over a high fence by the edge of the Blue Lake cliff near Mount Gambier, and to enjoy his tributes to the horse in stirring verse. Australia became the major supplier of horses for the British imperial armies, and many South Australian mounts served in India and the campaigns in South Africa and Palestine.

In sport, this Adelaide enthusiasm for horses expressed itself in hunting, and especially in racing. Early Adelaide magnates like Fisher, Kingston, and Morphett were ardent racing men. Inspector Tolmer was, by his own account, a veritable centaur. In his reminiscences, he tells some of his tallest stories about his success in steeplechasing over the foothills. He claims, to be the originator of trotting races in Adelaide with a magnificent animal which only he could tame and with which he won a large wager by trotting the length of the metropolitan beaches despite many obstacles within a set time.[12]

After some earlier haphazard racing in the parklands, a Thebarton paddock became in 1838 the centre of Adelaide racing. A meeting there in that year attracted a crowd of 800 out of a total population of little over 2,000. By 1839, one of the many short-lived turf clubs was offering purses of thirty sovereigns for flat races, and a little less for steeplechases and water jumps. The *Adelaide Observer* of 30 December 1843 gave notice of a "Tradesman's Pony Race" for ponies under fourteen hands. Entrants had to register at Mr. Malcolm's Black Bull Hotel in Hindley Street.

A typical racing advertisement in the *Register* ran as follows:

> Adelaide Races. Thursday and Friday 1st and 2nd of January 1846, The maiden Stakes—2 guineas entrance for maiden horses dropped in the Colony. Mares and geldings allowed 31 lbs. Once around and a distance—the second to save his stake ... Second Race—The Town Plate—five guineas entrance—for horses of every denomination. Heats two miles ...

The *Register* reported on the New Year's races of 1846:

> Our annual meeting commenced on Thursday, the company exhibiting a blaze of splendour never equalled on a South Australian course ... every grade of society was duly represented. The weather was delightful, and the sport of the very highest order. The course was kept in good order by a body of the mounted police, under the command of Inspector Tolmer. A division of the foot police was also in attendance to counteract the proceedings of the Van Diemen's Land conditionals who mustered very strong.

This reference to the Vandemonian "conditionals", ticket-of-leave men, is interesting. These were the dreaded Tiersmen whose general hell-raising agitated early Adelaide. The police had to "counteract the proceedings" of such gentry at many other race-meetings in the 1840s and 50s, where sideshows, gambling, and plentiful grog prevailed between races.

Racing was held at the Victoria Park circuit, yet another alienation of parklands, from 1847. Classics were instituted, like the St. Leger in 1858, the Derby in 1860, and the Adelaide Cup in 1864. The first Birthday Cup was run in 1878, and one of the jockey clubs opened a new course, with a track of sand and dirt, at Morphettville. It had what the *Advertiser* called an "elegant and delightfully situated stand", and it had a totalizator—a tiny cabin—from which the club deducted 10 per cent.

Racing enthusiasm was at least as strong in the country. On Easter Monday 1876, people drove their wagonettes and traps by the hundred up the winding roads to Oakbank to watch a steeplechase "over 2½ miles and eight fences 4½ ft. high, of 20 sovs." on a paddock owned by Johnson's brewery. The judges sat on a brewery wagon. This was the origin of the popular Oakbank race meeting (in 1885 the first Great

Eastern was run there) which annually pulls the punters with their picnics from Adelaide up into the bracing hills.

Supreme on the Adelaide racing scene, of course, was and is the Adelaide Cup, which is now a public holiday. Parliament always adjourned for Cup Day, and it served as a "wholesome diversion" during hard times like the depression of the 1890s. On this, the *Register* of 3 May 1893 observed:

> In due proportion, what the Cup Day of November is to Melbourne, the Cup Day of May is to Adelaide. This is our Cup Day, and if the somewhat capricious weather of the period be only propitious the success of the occasion is assured in all the sense which the enterprising S.A. Jockey Club wish to secure it. Banks may totter and may fall— the commercial world may be disturbed and even distracted; but Australians will have their sports in all circumstances. And to the extent to which today's exemplifications of the national pastime serves the purpose of a wholesome diversion from the prevailing business agitation of the moment, it will be a substantial advantage to the Community ... Therefore we shall not discuss the action of the Government in giving a sort of State recognition to the races by ordering Civil Servants and the bankers to make a partial holiday of the occasion and consequently at least suggesting the same course to the rest of the community.

The year 1885 was a hurtful one for the Cup, for it was raced in rival Melbourne. The *Register* of 11 May remarked tartly: "The Adelaide Cup. Once more the big racing event of South Australia has been run for, but South Australians were debarred from witnessing it unless they went to the expense and inconvenience of travelling to Melbourne."

During 1885, racing in Adelaide suffered one of its many crises of confidence. A correspondent to the *Register* of 29 January lamented this, and gave an interesting indication that the local interest in the sport was a social leveller of especial value in class-conscious Adelaide.

> The Decay of Racing in this colony will be regarded by thousands as a greater social than sporting loss ... The racecourse may be regarded as a Republic, where for the time all social distinctions are broken down, and where men meet on more equal terms than on any other platform in the world ... It is on the racecourse that old friendships are renewed and new ones formed ... There also may be seen the great and wealthy of the land exchanging kind greetings with the less fortunate but not less worthy of respect.

The correspondent need not have fretted. The "Republics" survived this and other difficulties and became so strong a feature of the Adelaide lifestyle that today the state's smallish population makes possible three major racecourses in the city—Morphettville, Victoria Park, and Cheltenham—trotting tracks, and several country racegrounds. As for the Adelaide Cup, it is now a mandatory public holiday.

HUNTING AND SHOOTING

> *The Adelaide Hounds*
> by Pink Coat
> Now welcome, welcome, masters mine,
> Thrice welcome to the noble chase
> Nor earthly sport, nor sport divine
> Can take such honourable place.
> The Register, *10 July 1893.*

By the time Pink Coat took to poetry as above, fox hunting had become extremely well established in the sporting scene. Fox hunting, as lovingly described by writers like R.S. Surtees and Anthony Trollope, was the supreme sport for gentry in the English shires through the nineteenth century and beyond. What more natural, then, than that it should flourish in Adelaide which took vigorous pride in both its English provincial connexion and in its homegrown gentility? There was no city in the Empire more passionate about horses than Adelaide, and the ancient ritual of hounds, horns, pink coats and stirrup cups had a special appeal in a province devoid, for a long time, of a sense of history, and always anxious to emulate Home ways.

Once they had acquired and bred up their horses, the settlers with leisure and pretensions to gentility soon organized themselves into hunting parties. At first, of course, there were no foxes to hunt. Dingoes made a poor alternative and the bush pastime of chasing kangaroos and emus on horseback and clubbing them with a stirrup iron grated on the English sporting instinct. Foxes were imported and released. They became devastating pests. The South Australian terrain was wild and rugged and as there were no gamekeepers to stop the earths, they proved almost impossible to hunt down in the traditional way. Moreover, the gullies and high fences, the stumps and wombat holes made the galloping pursuit of a real fox, thinking for himself, hazardous.

The result was that the foxes were left to the shooters and trappers and the Adelaide Hunt Club, like most other Australian hunts, became mainly a drag hunt: that is, a scented trail was dragged over a prescribed route, and the hounds bounded along it. All the rest of the ritual, costume, calls and so on, were religiously kept.

Trollope, than whom there was no one, novelist or otherwise, fonder of fox hunting, described at amusing length an outing with the Melbourne Hunt Club in the early 1870s in his *Australia and New Zealand*. Meetings of the Adelaide Hunt about that time must have been similar. The proceedings began with a hunt banquet in a marquee near the beach attended by "about two hundred men ... of whom perhaps a quarter were dressed in scarlet". They ate a large luncheon "with a violent clatter of knives and forks", after which they smoked cigars until three o'clock. Then they rode off over a heath, the middle-aged novelist mounted on "a stout ... well-bitted cob". No one seemed to know what was to be hunted—a "bagged fox", a deer from a cart, or whether they would "turn down", or release from a bag, a dingo. It turned out to be a drag hunt, and after half a mile's hard riding, Trollope approached "an obstacle such as in England would stop a whole field". This was a high post and rail fence "which seemed as though it had been built against ever rushing herds of wild bulls. At home, we are not used to such fences and therefore they are terrible to us".

Trollope had been advised by his colonial friends that the only way to get over Australian fences was to ride hard at them: either the horse would clear it or it would smash the top rail. If you went at it slowly, you would be thrown and the horse would roll on you. In this case, a lady rider broke the top rail, so Trollope was able to clear the second. Eventually, he became entangled in a wire fence and was left "alone and disconsolate" while his horse dashed on after the hounds.[13]

Some of the early *Registers* describe hunts at which dingoes, kangaroos, emus and, eventually, foxes were hounded over the Adelaide Plains. The sporting Governor Robe was an especially keen huntsman. The *Southern Australian* described at length "runs with the hounds" at Dry Creek, Glenelg, and Tapley's Hill. The beauty of the drag hunt was that it allowed the organizers to plan a good, reliable ride, with frequent agreeable rests at "hospitable houses", like Urrbrae, en route. The hunt often started from a spot on the parklands, watched by critical crowds, and headed off through orchards, woods, and open farmland to the foothills or the reedbeds.

The Adelaide Hunt Club still meets. Indeed it has been strengthened by the phenomenal recent growth of interest in riding. Of course the expansion of the suburbs has driven it from most of its old runs in the plains to the hills, where hunt clubs are based on centres like Strathalbyn. It is an exhilarating sight on a raw hills afternoon in winter to see fifty or so riders of the Adelaide Hunt galloping in scarlet, black, and white over bright green fields, leaping pre-arranged fences and thundering over the skyline, to hear the medieval sound of the horn and the hounds' music. It is a stirring and extraordinarily beautiful spectacle. And it represents, for a few strange moments, the transformation of Australian paddocks and scrub into an English shire, by the exercise of a kind of determined folk will.

Apart from fox hunting or its equivalent, the Adelaideans strongly manifested the Anglo Saxon urge to go out and kill something, for sport, or for the pot, or for both. From the beginning of settlement, the resident population of kangaroos and wallabies took a ferocious battering from hunters, farmers, and developers, so much so that the marsupials only survive now in the Adelaide region in zoos or in remote patches of scrub in the hills. The emus—and J.W. Bull, for example, used to hunt them from horseback in Brownhill Creek—have completely gone.

Some kangaroo hunts were organized on vaguely fox hunting lines. Trollope went out with one in Queensland. He described the kangaroo dog as "a large, rough greyhound, that hunts both by sight and by nose". The object was to single out the "old man" kangaroos, run them down, then cut their throats or club them while the dogs were worrying them. He concluded: "In this hunting, there is not much jumping; but what there is requires a very quick horse. The turns are rapid, and the ground is strewed by prostrate forest trunks. There is danger too of riding against trees. This on one occasion I did, with great force; and could not use my leg for six weeks after the accident. In default, however, of anything better, kangaroo hunting is good sport".[14]

Kangaroos were destroyed in this way round Adelaide, but the more common means were shooting and organized drives to a *battue*. This was an enclosure or fenced hollow in the scrub into which large mobs of kangaroos and wallabies were driven by horsemen and beaters. Once the marsupials were trapped therein, the sportsmen would shoot or batter them at their leisure. According to the *Illustrated Australian News* of 2 November 1868, 40,000 kangaroos were butchered in this way on three properties near Mount Gambier in one year.

There were several other things to shoot. Twopeny unconsciously demonstrates the indiscriminate bloodthirstiness of the nineteenth century Anglo-Australian:

> There are snipe to be shot in Australia; but wild duck is really the best kind of shooting we get, and far more easily obtainable. They are much more varied in kind than at home. Rabbits are generally too plentiful to afford much fun. I have pelted them by the score from the veranda of a station house in South Australia. At best they are poor sport. The kangaroos and wallabies are too tame. Amongst other animals shootable are the native bear—a sluggish creature looking like a small bear; the bandicoot ... the native cat, cockatoos, parrots, eagles, hawks, owls, parroquets; wild turkey, quail, native pheasants, teal, waterhens, and the black swan and the opossum.[15]

In other words, anything that moved and was not owned by a farmer. On opossums, Twopeny advised: "The opossum you shoot by moonlight, getting them between your gun and the moon as they jump from tree to tree". This was how Prince Alfred, no doubt, shot his large bag of possums in the Adelaide Hills in 1867.

SOME OTHER SPORTS

Like cricket, golf finds in the Adelaide area an ideal environment. The parklands, the crest of the ranges where there are noble links like Mount Lofty, and certain select pleasaunces on the plains like Kooyonga seem made for golf. It began in a substantial way in 1870 when Governor Sir James Fergusson had nine holes installed in the old racecourse. The maintenance of greens was a problem during the hot summers until quite recently, but courses were laid out on the north parklands, at Seaton, and at Glenelg. Now most of the hills towns have their links. The happy inspiration of the parklands has been a boon to golfers as well as other sportsmen. Thousands upon thousands of golfers, after a round on the north parklands, or on the par three course by the Torrens Lake, must have called blessings on to Colonel Light's head. For in how many of the world's cities is it possible to enjoy golf in leafy tranquillity hard by the skyscrapers of the central city?

Croquet, lawn tennis, and bowls also thrive under the Adelaide sun. Lawn tennis came over promptly after its invention in England in the 1870s, and it soon became a matter of pride for middle-class villa-owners to set up a tennis court amid the geraniums and orangeries of their spacious gardens. A club was formed at the Adelaide Oval, combining it with croquet, and later a strong lawn tennis association got a parklands grant outside the Oval and established excellent facilities where major tournaments can be played.

Senior Adelaideans are addicted to bowls, and meticulously dressed bowlers drive gingerly from one club to the other for contests. It is a serious business. From the headland at Port Elliot, I once watched a grand rally of south coast lady bowlers adorning the club lawns in their white uniforms, blazers, and shady hats. A rain squall blew in from the southern ocean, but the ladies stooped, bowled, and clapped indomitably on.

The Oxford and Cambridge rowing matches and the Henley on Thames Regatta inevitably caused emulation in loyal Adelaide. The annual rowing contests on the Torrens Lake was actually called Henley-on-Torrens during the high noon of Empire. Swimming used to be popular in the Torrens, but has now gravitated to the swimming pools and the splendid metropolitan beaches. Sea bathing, as has been noted before, had to struggle for many years against the Adelaide sense of propriety. It was long totally forbidden at Glenelg and one's heart goes out to those sweltering strollers on the beach in old photographs. When swimming was allowed, it was only with grisly restrictions. Ladies and gentlemen had to confine themselves to separate cages near the pier.

But even the bluest-nosed wowser could see nothing improper in sailing, although he might have disliked it for causing enjoyment. Thus yachting and dinghy sailing on the blue and generally safe waters of the gulf had early and untrammelled development. Nowadays on a sunny weekend the waters off the city beaches are flecked by myriads of pleasure boats.

Cycling was another immediate and popular English import. The stalwart Madame Franzina, tights and all, a "bicycle performer", enchanted Adelaide audiences in 1876 with her demonstration of the "boneshaker". Descended from the velocipede of the eighteenth century, the boneshaker was driven by a crank on the front wheel, and its wooden wheels had iron tyres. Shortly afterwards, the pennyfarthing appeared. It must have shaken the bones just as hard as members of the Adelaide Bicycle Club, in special caps, kneebreeches, and jackets, bumped and jounced over the execrable roads. Cycling soon became a craze. Moonlight rallies in the Oval were the thing, and there were races and expeditions into the bush. Cycling afforded some outlet for the stifled sporting energies of Adelaide women. The sport was considered respectable, so many ladies joined cycling clubs and pedalled off in flotillas as far afield as Burra. Special cycling tracks were installed in the Adelaide and Jubilee ovals.

Policemen were soon pursuing wrongdoers on bicycles, including cyclists and cart drivers who exceeded the twelve miles per hour speed limit in the city. The *Register* of 6 July 1893, reported that Commissioner Peterswald was "entirely satisfied" with the experiment of supplying the new "safety" bicycle to members of the force.

In the 1890s there began a craze for roller and ice-skating. The *Register* of 25 March 1910 reported: "One of the most popular attractions in the city on Thursday evening was the Elite Skating Rink in Pirie Street which was re-opened by Mr. F.W. Conybear after its summer recess. Notwithstanding the warm weather, there was a gratifying attendance and nearly 50 couples took part in the grand match ..."

Polo was popular early in this hard-riding province, which always responded strongly to any variation of equestrian sports. In 1975, Adelaide was the setting for the first equestrian Expo, and King William Street resounded to hooves once more as hundreds of riders made their way to the Oval. The procession was headed by contingents from the many pony clubs that flourish in and around Adelaide and especially in the hills where nowadays horses graze in practically every paddock.

In sum, Adelaide gives opportunities for sports followers of almost every leaning, from baseball to hockey, hare coursing to wild fowling. Enthusiasm for sport has always been a marked feature of the city. So much so that "One who will Join" in his letter to the *Register* of 25 April 1885 felt that Adelaide sportiness endangered the defences of the city. He wrote:

> As there seems at the present moment to be every probability of a war with Russia, with perhaps the involvement of the other Great Powers of Europe, and as it is almost universally acknowledged that the defences of this colony are insufficient for its protection, perhaps a hint as to a means of raising further means of defence would not be out of place. At the present moment we have hundreds of young strong healthy men members of the various cricket and football clubs in the city and suburbs who, I am sure, would be willing to join in any defence movement if it were not for the objection that they will be deprived of their Saturday afternoon's pleasure through being required to drill.

As it turned out, there was no war with Russia. But even had there been one, it seems that this or even worse cataclysms would have failed to divert Adelaide sports enthusiasts from their Saturday matches.

A powerful interest in sport is, of course, a common denominator in all Australian cities and towns. Adelaide's sense of difference in this area derives, perhaps, from that beautiful Oval and that unique swathe of parklands where there is tremendous opportunity for sport right by the heart of the city.

Newspapers

That Press which I calculated would be the means of promoting peace has, alas, fomented discord and disputes in the new colony. Why is this? *George Fife Angas, 1838*

This is essentially the land of newspapers ... the proportion of the population who can afford to purchase and subscribe to newspapers is ten times as large as in England.

R.E.N. Twopeny, 1882

Adelaide people were always avid newspaper readers. According to J. Arbuckle Reid's collection of articles, *The Australian Reader*, published in 1882, South Australia had 47 newspapers in the early 1880s. This, set against its modest population, gave the province a ratio of one newspaper for every 5,880 persons. By comparison, Britain had one newspaper for every 18,000 people. British population densities and large circulations explain some of this, and of course many of the colonial newspapers were ephemeral and of small circulation. Nonetheless, the inference is that Adelaide was always fond of its paper.

Indeed, and typically, the Wakefieldian founders were so seized with the importance of printed news and information that they printed the first number of the *South Australian Gazette and Colonial Register* in June 1834, more than two years before the settlers reached Holdfast Bay. A government printer, Robert Thomas, and a printing press arrived on the *Africaine*—the press is now displayed in the Historical Museum—and George Stevenson was the controversial first editor of the *Register*. A weekly at first, by 1837 it was selling an average of 300 copies a week, and by 1846 it had doubled its circulation. In 1841, for a population of under 20,000, the province had seven weekly newspapers, each published on a different day of the week. With the *Register*, these comprised the *Chronicle*, the *Advertiser*, the *Free Press*, the *Examiner*, the *Observer*, and the *Southern Star*. There was further spasmodic competition from the *Egotist* and the *Port Lincoln Herald* which began in 1839.

These early Adelaide newspapers had their faults. They were often confused, inaccurate, and prejudiced one way or the other. They fought fierce and abusive wars with each other. Libel suits and lawyers closed in on the livelier of them. Some were little more than mouthpieces for political or business factions.

As such, they were not dissimilar to some modern newspapers. But the early *Register*s and *Observer*s and their peers had their peculiar virtues. They exercised, sometimes to the point of their own financial ruin, their right to free speech and comment. Their closely packed columns were a modern lay-out man's nightmare, but they gave space for editor and contributor to stretch their legs. Generally, their grammar, syntax, and range of words put modern journalists to shame. They would call a spade a

spade; and if a public figure or a competitor seemed to them to be a knave then, ex-
uberantly at length, they would say so.

They were never really remunerative in the early decades and editors and
proprietors, like John Stephens of the *Register*, were sometimes in severe financial difficulties. The depression of the 1840s destroyed some of them. Nathaniel Hailes tried
and failed with the *Adelaide Independent* and the *Free Press*, and his intermittent
humorous paper, *Timothy Short's Journal of Passing Events* did not last long. The monthly
South Australian Magazine, owned by Alexander Macdougall and edited by James Allen
(who later edited the *Adelaide Times*) survived only three years, from 1841 to 1843. This
was a pity, for the magazine was more reflective and less obsessed with political controversy than the feuding newspapers. Its tone was thoroughly Australian, and concentrated upon the natural history and pursuits of the new country. The *Southern
Australian*, that vehement counterbalance to the *Register*, was forced to cease publication
in 1852. Its editor, Andrew Murray, a former draper, went on to edit the Melbourne
Argus which was to become Australia's most respected newspaper.

The early colonial press was often pompous. The genteel third person was generally used in advertisements. Characteristically, the *Register* pontificated on 27 July 1848:
"It may be said without any verbal impropriety that the facts in elucidation began to
thicken as to the clear practicability of steam communication between the vast colonies
of Australia and the Mother Country." This is almost as bad as modern Public Service
Australian English with its clots of meaningless jargon. But the pioneer journalists had
the excuse, which the public servants certainly do not, that they were short of staff,
time, and resources. Most of the editorial content of the four-page dailies was written
by the weary editor himself, so the padding is understandable. He and his colleagues
had no time to classify the advertisements or afford the luxuries of headlines and
special reporters. They were glad to fill columns with stale news of Home and Europe,
especially when the telegraph was established.

Yet the early newspapers had their strengths. They were society's watchdogs,
albeit self-appointed, against administrative incompetence, injustice, and governmental
high-handedness. They were the only regular means of providing information, news,
reports on such matters as government proceedings and shipping arrivals and depar-
tures, and advertisements for a small and isolated community. And in the last analysis,
the people themselves thought their newspapers indispensable. Twopeny remarked
that, apart from the Bible, Shakespeare, and Macaulay's *Essays*, "the only literature
within the bushman's reach are newspapers. The townsman deems them equally essential to his well-being. Nearly everybody can read and nearly everybody has leisure to do
so."

But perhaps their chief virtue was that they were authentic mirrors of early
Adelaide life. Citizens wrote letters to them about their problems or grievances just as
they saw them. The columns of advertisements give sharp insight into the fashions,
entertainments, and mores of the period. The people scarcely mentioned except in
general terms by official historians make their vigorous and complex presence felt
here—the working people, stallholders, publicans, and even the sinners. A gamey
Register of the 1840s, for instance, is a useful corrective to the governor-dominated pages
of Hodder, Blacket, Pascoe, and the rest. The newspapers tended to tell it like it was.
The official or semi-official recorders for posterity told it like it ought to have been.

The *Register* advertisements tell an intriguing story of their own, and show that the
long gone pioneers were not so very different from their successors in the 1970s. John
Bentham Neales, for example, the government auctioneer, placed advertisements
throughout the 1840s for goods to be auctioned ranging from real estate to "jams and

jellies of all kinds", "New novels, Trollope, Cooper etc." (he would have meant Anthony Trollope's mother, Frances), mould candles, grindstones, working bullocks, and "a capital iron bedstead". Among the "very great variety of merchandise and sundries" offered by E. Solomon in the *Register* of 19 July 1845 were "Gents' Chesterfield coats", pea jackets, sperm candles, cotton wick, and a "few bags of GOOD Sugar". Next week, Platt's Library and Bookshop of Hindley Street invited clients to buy "Playing cards, ready-reckoners, cigars, ledgers, Wesley's Hymns, Watt's Hymns, encyclopaedias, tops, marbles, backgammon boards, card cases, pocket books and small testaments". By lumping Wesley's Hymns with playing cards, Platts showed that they were ready to accommodate both saints and sinners.

On 6 December 1845 Robert Dodgson, "formerly of Liverpool", gave notice of the existence of "the Royal Adelaide Hot and Cold Baths for Ladies and Gentlemen", to be enjoyed "in the best style of accommodation" in Rundle Street. On 27 December Mr. Norman urged Adelaideans to apply for Daguerrotype Portraits and promised: "A perfect likeness, and unchangeable, is ensured, neither flattering nor detracting".

The lively Adelaide inns provided much of the advertising revenue for struggling editors. For instance, Mr. R. Pepperell of the City Arms Inn advised "Lovers of Good Cheer" attending the cattle show of September 1845 that for two and six they could have a dinner at his establishment with "all the delicacies of the season". A little later, Mr. Barnett of the Sturt Hotel informed the "officers and gentlemen of Adelaide" that his billiard room was open. Soon afterwards, the impetuous Mr. Barnett offered to pay 50 pounds to anyone who could prove that his billiard table was not the best in the colony.

There were many advertisements for entertainment, as has already been seen in the earlier section on popular amusements. The colonial editors tended to flatter local productions; indeed, I have been unable to find a really hostile review of any pantomime, circus, vaudeville act, melodrama, or musical comedy in nineteenth century Adelaide. The editors were well aware that, with so many newspapers competing for advertising revenue, realistic arts criticism was a liberty best overlooked.

But if they were kind to advertisers, the colonial editors were often ferocious about political or local government inefficiencies. The City Council, especially in its early years, was frequently the focus of editorial sarcasm and indignation. Sanitary matters and the state of the roads were hardy perennials here. For instance, the Adelaide *Observer* of 16 September 1843 printed a "Notice to Pedestrians": "The open state of wells in parts of this town has been the subject of remarks before, but now it has become more dangerous to foot passengers because of the absence or dilapidation of fences which were formerly entire. There is a well on an acre in Grote Street, opposite Ferguson's Iron Store, which is completely open, about 45 feet deep, with about 12 feet of water in it." There were sometimes reports about unfortunates, drunk or otherwise, but dead just the same, who fell down wells like this in the city. In July, 1843, the *Observer* waxed indignant about " ... the almost impassable state of the roads, particularly King William Street, and some parts of Hindley Street ... In many cases, to avoid being altogether swamped, persons have been obliged to go half a mile out of their way ... It is of no use to ask what our dormant or defunct Corporation is about ..." A correspondent to the *Observer* of 25 May 1843 was angry about another constant source of complaint, the Torrens water:

> It does appear strange to me that no steps are as yet taken to supply the town with cleaner water. It would be hard indeed to persuade me that the Torrens water is at all wholesome, if sheep washing with tobacco, tanning hides, and so forth, are allowed on its banks ... But

besides all this, the cows, goats, bullocks and horses kept in the town are taken to the Old Bridge to water and to wash ... In the neighbourhood of Currie Street, wells may be surrounded by water closets, within a few feet, and these wells are not dammed. This must be worse than drinking the Torrens water.

The *Register* of 1 January 1885 was sardonic about the government-supplied Christmas dinner at the Destitute Asylum: "The Government provided the usual dinner of roast beef and plum pudding for the inmates of the Destitute Asylum on Christmas Day. Two half barrels of beer were presented by Messrs. Haussen and Co. ... unfortunately the quantity was only sufficient to supply half the old people."

Outspokenness by the Adelaide press, and especially by the dominant *Register*, often brought trouble. In 1838, this paper called the contents of its political rival, *The Southern Australian*, "sixpence worth of scum ... nauseous and disgusting puddle". Accordingly, the *Register* was quite often on the brink of ruin because of libel actions. The year 1849 was a comparatively good one for its pugnacious editor, for while damages amounting to 12,950 pounds were claimed in nine libel actions at the Supreme Court, only 13 pence were awarded. Perhaps this indicates a certain community sympathy with the *Register*. Twopeny liked the *Register* placing it second in quality for the whole country only to the Melbourne *Argus*. He wrote of it:

> In style and get-up it is almost an exact copy of its Melbourne contemporary ... In reports and correspondence, it is quite as enterprising, but its leading columns and critiques being almost all written in the office, are necessarily weaker. The whole paper is less carefully edited, but its opinions are more liberal, and it is in no sense a party paper. It may, indeed, be said that not even the *Times* exercised so much influence in its sphere as does the *Register*.
>
> It not merely reflects public opinion, but, to a great extent, leads it, and it must be admitted that, on the whole, it leads very sensibly ... The extraordinary merits of this paper, in so small a community, are due partly to its having been, at a critical period in its existence, edited, managed and partly owned by the late Mr. Howard Clark, a man of great culture and ability, and also to the close competition of the South Australian *Advertiser*, a twopenny paper which is well sustained in every department, and noted for occasional leading articles of great brilliancy.[1]

The non-partisan "liberal opinion" and the occasional "great brilliancy" of the *Advertiser*, and the fact that two such dailies could exist "in so small a community" demonstrate a certain intellectual liveliness in this little colonial city. There was none of what Twopeny called that "fatal odour of respectable dullness"—which, in his opinion, afflicted intercolonial papers like the *Sydney Morning Herald*—about Adelaide's *Register* and *Advertiser*. They became, inevitably perhaps, bitter rivals and competitors. The *Advertiser* began on 12 July 1858, printed in offices behind an ironmonger's shop in Hindley Street. It survived difficulties to flourish under Sir Langdon Bonython and build a three-storey new home (since greatly expanded) on the corner of King William and Waymouth Streets where the *Advertiser* building is now one of Adelaide's familiar landmarks. There had been circuses and a timber yard on the site. The *Advertiser* absorbed the *Register* in 1932.

Indeed, the *Advertiser*, since the sad demise of the *Register*, is and has been for years *the* Adelaide newspaper, and plays the role that Twopeny defined for the *Register* in 1882. Many other newspapers—weeklies, monthlies, and evening papers—have appeared and died in the history of South Australian journalism. The current *News* and the *Sunday Mail* are indistinguishable, for good or ill, from interstate tabloids. But the *Advertiser* has kept going since 1858, imperturbably chronicling the vicissitudes of the city and the province. Now it is as integral a part of the Adelaide scene as Colonel

Light's statue or the meditative Torrens. As it has matured in the vat of passing years, the *Advertiser* has come to symbolize the distinctive ingredients of Adelaide life. The *Current Affairs Bulletin* on Adelaide of 1965 said of the *Advertiser*:

> It reflects in so many ways the tone of South Australian life. A comparison with one of the great dailies of the eastern states is instructive. The *Advertiser* is more restrained; the editorials are heavier; the headlines less exciting; the social columns more extensive; the reference to and reverence for the local institutions and the local dignitaries more pronounced ... There lingers about it still the aura of the nineteenth century provincial organ, the note of ponderous respectability, but also of ponderous responsibility.
>
> One pictures the ideal *Advertiser* reader and his wife as a couple with a modestly imposing residence in the upper middle executive brackets, hardworking, conscientious, with a proper interest in public affairs and some minor role in civic or community life, interested in sport and gardening, somewhat Philistine and somewhat disturbed by some aspects of comtemporary life but keen to keep up with what is going on; the woman, kindly, cheerful, efficient, connected with some improving organisation and with an eye to social distinctions.

This was perceptive for 1965 and has much relevance ten years later. The *Advertiser* has changed, and quickened its tempo a little with the times since then. But, like the majority of its faithful readers, it is still distinctive in the Australian context. Its leaders sometimes evoke the resonance and moral concern of the old *Register*. Strong on reviews, gardening, sport, features and social news, it is alert to deplore creeping socialism or encourage cautious improvement. It is not afraid to lecture its readers on solid topics, can relax with whimsy, and keeps an endearing, if diminished, interest in news of the Old Country.

To read the *Advertiser* is to have the essence of the Adelaide sense of difference before you in newsprint.

The Natural Environment

The Adelaide pioneers were quite conservationist, to use the modern term. Their appreciation, often expressed, for the natural beauty and character of the Adelaide area contrasts agreeably with the "if it moves, shoot it, if it stands still, cut it down" attitudes that prevailed in the other Australian colonies. The Wakefieldians wanted order, both social and environmental. Certainly, their tastes were formed by the close and ancient pattern of the English countryside, by Bath and the Cotswolds, Cambridge and Devonshire. Their ideal was the mansions of men like Samuel Davenport who built at Macclesfield a country house, where the tenants played cricket, which would have been quite at home in Wiltshire.

This Wakefieldian concern for harmony is manifest in other aspects of settlement, such as the regulations for land distribution and the moves for self-government.

The open savannah woodland of the Adelaide Plains and the stringybark forests of the ranges could never be trimmed to become another, better England. But at least they were not so alien to Englishmen as was, say, the eerie scrub of the Blue Mountains or the rain forest of the Dandenongs. With a little imagination, a settler in the Adelaide Hills could well think that he was in a sunnier Ayrshire or Shropshire, particularly after the planting of elms and oaks and the release of blackbirds and goldfinches into the bush.

Gnawed by a new found conscience about conservation, it is our habit nowadays to rail against the first generations of Australians as wreckers of the country's ecology. It is fair enough for us to be critical, so long as we do not make similar mistakes ourselves. In a few decades white settlement in Australia deforested whole mountain ranges, exterminated several native fauna species, and caused plagues of imported pests like rabbits, prickly pears, African daisies, foxes, and feral cats. Yet we should take care to remember that the pioneers were driven by different urges, and had not the knowledge available to us. The South Australian pioneers made many bad environmental mistakes, such as clearing large areas of native hardwoods when South Australia always was, and is, chronically short of such timber. They caused enormous soil erosion with their efforts to farm beyond Goyder's Line, and they polluted the Murray. The black whales were hunted so ruthlessly from the Victor Harbour Station that they virtually became extinct. The last whale was killed there in 1872. Yet the settlers acted according to their lights. It was the custom then to believe in endless progress and advancement. Men like Morphett had visions of an ever-growing population of improved Britons thriving under blue Adelaide skies. Providence for a long time seemed to encourage growth, as with the revelation of the copper wealth of the Burra and Moonta Wallaroo areas. Did not Holy Writ, as in Genesis, exhort the faithful to be fruitful and to multiply and have dominion over the earth? Nineteenth century ideas of progress towards increased comfort and material possessions remained supreme in Australia, the last frontier, until quite recent times. They certainly encouraged the huge immigration programme of the federal government which funnelled millions of people into Australia between 1947 and the early 1970s.

Thus we who pick up the pieces after the boom has burst, who shake wise heads over the Borrie Report and the concept of zero population growth, ought not to be too hard on our ancestors. What they did to the environment seemed to them to be common sense. And if they thought further about it, they could argue that it was ordained by the Bible and—an even more awful source—by the state and federal governments.

This being said, it is gratifying to see that the superior Adelaide sense of difference is manifest in environmental matters too—is and always was. To a marked degree, the Wakefieldians reflected the intellectual fashions of philanthropy, sentiment, romanticism, and scientific interest. Pioneers like Morphett and Stevenson were always alertly commenting on the local flora and fauna in their letters; governors like Gawler and Grey were ardent botanists and geographers when they could get away from the contentious capital. Officials like Light and Frome were skilled artists, with a sensitive response to the environment.

George French Angas, who could write as well as he painted, was perhaps the outstanding local example of a man of taste and sentiment. His *Savage Life and Scenes* (1847) is still remarkable for the immediacy of its evocations, literary and pictorial, of the South Australian landscape. Consider this description of the Australian night sky, so stunning to the newcomer: "The moon off the New Holland coast is exquisitely clear, and the mackerel sky most beautiful; it reminds one of a brilliant gem reposing on a cushion of the whitest and softest wool. The stars are twinkling out at every break in the spotted clouds, that steal like downy flocks along the upper regions of the atmosphere, with the cool night breeze for their shepherd."

Many other visitors and settlers, if less highflown, were just as enthusiastic about the beauties and curiosities of the Adelaide region. The pioneers on Proclamation Day "hailed with delight" familiar flowers in the grass, and marvelled at the richness of the soil, the abundance of parrots and waterfowl and the "splendid trees of the eucalypt species". The horticultural Stevenson remarked in an early *Register*: "New flowers are brought in every day."

The looming backdrop of the ranges, changing colour from brown to blue to violet as the light changed, from green in winter to tawny in summer, was often praised for its beauty. The settlers took pains to describe the magnificence of the ancient eucalypts, even when they were on the point of cutting them down. William Finlayson of Brownhill Creek, for instance, recalled: "Our land was thickly, I might say densely, timbered with peppermint or boxwood, and no part of the land could be cultivated without clearing. The roots spread far and were near the surface, and after the tree was cut or burnt down there was constant trouble in cutting up and digging out the roots, and oh!, what numbers of coulters and ploughshares were broken!"[1]

From the chance remarks and snippets of information left by the early settlers, we are able to gain an idea of the original landscape of the plains and ranges. Beyond the swamps round creeks like the Sturt, the grassy plain was dotted with trees of small stature, up to about six metres high, such as peppermint box, large stands of golden wattle, and clumps of native pines on sandy tracts. Mallee eucalypts stretched down from the dry north to the region of present day Enfield. Stands of peppermint box dominated the future city area, and a dense forest of these trees extended from South Terrace to Morphettville. This was called the Black Forest by the settlers and became popular with cattle duffers. The name survives in a suburb notable more for tiled roofs than trees. The western spurs of the ranges carried, in favoured parts, blue, red, and pink gums. On the rocky upper slopes, forests of messmate stringybark prevailed, together with patches of casuarina and yacca on the harsher exposures. Lovely white-stemmed candle bark gums grew beyond Mount Lofty.

With settlement, most of the great trees of the plains eventually went the way of Finlayson's peppermint gums. A timber-getting industry in the ranges was started by the Tiersmen and continued into living memory, and teams of Clydesdales strained to drag the trunks of mighty blue gums and stringybarks down the slopes to the sawpits. Too much was taken too quickly, and now a conservation conscious generation is anxious to safeguard the surviving pre-1836 giant eucalypts as they stand in solitary retirement in the ranges and in the metropolitan area. All that remains of the Big Gum Tree that stood near the Glen Osmond Toll House is a slice of it propped against the wall of the Museum of Economic Botany in the Botanic Gardens. At least two hundred years old, the tree was felled in 1960 in the interests of the new road.

The forests of the ranges and the tall grass of the plains, together with heat and searing north winds, posed the chronic threat of bushfire to the Adelaide people. The Aborigines had been accustomed to burn off patches of scrub to flush out game. Fire was always a worry to the colonists. During the summer of 1840, J.W. Bull saw the "smoking heaps" which had once been the government offices on North Terrace. Important public documents, maps, records, and Colonel Light's private and official papers all went up in the flames. Bull recalls: "Colonel Light felt the loss of his journal very deeply, and stated that he would not have parted with it for several thousand pounds." Osmond Gilles's Octagon Cottage was gutted soon afterwards.

Even more devastating were the bushfires that ravaged areas like the reedbeds and the stringybark forests of the ranges. Bull, driving cattle from Bull's Creek to Crafers, nearly perished in one bushfire that swept down the Onkaparinga valley near Echunga. Confronted by an oncoming wall of flame, he charged his cattle through it. "As I was close upon them, I followed over burning brushwood which had been a good deal trampled out by the bullocks, and passed on, over smouldering grass and bushes, at full gallop after the cattle, trees on all sides being on fire to their tops, and falling branches crashing in all directions, but was soon safe on the track again, on to which the cattle had turned; and soon after safely yarded them at Crafers."[2]

The South Australian flora and fauna were regarded by most of the pioneers with mixed feelings. C.H. Barton on 7 December 1853 wrote home about his first impressions of the South Australian vegetation:

> The first thing that struck me was the extraordinary appearance of the Bush covering that part. Not a tree, not a bush, not a blade of grass resembles those of England in the slightest degree. The trees are shrivelled up, dry bits of stick, the leaves thick, leathery, and without freshness. The bushes and smallest plants in that place are chiefly of the succulent sassafras tribe, many bearing beautiful flowers, but without smell.

Barton was, of course, describing the dreary flats round the port, and in midsummer.[3]

In general, the Adelaide region was kinder to the first immigrants than were the localities of the other Australian capital cities. The sandy soil round Sydney, for instance, made poor agricultural land and the infant colony almost died of starvation during drought. The harsh, forested ranges that formed a background to the first settlements by Sydney Cove, Moreton Bay, and the Derwent estuary must have seemed forbidding enough to the first citizens of Sydney, Brisbane, and Hobart. Moreover, the ubiquitous signs of the convict system—hangings, floggings, ironed gangs, redcoats, barracks—darkened an atmosphere of struggle and alienation.

It seems to have been quite different in Adelaide, and not only because of the self-consciously convict-free utopianism of the founders. The peppermint gum plains by the meandering Torrens, the long strands of white sand washed by a gentle sea, the rolling, verdant ranges under a beneficent sun offered a kindlier environment. Of course, some settlers, like settlers anywhere, bemoaned their fate and complained. Summertime Adelaide seemed "a dustheap". Muddy Port Misery provoked many jeremiads. There were maggots, white ants, scorching sun, drizzling rain, bumptious labourers and pretentious masters, dingoes, dust, fleas, sheep scab, and a climate that often seemed, in Pike's words, "more like gehenna than paradise". Pike concludes: "The new land was hard to love, although many praised its ever-green trees and sunshine in an effort to persuade themselves that they really liked the place. Some, intrigued by the curious, sent back parrots, butterflies, wildflowers and rocks. Others carefully tended roses, musk, violets and foxgloves in little gardens to remind them of home."[4]

I suspect that Pike sways a little from his accuracy of imaginative reconstruction when he says that the land was hard to love. Perhaps the reverse was true in most cases. It is salutary to stress the hardships and discomforts of pioneer life; certainly the bush is better appreciated with the help of a car and a caravan in 1976 than from beneath a leaking tarpaulin in the stringy bark scrub in the winter of 1840. It seems likely, too, that many of the settlers were anxious to convince themselves that they had done the right thing by tying their fortunes to Adelaide.

Yet in our eagerness to penetrate sentiment and self-deception, we should not overlook the fact that many, probably most, of the pioneers had left Britain because they were dissatisfied with their prospects there. Some of this discontent derived from a poor home environment—overcrowding, shortage of land and so on. The pleasure expressed in so many pioneer letters about South Australia rings true. Clearly, many of them were exhilarated by their new environment. Even the petulant Horton James rejoiced in the air of the ranges. "There is a Land where Summer skies," wrote Miss Carleton to Linger's stirring tune in "The Song of Australia", "Are gleaming with a thousand dyes ... " To generations of refugees from the grime of Liverpool and London, the sparkling vista of hills, plains and sea were welcome and refreshing. They eased the ache of homesickness.

Of course, the settler wanted to change this environment. Patriotism as well as indoctrinated taste dictated that they should superimpose busy streets and houses surrounded by English flowers and shrubs. To the progressive eye of what George French Angas called "the intelligent and Christianized European", the naturalness of the landscape was an affront. They were equally offended by the attitudes of what Angas called "the degraded citizen of the soil". They praised God and reached for the axe.

Wallflowers, petunias, geraniums, and many other homely plants were imported by gardeners like Stevenson. Keen "acclimatizers" released blackbirds and goldfinches among the wattles to anglicize the dawn chorus, and if a native bird looked remotely like an English one, then it was given the English name. Thus the melodious shrike became the magpie and a large sea perch became a salmon and even, in its immature phase, a salmon trout.

Each of the Australian colonies formed acclimatization societies during the second half of the nineteenth century. The South Australian Acclimatization Society was established on 23 July 1878. It was the ancestor of the Zoological Society, founded in 1893 when eight hectares of parklands by the Torrens were set aside for a Zoological Garden. The acclimatizers were determined to make the province more homelike by means of assisted faunal immigrants. The current director of the Zoological Garden, W.E. Lancaster, writes in his brief history of the society:

The first three or four years of the Society's activities were mainly concerned with the introduction of foreign fauna, and especially such birds as skylarks, thrushes, blackbirds, bullfinches, greenfinches, goldfinches, chaffinches, bramblings and linnets in the hope that, in the words of the 3rd Annual Report, "they may be permanently established here, and import to our somewhat unmelodious hills and woods the music and harmony of English country life."[5]

Of these feathered imports, only the goldfinches and blackbirds seem to have established themselves. So the Hills would remain "unmelodious" to the acclimatizers, although any settler with half an ear must have been more than content with the indigenous song of birds like the magpie and the harvest lark. The acclimatizers persisted with their ecological meddlings for some years until better sense prevailed. Hence undesirables like foxes, soursobs, Salvation Jane, prickly pear, sparrows, and rabbits— although the society was at pains to deny any connection with the introduction of the last two pests. They encouraged the release of trout, perch (redfin), and eels in the local creeks, and in 1883 the governor complained that the colonial trout would not take the fly in a well bred way, as "at home or in North America". They brought in the American bronze turkey and ostriches. Bishop Kennion even urged the release of mongooses in the bush "to war against the rabbits".

Here again, we should be chary of condemning the colonists from the judgment seat of our present commitments to conservation. The harmonious English landscape from which they had come was the end result of centuries of massive interference with nature by man. For instance, the Lakeland Hills had originally been forested, as had Rannoch Moor. The Weald and other lowland areas of Britain had been clothed by woods of oak and beech. Much of the beauties of the English scene hailed by Keats and portrayed by Constable were artificial, such as the hedgerows of the enclosed fields, the stone walls, the villages, the water mills, the canals. It was perfectly logical for the settlers to assume they were to improve the bush. The present Australian urge for "beautification" stems from the same root.

When a contented pioneer was groping for comparisons for the view of the ranges from his East Terrace home, he felt he could do no better than compare it with "the rich and verdant views of Cumberland". H.T. Morris, a *Buffalo* pioneer who settled at Kapunda, reminisced on his first impressions of the Adelaide Plains as they appeared in 1836:

> I remember my uncle saying to me: "Harry, run up the main rigging and tell me what you think of the country." I went up obediently, and had a good look. When I came down, I told him that ashore it looked quite like the Old Country. It looked as if it were covered with wheat fields, whose fences were the dark shadows made by the gullies in the hills. There was beautiful kangaroo-grass, which we found to be nearly hip-high when we walked through it.

Morris's choice of simile to describe the scene is interesting, and probably epitomizes the hopes of the pioneers. They must have felt lonely and frightened. They wanted to start making money from farming as soon as possible, to reassure themselves that they had decided rightly. So the best thing the wild hills and plains could possibly look like was a wheat field, which meant both home and profit. And they made every effort to convince themselves that the tawny wilderness before them was just like the Old Country. Or if it did not, then they would soon make it so.

This zeal for improvement, for making the Adelaide environment more homelike, led to many mistakes and a good deal of brash ugliness. The rank utilitarianism which led the citizens to use the Torrens as a sewerage drain, with such effect that the governor of South Australia, Sir Mark Oliphant, was able to lament in 1974 over the "unspeakable things floating down it", is now deplored. So are the attitudes which led to the levelling of the sand dunes along the metropolitan beaches, and the gouging of the hills face for building stone.

Bull talked of hunting emus in the valley of Brownhill Creek. Such fauna have long since recoiled before the thrust of settlement. The only kangaroos, wallabies, and emus to be seen within easy reach of Adelaide are in captivity at the zoo by the Torrens, at the Cleland Reserve or at the Parra Wirra and Belair recreation parks.

That the original wild life was decimated is not surprising. C.H. Barton's "three day excursion" to Mount Torrens in March 1854, brimful of the "if it moves, shoot it" ethos, must have been typical of many thousands of other gun-happy outings by the settlers. Barton wrote to his sister: "Having my Gun with me, I enjoyed the ramble very much, shooting a great quantity of birds unknown to me, and also some parrots, lories and a large white cockatoo, nearly as big as a goose, with a fine yellow crest." With some friends, Barton shot twenty-three "opossums" by night at Mount Torrens and gave them to the Aborigines to eat. Next day, he wrote, the natives "were naturally rather indisposed, and I saw two rolling and rubbing each other on the ground to relieve the extreme tension of their skins. Others adopted a mud bath as a cure, sitting in the creek up to their chins in the black mud, and their woolly heads resembling so many noxious fungi." One Aboriginal began to beat his wife with a club, broke her arm and "burst an eye in". The wretched woman told Barton: "Blackfellow plenty growl."[6]

Many of the bird species which intrigued the early settlers are now rare or vanished from the city scene. In his foreword to G.E. Archer Russell's collection of South Australian ornithological essays, *Wildlife in Bushland*, published in 1919, Ernest Whitington writes of the experiences of a birdwatcher by the Torrens fifty years ago:

> He ... strolls along the banks of the Torrens and he pictures the warbler attuning his music to the swaying reeds, the metallic blue Kingfisher shooting like a meteor through the willows, or the evermoving Pardalote "luting" by his tunnelled home. He wanders across the plains and by wheatfields near the foothills and he writes lovingly ... of the heavenly notes of the Brown Song Lark ... and of the superb gem among our feathered police—the Blue Wren ... and of the wise old Boobook Owl, with its insistent and melancholy "Mopoke".

You would be extraordinarily lucky to see a kingfisher by the urban Torrens now, blue wrens have retreated before the city pesticide puffers, and boobook owls are heard only in the hills. As for the larks, these, according to Ian Mudie, once abounded over the pastures and wheatfields of the foothills region. Since the farms have been dismembered by the developers, the larks have gone. Russell wrote of the lark in one of his essays:

> And when next you hear it, rained down from afar up, give an attentive ear to the song of the Australian song lark, or harvest bird. Thrilled, as I have often heard it, over the silent gullies of the foothills from Blackwood to the sea at Hallett's Cove, the harvest bird's song holds a wealth of melody excelled by none, and that is saying all that is to be said, for I have in mind the song of the English skylark sung over English fields ... Surely it is time for every one of us to know and to appreciate our own.[7]

Most of the Blackwood gullies, a chequerboard of housing, are silent no longer. And if there are any larks left in the surviving paddocks near Hallett's Cove, they will soon go, like the beauty of the cove itself.

The fate of Hallett's Cove, virtually wrecked as a beauty spot in the early 1970s, can serve as a paradigm for much of the Adelaide natural environment, for there used to be much more to it than Mr. Russell's trilling skylarks. There are steep cliffs to the north and south, but until recently these cut off the cove from the suburbia of Seacliff and the industrial crudities of the Port Stanvac Oil Refinery. There were a few houses by the sea, of course, and a seedy rind of shacks above the waterline. But there were broad grasslands inland, the sand was clean and white, there were scores of rockpools where children could plumb the crystalline mysteries of crab hunting. Adelaide people could still find peace and naturalness at Hallett's Cove, only about twenty-five kilometres from the city centre. The cove had other features of interest, notably some rare plants and, uniquely convenient to a major city, a concentration of geological remains including evidence of Permian glaciation. As a geological monument, part of the cove area will be preserved, for the state and federal governments are making strenuous and costly efforts to safeguard them. But these efforts were late, new houses have mushroomed over the southern area (and, indeed, will soon cover the inland plain) and the clay amphitheatre has been bulldozed flat. Hallett's Cove, which was once something tranquil and special, is degenerating to the status of a typical Australian seaside suburb.

Similarly, the entire Southern Vales region is becoming honeycombed with housing development. Most of the vineyards in the near metropolitan area have been engulfed. The sprawl has taken in Reynella and now threatens McLaren Vale. The orchards and the blossom are disappearing. As for the northern coastal area, the West Beach wilderness is now a glossy residential development and almost the very last portion of natural dune and heath, just south of Outer Harbour, is being built over.

There are a few reserves scattered about the metropolitan area which give some slight indication of what the natural environment of Adelaide was like. These include the Kingston Reserve, now dominated by a caravan park, Hazelwood Park in Burnside, and Heywood Park, with its fine trees, in Unley. Otherwise, the citizen in search of nature and tranquillity has to drive up into the hills and their reserves, or for forty or fifty kilometres through the suburbs of the plains.

In the end, one comes back to the wise choice of Colonel Light. He made sure that the city would be near the ranges. He laid out the parklands and reserved part of the Torrens valley. The founder's plan, the innate taste of many of Adelaide's citizens, and the economic forces—happy in this context—which restricted Adelaide's size in comparison with Melbourne and Sydney, all these allow a continuing consciousness of the natural environment which is rare in any city.

The Adelaide Hills

"The Tiers" ... they are called in the colony, from the step-like arrangement of the chains, one rising above the other, like a huge staircase of mountains.

C.H. Barton, 1854

Any history of Adelaide should make detailed reference to the neighbouring Adelaide Hills, the central portion of the Mount Lofty Ranges. They are, and always have been, the lovely and beloved background to the Adelaide scene. Adelaide without its hills would be Sydney without the harbour, or London without the Thames. From the beginning they have had a strong physical, economic, and aesthetic influence upon the city at their feet. Their highest point, the discreetly dominating Mount Lofty, has been Adelaide's sentinel and its symbol, as Mount Wellington is to Hobart, or the Wrekin to the people of Shropshire.

Their climate, flora and fauna have been described. We have seen how the wooded crests of the ranges impressed the founders. How the settlers saw the hills as a source of timber and building stone, as a barricade against the frightening dry vastness of the interior, as pastureland and water supply. How Hutchinson and his party scrambled through imagined hazards to the summit of Mount Lofty, and how the citizens soon learned to value the hills as a cool refuge from the heat of the plain. And how the hills, which they wistfully likened to the Cumbrian fells, reminded them of home, because there it was green and imported English trees, plants, birds and animals could flourish.

Light called them "the enchanted Hills" and, as home, recreation area, or landscape ornament they have been enchanting Adelaideans ever since. Had they never existed, the Adelaide plains would have merged with dreary saltbush and mallee such as grows north of the city, or beyond the ranges. But as it is, they almost enclose that pocket of fertile land which is the heartland of South Australia. They make possible much of the pleasantness of Adelaide.

While the founders were preoccupied with putting up tents and waiting for the allocation of city areas, the hills were left alone. A few energetic souls like the wandering Menge or immigrants determined on a country life explored the nearer gullies but, until horses arrived in quantity, this was an arduous business. Some of the overlanders from New South Wales crossed the hills with their weary herds from the east. With them came the ticket-of-leave men and ex-convicts, many of them Vandemonians who, either because they were not made welcome in respectable Adelaide, or because they preferred bush life, became the wild Tiersmen of Adelaide's brief and modest frontier era. As Inspector Tolmer tells us, the Tiersmen lurked in an area round Mount Lofty known as the Stringybark Forest, duffed cattle, which they salted and barrelled for brazen sale in the city, and hung about Crafer's grog shanty. But the dauntless inspector soon hunted down escaped convicts and saw them hanged or gaoled in Adelaide. The Tiersmen called the Adelaide gaol "the stone jug". And the Tiersmen proved invaluable to the townspeople with their bushcraft, showing them how to make post and rail fences and build good timber huts and become accomplished timber getters. It was a Tiersman wanted by the law for bushranging who led J.W. Bull to good pastoral country in the area now known as Bull's Creek.

EARLY SETTLEMENT

Then respectable immigrants began to move into the hills and parcel them up into farms. The first notable settler on the Burnside foothills was the gentleman farmer James Gleeson. At his prefabricated home "Gleeville" he was attended by a retinue of Indian servants. By the mid 1840s there were growing settlements at Mount Barker, Encounter Bay, Yankalilla, Crafers, Meadows, Strathalbyn, and the Barossa Valley. Many of these developed on convenient routes, such as Mount Barker on the track from Adelaide to the Murray Valley. The *Register* of 11 January 1840 reported that it was proposed

> to form a Township at the well-known Station first selected in the Mount Barker district by Mr. Coghil from New South Wales. This location is exceedingly central, being within two miles of Mount Barker, nearly the last well-watered spot on the Sydney road between Adelaide and the Murray, and much frequented by parties visiting the Mountain, and by travellers to and from the more Eastern Districts, the Lake, and the intervening country, both on the route from the Ford of the Angas, and the German Village. It is surrounded by extensive sheep and cattle runs, on which a great proportion of the stock brought overland is kept for sale. It is a good stage from Crafer's Inn on the Tiers, and any easy day's ride from Town ... As the climate is salubrious, and the elevation from the plains considerable, it is a most desirable spot for summer residences, particularly for persons requiring a change of air ...

The German Village was Hahndorf, for during this period the German religious refugees led by men like Captain Hahn and Pastor Kavel were moving resolutely into the hills to form their Lutheran New Jerusalems as at Tanunda and Lobethal. The German settlers comprised an industrious stratum in hills society. Insulated from more happy go lucky British ways by their language, religion, and self-contained culture, they gradually worked their way out of their debt to George Fife Angas and made the ranges as fruitful as the hills of Silesia. And they thanked God in their spired Lutheran churches so that an English visitor to Hahndorf wrote: "Scarcely a day passes but that some of the people repair to the place of worship, either early in the morning, or in the evening after work ... There is nothing more pleasing for the passer-by than to have the voices mingling in sacred song rise and fall upon the ear."

As for "persons requiring a change of air" and summer or permanent residences, there were obvious attractions in the hills. Some well to do settlers like Hack at Mount Barker, Hagen at Echunga, and the Davenport brothers at Macclesfield preferred to build their homes in the ranges from the beginning, and thought the advantages well worth the long ride into town. Elizabeth Davison, whose husband took up land near Mount Barker in 1840, was glad to escape from the high prices and heat of Adelaide— "The weather was so hot it was almost insupportable and not a blade of grass ... " But thirty-seven kilometres to the east and five hundred metres higher "the air felt so pure and invigorating that I could not think I was in the same country as Adelaide".

ARISTOCRATIC RETREAT

The urban aristocracy soon found it both pleasant and presitgious to have mansions both in town and in the hills. Sir Thomas Elder outdid them all and bought land as near as possible to the summit of Mount Lofty (no one could overlook *him*) and spent lavishly so that his architects, Black and Hughes, could build him a Scottish baronial castle. The grey, grim Carminow with its high tower was the result. Seen from the east, from the freeway, in the morning (the best way to see Mount Lofty), Carminow glowers from its height over forests and mist in a manner that would have warmed the heart of Sir Walter Scott. Mount Lofty House, Wonnaminta, Morialta House, Sir Edward Stirling's St. Vigean's, and Shurdington are other hills mansions in the grand style. The Barr-Smiths built on to Lachlan McFarlane's Oakfield Inn at Mount Barker, where the brightly painted Royal Mail coaches used to stop, re-named it Auchendarroch, and used it as their summer residence. The governors followed the hills fashion. In 1858, a thousand pounds was spent to build a "cottage residence" at Government Farm, now the Belair Recreation Park. Governors MacDonnell and Daly passed the summer months there, and "Old Government House" is still preserved. Later governors preferred to summer at Karatta, Robe, but Governor Sir William Jervois suggested a more grandiose return to the hills. In 1891 Marble Hill, a hugh Gothic viceregal summer residence, was built near Norton Summit for 36,000 pounds. It had forty rooms, two storeys, and a thirty-metre tower from which governors like Sir William Robinson, Lord Kintore, and Lord Tennyson (son of the poet) could contemplate their pleasant domain.

As always in the hills, however, summer bushfires were a worry, especially as Marble Hill stood in an exposed and heavily wooded area. There were near misses in 1912, when English test match cricketers in Adelaide at the time joined the firefighters, and again in 1939. Marble Hill's doom came on the infamous Black Sunday of March 1955 when a strong northerly wind drove fire through thousands of hectares of hills forest and grassland. Marble Hill was gutted as the vice regal party sheltered in a gully with wet blankets over their heads. Since then it has stood as a blackened ruin and as a warning how devastating a bushfire can be in the Mount Lofty Ranges—a warning still blandly ignored by many hills dwellers who surround their houses with combustible vegetation. Recently, the National Trust opened Marble Hill, its outer shell partly restored, to visitors.

While some of the rich valued the hills as a place for retirement, or as a kind of enormous country club for weekend and summer holidays, poorer people, yeomanry in Wakefield's terms, lived and made their living there. Market gardening to provide fruit and vegetables for the neighbouring city soon became important, together with grazing, cropping, and the timber industry. Ridley's Stripper, invented in 1843, made grain harvesting easier in the rugged paddocks. In 1855 there were thirteen flour mills operating in the hills, and four in the Barossa Valley, four at Encounter Bay, and one at Yankalilla. The planting of the famous hills vineyards, mainly by Germans, began in the 1850s.

TRANSPORT

Travel and transport across the ranges to and from the city was difficult at first because of the rough terrain. Pioneer travellers had to ride up and down the spurs through the stringybarks, nervous about encounters with Tiersmen. Samuel Stephens, first manager of the South Australian Company, broke his neck when thrown while riding down from the ranges by way of one of the Glen Osmond spurs. The Great Eastern Road, soon popularly known as the Mount Barker Road, was pushed through by Gawler in 1841 but it was not until 1847 that Port Elliot was linked by road to Adelaide via the Crow's Nest and Willunga. The Adelaide–Victor Harbour road was completed in 1860, winding round the spurs and down the gullies via Blackwood and Bull's Creek. Hills travel was tough enough on horseback—by buggy, cart, or bullock dray it was a jolting ordeal. It took a bullocky three days to drive his team from Adelaide to Victor Harbour. Most travellers to the south coast preferred to go by sea. Even when Cobb and Co. coaches began operating in 1867, it took nearly eight hours— barring frequent mishaps—to make the trip. The Green Hill road was opened in 1858 and the Magill Road to Norton's Summit in 1859.

Inns, of necessity, were quickly established along the hills roads, such as the Old Mountain Hut, the Eagle on the Hill, Crafer's Inn, and the Aldgate Pump along the Great Eastern Road. The *Register* of 3 January 1841 reported that the licensee of the Mountain Hut Inn, R. Spearman, had been convicted of highway robbery and sent to Van Diemen's Land.

The *Adelaide Observer*, of 17 March 1883 reported on the formal opening of the hills railway by Governor Robinson. "Panting convulsively" the engine wound its way through the tunnels and over the viaducts but could not pull its load of well wishers beyond Blackwood. Embarrassed officials uncoupled most of the carriages, so that the governor and the ministers proceeded on to Aldgate. The other stranded guests, over two hundred of them, had to walk back to Mitcham.

Mark Twain, during his breezy tour of Australia in 1895, approached Adelaide by rail from Melbourne, and liked the look of the hills. Twain left the train to travel down to the city in a horse drawn carriage, and wrote:

> It was an excursion of an hour or two, and the charm of it could not be overstated, I think. The road wound between gaps and gorges, and offered all varieties of scenery and prospect—mountains, crags, country homes, gardens, forests—colour, colour, colour everywhere, and the air fine and fresh, the skies blue, and not a shred of cloud to mar the downpour of brilliant sunshine. And finally the mountain gateway opened, and the immense plain lay spread out below and stretching away into dim distances on every hand, soft and delicate and dainty and beautiful. On its near edge reposed the city.[1]

Many before and since have unconsciously agreed with Twain that Adelaide is best approached from the hills, and best contemplated from their ridges.

MINING AND LAND USE

Mining gave a boost to hills economy. There was a gold rush to Balhannah, where Osmond Gilles built himself a country house, in 1850 and the ancient, geologically varied ranges were the scene for Adelaide's first minerals boom, such as the silver lead discoveries at Glen Osmond, the exciting if short-lived gold rush to Echunga in 1852, and the rich copper mine at Kapunda. Gold was found at various spots in the hills, including Woodside and Jupiter Creek. Unemployed men were still finding a few ounces of gold dust at Echunga in the depression of the 1930s. Copper at Kanmantoo, pyrite at Brukunga, slate at Willunga, limestone at Rapid Bay, and refractory clay at Williamstown were other minerals mined in the hills.

From the first, too, the hills have been a rich source of construction materials including clay, course aggregates, sands, rubble, and building and ornamental stone.

Physically, Adelaide has been quarried from the hills and the city has benefited greatly from having such a handy supply of building materials. Much of its architectual sense of difference derives from the locally quarried slate, bluestone, and free stone from the ranges. As a result, the hills in the Adelaide vicinity are pocked by quarries, some presenting a drear and lunar landscape to the air passenger flying overhead, but others, especially the older, smaller quarries, adding variety to the hillsface with rugged cliffs which glow in the setting sun.

Land use in the hills has changed considerably in emphasis. At first the farmers on their small blocks concentrated on wheat, varied here and there with stock grazing, market gardening, apple and pear orchards, and viticulture. It gradually became apparent that cereal crops could be more efficiently grown on the larger holdings of the northern plains. In fact, many hills farmers left the stony uplands to take up land further north. A further inducement to more stock raising was the advent of refrigeration in 1879, which allowed the export of frozen beef and mutton. So the farming pattern in the hills until recent times became pasturing stock for wool, meat, and dairy products and for specialized vegetable and fruit produce. Subterranean clover, first identified by A.W. Howard near Mount Barker in 1889, and the use of superphosphate after 1918, further enriched hills pasture.

"ENEMY PLACE NAMES"

One bizarre and, in retrospect, shameful episode in the history of the hills needs to be mentioned, if only as an indication of how war hysteria can distort reason. South Australia was as ardent as any Australian state to follow imperial banners into the horrors of the Great War. Warriors left at home, perhaps hoping to prove their loyalty without firing a gun, turned to the persecution of the descendants of the German settlers in the hills and the Barossa. No doubt some of these had a certain sentimental and harmless sympathy with Germany but the majority of them were Australians first and sent their sons in hundreds to die or be maimed in the trenches. This did not satisfy the zealous Anglo Saxon patriots who were irritated by the fact that the map of South Australia was scattered with the names of German pioneers and place names of German origin. It was forgotten that the Germans had settled many years before, that they had often come because they were dissatisfied with conditions at home, or that they had contributed greatly to the state's prosperity and cultural growth.

On 2 August 1916, the House of Assembly resolved: "The time has now arrived when the names of all towns and districts in South Australia which indicate foreign enemy origin should be altered, and that such places should be designated by names either of British origin or South Australian native origin." Apparently the House was unanimously behind this folly "which clearly has the whole of public opinion behind it". It was admitted that there would be "vexatious" effects from the re-naming, but only for the railways and postal services and legal documents. The feelings of the people of German descent were not considered. There was, of course, gross illogicality in this move. No one thought to suggest the abolition of the name Victoria so freely showered over Adelaide and the state. Yet Queen Victoria, as well as Prince Albert (after whom the Albert Tower in the Town Hall was named), Prince Alfred (Prince Alfred College), and even the original Queen Adelaide herself were all of overwhelmingly Germanic descent. Royalty, albeit German to the bootstraps, was above complaint—although a similar hysteria in Britain made it politic for the Royal Family to change their name from Saxe Coburg Gotha to Windsor and from Battenberg to Mountbatten.

A Nomenclature Committee on "enemy place names" was set up which pondered over the map of South Australia and finally gutted it of many of its historic connotations. Their recommendations were as sweeping as they were stupid. Hahndorf, the cradle of German settlement in the hills, became Ambleside; Lobethal became Tweedvale; Petersburgh became Peterborough. The ultimate insult to German pride was that replacement names were often chosen to honour British generals or British victories in the current war. Thus Kaiser Stuhl became, of all things, Mount Kitchener (and the Berliner bun the Kitchener bun!); the Rhine became the Marne; Blumberg became Birdwood; and German Town Hill and Gruenthal were named after German defeats— Vimy Ridge and Verdun. Hundreds named after German pioneers were renamed in a similar military way: von Doussa to Allenby, Homburg to Haig, Krichauff to Beatty, and Rhine to Jellicoe. The city suburb of Klemzig, site of the first German settlement in South Australia, was named Gaza. Other Germanic names were replaced by Aboriginal names of specious origin. Hergitt Springs became Marree, for instance, Siegersdorf became Bultawilta, and Hoffnungsthal Kirrawirra.

This witless Nomenclature Act gave mortal offence for at least a generation to people who had made the hills fruitful, who made the Barossa Valley a place of honour and pilgrimage, who helped give the province industry, backbone, and probity and who with men like Heysen, Linger, Schomburgk, Menge, and Thiele contributed so much to the arts and sciences.

The pendulum is swinging back again now. Gaza became Klemzig once more and Hahndorf and Lobethal re-emerged in 1936. In 1975, thanks to the efforts of a Barossa Valley historical society, such evocative names as Kaiser Stuhl, Hoffnungsthal, and Krondorf were restored and we must hope that the restoration will continue. The once bitter anti-German feeling in the hills has disappeared: indeed, villages like Hahndorf, with its annual Schuetzenfest, Tanunda, and Nooriootpa, in this tourist age, are now excessively Germanic on the surface with their *stube*, *wurst*, *kuchen*, and German restaurants. Tourists travelling Australia soon tire of gold towns and meat pies. The new look continental atmosphere, the cherished spired churches, museums, meticulous gardens, and knick knack shops of the German districts of the hills, for all their occasional excess, make for an agreeable—and profitable—change.

URBAN INFILTRATION

In fact, the Adelaide Hills in the 1970s have changed their emphasis once more. Orchardists, market gardeners, wine growers, and graziers and dairymen are still important, but the hills are now increasingly seen as part of the national estate. They will soon, I suspect, be treasured as an English-style national park, an area of special historic, scenic, and ecological interest, safeguarded as the British safeguard Snowdonia, or the Lake District, or the Yorkshire Dales. Close to the city, and exploited for generations for their natural resources, the hills have suffered much from European interference. Most of the great trees were logged, there was severe soil erosion, and pest infestation and mining and quarrying caused water pollution and disfigured landscapes.

In 1939 J.E. Monfries wrote in his *History of Gumeracha and District*:

Much that was definitely beautiful has fallen to the hand of man. Those of us ... who can look back over half a century or so will remember with regret the absence of those hedges of monthly roses and moss roses which used to adorn the front boundaries of so many of the cottages and also those fences of bright yellow and green English gorse which once

separated all the surrounding paddocks and which were abounding joy to members of the
Adelaide Hunt Club in the old days. And what also of the numerous stately gumtrees
which became the passive victims of axe and saw?

Yet it was not so much axe and saw as cream bricks and sub-divisions which have put
the hills in their most recent hazard. With improved transport and better roads, including the new hills freeway, the attractions of the ranges have brought a big com-
muter population to the uplands. The cool, fresh air, the scenery, the space, the gardening prospects (the hills allow semi alpine plants like azaleas, camellias, and
rhododendrons to thrive) were irresistable. During the late 1950s, the 1960s, and the
early 1970s the hills winced beneath a vibrant real estate boom. Desirable residences
proliferated on top of Mount Osmond, in the Aldgate Valley, Carey's Gully, Golden
Grove, Birdwood, and Woodside. There was a rollicking trade in eight hectare blocks
around townships like Mount Barker and Scott's Creek. Houses scrambled up the
foothills like a besieging army. Stirling and Aldgate (Crafers was riven in two by the
freeway) have become a rather exclusive highlands suburb, the houses divided from
each other by dense coppices of oak, silver birch, and Tasmanian Bluegum. Towns and
villages as far from Adelaide as Meadows, Clarendon, and Strathalbyn were affected by
the rush, the climb in land values, and higher ratings. There was a real danger of bad
ribbon development along the freeway which bisects the hills and which will terminate
near the projected city of Monarto. With the spreading commuters came supermarkets
and service stations, weekenders, hippy communes, nature trails, and bikies. There has
been a terrific horse explosion in the hills. Pony clubs abound as never before and harrassed parents search the numerous real estate offices for horse paddocks.

With the recent concern for conservation, affluence (which usually precedes the
concern), and the fact that many articulate and active people had settled in the hills
precisely because of their natural attractions, there has inevitably been a strong movement towards better protection of the ranges and more public control over their
development.

In the *Mount Lofty Ranges Study* (1974) published by the State Planning Authority,
the impact of increased settlement in the hills over recent years is graphically
described. Over 30,000 people, or 60 per cent of the hills population, live within 40
kilometres of Adelaide in the six district councils of East Torrens, Gumeracha,
Meadows, Mount Barker, Onkaparinga, and Stirling. The Stirling area, convenient to
the city, has been the one most affected, despite its wet and misty winters. Between
1961 and 1971, Stirling's population grew from a mere 1,273 to 8,348, 712 houses were
completed and 1,425 new allotments created. The majority of these new residents
worked in the city: approximately 56 per cent of Stirling's work force. There were
similar developments in the other hills districts.

Stringent planning regulations followed the population spread, but not before
some lamentable environmental damage was done, especially on the hillsface zone.
There are now strict deterrents to pollution, particularly in the water catchment areas.
No new subdivision is allowed under 33 hectares in the ranges and 4 hectares in the
hillsface zone. Most developments on properties, such as buildings, have to be approved
by a number of authorities, a lengthy and often frustrating process, but one necessary to
safeguard the essential character of the hills.

The population surge, coupled with the economic decline of the wool, lamb, beef,
and dairying industries, is having a strong and sometimes regrettable influence on the
character of the hills. Many of the villages are no longer self-supporting rural centres so
much as dormitory and recreation suburbs for city workers. Genuine full-time farmers
have been tempted to subdivide their ancestral acres and start again in the southeast.

Even if they wish to stay, despite falling farm incomes, they often cannot afford the higher rates that come with closer settlement. More dogs, children, open gates, trail riders, and bush fires are concomitant nuisances. There are now many scores of 8 hectare blocks in the hills. Some of these have not been built on and have become reservoirs of weeds and pests that trouble neighbouring farmers. There were, too, many "Rundle Street Farmers" who worked in the city but had very agreeable rebates as alleged primary producers on their handfuls of hectares until the Income Tax Department became less obliging.

The ousting of farmers by commuters in the more popular areas has not, however, caused a decline in the social vitality of the hills: quite the reverse. In general, people who take the trouble to build new houses there or painstakingly renovate old ones, to travel long distances to and from work, and accept other inconveniences to make a country home possible, are strongly motivated. They love the hills, and show this love in many ways. They plant trees in deforested areas, grub out gorse and African Daisy, mend fences, improve pastures, encourage native flora and fauna, and agitate for more national parks and reserves. Some of the older settlers, to be frank, abused the environment most miserably. Often the newcomers are more eager and better informed custodians.

CONSERVATION

The Belair National Park, latterly redesignated as a recreation park of 836 hectares, is probably the best known and most popular part of the hills to Adelaide citizens. Originally, much of the area was known as Government Farm and a summer residence for governors, now preserved as Old Government House, was built there in 1858. In 1891 Parliament resisted pressures from developers to set the area aside as "a national recreation and pleasure ground". Pleasure, in the Adelaide of 1891, meant something substantially different from its present connotations. The park's custodians laid down bitumen roads, tennis courts, and a golf links so that citizens could indulge in manly sports and barbeque their chops amid tamed bush.

For its time, the setting up of the national park was an imaginative venture and an indication that Adelaide's attitude to the environment was not entirely Philistine. This rugged, varied, and heavily forested reserve must have given immense enjoyment to millions of escapees from the heat and din of the city.

There are seven other recreation parks in the hills, of which Parra Wirra, 1,265 hectares, is the largest. Like Belair, Parra Wirra was first known as a national park. However, the National Parks and Wildlife Act of 1972 decreed that henceforth in South Australia only large parks "of national significance by reason of the wildlife or natural features" would be known as national parks. There are none such in the ranges although the *Mount Lofty Ranges Study* observes, hopefully perhaps: "The establishment of four national parks of up to 25,000 hectares each would ensure the conservation of the principal natural history features of the Ranges. One park should be established on the Fleurieu Peninsula, a second on the western escarpment of the Ranges, a third on the dry eastern escarpment and a fourth in the northern savannah woodland area in the vicinity of Kaiser Stuhl." There are nineteen conservation parks in the hills, "primarily for the purpose of conserving wildlife or natural or historic features", comprising almost 4,000 hectares in all.

The *Mount Lofty Ranges Study*, like a number of university seminars on the challenges of the ranges, comes to several high-minded conclusions. For instance, "protection of natural beauty should be the overriding policy governing all decisions relating to the development and use of land in the Mount Lofty Ranges". There should be "a clear distinction drawn between town and country", more national recreation and conservation parks, even more stringent zoning and planning regulations, and a series of "tourist roads ... walking, horse riding and pedal cycle trails". As well, "a prosperous agriculture" should be fostered in the hills, and the amalgamation of small holdings into economic farm units should be "actively encouraged".

Something like this may come about, for the state and local authorities have already made several strong moves towards conserving the hills. Moreover, the unexpected drop in Adelaide's population growth to less than 1 per cent a year has weakened the rationale of more housing and industrial development in the ranges—and, indeed, of Monarto. That project will probably tread water for a long time. My own hope is that the entire hills area will eventually become a national park, or a piece of the national estate, or something similar. There are many excellent precedents: in France, for instance, and Germany, and especially in Britain. Exmoor, the South Downs, and the Cotswolds, for example, are settled, beautiful regions now strictly preserved, with their natural and historic features safeguarded. The Adelaide Hills, like the Dandenongs and the Blue Mountains, are of special importance to their adjacent cities, and of special national importance. An overall authority, however, would need to be leavened with local participation by hills residents; for Australians have had quite enough of bureaucratic delays and arrogance, the reasons for which are usually hidden deep from ordinary mortals. As one who has had the good fortune to live for years in the English Lake District, a national park, and who now has the even greater good fortune to live in the heart of the Mount Lofty Ranges, I know that the overall national park system would work, and to the advantage of both resident and visitor. To take just one idea from the Lake District: if the authorities revived the old stone cutting and dressing industry of the hills and obliged all home builders to use only local material, half the battle would be won. Much of the aesthetic damage to the hills derives directly from the mania for cream and pink brick, set off by galvanized iron and variegated tiles.

Meanwhile the hills are always there over Adelaide. That looming outline is part of the city's consciousness. In the midst of the Rundle Street hubbub, people can raise their eyes to see, as at the end of a canyon, the hillsface. It is a backdrop to all the city's activities, from football at the ovals to the Royal Show. Even on the beaches, you need only glance inland and there, dramatically, is the lovely escarpment. It changes colour according to time and season: violet, blue, green, tawny, chequered with pastel shades. Winds herd the clouds in from the gulf to cluster round Mount Lofty, a landmark to sailors and immigrants since Matthew Flinders. A small mountain which to millions of people in a vague but tender and subtle way means simply, Adelaide.

73. John Martin & Company, which began humbly enough as Martin and Peters in 1861, gradually developed into a retailing Leviathan of Rundle Street. It became popularly known for its spectacular annual Christmas pageant.

74. The retailing heart of Adelaide, Rundle Street, in 1882 looking west from Gawler Place. Marshall & Co. and Birks were important stores, now replaced by Myers and David Jones respectively.

75. A flag bedecked Birks in Rundle Street in the 1890s during a Christmas rush.

76. The corner of King William and Grenfell Streets about 1910.

77. The East End Market in East Terrace in 1912.

78. The Grand Central Hotel, corner of Pulteney and Rundle Streets, around the turn of the century. This vigorous chunk of Victorian architecture, later the Foy and Gibson's store, was flattened in 1976 for a car park.

79. The Royal Adelaide Hospital, North Terrace at the turn of the century.

0. The Botanic Gardens in 1870 with the Lunatic Asylum in the background. The Gardens, kept locked up on the Sabbath until well into this century, are justly famous for their beauty.

81. Adelaideans relaxing, respectably, amid the statuary and leafy shade of the Botanic Gardens in 1901.

82. St. Peter's Cathedral from Pennington Gardens in the early 1900s. Bishop Short sensibly dismissed an architect who wished to build St. Peter's in brick.

83. Holy Trinity Church, North Terrace. Opened in 1838, it was Adelaide's first Anglican church and is still in excellent order. Photograph supplied by the Publicity Branch of the Premier's Department.

84. The fine Presbyterian Church at Strathalbyn, originally a mainly Scottish settlement on the far side of the Hills. In Anthony Trollope's opinion in the 1870s it was one of the prettiest and cleanest country towns in Australia. It still is. Photograph supplied by the Publicity Branch of the Premier's Department.

85. The German School in Wakefield Street, 1866. Adelaideans had mixed feelings about the clannish and prosperous Lutheran German settlers who made the Barossa Valley and parts of the Hills fruitful. The spiteful outburst of anti-German feeling during the First World War wiped many old German names from the state map. Some are being restored.

86. Norwood Model School, Norwood Parade, about 1870.

87. An almost totally solemn church group, about 1900, ruled no doubt with an iron hand by the mistress at the back left.

"The Government were a Government of promises, and all that was needed, was for a few old women to get up a deputation and they could obtain a promise from the Government."—*Hon. J. H. Howe in the S.A. Council.*

THE WHISPER OF A "SHRIEK."

Mrs. W.C.T.U. finds Chawles' ear an absorbing receptacle for all her crank fads.

88. Cartoon depicting the Woman's Christian Temperance Union speaking in Premier Kingston's ear, from the *Critic* of 22 October 1898. The W.C.T.U. had inordinate political influence; its members were unstoppable lobbyists.

89. "God's Police" in force—the annual conference of the Woman's Christian Temperance Union, about 1900. Smiles are not much in evidence but funereal clothing and grotesquely embellished hats are.

90. One of the city's innumerable pubs, which so upset the W.C.T.U. ladies, photographed about 1870.

91. Another typical Adelaide pub, the Oakfield in Flinders Street, 1929.

92. Exuberant, but respectable, Victoriana—West's Coffee Palace, Hindley Street, in 1929. Coffee was urged by the wowsers as an alternative to demon drink.

93. The Tivoli Theatre in 1920. Vaudeville and music hall, which flourished at the Tivoli, are staging a revival in some Adelaide pubs of the mid 1970s. The earliest Adelaide theatres often began as adjuncts to hotels. Photograph by courtesy of the Adelaide *Advertiser*.

94. Members of the Adelaide City Council at the governor's residence Marble Hill in 1895. This Gothic viceregal palace on the crest of the Mount Lofty Ranges was the Valhalla of Adelaide society until it was gutted by fire in 1955.

95. The burnt shell of Marble Hill, the governor's summer residence in the Hills, after the terrible bushfires of "Black Sunday", 1955. The ruins are now in the care of the National Trust. Photograph by courtesy of the Adelaide *Advertiser*.

96. The pleasant mansions of North Adelaide in their large, leafy gardens at the turn of the century, seen from St. Peter's Cathedral. From a postcard in the possession of Mrs. Sadie Pritchard.

97. The mayor's garden party in the parklands, 1903, with the assembled guests still resolutely dressed in the style of Victorian England.

98. The mayoral ball, Adelaide Town Hall, 1905. Against the backdrop of the mighty organ, this was the high point of the social year.

99. Boating on the Torrens in the 1890s. This is the pleasant section of the river flowing through the parklands between North and South Adelaide.

100. The Lady's Boat Club, 1895–96, in repose on the south bank of the Torrens.

101. Cyclists about 1890. Riding penny-farthings and "bone-shakers" was the trendy thing to do in the late nineteenth century. Elaborate uniforms, outings, and races were devised. The garb of the gentleman on the right seems to owe much to equestrian fashion.

102. Picnic party in the Hills during the late nineteenth century, probably on the Belair Road. The commercial potential of roadside advertising was appreciated from an early period.

103. A cricket match at St. Peter's College in 1880—Tom Brown's schooldays in the antipodes.

104. An Australia-England test match at the Adelaide Oval in 1901, seen from Montefiore Hill. Named after the famous Kennington Oval in London it is still one of the loveliest cricket grounds in the world. (See illustrations 126 and 127 for a modern test match at the oval.) The Jubilee Exhibition Building on the left (with the cupola) was demolished in the early 1960s.

105. Football clash between St. Peter's and Prince Alfred College at the Adelaide Oval about 1895. By this time football had become respectable. These two teams represented South Australia's Eton and Harrow.

106. An Adelaide race meeting, sketched by S.T. Gill in 1845. Like all Australians, Adelaideans soon displayed a passion for horse racing. Early newspaper editors deplored the appearance at such races of wild "Tiersmen" from the nearby Hills.

107. Racing today—the Great Eastern Steeplechase at the annual Oakbank Races, begun in 1876, in the Adelaide Hills. Photograph supplied by the Publicity Branch of the Premier's Department.

108. A tennis party, suitably posed, at North Adelaide about 1880. Speed around the court was a secondary consideration, judging by the fashionably bulky dress.

109. "Schuetzenfest"—shooting match at Hahndorf in the 1880s. The Schuetzenfest is now more popular than ever, although the German settlers in the Hills were probably closer to its original aims.

110. Ladies' baths at the Olympic Pool, King William Road, in the 1890s. The water was pumped directly from the Torrens.

111. Henley-on-Torrens regatta at the turn of the century. British to the bootstraps, these citizens visualized the Torrens as another Thames.

112. Applause for a good drive by Lord Mayor Lewis Cohen to open the Municipal Golf Links on 11 August 1923. The links were, of course, on the indispensable parklands.

113. Croquet players at Angaston in 1867.

114. The *South Australian Register* office posts colonial election results in the late nineteenth century. The *Register*, a fine newspaper and the first in Adelaide, was later absorbed by the *Advertiser*.

115. The village of Clarendon in the Adelaide Hills about 1870. Note the vineyard—this is near the famous Southern Vales country. Like other Hills villages, Clarendon is now becoming a haven for city commuters.

116. Part of an enclave of rich Adelaide citizens' mansions near Mount Lofty about 1900, seen from the railway line. Poorer folk made Sunday excursions into the Hills to peer over the hedges, especially in autumn, when the imported oaks, poplars, ash and maples daubed the ranges with vivid colours. From a postcard in the possession of Mrs. Sadie Pritchard.

4

ADELAIDE IN THE 1970s

The Dunstan Epoch

I'm trying to create in Adelaide ... the best urban conditions in
the world.   *Premier Dunstan, September 1975*

South Australia has a Labor party different from those in other
states; it also has a different premier.
                                                       Dr. Dean Jaensch, 1975

A delaide has always had its dominating personalities who have exercised strong
influence upon its development, who exemplified personally or expressed by official action some of the prevailing Adelaide attitudes, who have almost epitomized the
city in their time. Such influences have been encouraged, I suggest, by Adelaide's isolation and the resultant challenges imposed upon its leaders, as well as by the distinctive
philosophies planted in Adelaide by the founding fathers. These plants, as I have tried
to show, have grown deep roots and still, despite the buffetings of winds of change,
constitute the Adelaide sense of difference. Personal influences upon Adelaide's growth
and social directions would include successively those exercised by leaders like Gawler,
Fisher, Grey, Mayor Smith, and Premier Kingston. The most striking example of this
phenomenon of personal influence would have been that of Sir Thomas Playford, who
vigorously ruled the state as Premier for twenty-seven years (1938–65)—a record in the
history of the British Commonwealth—and who was the architect of its industrial
revolution. Would have been, I say, because the influence of the present premier, Don
Dunstan, might rival that of Playford. If there were, say, a Grey era and a Playford era
in Adelaide's history then assuredly in the mid 1970s we are in the throes of the
Dunstan epoch. To millions of interstate Australians, and to overseas observers who
take an interest in Australia, this forceful, stylish, busy, and many-sided premier,
described by John Gunther in 1972 as the "first fresh figure in Australian politics in a
wombat's age", *is* South Australia, *is* Adelaide.

Dunstan has been premier since 1970. Before that he had gone down in defeat in
1968 to the Liberal Country League headed by Steele Hall. Hall, honourably, but fatally
for conservatism, made an electoral redistribution in 1969 which abolished the
"Playmander" whereby a weighting of rural electorates allowed the long LCL
hegemony of a predominantly Labor state. Thus Dunstan and his supporters came back
to power and he has ruled so effectively that the July 1975 state elections, despite
nationwide discontent with Whitlam's federal Labor government, kept him, more
precariously, in power. Here again South Australia and its capital, voting against the
national trend, showed its tendency to differ.

Dunstan was secure, according to the *Advertiser* of 12 July 1975, in his "jazzy new
office in the State Administration Centre". The *Advertiser* sympathized with his Liberal
rival, Dr. Bruce Eastick, but made a telling point when it remarked: "It may be a sad

commentary on our society's values to say that a hard-working, honest man like Dr. Eastick would not have made a good premier. But these matters are relative. He compared poorly with Mr. Dunstan, and therefore with the sort of leadership South Australians are used to." Naturally, this charismatic premier has his critics. He is severally assailed for being too autocratic, trendy, humorless, self-opinionated, and so on. Max Harris baited him in the *Australian* of 19 July 1975: "Dunstan tends to see himself shining with a pure, pure light, like a little nuclear explosion burning in the night. South Australian cynics have sometimes thought of him as a small town Indira Gandhi, because of the ease with which he slips from declamation to homily." Yet the national admiration for Dunstan remained strong. Even Adelaide Liberals could feel a pride in a man so eloquently proud of Adelaide, a scion of St. Peter's College and the university who was described by the *Australian* of 20 September 1975 as "the man many voters see as a future Prime Minister".

When he won his last election there was general agreement among the media that Dunstan was one of the most able and effective politicians in Australia. "Australian socialism's success story", the *Bulletin* called him on 28 June 1975. He has often been compared to the younger Trudeau. Peter Heyworth in the British *Observer* of 25 April 1976 considered Dunstan to be "an unusual politician in any country" but in Australia, with his "allure of a matinee idol", he was "a positive exotic". Yet the South Australian branch of the Labor Party, largely the creation of Senator Jim Toohey and the left-winger, Clyde Cameron, is more than usually dominated by big trade unions. Over two thirds of the executive are or were trade union leaders. The "card vote", which gives power to unions with large "book" membership, has prevailed in all elections to party office or parliamentary pre-selection since 1946. If the party can be controlled by union leaders, how then has Dunstan managed to capture the vital middle ground in state elections, the votes of the urban middle class? I suggest that it is because of his sensitive touch on the pulse of Adelaide; his understanding of how far the city wants to and will go.

Dunstan has been described as "centre right" on economics and "centre left" on social reform. This accords with the Adelaide tradition of caution over business matters and radicalism on social issues. Moreover it was politic in that the Playford ministries had been strong on economics but weak on social reform. Dunstan told a *Bulletin* interviewer of the events in Adelaide which turned him to politics and his interpretation of democratic socialism: "As a small boy, I spent my holidays with my great uncle who was then the Lord Mayor of Adelaide. That was during the great depression and most of his time was spent in measures for the under-privileged, the workless and the starving. I saw then the horror that could occur in an industrial society and the need for people of good will to do whatever they could to assist the under privileged."

In his Labor policy speech in 1970, Dunstan promised "the most comprehensive plans for change and growth any state has had since Federation". Adelaide would become "the technological, the design, the social reform and the artistic centre of Australia". "New ideas" were promised for education, the environment, law reform, freedom, and so on. To achieve all this he set up a streamlined system of communication, a large entourage of able aides and press officers, and coaxed his cabinet, many of whom had hitherto seen the world through trade union blinkers, down strange new paths. He recommended the appointment in 1971 of Sir Mark Oliphant as governor. This distinguished nuclear physicist has shown how effective a state governor can still be, if he has drive, ability, and commitment. Sir Mark, an eloquent champion of conservation, was busy and outspoken. He was almost certainly the most popular and best known of modern governors. The appointment in late 1976 of Sir Douglas Nicholls, the Aboriginal pastor, as Sir Mark's successor was an even more vivid example of the premier's penchant for the remarkable.

Dunstan's most obvious influence upon Adelaide has been in the areas of social reform and artistic innovation. South Australians now have the most comprehensive laws concerning consumer protection and trade practices in the country. The introduction of a state lottery, the T.A.B., late closing for hotels, special beaches for nudists, R certificate films, relaxed book censorship—all these measures took the starch from the Adelaide image.

The beauty, efficiency, and success of the new Festival Theatre is also generally seen as another feather in the Dunstan cap, although it should be remembered that the project was pioneered by the City Council and encouraged by Hall's reformist government. In September 1974 the 600 seat Playhouse, the revolutionary 350 seat Space, and the 800 seat Amphitheatre were opened as stage two of the cultural complex by the Torrens Lake. "The feel of the whole complex", declared Anthony Steel, general manager of the Festival Centre Trust, "is one of flexibility and intimacy". George Ogilvie of the South Australian Theatre Company stated: "The State Government has achieved its dream. It's most unusual in my experience for a Government to take so much interest in a theatrical company." In addition, the Dunstan government has increased state help and encouragement to the arts in general. It established a Film Corporation, which has earned admiring comment with its feature films "Sunday Too Far Away" and "Picnic at Hanging Rock". Within six years it raised state expenditure on the arts seven fold.

Such reforms and innovations were comparatively easy, at least partly popular, and sometimes cheap. There was no concerted grumbling in Adelaide over the cost of the Festival Theatre Centre, ($16 million all told), partly because some federal money helped and partly because it added so substantially to civic self-esteem, won much praise, and was so conspicuously more successful—and cheaper—than Sydney's blunderings over its Opera House.

Again, the relaxations of censorship and drinking restrictions were easy to bring about and generally popular. Adelaide wowserism made occasional noises and managed to stop the staging of "Oh! Calcutta!", for example, but it mustered little of its previous force. Like all the Australian cities, Adelaide is now washed over by permissive waves. True, Dunstan went further than other premiers dared, or wanted to, on such issues as nudist beaches and reducing the penal sanctions against homosexuality, but even here he had a sharp ear for the consensus of the electorate. There has been vehement opposition from such groups as The Right To Life, The Festival of Light, and The Community Standards Organization, but they have been outmanoeuvred and outnumbered.

The general cultural atmosphere generated by Dunstan and his fellow spirits, especially strong round the Festival Theatre Centre and such distinguished new restaurants as Ayers' House, attracted admiring comments from visiting bon vivant journalists and intellectuals. There was quite a migration of artists, craft workers, actors, and writers to Adelaide, settling rapturously on mellow hills cottages and the now trendy villas and terraces of North Adelaide. *Vogue* magazine printed a glossy feature on Adelaide's cultural blooming. Bob Ellis burst into evocative prose on the "Adelaide civilization" in the *Bulletin* of 26 July 1975: "Under calm skies, it seemed, men of moderation and culture pursued their honourable visions unflurried by the world as Ellis knew it. The Arts Centre, the gallery restaurants, the firelit hospitality, the tranquil streets, the Spanish light seemed just right, and when he saw the house prices, Ellis resolved to move there." He thought that "the Dunstan civilization" was suffused with "some quality of elegant mercy, some quality of ultimate civility". These cultured wine bibbers surrounded by Spanish light seemed a far cry from the trilby hatted men and begloved ladies who went to church and pruned their roses in Playford's Adelaide, just a few short years before.

Ellis's reference to Adelaide's comparatively cheap housing indicates another of the Dunstan successes: his general ability to keep land and building costs to levels well below that of most other Australian capitals by adroit legislation and use of federal money through the Land Commission.

Yet many Adelaideans believe, and a revivified Liberal Party led by Dr. Tonkin and a gadfly Liberal Movement concentrate the criticism, that Dunstan is far from infallible, and that there is some clay beneath the glitter. Despite the glossy booklets, admirable planning, and confident statements, Monarto could be a costly bellyflop, as illusory as the Redcliff petro-chemical complex vision. Promised federal support was cut to a derisory $600,000 during the last months of the Whitlam government. At least $16 million has been spent on Monarto at the time of writing, but there is little to show for it beyond a few signs, a commission, some tree plantings, and maps and models in a city office display. Public servants jib at suggestions of their being "conscripted" to Monarto. There have been embarrassing revelations that the Monarto soil may be too saline, and its bedrock too hard for deep drainage. A number of ecological questions remain inadequately answered, not least the effects of the new city on an already grossly polluted Murray. Most damaging of all, there is no longer the demographic pressure to justify a brand new city on those dry and windy plains beyond the ranges.

The Department of Environment and Conservation, started with many pace-making promises and inspired statements on environmental protection, seems to have become ponderous. Some good progress has been made, such as the establishment of new conservation and recreation parks—on average ten a year. Yet, for all the promises, some grievous environmental damage has been done under the Dunstan regime. It allowed the South Australian Hotel to be demolished. Hallett Cove has been "developed", although the government has made strenuous efforts to preserve the rump.

At the time of writing, an infernal machine is ripping up vines at old, famous, and productive vineyards in Tea Tree Gully and Reynella and tossing them into a hopper. The vineyards have been compulsorily purchased for Housing Trust homes, a conflict with an inevitable result between the government's promises of more housing and more conservation. The government has acquired compulsorily the old Hamilton Ewell vineyard at Morphettville as a site for a bus depot. A costive bureaucracy allowed the last harvest of grapes to rot on the doomed vines. The Land Commission has acquired— compulsorily again—390 hectares owned by four major wineries in the Modbury area. The famous Stonyfell vineyard on the foothills at Burnside and Magill are dwindling before the pressures of subdivision, rising land values, and increased rates. There is something tragic and illogical in all this. Tragic because these vineyards are, or were, productive, provided pleasant patches of green in suburbia, and have considerable historical importance. Dr. Christopher Rawson Penfold, one of the pioneer vignerons, built his "Grange" homestead in the Magill vineyard, and it still stands. Some of the vines planted by Richard Hamilton and John Reynell in the late 1830s are still growing. Illogical, because the vineyards attract wine lovers and tourists, and the government is very much in favour of both. And illogical because Mr. Dunstan has frequently expressed his sympathy with the need to conserve the old vineyards. At the first Bushing Festival in 1974 at McLaren Vale, for instance, he declared that no government should allow that beautiful and productive wine-growing region to disintegrate among sub-divisions. Yet its zoning for residential development still stands, and sad inroads are being made. "We are losing them," John Miles lamented in the *Advertiser* of 25 March 1975. "The good wines of the plains are going." When I asked Mr. Dunstan about this in an interview on 7 October 1975, he stated that some productive vineyards would certainly be preserved at Reynella and Modbury.

The Dunstan government deserves the thanks of posterity for abandoning the Hall government's infamous M.A.T.S. plan, which would have disembowelled much of the urban area for freeways. But whether posterity will thank it for the extension of the South Eastern Freeway is a moot point. The link to Monarto, which bisects the Mount Lofty Ranges, is a magnificent highway, but it could stimulate further development inroads into a particularly lovely part of the hills. (Playford actually initiated the freeway, and drove it ruthlessly through the middle of Sir Alexander Downer's pleasant demesne of Raybrook, now an educational conference centre.)

On 23 September 1974, the governor, Sir Mark Oliphant, opened the Australian Institute of Parks and Recreation conference in Adelaide. He justified his reputation as a doughty champion of the South Australian environment. According to Sir Mark, the Torrens was "a sewer", as murky as the Yarra and as polluted as the Rhine. In the national parks "Picnickers leave their rubbish just where they sit". He lamented the damage being done to the Flinders Ranges, and Hallett Cove was suffering "the irreversible destruction of sandhills, rocks and foreshore". The hills, "which were the glory of Adelaide's setting", were still being eaten away by quarries and housing. "Despite limitations placed on development, the remaining open land on the Adelaide Plains and the last vestiges of bush in the foothills are disappearing rapidly into the rapacious maw of the developers ... I know members of the present South Australian Government are anxious to preserve the environment and preserve pollution, but they seem as powerless to prevent the destruction of open spaces as they are to control inflation." Government departments such as Highways and Engineering and Water Supply "can acquire land, erect unsightly structures and lop or remove trees at will". As for the Jordan Report on the environment, specially commissioned by the government and containing wise guidelines on environmental protection, its "recommendations have been largely ignored".

This was a swingeing indictment, although the governor was sympathetic to some of the problems faced by the government. The Hon. Glen Broomhill, minister for the environment, was well in advance of his interstate counterparts in the early 1970s and some fine legislation has been enacted to conserve the South Australian environment. There have been bureaucratic delays and confusions, and Broomhill has been unfairly blamed for some developments which were approved by previous governments. Like all politicians committed to economic growth, more jobs, and more housing, the Dunstan ministers are in a cleft stick on conservation. It is an increasingly popular cause with the voters—as Dunstan was characteristically quick to recognize in 1970. But then, a second oil refinery at Port Stanvac, for instance, making necessary still more housing estates in the Southern Vales, is also politically desirable for a union-backed party.

Still, it seems fair to conclude that the Dunstan government has been unprecedentedly imaginative on environmental matters. It came to the rescue of the fine A.N.Z. Bank building (originally built for the Bank of South Australia and designed by Edmund Wright) in King William Street. Private groups and the National Trust had fought an exhausting battle to prevent it being replaced by a highrise office block by the Mainline Corporation. When all seemed lost, the government stepped in and bought the bank. Renamed Edmund Wright House its future is secure as one of the most pleasing nineteenth century survivors in Adelaide's architecture. More recently, in late 1975, the government bought the historic Customs House at Semaphore. The Port Adelaide Council, unable to allot the large sum necessary for restoration, was about to demolish it for flat development.

Perhaps the pressures and tensions of the conservation/development confrontation will be eased by quite fortuitous factors beyond the control of state politics. Adelaide's population growth is slowing. Throughout Australia there has been a sharp downturn in the number of births since 1971. Moreover, the flow of assisted migrants has been drastically reduced. The 1962 Town Planning Report, which had zoned as residential large sections of the Southern Vales, for instance, had postulated a population of approximately 1.3 million for metropolitan Adelaide by 1991. The Jordan Report had suggested a much lower ceiling would be more likely in view of demographic trends and more desirable environmentally. On 26 February 1975, Mr. Dunstan defined a compromise: "A ceiling population of around a million would make Adelaide of the future a very comfortable place in which to live."

The premier has had least success with his economic policies. Adelaide's economy is now based on the consumer durables industries. It has therefore been severely affected by recent national economic trends. Dunstan, through his new Department of Industrial Development, has worked as hard as Playford ever did to diversify the economy and attract new industries, but the general economic climate, in a period of national and international inflation and recession, has been unfriendly. In three years, state taxation has almost doubled through new imposts on public transport fares, electricity, water rates, and so on. State revenue from taxes has risen from $107.8 million in 1972–73 to $208.9 million in the 1974–75 budget. Yet Dunstan usually managed reasonably to claim that such inflation has been caused by the flounderings of the Whitlam administration in Canberra. And at least, unique among state premiers, he finished the 1975 budgetary year with a surplus thanks to an adroit sale of the chronically expensive country railways to the commonwealth.

How much is mere charisma with Dunstan and how much real administrative effectiveness is debatable. It is argued that similar reforms and progress would have come had he never existed. The South Australian mood has been reformist for some years now, as the Hall government showed. The City Council began some ambitious ventures in the 1970s, and the council guards its autonomy and is not influenced, directly at least, by the trendy premier with his impeccably dressed hair and Nehru jacket. There is nothing new, either, in his paternalistic leadership. Playford was a decisive father figure too, and political paternalism is an Adelaide tradition stretching right back to Grey and Gawler.

But when all this is said, it is hard to imagine the Adelaide of the 1970s without Don Dunstan. It is equally as hard to imagine a politician of his particular style and eccentricity succeeding so well in any other Australian capital. As it is, Dunstan's urbanity is that of Adelaide, and he represents his city just as Lorenzo dei Medici encapsulated the spirit of his Florence. The analogy, if closely examined, is not fanciful.

The City Revival

Like most Australian inner city areas, the city of Adelaide suffered a steady decline in its residential population, from about 33,000 in the 1920s to about 17,000 in 1971. The number of privately occupied dwellings fell from 8,152 in 1947 to 4,227 in 1971, most of these in North Adelaide and the southeast and southwest corners of South Adelaide. Flat dwellers, transients, elderly people, and young people, often socially disadvantaged, have become prominent in the resident population. The displacement of dwellings by commercial buildings, car parks, and public works, the extreme difficulty of borrowing money for old houses, and the notion that it was healthier and more fashionable to live in a suburb were the main causes of this decline.

Much anguish is expressed by city fathers all over the western world about the "dead hearts" of old cities. Adelaide's City Council is one of the minority who are planning realistically to reverse the trend away from inner city living and to revive their city's heart. In this, the council had a number of factors in its favour. Thanks to Colonel Light, once again, Adelaide had a spacious and basically attractive urban heartland, with the parklands as a long established and exemplary green belt. This spaciousness needs to be thankfully stressed. The town clerk has remarked to me that the City of Sydney proper would fit comfortably into the area between the Torrens and South Terrace. The central area of the City of Melbourne is only about two thirds the size of Adelaide within the terraces. This has pleasant implications for the retention of large residential enclaves within the Adelaide city limits. Adelaide had a comparatively modest population increase and had not suffered as severely as many other cities from industrial growth. The Adelaide tradition of a reasonable concern for the urban environment is propitious. Finally, it seems most significant to me that Adelaide's is one of the very few city councils anywhere in the world unplagued by the irrelevancies of party politics. The councillors, as councillors, are non political; they are pragmatists looking to the affairs of their city. Another, probably unique, aspect of the council is that the lord mayor is elected annually and the aldermen triennially by *all* the electors in the city. The councillors are elected biennially by the electors of the six wards. Thus a nice balance is preserved between the parochial and the broader views, and the system works well.

The physical and psychological limits to suburban expansion round Adelaide have probably been reached. It is becoming harder for developers to convince home buyers that their future lies in a sometimes shoddily built house in a raw estate thirty or forty kilometres away from the city centre and costing, in 1975, about $25,000. Commuting is becoming increasingly fatiguing and unpleasant. Alternative housing, including flats, terraces, and cluster housing, in the inner suburbs or city centre has a growing appeal. Large parts of the city proper, especially in South Adelaide, have become so thoroughly run down and seedy that a policy of renovation and revival has obvious force. The Adelaide City Council has been in worsening financial difficulties for some years. The costs of providing services for the city are rising steeply and prime areas are occupied by organizations, such as federal government departments, churches and schools, which do not pay rates.

To improve the situation, resuscitate the city, and build up the rate paying residential population to a hoped for 30,000 the council has accepted the bold new City of Adelaide Plan. Drawn up by the council's planning consultants, Urban Systems Corporation, the plan was first published in 1974 after months of study and discussions with community groups and individuals. Lord Mayor R.W. Clampett that year stated that "it proposes a change in direction ... a change in emphasis". Some of the plan's implications are described in the sections on the parklands and on architecture and town planning, and need not be repeated here.

There have been seminars, exhibitions, and many public statements on the plan. The council has gone out of its way to invite public comment and suggestions before accepting its proposals. For example, the town clerk, Russell Arland, wrote in the *News* of 2 December 1974: "It is of great importance that the people of Adelaide should be able to choose the City they want. Melbourne and Sydney are rushing headlong towards saturation point, but with Adelaide's modest rate of growth, there is time to consider and plan the direction in which we would like to move ... Adelaide ... is unique in many respects. It can remain so if we have the will."

In brief, the plan is remarkably sweeping. It will ban, or at least seriously curb, the intrusive motor car from parts of Adelaide and restore them to pedestrians and cyclists. It will close or narrow several kilometres of roads now groaning under traffic. It will restore the squares and make the parklands even more pleasant than they were when Colonel Light first moved across them with his theodolyte. It will bring back people, life, and colour to the dingy purlieus of South Adelaide. It will create "a city within a city" in the down at heel southwestern section. The commercial city heart is to be concentrated and refined. Adelaide's history, its distinctive buildings, vistas, and atmosphere, for so long neglected and eroded as during the decades of development under Playford, will be preserved or restored. The plan is full of such proposals and it appears that most of them at least will be implemented. The old equations of progress with development, of old with bad and good with new, are being discarded for a more reasonable concept of conservation, of balanced development within the guidelines of a humane plan conscious of the past as well as the future.

Studies for the City of Adelaide Plan began in 1972. That they started at all showed a new feeling in Adelaide, and one by no means confined to the City Council. For an interim period an active City of Adelaide Development Committee worked in conjunction with the Council. The growing interest in and appreciation of the city is pervasive throughout the community, and becomes stronger. As an indication of this, between July 1972 and June 1976 five hundred residential units were approved by the Adelaide City Council, to replace just over one hundred existing dwellings, giving a net gain of four hundred housing units in that four year period of interim development control. Many more old houses have been upgraded, some of them by the South Australian Housing Trust which has restored a number of decrepit cottages. Renovations have been especially marked in the Carrington Street, Hurtle Square, and Margaret Street areas. North Adelaide, which has generally preserved its charms better than the southern part of the city, has experienced a marked growth in both population and restoration projects since the late 1960s.

Apart from refurbishing old homes, citizens of both North and South Adelaide are showing interest in new houses with strata titles, town houses, even terrace houses that harmonize with the environment. Courtyards, old trees, retricked stonework, vines, wistaria, mellow vistas all round, the parklands hard by, and only a short walk to the city centre—these are all agreeable aspects of inner city lifestyle. Moreover, the residential parts of the city have become popular with artists and intellectuals, and to retailers with a weather eye for trends and the new mode for the old fashioned, as in Melbourne Street. In 1975, a row of new shops were opened in Hutt Street, designed to look as Victorian as possible.

There are the occasional gimmicks, but usually the restorations have been done with taste. Fortunately, the genuine indigenous atmosphere is still strong and soon influences the newcomers. It is a delight, which few seem to recognize, to wander round the backstreets of the city, especially those which have not become trendy. Round the crumbling byways of McLaren Street, in South Adelaide, for instance, the saunterer will often be intrigued by examples of the pretty, the quaint, the ugly, the picturesque, and the nasty—all indestructibly Adelaidean, all somehow unique to the old city. In the McLaren Street region, for example, he will see terrace houses that seem to have grown out of the soil like ancient hobbit houses of Mount Lofty stone. Old ladies sit in the sun in tiny front gardens where geraniums twine over cyclone wire and painted galvanized iron, and discuss the pensions—and passers by. One odd little cottage is now Adelaide University's Department of Ethnomusicology, and when I passed it some Aboriginal elders, who lecture on their songs and music, were amiably disentangling themselves from the back of a Landrover. Nearby is the office of the Amalgamated Metalworkers Union, and the General Havelock Hotel, presumably built at the time of the Indian Mutiny and named after its imperial hero. By the Biscuit Box Factory community centre, a faded advertisement on a brick wall states that Viceroy Tea is British and Best.

There was a gap where a cottage had collapsed in the middle of one terrace, but its neighbours were propped up by bent girders. Climbing with dignity up one of these girders was a magnificent marmalade alley cat tom, whose territory all this area really is, what ever the City Council may imagine. There is more character in an area like McLaren Street than in a dozen of the Playford suburbs.

There are many pockets of undiluted old Adelaide, as round Margaret Street, along Carrington Street, and west of Colonel Light Square.

The City of Adelaide Plan's acceptance has stimulated interest in commercial and industrial real estate in Adelaide. Mr. Kevin Hepenstall, vice-president of the Real Estate Institute, claimed in the *Advertiser* of 21 October 1975 that the city's property market was better than it had been for fifteen years. He went on: "It indicates that the public is being motivated by the new City of Adelaide Plan. There have been more large sales of city real estate in the past 12 months than since the late 1950s."

Perhaps the most striking signs of the plan's implementation thus far are in the "core", the commercial centre where the highest buildings are concentrated. Here the transformation of Rundle Street, Adelaide's most congested shopping street, into a pedestrial mall "with a 19th century air" has been triumphantly achieved. In September 1976, Premier Dunstan, who initiated the mall idea and vigorously supported the group of traders and councillors interested in the project, declared the mall open by a fountain flowing with champagne. A street that once signified crowds, noise, exhaust fumes, and an ailing retail trade has been turned by imaginative planning into one of Adelaide's most attractive features. There are trees, flowers, seats, fruit and flower stalls and weekend entertainments that range from pony rides to Italian feasts. The 540 merchants operating in the mall, many of whom initially opposed the scheme, now rejoice in it, as does everyone else. It is, incidentally, much the biggest inner city retail trade concentration in Australia. The appearance of surviving old buildings, such as the splendid exterior of the Adelaide Arcade, cupola, coat of arms and all, has been preserved and enhanced. New buildings like the King William Tower and the projects round the Stock Exchange Plaza will soon out top everything round them.

The Sense of Difference:
A Summary

This, then, is the Adelaide of the mid 1970s. The very appearance and feel of the city now, the creativity of the new plan and its supporting attitudes show I think that the city's confidence and self-esteem are higher than ever; and Adelaide has always esteemed itself highly. They show further that the Adelaide sense of difference still lives and thrives.

One could I suppose overstress this theme, or disagree with it altogether. All cities are different. Of course there are many common denominators in the histories of all Australian cities. They have all had their colourful formative eras, their strong personalities, their booms and depressions, their periods of wowserism. Some of the sections in this book, such as those on sport or popular amusements, could roughly apply to, say, Melbourne or Perth, with the only differences being local detail. All the Australian cities have had their political heroes and political villains, their scandals, triumphs, strikes, royal visits, charlatans and philanthropists. All, at present, are concerned about new urban plans, conservation, and inner city renewal.

Yet in all cases I suggest the differences between the capital cities are often stronger than the similarities. It has been a tradition of Australian historiography since federation to write of Australia as if it were a closely united and centralized single nation, like some of the older countries of Europe. In effect, this has usually meant emphasis on New South Wales and Victoria with a few hurried sentences on the other states here and there.

Such national histories are therefore often misleading, save where they deal with foreign policy and other strictly federal matters. They gloss over the strong particularism that characterized Australian history up to federation, and which is still powerful in the 1970s. The Australian colonies looked first to Britain. Their neighbours came a poor second. In many matters, they made their own way. Since 1901, the states have tended to look first to their own interests and have erected a panoply of state bureaucracy, states' rights, and state parliaments to ensure their individuality remains. It would therefore be valid to write Australian history as a chronicle of a group of city states joined only by geography and some matters of national concern. In wartime only did they become an enthusiastic unit. This particularism explains in 1975, for instance, the diverse state policies on Medibank and their chaotic attitudes to constitutional reform.

If this is accepted, then a case can be made for studying the history of any of the capitals mainly in isolation, especially during colonial times. Sydney, Melbourne, Hobart, Brisbane, and Perth were all strongly individualistic. And Adelaide, I have tried to show, more so than all of them.

To summarise, I have tried to prove that this sense of difference developed partly by accident, partly by design. It was a lucky geographical accident that Adelaide had its climate, setting, and topography—although it took the artistic and decisive Light to place and plan the city. Adelaide's location—the hills, the plain, the blue gulf—has always excited and pleased the approaching traveller. It still does. In the 1840s, George French Angas wrote vividly in his *Savage Life and Scenes* of how he first saw Adelaide from a ship sailing up the gulf: "At daybreak we saw the red sun come up from behind the darkly purple hills. How gloriously it gilded the land of our hopes! We gazed on South Australia: that high, jagged ridge was Mount Lofty; yonder the mouth of the Onkaparinga River; and before us was Holdfast Bay. At last the buildings of the City of Adelaide were descried, glittering in the sunshine, and a shout of joy arose from the vessel's deck." Suburban spread and, occasionally, air pollution have marred the view once enjoyed by Angas, and anyway now only yachtsmen and anglers out in the bay can see it. Yet the beauty of Adelaide's setting can be appreciated from another view-point by air travellers flying in over the ranges, and even by motorists who stop at lookouts on the escarpment, or on Mouth Lofty itself, to contemplate the city.

Given the splendid setting, it was human design, of course, which made a distinctive city. The Wakefieldian founders wanted a model city and a model community. They were discontented with England and appalled by New South Wales. Laissez faire as a policy did not appeal to them: it gave free rein to the devil and the Old Adam as Sydney, in their opinion, showed. Their province and its capital would be a planned prototype for all communities which might wish to learn by their example.

When no one showed much interest, they raised a psychological drawbridge round their province, and the boundary of the inner keep was the parklands. Free communication was encouraged only with the Mother Country; but this was an England idealized by sentiment and distance almost out of recognition. In their Adelaide, the founders tried to do everything by design. Their policies on land ownership, self-government, freedom of conscience (they adroitly rid themselves of the true meaning of Dissent and Nonconformity by not permitting a denominational norm), business probity and so on were all idealistic. Some failed, or were abandoned with the abolition of dual government, but some achieved a high measure of success. Most obviously, they achieved a fully planned city, and the happy accident of Light's appointment made this perhaps their most signal success.

I have argued that this consequent sense of difference about Adelaide kept its impetus right through the decades of the city's growth. A curious compound of moral conservatism and legislative audacity, it has manifested itself often in Adelaide's history. This city was one of the very few in the world which allowed full, unfettered expression to the British Nonconformist conscience. Torrens, Grey, Sir Edwin Smith, Kingston, Playford, advanced policies on a range of issues from votes for women to deep drainage. The John Martin's Christmas Pageant, the long moral hegemony of the Woman's Christian Temperance Union, sabbatarianism, an excess of churches and insurance companies, the dynastic Old Adelaide Families with their mansions and their protocol, the agreeable vistas of North Terrace and the statue of King Edward VII gazing across it at the Bank of Adelaide—these are all exemplars of this sense of difference.

It is often hard to define this Adelaide distinctiveness, a thing of nuances and emphases, and it can strike different people differently. You may feel it wandering among the villas and terraces of North Adelaide, or by the Torrens, or by the old warehouses, pubs, and workshops near Colonel Light Square. It makes its subtle presence felt in the Adelaide Oval when the cricketers come out on a warm day, or in the cool recesses of the Botanic Garden, or in the Rundle Mall, undoubtedly one of the most agreeable urban sauntering places anywhere. Adelaide's statues—Elder and Hughes solemn before their university, Robert Burns in front of the library, McDouall Stuart in Victoria Square, the pure maid in the Women's Garden of Remembrance, the bronze angel by the river who draws your attention to the memorial to the Angas family, and Light himself gesturing from Montefiore Hill—all bespeak this difference.

I suggest finally that this sense of difference still shows its vigour in recent years in buildings such as the Festival Theatre, in ideas such as the City of Adelaide Plan, and in people such as a premier who jogs, discusses Yeats and Burke on television, reads poetry to children in the zoo, and wears a white polo neck sweater with a dinner jacket with as much aplomb as he governs.

And it is this distinctiveness of an old but young, cautious but bold, prudent yet swinging city which awakens what Harry Miller has called "a special kind of affection" from visitors not fortunate enough to live in Adelaide. It has always encouraged travellers, as we have seen, to strain for comparisons between Adelaide and Athens, or Florence, or Weimar. They miss the point. Adelaide is Adelaide is Adelaide.

Elizabeth Riddell wrote in the *Australian* in November 1974 about the opening of the Playhouse by Mr. Dunstan "in an atmosphere of flowers, birdsong and splendid weather". From the stage, the premier read some iambic pentameters written by the Chief Justice, Dr. John Bray. After the opening, Miss Riddell watched children chasing each other round the sculpture on the Festival Centre plaza. She concluded: "Up in busy Hindley Street I saw women carrying bunches of sweet peas, still dewy. And on the bus the driver answered my questions politely, told me where to alight and warned me to be careful of traffic when crossing the road. That's Adelaide for you. Not to mention a Premier who can speak blank verse, and a Chief Justice who can write it."

Another distinguished journalist, Peter Heyworth of the British *Observer* of 25 April 1976, added further plaudits. He wrote that Adelaide's "biennial festival expresses much of the country's new found cultural vigour", praised the vitality and variety of the 1976 festival, and said of the gleaming white Festival Centre:

> That the Adelaide Centre has so rapidly achieved a status beyond controversy in a country once famed for its philistinism is not only due to the fact that it cost approximately one-tenth of its counterpart in Sydney. It is a popular success because it works. Unlike the remote, grey temples that have arisen on London's South Bank, it opens its arms to human beings ... its scale relates to the people who at all hours of the day throng its terraces, auditoriums and eating places. Both in design and function it challenges the notion of culture as a ritual separate from the rest of life. Unlike any other centre I have seen, it approaches the arts with an open mind ... At its box office the public does not appear as a suppliant before a small gap in a glass barrier, but at an open counter.

Heyworth went on to praise, as so many do, the agreeable urban context in which the festival flourishes, especially the "sand, sea and an abundant flow of sound local wine" enjoyed in "a climate as close to perfection as any I have experienced on this imperfect globe".

Perhaps, then, the utopian founders of a special city in a special province in 1836 did in the end have more success than the world usually accords to its visionaries. They had great expectations and naturally the reality fell short of them, often far short. They dreamed some impossible dreams, but many of their plans were practical and striking and all were warmed by a refreshing belief in the essential goodness of people.

Maybe it is wrong to stress the gap between doctrine and achievement. Maybe we should emphasize the hopes that were in the main realized. The founders hoped for freedom, fresh horizons, the chance to earn comfort and security. Modest and mundane hopes, perhaps, but rarely fulfilled, the world over, so well and so often, from the first, as in South Australia. Had that been all there was to it—the classical Australian pursuit for comfort and convenience, the solid home, the good job, the holidays, the union— then the Adelaide dream might have seemed an understandable but philistine *summum bonum*. But, as we have seen, that tincture of founding idealism always coloured and still colours the Adelaide ethos.

Given that the expectations of Wakefield, Angas, Gawler, and Light would have been different had they lived in this century we can, I think, assume that their shades look with approval on the city shaped and lived in by their followers. Angas must surely recognize a fellow spirit in Playford, Wakefield in Dunstan, Governor Gawler in Governor Oliphant, and the immortal Colonel Light must nod approvingly from Elysium at the Festival Centre and the City of Adelaide Plan, whatever he feels about the suburbs.

In the last analysis, the founders succeeded in starting on its way a city and an urban community that in many pleasant ways would be different from the norm. The Adelaide of the 1970s is still vigorously, elegantly, and comfortably different. *Vive la différence!*

117. Aerial view of modern Adelaide looking over North Adelaide to South Adelaide, the suburbs, and the Hills (wearing a quarry scar top left). The insulating swathes of parklands are evident, as are the pleasant avenues of North Adelaide. Photograph supplied by the Publicity Branch of the Premier's Department.

118. The gracious South Australian Hotel early this century. It was demolished in 1971 to make way for a high-rise motel. The "South" was by far the finest hotel in Adelaide for many years and its destruction is now bitterly and hopelessly regretted.

119. Edmund Wright House, King William Street. This superb building, then a branch of the A.N.Z. Bank, was saved from the wreckers by the Dunstan Government in 1972 after a long battle by conservationists. Now used mainly for civil marriages, Edmund Wright House preserves the name of the former mayor who designed the Town Hall. Photograph supplied by the Publicity Branch of the Premier's Department.

120. The magnificent italianate ceiling of the main marriage room of Edmund Wright House. Like the Town Hall, this building was also designed by Wright and was built between 1875 and 1878. Photograph supplied by the Publicity Branch of the Premier's Department.

121. Carclew, outstanding, even among North Adelaide villas, as a vigorous example of Victorian domestic Gothic. Once a mansion of the Bonython family, it is now a state government owned drama centre for children. Photograph supplied by the Publicity Branch of the Premier's Department.

122. Captain Sturt's house, Grange. This old home of the great explorer and surveyor is now a tourist attraction near Adelaide's beachfront. Photograph supplied by the Publicity Branch of the Premier's Department.

123. Ayers' House, North Terrace. Sir Henry Ayer prospered on Burra copper, became premier, and built this fine mansion. It was purchased and restored by the Dunstan government and turned into a restaurant. The National Trust is also based here. Photograph supplied by the Publicity Branch of the Premier's Department.

124. Beautifully restored terrace houses in Archer Street, North Adelaide.

125. Government House, looking across the parklands and river to St. Peter's Cathedral and North Adelaide where high-rise buildings are beginning to sprout among the villas. Photograph supplied by the Publicity Branch of the Premier's Department.

126. England versus Australia test match at the Adelaide Oval in 1970, against the backdrop of the new Festival Theatre (across the river) and still growing city towers. Photograph supplied by the Publicity Branch of the Premier's Department.

127. A section of the crowd for the same test match. It is interesting to compare this crush of bare or lightly clad torsos with the spectators at an earlier test (see illustration 104). The Adelaide Oval is also used for Australian Rules football, Highland Games, and even equestrian events, but it is first and foremost a cricket ground. Photograph supplied by the Publicity Branch of the Premier's Department.

128. North Terrace near the Art Gallery, surely the pleasantest boulevard in Australia. Photograph supplied by the Publicity Branch of the Premier's Department.

129. Sculptor's eye view of the Festival Theatre through the sun dial on the terrace of the Festival complex. The Athens of the South, but with an eye to the future. Photograph supplied by the Publicity Branch of the Premier's Department.

130. The tall eucalypts section of the Botanic Gardens. Photograph supplied by the Publicity Branch of the Premier's Department.

131. Adelaide's commercial heartland from the municipal golf course on the parklands. Adelaide is now rather a city of insurance, banking, and bureaucracy than of churches. Photograph supplied by the Publicity Branch of the Premier's Department.

132. Removing the scale of charges from one of the south parkland pounds in 1968. The herds of sheep and cattle that grazed on the parklands, by carefully guarded right, since the late 1830s are now a memory. Some saddle horses still graze on the north parklands. Photograph by courtesy of the Adelaide *Advertiser*.

133. Two statesmen who have shaped the course of Adelaide and South Australia since the Second World War—Sir Thomas Playford and Don Dunstan, in 1972. Photograph by courtesy of the Adelaide *Advertiser*.

134. "Captain Adelaide"—a painting of Premier Dunstan as Superman, by Nigel Murray-Harvey, which hangs in the Flinders University students' refectory. Photograph by courtesy of the Adelaide *Advertiser*.

135. Sir Mark Oliphant communicates with a three-year-old girl at the opening of a school for deaf and blind children in 1976. A distinguished nuclear scientist and outspoken on many issues, he has been probably the most effective and genuinely popular South Australian governor. Photograph by courtesy of the Adelaide *Advertiser*.

136. The old toll house near the remains of the Glen Osmond silver lead mine, the first substantial mine in Australia. In the 1840s tolls were charged on people using Governor Gawler's road into the Hills. Those travelling to divine service were allowed through free. It now stands at the entrance to the South Eastern freeway. Photograph supplied by the Publicity Branch of the Premier's Department.

137. An idyllic scene in the Adelaide Hills, only twenty kilometres from the city centre. Colonel Light described the Mount Lofty Ranges as "the enchanted hills". Parts of the Hills have suffered from suburban spread but rigorous environmental controls now apply. Photograph supplied by the Publicity Branch of the Premier's Department.

138. The view north from Mengler's Hill over the famous Barossa Valley, named by Light after a Peninsular War battle (spelt Barrosa). Here Lutheran refugees from religious persecution in northern Germany settled and planted their celebrated vineyards. The first village, Bethany, is in the left middle distance. Tanunda is on the right. Photograph supplied by the Publicity Branch of the Premier's Department.

Notes to Text

1. FOUNDATION

Proclamation

1. John Morphett to the Commissioners. Letter dated 6 December 1837. South Australian Archives. See also G.C. Morphett, *The Life and Letters of Sir John Morphett* (Adelaide, 1936).
2. Anthony Trollope, *Australia*, preface.
3. Letter dated 25 November 1836. South Australian Archives, Adelaide.
4. Ibid.
5. Auckland to Glenelg, 31 May 1836. C.O. 13/3 Public Records Office, London.
6. Quoted in Edwin Hodder, *The History of South Australia*, vol. 1, pp. 170–71.
7. Letter of October 1835. Quoted in A.G. Price, *Founders and Pioneers of South Australia*, p. 97.
8. A good biography is Geoffrey Dutton, *Founder of A City* (1960), reissued in paperback. See also the Light material in the South Australian Archives and the Adelaide Town Hall.
9. W. Napier, *History of the War in the Peninsula*, vol. vi, p. 146.
10. Dutton, *Founder of A City*, p. 161.
11. See generally E.K. Thomas, ed., *The Diary and Letters of Mary Thomas* (Adelaide 1915) and E. Hodder, ed., *The Founding of South Australia as recorded in the journals of Mr. Robert Gouger* (London, 1898).
12. Royal Geographical Society of Australasia, South Australian Branch, *Proceedings* vol. 30, pp. 21–23. *Extracts from the Diary of G. Stevenson.*
13. William Light, *Brief Journal*, p. 38.

The Physical Setting

1. The appropriate sections of the *South Australian Year Book* (Adelaide: Government Printer, published annually) are informative on the physical background of the state, as well as on many other matters appertaining to South Australia.
2. J. Backhouse, *A Narrative of a Visit to the Australian Colonies*, p. 512.
3. R. Schomburgk in William Harcus, ed., *South Australia: its History, Resources and Productions*, p. 215.
4. Quoted in Edwin Hodder, *The History of South Australia*, vol.1, pp. 88–89.

Discovery

1. Quoted in Edwin Hodder, *The History of South Australia*, vol. 1, p. 6.
2. Charles Sturt, *Two Expeditions into the Interior of Southern Australia* (London, 1833), vol. 2, p. 245.
3. Hodder, *The History of South Australia*, vol. 1, p. 17.
4. Sturt, *Two Expeditions*, vol. 2, p. 246.

The Background to Settlement

1. A useful account of Wakefield is given in R.C. Mills's introduction to E.G. Wakefield, *A Letter From Sydney*, (London: Dent, 1929, Everyman's Library). The quotations in the following pages are taken from this.

2. Prinsep, *Letters from Van Diemen's Land*, quoted in Edwin Hodder, *The History of South Australia*, vol. 1, pp. 45–46.

3. *Hansard's Parliamentary Debates*, New, vol. xvi, p. 495.

4. A superb account of Angas and his influence on South Australia is given in Douglas Pike, *Paradise of Dissent, South Australia 1827–1857* especially in the section beginning *p. 124*.

5. *See Pike, Paradise of Dissent*, especially chapters 5 and 6 for more details on the characters of prominent founding fathers.

Settling In, 1836–1840

1. Quoted in Geoffrey Dutton, *Founder of a City*, p. 189.

2. Some later over-ambitious settlements in South Australia, often doomed to be ghost towns, had Light-like original plans with parklands and wide streets. A good example is Hammond in the mid north, now almost deserted.

3. Quoted in Dutton, *Founder of a City*, p. 202.

4. Ibid., p. 207.

5. William Light, *Brief Journal*, p. 67.

6. Ibid., p. 69.

7. Quoted in A. Grenfell Price, *The Foundation and Settlement of South Australia, 1829–1845*, pp. 64–65.

8. Quoted in John Blacket, *History of South Australia*, p. 66.

9. Gawler, despatch, 11 October 1839, Colonial Office records, London.

10. Light, *Brief Journal*, p. 43.

11. Price, *Foundation and Settlement of South Australia*, pp. 68–69.

12. Quoted in Blacket, *History of South Australia*, p. 66.

13. Quoted in Dutton, *Founder of a City*, pp. 286–87.

14. Ibid., p. 289.

15. R.M. Hague, *Sir John Jeffcott*, p. 30.

16. Quoted in Royal Geographical Society of Australasia, *Centenary History of South Australia*, p. 234. The original of this letter is in the Mitchell Library, Sydney.

17. Quoted in Douglas Pike, *Paradise of Dissent*, p. 214.

Life in early Adelaide, 1837–41

1. T. Horton James, *Six Months in South Australia*, p. 193.

2. Geoffrey Dutton, *Founder of a City*, p. xii.

3. Morphett papers, South Australian Archives, Adelaide.

4. George French Angas, *Savage Life and Scenes in Australia and New Zealand*, vol. 1, pp. 214–15.

5. William Smillie, *The Great South Land*, p. 23.

6. Quoted in John Blacket, *History of South Australia*, p. 74.

7. Alexander Tolmer, *Reminiscences*, pp. 130–31.

8. J.W. Bull, *Early Experiences of Life in South Australia*, p. 51.

9. J. Stephens, *The Land of Promise*, pp. 108–9.

10. Quoted in Blacket, *History of South Australia*, pp. 77–78.

11. Ibid., p. 79.

12. Light to Palmer, 14 March 1839, quoted in Dutton, *Founder of a City*, p. 283.

13. Quoted in Blacket, *History of South Australia*, p. 80.

14. Ibid., p. 84.

15. Ibid., p. 84–85.

16. Ibid., p. 86.

17. Elizabeth Davison's diary, South Australian Archives.

18. Blacket, *History of South Australia*, p. 79.

19. George French Angas, *South Australia Illustrated*, p. 27.

20. See generally Tolmer, *Reminiscences*, vol. 1, chapters 16 and 17 for his own accounts of his derring do.

21. Ibid., p. 190.

22. George French Angas, *South Australia Illustrated*, p. 38.

23. Bull, *Early Experiences*, p. 34.

24. Ibid., p. 32.

25. Anthony Trollope, *Australia*, p. 113.
26. Bull, *Early Experiences*, p. 72.
27. Ibid., p. 65. Bull is informative on Aborigines in early South Australia, and a more objective commentator than most. See especially chapter 9.

Responsible Government

1. Thomas Worsnop, *History of the City of Adelaide*, p. 19.
2. Ibid., p. 44.
3. Ibid., p. 2, footnote.
4. Ibid., p. 77.
5. J.J. Pascoe, ed., *History of Adelaide and Vicinity*, p. 92.
6. J.W. Bull, in his *Early Experiences of Life in South Australia*, gives good examples of the ruin of country settlers, especially, at this time.
7. Actually, J.W. Bull selected this land first, but Gilles, shrewd as ever, appears to have talked him into a transfer. See ibid., pp. 137–39.
8. Douglas Pike, *Paradise of Dissent*, p. 332.
9. Ibid., p. 333.
10. Francis Dutton, *South Australia and Its Mines*, p. 133.
11. Perhaps the finest German buildings extant in the state are the houses and barns at Paechtown, near Hahndorf.
12. Quoted in A. Grenfell Price, *The Foundation and Settlement of South Australia, 1829–1845*, p. 233.
13. Quoted in Edwin Hodder, *The History of South Australia*, vol. 1, p. 260.
14. Bull, *Early Experiences*, p. 312.
15. Hodder, *History of South Australia*, vol. 1, p. 265.
16. Tolmer's own account of the gold escort is interesting. *Reminiscences*, vol. 11, chapters 17 and 18.
17. Quoted in R.M. Gibbs, *A History of South Australia*, p. 116.
18. Quoted in Max Colwell, *Adelaide: An Illustrated History*, p. 49.
19. Quoted in Blacket, *History of South Australia*, p. 379–80.
20. Worsnop, *History of the City of Adelaide*, p. 97.
21. Ibid., p. 100.
22. C.H. Barton, Letter book, Town Hall Archives.
23. Pike, *Paradise of Dissent*, pp. 495–96.
24. Pascoe, *History of Adelaide and Vicinity*, p. 125.

2. ADELAIDE, 1859–1970: A BRIEF CHRONICLE

Introduction

1. Edwin Hodder, *The History of South Australia*, vol. 2, p. 206.

The 1860s

1. Edwin Hodder, *The History of South Australia*, vol. 2, p. 207.
2. Ibid., p. 209.
3. J.J. Pascoe, ed., *History of Adelaide and Vicinity*, pp. 138–40.
4. On the Adelaide Town Hall, see generally Thomas Worsnop, *History of the City of Adelaide*, ch. 22, pp. 321–41.
5. An excellent account of Prince Alfred's visit is contained in Brian McKinlay, *The First Royal Tour, 1867–68*. Worsnop devotes two adoring chapters to the visit.
6. Hodder, *History of South Australia*, vol. 1, p. 387.

The 1870s

1. Worsnop, *History of the City of Adelaide*, p. 332.
2. See generally the section on South Australia, chs. 42 and 43, pp. 621–46, in Trollope,*Australia*, (1967 ed.).
3. William Harcus, ed., *South Australia: Its History, Resources and Productions*, p. 24.
4. Ibid., p. 26.
5. Ibid., pp. 27–28.
6. Ibid., p. 25.
7. *Mark Twain in Australia and New Zealand*, pp. 190–93. See generally chs. 18 and 19 of this book for Twain's comments on South Australia.
8. For further information on the foundation of the university, see W.G.K. Duncan and Roger Ashley Leonard, *The University of Adelaide, 1874–1974*.
9. These and the quotations immediately following are taken from the Mayor's report, 1879–80, Town Hall Archives.

1880–1900

1. Regulations on the compulsory school age (6–13) were passed in 1875 and 1878, and prevailed until well into this century.
2. Edwin Hodder, *The History of South Australia*, vol. 2, p. 107.
3. Quoted in Michael Cannon, "Boom and Bust, Boom and Bust," *National Times* magazine's *History of the Australian People*, p. 12.
4. Ibid.

1945–70

1. Donald Horne, *The Lucky Country*, p. 37.
2. Jeanne MacKenzie, *Australian Paradox*, p. 160.

3. MOSAIC OF A COMMUNITY

Commerce and Industry

1. J. Stephens, *The Land of Promise*, preface.
2. A.A. Simpson, "Manufactures and Commerce", in the Royal Geographical Society of Australasia's *Centenary History of South Australia*, p. 189.
3. A useful account of the chamber's history is John Miles, *A Richness of People*.
4. Ibid., p. 15.
5. Ibid.
6. R.E.N. Twopenny, *Town Life in Australia*, p. 201.

Immigration, Working and Living Conditions

1. Information from the South Australian and commonwealth *Yearbooks*.
2. Grey papers, South Australian Archives, Adelaide.
3. See generally Douglas Pike, *Paradise of Dissent*, ch. 13.
4. Quoted in ibid., p. 181.
5. Quoted in ibid., pp. 182–83.
6. Letter, Henry Grinham to John Kellick Bathurst. Original in the possession of Hubert Bathurst Perry, Rosudgeon, Cornwall, great grandson of John Kellick Bathurst.
7. C.H. Barton, letter book, Town Hall Archives, Adelaide.
8. John Blacket, *History of South Australia*, p. 87.
9. William Harcus, *South Australia: Its History, Resources and Productions*, p. 19.

10. J.D. Gordon, *Handbook of South Australia*, pp. 72–76.
11. Edwin Hodder, *History of South Australia*, vol. 1., p. 291.
12. Ibid., p. 293.

Architecture and Town Planning

1. James Stephens, *The Land of Promise*, p. 9.
2. Ibid.
3. One Manning house, at least, still survives, still in use and well preserved. It is the Quaker meeting house by St Peter's Cathedral.
4. C.H. Barton, letter book, Town Hall Archives, Adelaide.
5. *Mark Twain in Australia and New Zealand*, p. 187.
6. There are a number of recent suburban histories, including W.A. Norman, *The History of the City of Mitcham*, and Max Lamshed, *Prospect, 1872–1972. A Portrait of a City*. See bibliography.
7. Information on the proposed city may be obtained from the Monarto Development Commission, Adelaide. The Department of Adult Education at the University of Adelaide has printed the proceedings of three seminars on Monarto.

The Parklands, Squares, and Botanic Gardens

1. William Harcus, *South Australia: Its History, Resources and Productions*, p. 25.

The Churches

1. J.J. Pascoe, ed., *History of Adelaide and Vicinity*, p. 125.
2. Quoted in Edwin Hodder, *History of South Australia*, vol. 1, p. 80.
3. Quoted in Douglas Pike, *Paradise of Dissent*, p. 138.
4. Ibid., p. 79.
5. See ibid., pp. 275–76.
6. Hodder, *History of South Australia*, vol. 1, p. 197.
7. William Harcus, *South Australia: Its History, Resources and Productions*, p. 137.
8. Quoted in John Blacket, *History of South Australia*, pp. 377–78.
9. Ibid.
10. Pike, *Paradise of Dissent*, p. 133.
11. Quoted in ibid., p. 130.

Culture

1. A good survey of the South Australian cultural scene is the *Report of the Arts Inquiry Committee*, S.A. Government, roneoed, 1962.
2. For details of the mechanics' institute in Australia, including South Australia, see Derek Whitelock, *The Great Tradition: A History of Adult Education in Australia*, ch. 3.
3. A.G. Austin, ed., *The Webbs' Australian Diary, 1898*, (Melbourne: Pitman, 1965), p. 93.
4. R.E.N. Twopeny, *Town Life in Australia*, p. 92.

Adelaide Respectability, Virtue and Vice

1. R.E.N. Twopeny, *Town Life in Australia*, p. 123.
2. See Douglas Pike, *Paradise of Dissent*, pp. 414–15.
3. Letter dated 22 August 1844, South Australian Archives, Adelaide.
4. Pike, *Paradise of Dissent*, p. 500.
5. Ibid., p. 503.
6. Ibid., p. 500

7. Ibid., p. 510.

8. Hugh Stretton, *Ideas for Australian Cities* (Adelaide: Griffin Press, 1970), p. 143.

9. There are copies of this remarkable pamphlet in the South Australian Archives, and the Special Collection of the Barr Smith Library, University of Adelaide. It ought to be reprinted.

10. C.H. Barton, letter book, Town Hall Archives, Adelaide.

11. Published by the W.C.T.U. itself. Most of the quotations about the W.C.T.U. in these pages are taken from this extraordinary book.

12. Pike, *Paradise of Dissent*, p. 514.

Sport

1. The R.E.N. Twopeny quotations in this section are taken from his excellent chapter on "Amusements" in his *Town Life in Australia*, pp. 202–14.

2. Anthony Trollope, *Australia*, p. 733. See generally ch. 51, "Australian Sports".

3. Twopeny, *Town Life in Australia*, p. 204.

4. A.G. Moyes, *Australian Cricket: A History*, p. 55.

5. Quoted in ibid., p. 150.

6. Ibid., p. 54.

7. Ibid., pp. 50–51.

8. Twopeny, *Town Life in Australia*, p. 206.

9. Ibid., p. 206.

10. Max Lamshed, "The Bushmen" section, *South Australian Story*.

11. Twopeny, *Town Life in Australia*, p. 214.

12. See generally Alexander Tolmer, *Reminiscences*, vol. 2, ch. 3, pp. 19–30.

13. See Trollope, *Australia*, pp. 736–40, for an account of this hunt.

14. Ibid., p. 741.

15. Twopeny, *Town Life in Australia*, pp. 209–10.

Newspapers

1. R.E.N. Twopeny, *Town Life in Australia*, pp. 232–33.

The Natural Environment

1. Quoted in W.A. Norman, *The History of the City of Mitcham*, p. 11.

2. J.W. Bull, *Early Experiences of Life in South Australia*, pp. 130–33 is informative on early bush fires.

3. C.H. Barton, letter book, Town Hall Archives, Adelaide.

4. Douglas Pike, *Paradise of Dissent*, p. 498.

5. Records, Adelaide Zoological Gardens.

6. Barton, letter book.

7. G.E. Archer Russell, *Wildlife in Bushland*, p. 43.

The Adelaide Hills

1. *Mark Twain in Australia and New Zealand*, p. 190.

Sources

Among books, Douglas Pike's magnificent long study, *Paradise of Dissent: South Australia 1829–1857* was first and foremost among my reference. A huge compendium of research, details, and judicious but forthright opinion, it must be an indispensable companion to all students of early South Australian history.

Other useful sources included Edwin Hodder's two volume *History of South Australia*, A.G. Price's two studies of the foundation period, *Founders and Pioneers of South Australia* and *The Foundation and Settlement of South Australia*, Geoffrey Dutton's elegant *Founder of a City*, and the Rev. John Blacket's confused but lively *History of South Australia*. Harcus, Pascoe and Worsnop were often helpful.

Bull and Tolmer were the most informative of the early writers on South Australia. William Light's *Brief Journal* ought to be read—a short and pleasant task—before the many commentaries on it. Crowley's survey of sources on South Australian history is admirable and saves many weary hours of reference hunting. Ron Gibbs's *History of South Australia* is much the best of the recent studies.

The newspaper archives of the State Library of South Australia is a mine of journalistic information on South Australian history and richly repays many visits. The South Australian Archives and the Special Collections Room at the Barr Smith Library, University of Adelaide, are packed with primary and secondary research sources, many of them still untapped. The recently established records room at the Adelaide Town Hall has quantities of fascinating historical material, much of which has only been catalogued in the last year or two.

I also talked to many reminiscing Adelaide veterans and became sadly aware of the folk memory wasting away, neglected, in senior citizens' homes.

Select Bibliography

Adelaide City Council Mayoral Annual Reports, Records, Minute Books, etc.

Angas, George French. *Savage Life and Scenes in Australia and New Zealand: Being an artist's Impression of the Countries and People at the Antipodes*. 2 vols. London: Smith, Elder & Co. 1847. State Library of South Australia facsimile, 1969.

————. *South Australia Illustrated*. London: Smith, Elder & Co. 1847.

Backhouse, James. *A Narrative of a Visit to the Australian Colonies*. London: Hamilton, Adams & Co., 1843.

Blacket, Rev. John. *History of South Australia, a Romantic and Successful Experiment in Colonization*. Adelaide: Hussey & Gillingham, 2nd ed., 1911.

Brown, Tom. *Glenelg: An Urban Village, 1836–1972*. Adelaide: Strehlow, 1973.

Bull, J.W. *Early Experiences of Life in South Australia, and an Extended Colonial History*. London & Adelaide: E.S. Wigg and Sampson Low, 2nd ed, 1884. State Library of South Australia facsimile, 1972.

Cannon, Michael. *Life in the Country: Australia in the Victorian Age*. Melbourne: Lansdowne, 1973.

Capper, Henry. *South Australia, Containing Hints to Emigrants, Proceedings of the South Australian Company, a Variety of Authentic and Useful Information* London: Tyas, 1838.

Charlton, Rob. *The History of Kapunda*. Melbourne: Hawthorn Press, 1971.

Clark, C.M.H. *Select Documents in Australian History, 1788–1850*. Sydney: Angus & Robertson, 1950.

Coleman, Dudley, ed. *The First Hundred Years: A History of Burnside in South Australia*. Adelaide: Griffin Press, 1956.

Coleman, Dudley and Miles, John. *A Richness of People*. Adelaide: Griffin Press, 1969.

Colwell, Max. *Adelaide: An Illustrated History*. Melbourne: Lansdowne, 1974.

Committee on the Environment. *The Environment in South Australia: A Report*. Adelaide: Government Printer, 1972.

Conigrave, Mrs. J. Fairfax. *My Reminiscences of the Early Days: Personal Incidents on a Sheep and Cattle Run in South Australia*. Perth: Brokensha and Shaw, 1916.

Crowley, F.K. *South Australian History: A survey for Research Students*. Adelaide: Libraries Board of South Australia, 1966.

Duncan, W.G.K. and Leonard, Roger Ashley. *The University of Adelaide, 1874–1974*. Adelaide: Rigby 1973.

Dutton, Francis. *South Australia and Its Mines, with an Historical Sketch of the Colony*. London: T & F Boone, 1846.

Dutton, Geoffrey. *Founder of a City: The Life of Colonel William Light*. Melbourne: Cheshire, 1960.

Gibbs, R.M. *A History of South Australia*. Adelaide: Ballara Books, 1969.

Gordon, D.J., ed. *Handbook of South Australia*. Adelaide: Government Printer, 1914.

Gunther, John. *Inside Australia and New Zealand*. London: Hamish Hamilton, 1972.

Hague, R.M. *Sir John Jeffcott: Portrait of a Colonial Judge*. Melbourne: Melbourne University Press, 1963.

Harcus, William, ed. *South Australia: Its History, Resources and Productions*. London: Sampson, Low, 1963.

Hirst, J.B. *Adelaide & The Country, 1870–1917: Their social and political relationship*. Melbourne: Melbourne University Press, 1973.

Hodder, Edwin. *The History of South Australia, from Its Foundation to the Year of Its Jubilee*. 2 vols. London: Sampson, Low, 1893.

Horne, Donald. *The Lucky Country: Australia in the Sixties*. Penguin, 1964. Sydney: Angus & Robertson, rev. ed., 1965.

James, T. Horton. *Six Months in South Australia with Some Account of Port Philip and Portland Bay in Australia Felix*. London: Cross, 1838.

Lamshed, Max. *The South Australian Story*. Adelaide: Advertiser, 1958.

————. *Prospect, 1872–1972: A Portrait of a City*. Adelaide: Prospect Corporation, 1972.

Lamshed, Max and McLeod, Jeanette. *Adelaide Sketchbook*. Adelaide: Rigby, 1967.

————. *Adelaide Hills Sketchbook*. Adelaide: Rigby, 1971.

Leaney, John T. *Campbelltown, 1868–1968*. Adelaide: Campbelltown Corporation, 1968.

Light, William. *A Brief Journal of the proceedings of William Light, later Surveyor-General of the province of South Australia, with a few remarks on some of the objections that have been made to them.* Adelaide: Archibald Mac-Dougall, 1839. State Library of South Australia facsimile, 1963.

McCorkindale, Isabel, ed. *Torch-Bearers; The Woman's Christian Temperance Union of South Australia, 1886–1948.* Adelaide: Woman's Christian Temperance Union of South Australia, 1949.

McGregor, Craig. *Profile of Australia.* London: Hodder & Stoughton, 1966.

MacKenzie, Jeanne. *Australian Paradox.* London: Macgibbon & Kee, 1962.

McKinlay, Brian. *The First Royal Tour, 1867–68.* Adelaide: Rigby, 1970.

Mayer, Henry. *The Press in Australia.* Melbourne: Cheshire, 1964.

Miles, John. *A Richness of People.* Adelaide: Griffin Press, 1969.

Morphett, G.C. *When Adelaide Was Very Young: Trials and Hardships of the Pioneers.* Adelaide: Pioneer's Association of South Australia, 1939.

Moyes, A.G. *Australian Cricket: a History.* Sydney: Angus & Robertson, 1959.

Nagel, Paula. *A Social History of North Adelaide, 1837–1901.* Adelaide: Austaprint, 1974.

Newland, Simpson. *Paving the Way: A Romance of the Australian Bush.* London: Gay & Bird, 1893.

Newnham, W.H., and McLeod, Jeannette. *Old Adelaide Hotels Sketchbook.* Adelaide: Rigby, 1971.

Norman, W.A. *The History of the City of Mitcham.* Adelaide: Mitcham Corporation, 1953.

Old Colonist. Edited by E.M. Yelland. *Colonists, Copper and Corn in the Colony of South Australia.* Reprint. Melbourne: Melbourne University Press, 1970.

Pascoe, J.J., ed. *History of Adelaide and Vicinity, with a General Sketch of the Province of South Australia and Biographies of Representative Men.* Adelaide: Hussey and Gillingham, 1901.

Payne, G.R. and Cosh, E. *History of Unley, 1871–1971.* Adelaide: Unley Corporation, 1971.

Pike, Douglas. *Paradise of Dissent: South Australia 1829–1857.* Melbourne: Melbourne University Press, 1957.

————, ed. *Australian Dictionary of Biography.* Melbourne: Melbourne University Press, 5 vols. so far, 1966–74.

Price, A. Grenfell. *Founders and Pioneers of South Australia.* Adelaide: Preece, 1929.

————. *The Foundation and Settlement of South Australia, 1829–1846.* Adelaide: F.W. Preece, 1924.

Report of the Arts Enquiry Committee for South Australia. Adelaide: Government Printer, 1962.

Royal Geographical Society of Australasia, South Australian Branch. *The Centenary History of South Australia.* Adelaide: Hassell Press, 1936.

Russell, G.E. Archer. *Wildlife in Bushland.* Adelaide: Thomas, 1919.

Scales, Marjorie. *John Walker's Village: A History of Walkerville.* Adelaide: Rigby, 1974.

Scott, H.J. *South Australia in 1887–88. A Handbook Compiled for the Centennial International Exhibition, Melbourne, 1888.* Adelaide: Government Printer, 1888.

Scott, Theodore. *Description of South Australia, with Sketches of New South Wales, Port Philip and New Zealand.* Glasgow: D. Campbell, 1839. State Library of South Australia facsimile, 1962.

Sierp, Allan. *Colonial Life in South Australia: Fifty Years of Photography. 1885–1905.* Adelaide: Rigby, 1969.

Smillie, William. *The Great South Land: four articles on emigration, designed to exhibit the principles and progress of the new colony of South Australia.* Adelaide: Stirling Observer Office, 1838. State Library of South Australia facsimile, 1962.

Smith, Russell. *1850. A Very Good Year in the Colony of South Australia.* Sydney: Shakespeare Head Press, 1973.

Spence, Catherine Helen. *Clara Morrison: A Tale of South Australia During the Gold Fever.* London: Parker, 1854.

Stephens, J. *The Land of Promise; Being an Authentic and Impartial History of the Rise and Progress of the New British Province of South Australia.* London: Smith, Elder & Co., 1839.

Sutherland, George. *The South Australian Company. A Study in Colonization.* London: Longmans, Greer and Co., 1898.

Thiele, Colin. *Grains of Mustard Seed: A Narrative Outline of State Education in South Australia 1875–1975.* Adelaide: Government Printer, 1975.

Tolmer, Alexander. *Reminiscences of an Adventurous and Chequered Career at Home and at the Antipodes.* 2 vols. London: Sampson Low, 1882. State Library of South Australia facsimile, 1972.

Trollope, Anthony. *Australia and New Zealand.* London: Chapman & Hall, 1873. Abridged, edited, and introduced by P.D. Edwards and R.B. Joyce as *Australia.* Brisbane: Queensland University Press, 1967.

Twain, Mark (Samuel Clemens). *Mark Twain in Australia and New Zealand.* Penguin Colonial Facsimiles, 1973. Original edition, *Follow the Equator,* 1897.

Twopeny, R.E.N. *Town Life in Australia.* London: Stock, 1883. Sydney: University Press facsimile, 1973.

Vivienne, May. *Sunny South Australia.* Adelaide: Hussey & Gillingham, 1908.

Whitelock, Derek. *The Great Tradition: A History of Adult Education in Australia.* Brisbane: University of Queensland Press, 1974.

Whitelock, Derek, ed. *City Living, with Emphasis on North Adelaide.* University of Adelaide, seminar proceedings, 1971.

Wakefield, E.G. *A Letter from Sydney The Principal Town of Australasia; & Other Writings on Colonization.* London 1829. Everyman's Library edition London: Dent, 1929.

Whitington, F.T. *Augustus Short. First Bishop of Adelaide. The Story of a Thirty-four Years' Episcopate*. London: Wells Gardner, Daiton & Co., 1888.

Wilkinson, G.B. *South Australia: Its Advantages and Resources, Being a Description of that Colony and a Manual of Information for Emigrants*. London: Murray, 1848.

Worsnop, Thomas. *History of the City of Adelaide, from the Foundation of the Province of South Australia in 1836, to the end of the Municipal Year 1877*. Adelaide: J. Williams, 1878.

Index